Patent Patterns

EDITED AND PHOTOGRAPHED BY
JIM SCHOLLMEYER

Patent Patterns

EDITED AND PHOTOGRAPHED BY
JIM SCHOLLMEYER

Frank Amato
PORTLAND

Dedication

To all the tiers whose flies made this book possible.

Published in 2003 by Frank Amato Publications, Inc.
P.O. Box 82112, Portland, Oregon 97282
(503) 653-8108
www.amatobooks.com

Softbound ISBN: 1-57188-279-0
Softbound UPC: 0-66066-00512-0
Spiral Hardbound ISBN: 1-57188-280-4
Spiral Hardbound UPC: 0-66066-00513-7

Flies photographed by Jim Schollmeyer

Book design and layout: Tony Amato

Printed in Hong Kong
1 3 5 7 9 10 8 6 4 2

Contents

INTRODUCTION

"Patent Patterns" is the name of a fly tying contest that runs in each issue of *Flyfishing and Tying Journal*. I am not sure of the origin of the contest's name, or what it was originally supposed to mean, but the word patent often refers to an exclusive right or title. Nevertheless, while some fly tiers are possessive or secretive with their flies, most are willing to share their knowledge and new fly designs with others. This hints at another usage of the word patent: "to make something open to observation or inspection." I think this definition better fits the contest.

During the early years of the contest we did not ask for the dressings of the flies because there was only so much space in the magazine and this was used to show as many photographs of flies as possible—which meant omitting their dressings. This was a disappointment to many tiers; while an experienced fly tier might be able to work out some of the fly dressings, many were a mystery. This absence of specific fly recipes bothered me as it did a good number of other fly tiers who also wanted to see the dressings. That is how the idea for this book came about.

Beginning in the spring of 1999, I asked fly tiers to send a recipe for each fly they'd entered, asking their permission to use the fly with its dressing in a feature book. In the fall of 2002, I closed the entries for patterns, and since then, have been at work collecting those patterns to be put into book form. Most of the patterns that were pictured in the magazine are included in this book, though again, because of limited space in the magazine I was not able to show them all.

I also asked the fly tiers to send along any comments on how they tie or fish the fly. But, again, because of limited space, the only comments shown are those used to construct the fly. The fishing comments that came with many of the flies showed how attuned the fly tiers were to their craft and their fishing, and it was a pleasure to read their remarks. But even without the fishing comments, the skill of the fly tiers are shown by the quality of the flies sent.

The tiers range from beginners to experts; some are well-known, but most are just people that love to tie flies and are willing to share them. The contest did not ask for flies that would catch fish, but from reading the comments, I believe most of tiers fished their flies. Many of the patterns are variations of well-known patterns, and this is appropriate because it opens the door to modifications or the use of new or different fly tying materials in established patterns. A large number of patterns are new, and only time will tell whether they become standards.

I hope the fly patterns, knowledge, and skills shared by the fly tiers will help you with your fly tying and fishing. If you happen to meet one of them, be sure to thank them. I know I will.

—*Jim Schollmeyer*

Basic Nymph

Tied by: Dustin Harris, Monmouth, OR
Hook: TMC 2457, #10-#14
Thread: Green, or match body color
Tail: Pheasant tail feather fibers, natural or dyed to match body color
Body: Green Nymph Cord, or other color to match the natural
Thorax: Peacock herl
Wing Case: Pheasant tail fibers, natural or dyed
Head: Brass bead

Bill's Hybrid Nymph

Tied by: William Urban, Bound Brook, NJ
Hook: Mustad 94840 or TMC 5210, #10-#20
Thread: Olive 6/0 or 0/8, or color to match the natural
Rib: Copper or gold wire
Abdomen: Rusty brown dubbing, or color to match the natural
Tail/Shellback: Pheasant tail feather fibers
Wing Case: Peacock herl strands
Thorax: Rusty brown dubbing, picked out, or color to match the natural

Bill's Nymph

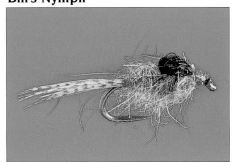

Tied by: Bill's Keister, Marlborough, CT
Hook: Mustad 3906, #10-#14, weighted
Thread: Tan
Tail: Wood duck feather fibers
Rib: Fine gold wire
Body: Light beaver dubbing
Wing Case: Black poly yarn

Biot Mayfly Nymph

Tied by: Steve Potter, Tracy, CA
Hook: TMC 3761, Mustad 3906B, #12
Thread: Black
Tail: 3 moose mane hairs
Abdomen: Light brown peacock wing feather biot
Wing Case: Pheasant tail feather fibers
Thorax: Hare's ear dubbing with guard hairs
Rib: Fine gold wire, through thorax
Legs: Emu feather fibers
Collar: White ostrich herl

Bird's Nest (Modified)

Tied by: Neil Selbicky, Talent, OR
Hook: Mustad 3906B or TMC 3761, #8
Thread: Olive
Tail: Wood duck feather fibers
Rib: Fine oval gold tinsel
Abdomen: Beaver, mixed with dark rust translucent dubbing
Legs: Wood duck feather fibers
Wing Case: Wood duck feather fibers, short
Thorax: Same as abdomen

Blue Quill Nymph

Tied by: Sheldon G. Fedder II, Millville, PA
Hook: Mustad 3906B, #18
Thread: Dark brown
Tail: Mallard-flank feather fibers, dyed dark brown
Rib: Fine copper wire
Body: Olive-brown squirrel dubbing, thorax area picked out
Wing Case: Gray duck wing feather fibers
Head: Gold bead

Borjas' Mayfly Nymph

Tied by: Dave Borja, Dillon, MT
Hook: Daiichi 135, #18
Thread: UNI 8/0, orange
Tail: Pheasant tail feather fibers
Abdomen: Brown goose biot, coated with head cement
Wing Case: Pheasant tail feather fibers
Thorax: Cream Antron dubbing
Legs: Tag ends of wing case fibers divided, folded back and crimped 1/3 from ends for joints

Curneal's Mayfly Nymph

Tied by: David Curneal, S. Solvan, NJ
Hook: Mustad 3761 or TMC 3906B, #10-#14
Thread: Green 6/0
Tail: Brown hen feather fibers
Rib: Green thread, counter wrapped
Gills: Amber ostrich herl
Shellback/Wing Case: Brown Antron yarn
Abdomen: Amber dubbing, picked out; bottom, tan Antron yarn, pulled forward and tied off at front of abdomen
Thorax: Brown Antron dubbing
Legs: Hen feather, drawn feather style

Egan's PMD Nymph

Tied by: Lance Egan, Sandy, UT
Hook: TMC 3761, #16
Thread: Yellow 8/0
Tail: 3 pheasant breast feather fibers
Rib: Fine gold wire, counter wrapped
Abdomen: Natural gray ostrich herl—between yellow turkey biots—mounted on the top and bottom of the hook shank, and pulled forward
Wing Case/Head: Mottled yellow Thin Skin
Legs: Tan hen feather, drawn feather style
Eyes: Small mono eyes
Thorax: Yellow Superfine dubbing

Brown Chickabou Mayfly Nymph, Flash Back

Tied by: Henry Hoffman, Warrenton, OR
Hook: Hook TMC 3761, Mustad 3906B, #10-#16
Thread: Brown
Tail: Barred brown chickabou feather fibers
Rib: Gold wire, counter wrapped
Abdomen: Barred brown chickabou feather, wrapped
Wing Case: Green Bill's Bodi-Braid
Hackle: Barred brown chickabou, top and bottom fibers trimmed

Dubbing Brush Nymph

Tied by: Floyd N. Franke, Roscoe, NY
Hook: Partridge K2B
Thread: Brown, 8/0
Tail: 3 pheasant tail feather fibers
Abdomen: Squirrel Plus Dubbing Brush or Special Natural Dubbing Brush and 12-15 pheasant tail feather fibers, woven, extended
Thorax: Squirrel Plus Dubbing Brush or Special Natural Dubbing Brush
Wing Case: Mottled hen saddle feather, lacquered, let dry, cut to shape
Legs: Turkey tail feather fibers, knotted
Eyes: 2 mm black (plastic or brass) bead chain

Ever Green

Tied by: Robert Schreiner Jr., Southampton, PA
Hook: Mustad 38941, #12
Thread: Black
Tail: 3 moose mane hairs
Rib: Stripped peacock herl with fine gold wire
Abdomen: Light green floss
Wing Case: Peacock sword herl strands
Thorax: Light green dubbing
Legs: Partridge feather fibers

Callibaetis Nymph

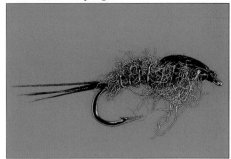

Tied by: Robert Kopp, Williams Lake, BC
Hook: Mustad 94840 or TMC 5210, #10-#14
Thread: Brown 6/0
Tail: Pheasant tail feather fibers
Rib: Fine copper wire
Body: Light hare's ear dubbing, thorax picked out
Wing Case: Pheasant tail feather fibers

Comments: Prefabricate the extended abdomen using a single strand of Dubbing Brush, weaving it around a bundle of pheasant tail fibers as follows. Hold a bundle of 12 to 15 pheasant tail fibers by their tips, coating the lower 3/4 of their length with thick head cement and let dry. Bend a 3-inch length of Dubbing Brush into the shape of a "V", then holding the pheasant tail fibers by their tips, place the "V" of the Dubbing Brush over the bundled fibers at a point about 1/4 its length. Start the weaving process by crossing the tips of the Dubbing Brush under the bundle and then cross the tips over it. Repeat this under and over and cross weaving sequence 2 times, then, using your fingernail and thumbnail, push the wraps of dubbing together. Continue the weave until the abdomen is equal to half the fly's total length. Next, trim off all but 3 of the pheasant tail tips for the tail. Now the abdomen is ready to be mounted on the hook shank. You will find the extended abdomen to be quite bendable. Try changing its curvature in order to change the fly's action. For slow water use more of a curve then for fast water.

Hare's Ear Nymph

Tied by: Mike Telford, Fresno, CA
Hook: TMC 200R
Thread: Black
Tail: Golden pheasant tail feather fibers
Rib: Gold wire, counter wrapped
Abdomen: March brown Australian possum dubbing
Thorax: Same as abdomen, picked out
Wing Case: Golden pheasant tail feather fibers
Legs: Tips of wing case fibers

Hendrickson Nymph

Tied by: Tim O'Sullivan, Elora, ON
Hook: TMC 200R, #16-#18
Thread: Brown UNI, 8/0
Tail: Dark partridge feather fibers
Rib: Medium gold wire, counter wrapped
Body: Brown New Dubb (dubbing brush)
Wing Case: Dark turkey feather section
Legs: Dark partridge feather fibers

Hendrickson Wet Fly

Tied by: Tim O'Sullivan, Elora, ON
Hook: Kamasan B-830, #16-#18
Thread: Brown 8/0
Tail: Dark partridge feather fibers
Rib: Gold wire, counter wrapped
Abdomen: Brown New Dubb (dubbing brush)
Thorax: Peacock herl
Hackle: Speckled brown hen saddle

King's BWO Nymph

Tied by: Matt King, Victoria, BC
Hook: Daiichi 1150, #12-#20, hoop point-up
Thread: Danville olive 6/0
Tail: Bronze mallard feather fibers
Rib: 2lb. mono and ostrich herl twisted together
Abdomen: Light olive SLF dubbing, or match the hatch
Shellback: Light olive Thin Skin
Thorax: Olive SLF squirrel dubbing
Wing Case/Head: Mottled Thin Skin, cut to shape
Legs: Picked out thorax guard hairs

Light Cahill Nymph

Tied by: Troy Standish, Williamsville, NY
Hook: Partridge, #12
Thread: Brown
Tail: Pheasant tail feather fibers
Shellback: Golden pheasant secondary feather fibers
Body: Ginger ostrich herl and copper wire, twisted together
Thorax: Ginger squirrel dubbing
Wing Case: Golden pheasant secondary feather fibers
(tied in at front of thorax and continued to bind fibers to hook eye)
Eyes: Mono
Head: Ginger squirrel dubbing, topped with butt ends of wing case fibers folded back and tied off at start of thorax

March Brown (*Stenonema* Genus)

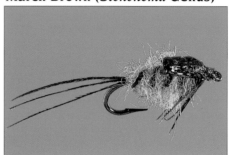

Tied by: Jack Pangburn, Westbury, NY
Hook: Mustad 3906B, #10
Thread: Brown
Tail: Pheasant tail feather fibers
Rib: Heavy brown thread
Body: Amber/tan Seal-Ex dubbing, picked out
Wing Case: Dark brown Swiss straw, lacquered
Legs: Brown partridge feather fibers

Mullin's Green Drake

Tied by: J.E. Mullin, Casper, WY
Hook: Mustad 9671, #8, weighted
Thread: Black
Tail: Gold Krystal Flash strands
Rib: Copper wire
Body: Olive wool
Wing Case: Pheasant tail feather fibers
Legs: Pheasant tail feather fibers
Head: Black glass bead

Para Nymph

Tied by: Steve Harryman, Sandy, UT
Hook: TMC 2487, #14-#16
Thread: Green 6/0 or 8/0
Tail: Partridge feather fibers
Rib: Gold wire
Body: Olive dubbing
Wing Case: High Luster wing material
Legs: Ostrich herl, wrapped over thorax

Plastic Mayfly

Tied by: Kyle Hicks, Berwick, NS
Hook: Mustad 94859 or TMC 100, #10
Thread: Black 6/0
Tail: Mallard flank feather fibers
Underbody: Cream dubbing
Overbody: Plastic bag strip, leave butt end long enough for wing case
Thorax: Peacock herl
Legs: Mallard flank feather fibers
Wing Case: Plastic bag strip, butt end from overbody

Poxyback Green Drake

Tied by: Gregory Krause, Coopersburg, PA
Hook: Mustad 79589, #8, weighted
Thread: Green
Tails: Green goose biots
Rib: Green wire
Shellback: Tan Raffia
Body: Olive Antron dubbing
Gills: Olive filoplume, pulled over top of abdomen
Wing Case: Mottled turkey feather section, coated with epoxy
Legs: Dark grouse feather, drawn feather style

Roth's March Brown Nymph

Tied by: Scott Roth, Andover, NJ
Hook: TMC 2487, #8-#12
Thread: Brown
Tails: Brown goose biots
Abdomen: Tan foam, color top with brown permanent marker
Wing Case: Brown fur foam
Thorax: Brown dubbing
Legs: Emu herl, wrapped, top and bottom fibers clipped
Head: Black cone

Schneider's Mayfly Nymph

Tied by: Alan Schneider, Penticton, BC
Hook: Mustad 94845, #16, weighted
Thread: Olive
Tails: 3 horsetail hairs
Body: Olive brown dubbing
Gills: Grizzly hackle
Wing Case: Brown Swiss straw
Legs: Pheasant tail feather fibers
Eyes: Monofilament, melted but not burned
Head: Olive Swiss straw, folded back

Simple Nymph

Tied by: John Roper, Jasper, GA
Hook: Mustad 9671, #12-#18, weighted with lengths of lead wire mounted to the sides of the hook shank, thread wraps CA glued after securing the lead
Thread: Tan 6/0
Tail: Pheasant tail feather fibers
Rib: Rust 6/0 thread, counter wrapped
Body: Light Antron hare's ear dubbing, thorax area picked out
Wing Case: Turkey feather section, cut to shape, coated with Flexament

Todd's Mayfly Nymph

Tied by: Todd Turner, Fort Lauderdale, FL
Hook: TMC 3761, #16-#20
Thread: Olive, 8/0
Tail: Brown marabou feather fibers
Rib: Tying thread
Shellback/Wing Case: Brown Scud Back
Body: Brown-olive dubbing
Legs: Brown marabou feather fibers
Head: Wing case material folded back

Tony's Wiggle Nymph

Tied by: Tony Kaminski, Victorville, CA
Hooks: Rear: #10, 3X long, clipped off at tail after tying on abdomen.
Front: TMC 2457, #12, weighted with .15 lead-free wire, mounted on top of hook shank and looped through eye of rear hook after abdomen is completed.
Thread: Light olive
Tail: Gray partridge feather fibers
Rib: Fine gold oval tinsel, counter wrapped
Abdomen/Rear Hook: Tan Squirrel Brite Dubbing
Thorax/Front Hook: Gray partridge flume to cover wire connection, tan Squirrel Brite Dubbing
Wing Case: Mallard flank feather section
Legs: Gray partridge feather, drawn feather style

Tough Nymph

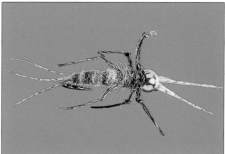

Tied by: Mike O'Neill, Sandy, OR
Hook: TMC 3761, Mustad 3906B, #12-#16
Thread: Olive
Tails: Wood duck flank feather fibers, separated and glued
Rib: Stripped grizzly feather stem
Body: Olive dubbing
Legs: Pheasant tail feather fibers, glued, then when dry, tied in knots to make joints
Thorax: Olive dubbing
Head: Gold bead
Antennae: Wood duck feather fibers, separated and glued

Mayfly Emergers

A-2-Z Emerger

Tied by: Ron Raykowski, Jackson Hole, WY
Hook: Nymph, #12-#18
Thread: Gray
Tail: Olive and yellow Z-lon fibers
Rib: Fine red wire
Abdomen: Silver gray Super Floss
Post: Super Floss, pulled forward and secured after hackle is wrapped
Hackle: Badger, parachute style
Thorax: Peacock herl

Al's Sulphur Emerger

Tied by: Al Milano, Bronx, NY
Hook: Partridge GRS15ST, #16
Thread: Yellow 8/0
Tail: Yellow pheasant tail feather fibers
Abdomen: Yellow pheasant tail feather fibers
Wing Post: Yellow calf tail
Thorax: Yellow peacock herl
Hackle: Ginger

Annie's Emerger

Tied by: Chris Currve, Naples, ID
Hook: Dry fly
Thread: Olive 8/0
Tail: Grizzly feather tip, mounted flat
Body: Olive Antron dubbing
Body Hackle: Brown, top fibers trimmed
Wing: Turkey feather section

B*aetis* Emerger

Tied by: Jack J. Johnson, Concord, CA
Hook: TMC 2487, #16-#18
Thread: Black
Tail: Brown Z-lon fibers
Abdomen: Brown Super Floss
Thorax: Olive dubbing
Hackle Post: Brown Super Floss
Hackle: Medium dun, parachute style, pulled forward

Basic Emerger (Green Drake)

Tied by: Dustin Harris, Monmouth, OR
Hook: Mustad 3906B or TMC 3761, #10-#14
Thread: Olive or to match body color
Tail: Olive pheasant tail feather fibers, or to match body color
Rib: Fine yellow Nymph Cord
Body: Olive Nymph Cord, or color to match the natural
Shellback: Pearl Krystal Flash strands
Thorax: Olive-brown dubbing, or color to match the natural
Wing Case: Olive pheasant tail feather fibers (or color to match the natural), pearl Krystal Flash strands from shellback
Wing: Pheasant tail feather fibers and Krystal Flash strands from wing case

Bead Head BWO

Tied by: Jack Pangburn, Westbury, NY
Hook: TMC 2487, #16-#18
Thread: Olive 8/0
Tail: Brown feather fibers
Abdomen: Olive thread
Wing: Dun CDC feather fibers
Thorax: Olive dubbing
Legs: Black yarn fibers
Head: Black glass bead

Berge's Pop-Up Hex Emerger

Tied by: Dick Berge, Iron River, WI
Hook: Mustad 94831, #10
Thread: Brown 6/0
Tail: Gray Antron yarn fibers, pheasant tail feather fibers
Rib: Fine gold wire
Body: Yellow dubbing
Wing: Pheasant tail feather fibers, gray poly yarn fibers
Wing Case: Tan foam
Legs: Yellow grizzly feather fibers

BH Flashback *Callibaetis* Emerger

Tied by: Elliott Gritton, Reno, NV
Hook: Daiichi 1260, #12-#16
Thread: Black
Tail: Gray marabou feather fibers, 4 strands of pearl Krystal Flash
Rib: Fine silver wire
Shellback: Silver holographic tinsel
Abdomen: Light turkey feather fibers, wrapped
Thorax: Peacock herl
Legs: Partridge feather fibers
Head: Gold bead

Big & Brown (March Brown Emerger)

Tied by: Philip Kee, Brooklyn, NY
Hook: Partridge CS 10/1, #10
Thread: Rust 6/0
Tail: Brown Antron yarn fibers
Body: Rusty brown dubbing
Wing: Snowshoe rabbit foot fur
Legs: Brown grouse flank feather fibers

Black & Gray Emerger

Tied by: A.J. Courteau, Erie, PA
Hook: TMC 2487, #14-#18
Thread: Gray 8/0
Tail: White Antron yarn fibers
Abdomen: Gray goose biot
Wing: Black CDC feathers fibers, looped over thorax
Thorax: Gray Hare Tron dubbing
Head: Butt ends from wing material

Blue Quill Emerger

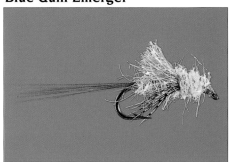

Tied by: Sheldon G. Fedder II, Millville, PA
Hook: Mustad 94840, #18
Thread: Dark gray
Tail: Dark dun Micro Fibetts
Rib: Fine silver wire
Body: Creamy gray dubbing
Legs: Partridge feather fibers
Wing: Dun poly yarn fibers
Head: Creamy gray dubbing

Blue Wing Olive Emerger

Tied by: Don Heydon, Bozeman, MT
Hook: Mustad 94845, #18
Thread: Olive 8/0
Tail: Teal or mallard flank feather fibers
Rib: Fine gold wire
Body: Olive poly dubbing
Wing: Light dun Antron yarn fibers, light dun CDC feather
fibers

Borjas' Mayfly Emerger

Tied by: Dave Borjas, Dillon, MT
Hook: Daiichi 135, #18
Thread: Tan 8/0
Tail: Wood duck flank feather fibers
Abdomen: Cream Antron dubbing
Legs: Wood duck flank feathers
Wing: Bleached coastal deer hair
Hackle: Bleached grizzly

BWO Para-Emerger

Tied by: Jonny King, New York, NY
Hook: TMC 101, #22
Thread: Olive 8/0
Tail: Brown Z-lon fibers
Abdomen: Olive stripped feather stem
Thorax: Tan dubbing
Wing Post: Light dun Z-lon fibers
Hackle: Dun

Callibaetis Emerger

Tied by: Robert Kopp, Williams Lake, BC
Hook: Mustad 94840 or TMC 5210, #10-#14, hook point-up
Thread: Olive and black, 8/0
Tail: 3 moose mane hairs
Rib: Olive thread
Body: Rust brown deer hair
Wings: Brown feather tips
Hackle: Grizzly

Carl's Mayfly Emerger

Tied by: Carl Mohney, Boston, MA
Hook: Mustad 94840, #14-#18
Thread: Pale yellow, 8/0
Tail: Bronze mallard feather fibers
Abdomen: Reddish-brown horsetail hair, coated with head
cement
Wing: Gray CDC feather fibers
Hackle: Dun hen, 2 turns, parachute style
Thorax: Pale yellow dubbing

CDC-Biot Emerger/Cripple

Tied by: Ben Byng, Tracy, CA
Hook: TMC 100, #12-#16
Thread: Yellow 8/0
Tail: Olive golden pheasant tippet fibers
Abdomen: Rusty-brown biot
Thorax: Fine yellow dubbing
Wing: CDC feather fibers
Hackle: Dun

CDC-PMD Cripple

Tied by: Jerry Jeffery, Long Beach, CA
Hook: Mustad 94840
Thread: Yellow 8/0
Tail: Olive mallard flank feather fibers, rust and white
Antron fibers
Abdomen: Brown dubbing
Wing: White CDC feather fibers
Thorax: Yellow dubbing

Cliff's Pullover Emerger

Tied by: Clifford Sullivan, Tracy, CA
Hook: Daiichi 1250, #8-#18
Thread: Olive 8/0, or color to match the natural
Tail: Peacock Krystal Flash, or color to match the natural,
3-6 strands
Underbody: Tail material
Overbody: Small clear Vinyl Rib
Post: Olive Super Floss
Hackle: Cree, 8-16 wraps
Thorax: Olive Antron dubbing, or color to match body
Comments: The hackle is wrapped on a stretched post then
the post is relaxed, pulled forward, and secured.

Craig's Mayfly Emerger

Tied by: Craig Knoll, Salem, OR
Hook: TMC 100, #12-#16
Thread: Tan 8/0
Tail: Pheasant tail feather fibers
Rib: Fine copper wire
Abdomen: Pheasant tail feather fibers, wrapped
Wing Case: Pheasant tail feather fibers
Thorax: Pheasant aftershaft feather, wrapped
Wing Bud: Cream Antron yarn fibers, looped
Head: Clear glass bead

Curneal's Mayfly Emerger

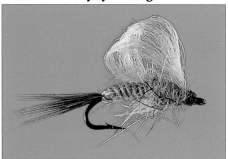

Tied by: David Curneal, S. Solvan, NJ
Hook: TMC 200R, #14-#16
Thread: Green
Tail: Hen feather fibers
Abdomen: Tan Antron yarn, twisted
Wing: Tan Antron yarn, looped
Thorax: Tan dubbing, picked out

Davis Lake Emerger

Tied by: Wade Malwitz, Portland, OR
Hook: Mustad 94840, #14
Thread: White 8/0
Tail: Olive Krystal Flash strand
Rib: Olive Krystal Flash strand, counter wrapped
Body: Ginger Sparkle Blend dubbing, optional colors:
   green, brown, and black
Post: Yellow Antron yarn
Hackle: Grizzly

Don's March Brown Emerger

Tied by: Don Heyden, Bozeman, MT
Hook: Mustad 80250, #12
Thread: Camel 8/0
Tail: Brown Z-lon fibers
Rib: Fine copper wire
Body: Light brown raccoon fur and Antron yarn fibers,
   blended, or light brown Hare-Tron dubbing
Wing: Natural snowshoe rabbit foot fur, mallard flank
   feather fibers

Don's PMD Emerger

Tied by: Don Heyden, Bozeman, MT
Hook: Mustad 94845, #14
Thread: Camel 8/0
Tail: Amber Z-lon fibers
Rib: Fine copper wire, counter wrapped
Abdomen: Pheasant tail feather fibers, wrapped
Wing: Tan CDC feather fibers
Thorax: Pale yellow dubbing

Doug's BWO Emerger

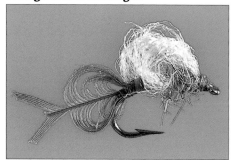

Tied by: Doug MacIver, St. Albert, AB
Hook: Mustad 80250BR, #14
Thread: Olive 8/0
Tail: Green feather, reverse hackle style, trimmed to shape
Abdomen: Olive goose biot
Wings: Dun Z-lon fibers, looped
Thorax: Olive rabbit dubbing mixed with chopped olive
   tinsel

Eastern Drake Emerger

Tied by: Stephen Lopatic, Harrisburg, PA
Hook: Mustad 37160, #10-#14
Thread: Black
Tail: Olive grizzly feather marabou fibers
Abdomen: Tail fibers wrapped forward
Tailing: Moose mane, 3 fibers
Thorax: Olive Antron dubbing
Hackle: Black
Wing Case: Black foam, pulled between wings
Wings: Grizzly feathers
Eyes: Red Amnesia mono, melted

Egan's PMD Emerger

Tied by: Lance Egan, Sandy, UT
Hook: TMC 100, #16
Thread: Yellow, 8/0
Tail: Rust Z-lon fibers
Abdomen: Yellow turkey biot
Wing Case: Deer hair, pulled forward after wrapping
   hackle around its base
Thorax: Yellow Superfine dubbing
Hackle: Dun, wrapped around base of wing case

Emerging Bubble

Tied by: Robert Schreiner Jr., Southampton, PA
Hook: TMC 200R, #14
Thread: Gray
Tail: Partridge feather fibers
Body: Moose mane hair
Wing: Light dun CDC feather fibers
Legs: Partridge feather fibers
Head/Bubble: Gray Antron yarn fibers pulled over gold
   tinsel

Emerging Hendrickson

Tied by: Bill Keister, Marlborough, CT
Hook: TMC 2487, #12-#14
Thread: Black 8/0
Tail: Pheasant tail fibers
Abdomen: Tan or brown turkey biot
Post: White poly yarn, knotted style, cemented
Wings: Brown molted Thin Skin, cut to shape, mounted
   spent
Legs: Partridge feather fibers
Hackle: Dark dun
Thorax: Fine dark brown or gray dubbing

EZ-Sight Cripple

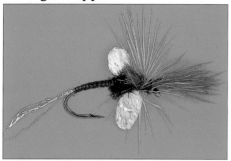

Tied by: Richard W. Murphy, Sr., Manitou Springs, CO
Hook: TMC 2487 or TMC 206BL, #18-#20
Thread: Black, 8/0
Tail: White SAPP Body Fur or Antron yarn, 6 to 8 fibers
Abdomen: 6/0 olive-brown Danville thread
Thorax: Peacock herl
Wings: 1/32 Evasote foam or Ethafoam, cut to shape, spent wing style
Fore Wing: Fluorescent orange calf body hair
Hackle: Dun, 1 or 2 wraps
Comments: This fly is great for the Spring and Fall BWO hatches in size 20 and also does well in a size 18 for PMD hatchs that occurs in the summer. Use floatant on the front half of the fly only so the tail and abdomen sink.

Fancy PMD Emerger

Tied by: Stephen Lopatic, Harrisburg, PA
Hook: Mustad 80260BR, #12-#16
Thread: Black 8/0
Tail: Olive marabou feather fibers
Rib: Green copper wire
Body: Yellow Antron dubbing
Wing: Yellow mallard flank feather fibers
Hackle: Dark dun, bottom fibers trimmed

Frank's Mayfly Emerger

Tied by: Frank dePrume, New Egypt, NJ
Hook: Mustad 94840, #16
Thread: Tan 8/0
Tail: Mallard flank feather fibers
Body: Amber Antron yarn
Wings: White Antron yarn fibers

Fred's Mayfly Emerger

Tied by: Fred Iacoletti, Albuquerque, NM
Hook: Dry fly, 2X long, #14
Thread: Brown, 8/0
Shuck: Grizzly feather, reverse style
Rear Hackle: Brown and grizzly
Body: Gray dubbing
Wings: Duck feather sections
Legs: Tan CDC feather, 1 turn
Front Hackle: Grizzly

Fuzzy Top

Tied by: Robert Schreiner, Southampton, PA
Hook: TMC 200R, #16
Thread: Brown
Tail: Partridge feather fibers
Abdomen: Stripped peacock herl, lacquered
Thorax: Peacock herl
Legs: Partridge feather fibers
Wing: Dun CDC feather fibers

General Purpose Flashback Mayfly Emerger

Tied by: Elliot Gritton, Reno, NV
Hook: Daiichi 1269, #12-#16
Thread: Camel 6/0
Tail: Grizzly feather marabou fibers, small white rubber strands
Rib: Fine copper wire
Shellback: Red holographic tinsel
Abdomen: Brown turkey feather fibers, wrapped
Thorax: Peacock herl
Wings: Small white rubber strands
Hackle: Brown partridge
Head: Orange glass bead

Gold Dust Emerger

Tied by: Ron Raykowski, Jackson Hole, WY
Hook: Nymph, #12-#18
Thread: Yellow
Tail: Gold Antron yarn fibers
Body: Rusty olive Super Floss
Wing: Gold Antron yarn fibers
Wing Buds: Packing foam, looped

Gold Ribbed Hare's Ear Emerger

Tied by: Rich Bogardus, Schenectady, NY
Hook: Mustad 3906B, #10-#16
Thread: Tan
Tail: Ginger feather fibers
Rib: Fine gold tinsel
Abdomen: Light Hare's ear dubbing
Wing Case: Mottled turkey tail feather section
Thorax: Dark hare's ear dubbing
Wings: White duck feather sections

Goodyear Hex Emerger

Tied by: John Gribb, Mt. Hored, WI
Hook: Mustad 3366, #6
Thread: Black 3/0
Tails: Mono strands
Rib: Black tying thread
Body: Yellow 2mm foam, cut to shape, color with brown marker
Wing: Light elk hair
Legs: Black round rubber
Head: Body material folded back

Guttulata Emerger

Tied by: Scott Roth, Newton, NJ
Hook: Orvis 1512, #10
Thread: Brown 14/0
Tails: Brown duck biots
Abdomen: Tan sheet foam strip, ironed flat, top half colored
with brown marker, coated with Softex
Gills: Brown Furry Foam
Wings: Olive CDC feathers
Wing Case: Partridge feather, coated with Softex, top half
split in middle
Legs: Emu feather fibers
Eyes: Black plastic barbell

Harrop's Baetis Emerger

Tied by: Neil Selbicky, Talent, OR
Hook: Mustad 94840 or TMC 5210, #18
Thread: Black, 8/0
Tail: 3 wood duck feather fibers
Rib: Fine gold wire
Body: Olive dry fly dubbing
Wing: Light dun CDC feather fibers, wood duck flank
feather fibers
Head: Black beaver dubbing

Hendrickson Emerger

Tied by: Tim O'Sullivan, Elora, ON
Hook: Kamasan B-100, #16-#18
Thread: Brown UNI, 8/0
Tail: Dark partridge feather fibers
Rib: Gold wire, counter wrapped
Abdomen: Brown New Dubb (dubbing brush)
Wing Case: Turkey tail feather fibers
Wing: Gray over white CDC feather fibers, loop style
Thorax: Peacock herl
Legs: Dark partridge feather fibers

Hendrickson Looped Usual Emerger

Tied by: Jonny King, New York, NY
Hook: TMC 2487, #14
Thread: Tan 8/0
Tail: Brown Z-lon fibers
Abdomen: Tan goose biot
Wing: Dun snowshoe rabbit fur, looped forward
Legs: Dun hackle, 3 turns over thorax, top and bottom fibers
trimmed
Thorax: Tan dubbing

Hendrickson Usual Emerger

Tied by: Jonny King, New York, NY
Hook: TMC 2487, #14
Thread: Tan 8/0
Shuck: Brown Z-lon fibers, veiling rear 1/3 of abdomen,
knotted, leaving a few fibers behind knot
Body: Tan dubbing
Wing: Dun snowshoe rabbit fur

Hexagenia Emerger

Tied by: Nadeer Youssef, Pullman, WA
Hook: TMC 2487, #12
Thread: Cream 6/0
Shuck: Cream Antron yarn, knotted
Rib: Olive 3/0 thread
Body: Gray dubbing, extended over mono core
Wings: Plastic, cut to shape
Hackle: Cream

Hill's Mayfly Emerger

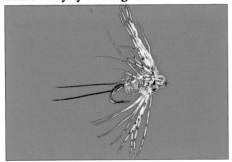

Tied by: Stephen Hill, Veneta, OR
Hook: Nymph, #12-#16
Thread: Olive
Tail: Pheasant tail feather fibers
Rib: Fine brass wire
Body: Light olive Ice Dub UV dubbing
Hackle: Partridge
Head: Clear glass bead

King's BWO Emerger

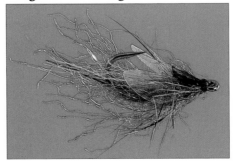

Tied by: Matt King, Victoria, BC
Hook: Daiichi 1150, #14-#20, hook point-up
Thread: Danville olive 6/0
Tail: Bronze mallard fibers
Rib: 2 lb. mono, counter wrapped
Shellback: Light olive Thin Skin
Abdomen: Light olive SLF dubbing, olive ostrich herl
Tailing Shuck: Sparse olive Antron dubbing, pearl Angle
Hair fibers
Thorax: Olive and brown squirrel SLF dubbing, blended
Wing Buds: Prismatic Pliable sheeting, cut to shape
Wing Case: Mottled Thin Skin

Krystal Mayfly Emerger

Tied by: Don Heyden, Bozeman, MT
Hook: Mustad 880250, #16
Thread: Gray 8/0
Tail: Gray Antron yarn fibers
Abdomen: Peacock Krystal Flash strands, wrapped flat
Wing: Dark dun CDC feather fibers
Thorax: Light brown raccoon fur and beige Antron yarn
fibers, blended, or light brown Hare-Tron dubbing

Last Stage Emergence

Tied by: Wade Malwitz, Portland, OR
Hook: Mustad 94840, #12
Thread: Olive 8/0
Tails: Moose mane hairs
Body: Yellow deer hair, tied, extended
Shuck: Clear Mylar tinsel, 1 strand per side
Wings: Clear Mylar tinsel, short, 2 strands per side
Post: Yellow yarn
Hackle: Grizzly

Leo's *Callibaetis* Emerger

Tied by: Leo Schlumpf, Redding, CA
Hook: Dai-Riki 135 or TMC 2487, #16
Thread: Olive 8/0
Tail: Light olive Z-lon fibers
Body: Olive Antron dubbing
Wing: Deer hair
Legs: Antron dubbing fibers

Little Olive Emerger

Tied by: Jerry Jeffery, Long Beach, CA
Hook: Mustad 94845, #16-#20
Thread: Black 8/0
Tail: Dun feather fibers
Body: Olive dubbing
Wing Bud: Light olive dubbing ball

Loop-wing March Brown

Tied by: Jack Pangburn, Westbury, NY
Hook: Mustad 94840, #12
Thread: Brown 6/0
Tail: Brown and wood duck flank feather fibers, mixed
Body: Cream/tan dubbing
Legs: Grizzly hackle, top and bottom clipped
Loop Wing: Brown Swiss straw, lacquered

Loren's Mayfly Emerger

Tied by: Loren Ipsen, Boise, ID
Hook: TMC 2457, #12-#14
Thread: Brown
Tail: Pheasant tail feather fibers, short
Body: Brown dubbing
Wing: Tan hare's foot hair

March Brown Emerger

Tied by: Richard Wager, Gloversville, NY
Hook: TMC 2487, #12-#14
Thread: Brown
Tail: Brown Z-lon fibers
Body: Tan Hare-Tron dubbing
Wing: Brown and gray CDC feather fibers
Head: Bronze Arizona Peacock Dubbing

March Brown Flymph

Tied by: Al Milano, Bronx, NY
Hook: TMC 3761, #10
Thread: Pearsall's claret silk
Tail: Brown hen feather fibers
Rib: Small gold oval tinsel, counter wrapped
Body: Dark hare's ear dubbing
Hackle: Brown hen

Michael's Mayfly Emerger

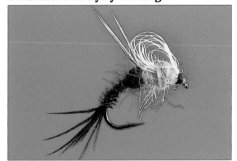

Tied by: Michael Bates, Steamboat Springs, CO
Hook: TMC 2487, #16
Thread: Black 8/0
Tail: Pheasant tail feather fibers
Abdomen: Rust turkey feather biot, rust dubbing
Wings: Dun feather tips
Wing Buds: White calf tail hairs, looped
Thorax: Yellow dubbing

Mr. Light Side PMD Emerger

Tied by: Joseph Burket, Bozeman, MT
Hook: TMC 101, #18-#20
Thread: Light yellow 8/0
Shuck: White or amber nylon webbing strip, or Z-lon
Shiny Sides: Small amber tubing, pulled forward
Abdomen: Pale yellow dubbing
Thorax: Rusty brown Ice Dub
Wings: CDC feathers, delta style

Ozark Quill Adam Emerger

Tied by: Randy Boyce, St. Louis, MO
Hook: Dai-Riki 135, #14-#18
Thread: Rust 8/0
Tail: Rust Antron yarn fibers
Abdomen: Blue and red stripped feather stems
Wing: White Antron yarn fibers, CDC feather fibers
Legs: CDC feather fibers
Thorax: Brown dubbing

Parachute Emerger

Tied by: Clifford Sullivan, Tracy, CA
Hook: TMC 206BL, #8-#18
Thread: Black 8/0
Tail: Dark moose hair
Rib: Tag end of tying thread
Body: Brown, tan, and gray dubbing, mixed
Wing: Deer hair
Wing Case: Moose hair
Legs: Tag ends from wing case
Hackle: Cree

Para Stuck Shuck Emerger

Tied by: Henry Hoffman, Warrenton, OR
Hook: Mustad 80150BR, #14
Thread: Tan 8/0
Tail: Barred light golden brown chickabou feather fibers
Abdomen: Barred light golden brown chickabou feather fibers, wrapped
Thorax: Tan beaver dubbing
Wings: Ginger grizzly feathers, reverse hackle style
Hackle: Ginger grizzly

Pete's Reel Mayfly Emerger

Tied by: Pete Toscani, Bristol, CT
Hook: Orvis, #14
Thread: Black 8/0
Tail: Copper Lite Brite fibers
Body: Gray dubbing
Wing: Pearl Lite Brite fibers, looped
Head: Epoxy with green glitter

Pheasant Emerger

Tied by: John Baracchi, E. Hartford, CT
Hook: Mustad 3906, #10-#14
Thread: Black
Tail: Pheasant tail feather fibers
Rib: Fine copper wire, counter wrapped
Abdomen: Pheasant tail feather fibers, wrapped
Wing Case: Pheasant tail feather fibers
Thorax: Marabou fibers from pheasant rump feather, dubbed
Hackle: Pheasant rump feather

Piller's Emerger

Tied by: Giuseppe Nova, Bollate, Italy
Hook: TMC 101, #14-#20
Thread: Black 8/0
Tail: Gray CDC feather fibers, optional
Underbody: Black thread
Body: Gray CDC feather, palmered, fibers pulled forward
Wing: CDC fibers, tips from body feather

PMD EM

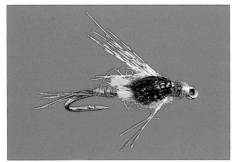

Tied by: Gary Dewey, Morrison, CO
Hook: TMC 200R, #14-#18
Thread: Gray
Tail: Pheasant tail feather fibers
Abdomen: Olive floss
Gills: Yellow floss fibers
Wing Case: Turkey feather section, coated with head cement
Thorax: Light olive dubbing
Legs: Partridge feather fibers

PMD Foam Emerger

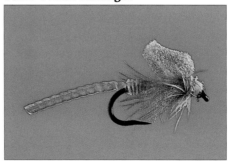

Tied by: Joseph Burket, Bozeman, MT
Hook: TMC 900BL, #18
Thread: Pale yellow 8/0
Shuck: Stalcup's light orange Trailing Shuck
Abdomen: Light yellow stripped feather stem
Thorax: Yellow-amber dubbing
Wing Bud: Gray foam, cut to shape
Wings: Dun CDC feathers
Hackle: Dun, top and bottom fibers trimmed

PMD Shiny Tail Emerger

Tied by: Joseph Burket, Bozeman, MT
Hook: TMC 2487G, #18
Thread: Light yellow 8/0
Tail: Amber Z-lon fibers, looped over copper wire and pulled into abdomen tubing
Abdomen: Amber tubing
Thorax: Rust brown Ice Dub
Wings: Dun CDC feather fibers, delta style
Legs: Brown micro rubber

Pop-Up Emerger

Tied by: Peter Frailey, Carlisle, MA
Hook: TMC 2487, #10-#18
Thread: Gray, or color to match body
Tail: Amber Antron yarn fibers
Body: Gray dubbing, or color to match the natural
Post: White Rainy's Foam Post material, colored with pink marker
Hackle: Brown, or color of choice, each hackle wrapped and turned tightly against the base of the post to splay out the fibers, bottom fibers trimmed flush with hook point

Powell's Mayfly Emerger

Tied by: Roy Powell, Danville, CA
Hook: TMC 400T, #14
Thread: Black 8/0
Tail: Woodduck feather fibers
Underbody: Silver Flashabou strand, wrapped
Abdomen: Small smoky gray or burnt orange Vinyl Rib
Gills: Pheasant aftershaft feather, 1 wrap
Thorax: Gray or yellow fine dubbing
Wings: Duck wing feather sections, cut to shape, inside of each wing coated with Softex or Flexament
Hackle: Brown or cream, bottom fibers trimmed

Quill & Cahill CDC

Tied by: Jack Pangburn, Westbury, NY
Hook: TMC 100, #14-#16
Thread: Dun 8/0
Tails: Dun Micro Fibetts
Abdomen: Olive biot
Thorax: Dun dubbing
Wing: Dun CDC fibers, mallard flank feather fibers

Rock Clinging Mayfly Nymph Emerger

Tied by: Rich Bogardus, Schenectady, NY
Hook: Mustad 3906B, #13-#16
Thread: Black
Tails: Tan Micro Fibetts, spotted with black marker
Abdomen: Brown latex strip, colored with dark brown marker
Thorax: Fine brown dubbing
Legs: Olive ostrich herl strands, singed, bent to shape
Wing Case/Head: Brown latex strip
Wings: White duck feather sections, cut to shape

Roth's March Brown Emerger

Tied by: Scott Roth, Andover, NJ
Hook: TMC 206BL, #8-#12
Thread: Brown
Tail: Brown goose biots
Abdomen: Tan foam, top half marked with brown permanent marker
Wing Case: Gray foam, topped with 3 gray ostrich herl
Thorax: March brown dubbing

Royal Parachute Emerger

Tied by: Jack Pangburn, Westbury, NY
Hook: Mustad 37160, #12-#18
Thread: Black
Rib: Red floss
Body: Peacock herl
Wing Post: White Antron yarn fibers
Hackle: Coachman brown

Roy's Mayfly Emerger

Tied by: Roy Powell, Danville, CA
Hook: TMC 400T, #14
Thread: Pale yellow 8/0, or color to match the natural
Tail: Rusty brown marabou feather fiber tips
Rib: Copper wire, counter wrapped
Abdomen: Rusty brown marabou feather fibers, butt ends from tail, wrapped forward
Thorax: Yellow fine dubbing, or color to match the natural
Wings: Duck wing feather sections, cut to shape, inside of each wing coated with Softex or Flexament
Hackle: Dun or cream, bottom fibers trimmed

Sadie's Green Drake Emerger

Tied by: David McCants, Pleasant Hill, CA
Hook: TMC 200R, #12
Thread: Yellow
Tail: Green grizzly feather marabou fibers
Rib: Yellow 3/0 thread, counter wrapped
Body: Olive dubbing
Wing: Golden retriever fur (Sadie) or substitute, white CDC feather fibers, looped
Hackle: Ginger grizzly

Sadie's Green Drake Pre-emerger

Tied by: David McCants, Pleasant Hill, CA
Hook: TMC 200R, #12, de-barbed
Thread: Yellow
Tail: Green grizzly feather marabou fibers
Rib: Yellow 3/0 thread, counter wrapped
Body: Olive dubbing
Hackle: Ginger grizzly

Scott's CDC Quill Emerger

Tied by: Scott Riddle, Tyler, TX
Hook: Mustad 94840, #14-#16
Thread: Gray 8/0
Tail: Woodduck flank feather fibers
Body: Olive stripped feather stem
Wing: White CDC feather fibers, white Antron yarn fibers
Hackle: Dun hen

Sean's *Callibaetis* Emerger

Tied by: Sean Davis, Gresham, OR
Hook: TMC 5262, #16-#18
Thread: Tan 8/0
Tail: Partridge feather fibers
Abdomen: Tan turkey biot
Thorax: Tan hare's mask dubbing
Wing: Partridge feather fibers

Shuck-kicking Emerger (BWO)

Tied by: Jack Pangburn, Westbury, NY
Hook: TMC 100, #12-#16
Thread: Olive 8/0
Tail/Shuck: Olive poly yarn bubble over braided pearl Mylar cord core
Abdomen: Olive thread
Wing Case: Deer hair
Thorax: Olive dubbing
Wing: Deer hair tips from wing case

Snowshoe Rabbit's Foot-Eastern Green Drake Emerger

Tied by: Doug Kerr, Glenfield, NY
Hook: Mustad 79580, #10-#12
Thread: Olive 8/0
Tail: Natural snowshoe rabbit's foot fur, wood duck flank feather fibers
Abdomen: 40% cream, 40% light olive, and 20% insect green substitute-seal dubbing, mixed
Wing: Snowshoe rabbit fur, colored with gray and yellow permanent marks
Thorax: Cream substitute seal and cream/red fox dubbing, mixed

SOH Emerger

Tied by: Bill Yale, Easton, PA
Hook: Mustad 94831, #12-#16
Thread: Olive 8/0
Tail: Light gray ploy yarn fibers
Abdomen: Fine olive and natural hare's ear dubbing, mixed
Wing Bud: CDC feather, looped forward over thorax
Thorax: Fine olive and dark hare's ear dubbing, mixed

Stuck-Shuck Emerger

Tied by: Henry Hoffman, Warrenton, OR
Hook: Mustad 80150 BR, #10-#16
Thread: Gray
Tail: Barred brown chickabou feather fibers
Shuck: Tag ends of tail fibers, wrapped
Body: Gray beaver dubbing
Hackle: Medium dun
Wing: Deer hair, clipped to shape

Sub-Merger (Green Drake)

Tied by: Jack Pangburn, Westbury, NY
Hook: Mustad 80050, #12-#18
Thread: Tan 6/0
Rib: Pearlescent Flashabou
Abdomen/Submerged Shuck: Tan Antron dubbing
Thorax: Black, brown and red Antron dubbing, mixed
Hackle: Badger
Comments: This fly float floats vertically, support it with the dry fly hackle.

Sulphur Emerger

Tied by: Bruce Raymond, Woodridge, IL
Hook: Kamasan B100, #14
Thread: Light yellow 8/0
Tail: Brown Antron yarn fibers
Abdomen: Sulphur orange turkey biot
Wing: CDC feathers, 2 short dark gray feathers inside, 2 long light gray feathers outside
Thorax: Yellow Hare-Ton dubbing

Tight Grip

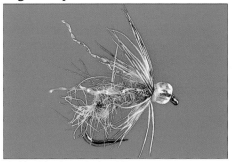

Tied by: Tyler Cote, Winslow, ME
Hook: TMC 2457, #14
Thread: Tan 8/0
Tail: Chartreuse Antron fibers
Rib: Pearl Krystal Flash strand, counter wrapped
Body: Olive dubbing
Wings: Pearl Krystal Flash, 2 strands
Hackle: Partridge
Head: Clear glass bead

Turkey Creek Emerger

Tied by: Ron Beasley, St. Louis, MO
Hook: Mustad 80250BR, #10-#18
Thread: Black
Tail: Pearl Krystal Flash, 3 strands
Abdomen: Olive Larva Lace
Thorax: Olive dubbing
Wing: White Antron yarn
Hackle: Olive CDC

Urban's Emerger

Tied by: William Urban, Bound Brook, NJ
Hook: TMC 2487 or TMC 206BL, #10-#22
Thread: 6/0 or 8/0, color to match the natural
Tailing Shuck: Brown Antron yarn, tied with an overhand knot, clipped and touched with Super Glue on knot
Thorax: Dubbing, color to match the natural
Wing: Dun poly yarn, looped
Hackle: Partridge, 2 wraps, bottom fibers clipped

Vertical Hendrickson Parachute

Tied by: Jack Pangburn, Westbury, NY
Hook: TMC 101, #14, hook point-up
Thread: Tan 8/0
Tail: Tan Antron yarn fibers
Rib: Fine copper wire
Abdomen: Dark Hendrickson dubbing
Post: White closed-cell foam
Thorax: Tan red dubbing
Hackle: Dun

West Branch Emerger (March Brown)

Tied by: Jack Pangburn, Westbury, NY
Hook: TMC 3761, #14
Thread: Brown 8/0
Tail: Tan Antron yarn fibers
Rib: Fine copper wire
Body: March brown dubbing
Wing: Snowshoe rabbit's foot hair, wood duck flank feather fibers
Head: Brass bead

Wilson's Light Cahill Emerger

Tied by: Brad Wilson, Millerton, PA
Hook: Mustad 37160, #16
Thread: Brown
Tail: Pheasant tail feather fibers
Rib: Brown embroidery floss
Body: Light brown dubbing
Wing: Woodduck flank feather fibers
Shellback: Mottled Thin Skin
Legs: Pheasant tail feather fibers
Eyes: Black paint

Yellow Emerger

Tied by: Mike Giavedoni, Maple, ON
Hook: Mustad 80050BR, #16
Thread: Tan 8/0
Tail: Lemon wood duck flank feather fibers
Rib: Amber Larvae Lace
Body: Tan dubbing
Hackle: Gray partridge aftershaft feather

Mayfly Duns

Adhesive Extended Body Mayfly (Green Drake)

Tied by: Earl A. Stanek, Cotter, AR
Hook: TMC 900BL, #10
Thread: Light olive 10/0
Tail: 3 bristles from polyester paint brush
Abdomen: 3M Scotch Brand Adhesive Transfer Tape #919, rolled with tail bristles, marked with permanent marker pens: Chartpak #P126 "Celery" and Berol #PM98 "Black," then coated with 3M Brand Pronto CA40, similar to a thin layer of Super Glue
Thorax: Pale olive dubbing
Eyes: Melted mono
Wing: Gadwall flank feather fibers
Hackle: Iron blue dun
Comments: It is possible tie any mayfly from a size 6 *Hexagenia limata* to a size 22 Trico with this type of abdomen. All that is required is the correct color of permanent markers.

American March Brown (*Stenonema* vicarium)

Tied by: Jack Pangburn, Westbury, NY
Hook: Mustad 94840, #12
Thread: Tan/brown (fawn), 6/0
Tail: Ginger Micro Fibetts
Body: Thread
Wing: Brown wood duck and mallard flank feather fibers, mixed, single wing
Hackle: Grizzly and dark ginger

Bill's P.E.D. Dun

Tied by: William Urban, Bound Brook, NJ
Hook: TMC 2487 or TMC 206BL, #10-#22
Thread: Tan 6/0 or 8/0, or color to match the natural body color
Tail: 3 or 4 hairs from abdomen
Abdomen: Yellow deer hair or color to match the natural, mounted even with hook point, then cross-wrapped length: approximately twice that of the hook shank
Thorax: Yellow dubbing or color to match the natural
Wing: Yellow poly yarn or color to match the natural or a color for better visibility
Hackle: Cream or color to match the natural

Biot Mayfly Dun

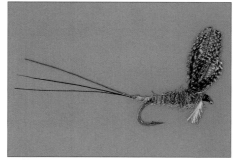

Tied by: Steve Potter, Tracy, CA
Hook: TMC 5210, Mustad 94840, #12
Thread: Black
Tail: 3 moose mane hairs
Abdomen: Tan peacock wing feather biot, wrapped starting behind hook bend over tail hair and thread core
Thorax: Hare's ear dubbing
Wings: Widgeon flank feathers, reverse style, divided
Legs: 2 emu feather fibers, cut short

Bivisible Dun

Tied by: Neil Selbicky, Talent, OR
Hook: Mustad 94840 or TMC 5210, #16
Thread: Olive
Tail: Dun CDC feather fibers
Body: Olive dry fly dubbing
Wing Post: Black calf tail and white goat body hair
Hackle: Dun

Black and White

Tied by: Robert Schreiner Jr., Southampton, PA
Hook: Mustad 94840, #12
Thread: Black
Tail: 2 moose mane hairs
Rib: Black thread
Abdomen: Stripped peacock herl, dyed black, coated with head cement
Wings: White duck quill sections, edged with black duck quill sections
Thorax: Black dubbing
Hackle: Black

Blue Quill Dun

Tied by: Sheldon G. Fedder II, Millville, PA
Hook: Mustad 94840, #18
Thread: Dark gray
Tail: Dark dun Micro Fibetts
Rib: Fine silver wire
Body: Creamy gray dubbing
Wings: Dark dun feather tips, divided
Hackle: Dark dun

Borjas' Mayfly Dun

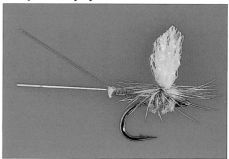

Tied by: Dave Borjas, Dillon, MT
Hook: Daiichi 1140, #18
Thread: Tan 8/0
Tails: Cream Micro Fibetts
Abdomen: Bleached porcupine guard hair, wrapped over cream McFly Form, extended
Thorax: Cream Antron dubbing
Wings: Tan poly yarn, divided, glued, pinched flat with pliers before drying, then cut to shape when dry
Hackle: Bleached grizzly

Budwill's Mayfly Dun

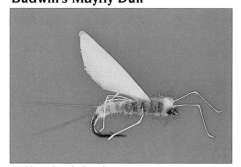

Tied by: Erik Budwill, Red Deer, AB
Hook: TMC 9300, #12
Thread: Dun 6/0
Tails: White Micro Fibetts
Legs: Elk rump hair, bent to shape
Abdomen: White beaver dubbing
Thorax: Cream beaver dubbing
Wings: White hen saddle feathers, cut to shape
Eyes: Mono

Charles' Golden Pheasant Tail

Tied by: G. Charles Costner, Sacramento, CA
Hook: TMC 5210, Mustad 94840, #12-#16
Thread: Black
Tails: Moose mane hairs, split
Body: Golden pheasant tail feather fibers, wrapped
Wing: White calf body hair
Hackle: Cree

David's Green Drake

Tied by: David Williams, Bloomington, IN
Hook: Mustad 98480, #10
Thread: Brown 6/0
Tail: Moose mane hairs
Body: Dark olive dubbing
Wings: Olive black-laced hen feathers
Hackles: Olive black-laced grizzly

Doc's BWO

Tied by: Mark B. Clack, Pueblo, CO
Hook: Mustad 94840, #16-#20
Thread: Gray
Tail: Gray deer hair
Body: Gray-olive Antron dubbing
Wing: Deer hair, cut to shape
Hackle: Light dun

Egan's PMD Dun

Tied by: Lance Egan, Sandy, UT
Hook: TMC 200R, #16, hook point-up
Thread: Yellow, 8/0
Tail: Yellow Micro Fibetts
Abdomen: Yellow turkey biot
Wings: Gray Air-Flow, cut to shape
Hackle: Dun
Head: Yellow Superfine

Extended Dun

Tied by: John Roper, Jasper, GA
Hook: Mustad 94840, #10-#16
Thread: Cream
Tail: White Micro Fibetts
Rib: Cream thread
Abdomen: Bleached elk hair, tied extended
Wings: Cream feathers, half feather style, folded and trimmed
Thorax: Cream dubbing
Hackle: Cream

Foam Parachute Adams

Tied by: Mike Telford, Fresno, CA
Hook: TMC 2487, #12
Thread: Gray
Tail: Golden pheasant tail feather fibers
Body: Gray Fur Foam, folded foam extension style
Wing: White Antron yarn fibers and 3 strands of pearl Krystal Flash, looped
Hackle: Brown and Grizzly

Foam Para Green Drake

Tied by: Perry Tupper, Salem, OR
Hook: TMC 103BL, #13
Thread: Black, 6/0
Tail: Dun Micro Fibetts
Body: Packing foam (Ethafoam) colored green with a waterproof marker, folded foam extension style
Wing: Deer hair
Hackle: Olive grizzly

Goodyear Hex Dun

Tied by: John Gribb, Mt. Hored, WI
Hook: Mustad 3366, #6
Thread: Black 6/0
Tails: Mono, 2 strands
Rib: Tying thread
Body: Yellow 2mm foam, cut to shape, colored with brown marker
Wing: Light elk hair
Legs: Black round rubber
Head: Body material folded back

Goto Mayfly

Tied by: Jim Riley, Grass Valley
Hook: TMC 101, #12-#20
Thread: Brown
Tail: Mallard flank feather fibers
Body: Olive brown Antron dubbing, or color of choice
Wing: White closed-cell foam noodle, looped
Hackle: Grizzly, natural or dyed
Comments: This is my "go to" fly. When there is no bug life showing, this is the fly I use. It can be used as an emerger or a low floating dun or spinner. I tie this pattern in different sizes and colors.

Hexagenia Dun

Tied by: Nadeer Youssef, Pullman, WA
Hook: TMC 2488, #10, hook point-up
Thread: Gray
Tail/Shellback: Moose main hairs
Rib: Black 3/0 thread
Body: Elk hair, extended
Wings: Plastic bag material, cut to shape
Hackle: Ginger, bottom fibers trimmed
Eyes: Red mono
Head: Elk hair, pulled back

Hoffman's Parachute Mayfly

Tied by: Henry Hoffman, Warrenton, OR
Hook: TMC 5210, Mustad 94840, #10-#16
Thread: Gray
Tail: Ginger grizzly feather fibers
Body: Stripped quill from feather used for tail fibers
Thorax: Tan beaver dubbing
Wings: 2 feathers, same color as tail, reverse-hackle, divided
Hackle: Same color as wing feathers, parachute style

Inverted Hook Bottom Hackled Mayfly

Tied by: Charles H. Robbins, Tracy, CA
Hook: TMC 200, #12-#20, hook point-up
Thread: Camel 6/0 or match body color
Tails: Woodduck flank feather fibers
Abdomen: Goose biot on the small hooks, turkey biot on the larger hooks, brown or color to match the natural
Thorax: Brown dry fly dubbing or to match abdomen color
Wings: Duck quill sections, divided, tied on inverted hook
Hackle: Tied parachute style, posted on a Super Floss band stretched to a gallows. When Super Floss is relaxed, it will swell to hold the hackle, it can then be cut off short, with just a small piece showing.
Comments: By inverting the hook the mayfly takes on the natural curved shape with the hackle on the bottom; this lets it rest on the water like a natural.

Parachute Louis

Tied by: Mike Murphy, Bozeman, MT
Hook: Mustad 94840 or TMC 5210, #10-#24
Thread: Color to match the natural
Tail: Yellow Labrador retriever "Louis" tail fur, 2 or 3 hairs
Body: Olive-brown or color to match the natural
Wing Post: Yellow Labrador retriever "Louis" tail fur
Hackle: Grizzly or color to match the natural

Royal May

Tied by: Roy D. Powell, Danville, CA
Hook: TMC 2487, #14-#16
Thread: Black 8/0 or to match the natural
Tails: Betts Tailing Fibers
Body: San Juan Chenille, medium dun, olive or black
Wings: Duck quill sections, treated with Softex
Thorax: Gray, olive or black Hare-Tron dubbing
Hackle: Grizzly hackle, palmered through thorax
Comments: To form body and tail section, heat 1/2 inch of chenille and mold into a tapered body. With a needle, form a hole in the narrow end of the chenille, then, insert the tail fibers. Pinch the end of the body with your fingers, spread the tail fibers, and add a very small amount of Super Glue.

King's BWO

Tied by: Matt King, Victoria, BC
Hook: Daiichi 1150, #14-#20, hook point-up
Thread: White 6/0
Tail: Blue eared pheasant feather fibers
Underbody: White thread, top colored with permanent black marker
Abdomen: Light olive Thin Skin
Thorax: Light olive SLF dubbing, picked out
Wings: Prismatic Pliable sheeting, cut to size
Hackle: Dark dun

Ralph's Green Drake

Tied by: Ralph D'Errico, Jr., Tucson, AZ
Hook: TMC 5230, #14
Thread: Green 8/0
Tail: Yellow and green feather fibers
Underbody: Yellow dubbing
Body: Yellow stripped peacock herl
Wings: Olive-yellow Medallion sheeting cut to shape
Hackle: Golden-olive grizzly

Schneider's Mayfly Dun

Tied by: Alan Schneider, Penticton, BC
Hook: TMC 2487, #20
Thread: Black
Tails: Mallard flank feather fibers
Abdomen: Black fabric ribbon, extended over mono core
Wings: Clear Swiss straw, shaped with wing burner, mottled with black permanent marker
Eyes: Mono
Legs: 4 pheasant tail feather fibers
Thorax: Brown dubbing

March Brown Extended Body Mayfly Dun

Tied by: Joe Sudman, Poulsbo, WA
Hook: TMC 2487, #10-14
Thread: Black, 6/0
Tail: Moose mane hairs
Rib: Black floss
Body: Light brown floss, extended body core is 15 lb. Maxima leader, dubbed
Wings: Bronze mallard flank feather fibers, looped wing style
Hackle: Cree

Roth's March Brown Para Dun

Tied by: Scott Roth, Andover, NJ
Hook: TMC 206BL, #10-#14
Thread: Tan
Tails: Mallard flank feather fibers
Abdomen: Tan foam, extended body with 12lb. mono core, mark top of body with brown permanent marker
Wing: 4 dun CDC feathers
Thorax: Tan dubbing mixed with chopped fine Mylar tinsel
Hackle: Medium dun

Sparkle Wing Dun—Extended Body

Tied by: David Curneal, S. Solvan, NJ
Hook: TMC 2487, #12-#16
Thread: Green
Abdomen: Tan and brown Antron yarn, twisted then furled, extended
Thorax: Tan dubbing
Wing: High Luster Sparkle Wing
Hackle: Brown, palmer over thorax, bottom clipped

Mayfly Spinners

The Unsinkable Mayfly

Tied by: Kyle Hicks, Berwick, NS
Hook: Mustad 3906 or TMC 3769, #14
Thread: White 6/0
Tail: Mallard flank feather fibers
Rib: White thread
Body: White foam
Wing: Mallard flank feather fibers
Hackle: Grizzly, wrapped between foam and hook shank

Wulff Green Drake

Tied by: Dustin Harris, Monmouth, OR
Hook: Mustad 94840 or TMC 900BL, #10-#14
Thread: Olive or color to match body
Tail: Brown-olive dyed deer hair, or color to match body
Rib: Yellow Nymph Cord
Body: Brown-olive dubbing or match color of natural
Wing: Brown-olive dyed deer hair
Hackle: Grizzly hackle dyed olive

Basic Spinner (Green Drake)

Tied by: Dustin Harris, Monmouth, OR
Hook: Mustad 3906B, TMC 3761, #10-#14
Thread: Olive or color to match body
Tail: Brown-olive dyed deer hair
Rib: Yellow Nymph Cord
Body: Olive Nymph Cord
Wing: Brown-olive dyed deer hair, spent
Hackle: Brown-olive grizzly, top and bottom fibers clipped

Bill's P.E.D. Spinner

Tied by: William Urban, Bound Brook, NJ
Hook: TMC 2487 or TMC 206BL, #10-#22
Thread: Brown 6/0 or 8/0 or color to match the natural
Tail: 3 or 5 strands of deer hair from abdomen
Abdomen: Brown deer hair or color to match the natural, extended approximately twice the hook length
Thorax: Brown dubbing or color to match the natural
Hackle: Light dun or white, top and bottom fibers clipped

Blue Quill Spinner

Tied by: Sheldon G. Fedder II, Millville, PA
Hook: Mustad 94840, #18
Thread: Dark brown
Tails: Dark brown Micro Fibetts
Body: Red-brown dubbing
Wings: Dark dun poly yarn

Borjas' Mayfly Spinner

Tied by: Dave Borjas, Dillon, MT
Hook: Daiichi 1140, #18
Thread: Tan 8/0
Tails: Cream Micro Fibetts
Abdomen: Brown porcupine guard hair, wrapped over cream McFly Foam
Thorax: Brown Antron dubbing
Wing: Tan poly yarn, glued, pinched flat with pliers before dry, dried, cut to shape

Budwill's Mayfly Spinner

Tied by: Erik Budwill, Red Deer, AB
Hook: TMC 9300, #12
Thread: Dun 6/0
Tails: White Micro Fibetts
Abdomen: White beaver dubbing
Thorax: Cream Beaver dubbing
Wing Case: Packing foam strip, colored brown
Wings: White hen saddle feathers, cut to shape
Eyes: Mono, burnt
Head: Same as abdomen

Callibaetis Spinner

Tied by: Robert Kopp, Williams Lake, BC
Hook: Mustad 94840 or TMC 5210, #10-#14, hook point-up
Thread: Brown 8/0
Tail: 3 moose mane hairs, tips from body
Rib: Brown thread
Body: Rusty brown deer hair
Wings: Badger feathers, spent style
Hackle: Grizzly, bottom fibers trimmed

CDC Biot Spinner

Tied by: Neil Selbicky, Talent, OR
Hook: Mustad 94840 or TMC 5210, #14
Thread: Tan
Tail: 3 light-colored deer hair fibers
Abdomen: Tan turkey biot
Wings: CDC feather fibers, white poly yarn fibers, spent style
Thorax: Tan translucent dubbing

Egan's PMD Spinner

Tied by: Lance Egan, Sandy, UT
Hook: TMC 100, #14
Thread: Yellow, 8/0
Tails: Yellow Micro Fibetts
Abdomen: Yellow turkey biot
Thorax: Yellow Superfine
Wings: Pearlescent Mylar, cut to shape, spent
Hackle: Dun, top and bottom fibers trimmed

Egg Laying Green Drake

Tied by: Troy Standish, Williamsville, NY
Hook: Partridge Fly Body, #10, bent down
Thread: White
Tails: Black Chinese Boar hairs
Egg Sac: Yellow Antron dubbing
Rib: Pearl tinsel
Body: White rabbit dubbing
Wing Pad: Black goose feather fibers
Wings: White hen feathers
Hackle: Grizzly

Feather Spinner

Tied by: John Roper, Jasper, GA
Hook: Mustad 94840, #14-#20
Thread: Rust
Tail/Abdomen: Brown feathers, pulled body style, abdomen coated with Flexament after mounting
Wings: Medium dun feather, pulled style, folded and trimmed after mounting
Thorax: Rust dubbing

Goodyear Hex Spinner

Tied by: John Gribb, Mt. Hored, WI
Hook: Mustad 3366, #6
Thread: Black 6/0
Tails: Mono, 2 strands
Rib: Tying thread
Body: Yellow 2mm foam, cut to shape, colored with brown permanent marker
Wings: Light elk hair
Head: Body material folded back

Hendrickson Spinner

Tied by: Tim O'Sullivan, Elora, ON
Hook: Daiichi 2460, #16-#18
Thread: Tan UNI, 8/0
Tails: Dun Micro Fibetts
Abdomen: Brown colored plastic strip
Thorax: Light hare's ear dubbing
Wings: Gray CDC feathers, spent style, cut to shape

Hexagenia Spinner

Tied by: Nadeer Youssef, Pullman, WA
Hook: TMC 2487, #10
Thread: Tan 6/0
Tail: Elk mane hair
Rib: Pearl Krystal Flash strand
Abdomen: Elk mane hair, wrapped
Wings: Black and pearl Krystal Flash strands, looped
Thorax/Head: Deer hair

King's BWO Spinner

Tied by: Matt King, Victoria, BC
Hook: TMC 101, #14-#22
Thread: White 6/0
Tails: Betts Tailing Fibers
Underbody: White thread, marked on top with black permanent marker
Abdomen: Light olive Thin Skin
Wing Case: Mottled Thin Skin
Thorax: SLF squirrel dubbing, picked out
Underwings: Dun CDC feather fibers
Wings: Prismatic Pliable Sheeting, cut to shape

March Brown Parachute (Spinner)

Tied by: Jack Pangburn, Westbury, NY
Hook: Mustad 94840, #12
Thread: Brown/tan (fawn), 6/0
Tail: Ginger Micro Fibetts
Body: Thread
Wing Post: Dark brown and gray poly yarn, mixed
Wing: Brown wood duck and mallard flank feather fibers, mixed
Hackle: Dark ginger

Roth's March Brown Spinner

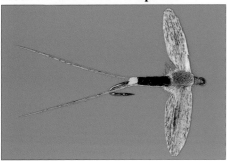

Tied by: Scott Roth, Andover, NJ
Hook: TMC 101, #10-#12
Thread: Tan
Tails: Mallard flank fibers
Abdomen: Tan foam, top colored with brown permanent marker, end colored with yellow waterproof paint
Thorax: Tan dubbing with chopped fine Mylar tinsel
Wing: Mottled plastic, preformed or cut to shape, spent
Thorax Shellback: Light brown foam

Rusty Quill

Tied by: Robert Schreiner, Southampton, PA
Hook: Mustad 94840, #12
Thread: Black
Tails: Moose mane hairs
Abdomen: Stripped peacock herl, lacquered
Wings: White feathers, pulled style, folded and trimmed
Thorax: Black dubbing

Sparkle Wing Spinner (Extended Body)

Tied by: David Curneal, S. Solvan, NJ
Hook: TMC 2487, #12-#16
Thread: Green
Abdomen: Tan and brown Antron yarn, twisted then furled, extended
Thorax: Tan dubbing
Wings: High Luster Sparkle Wing, tied spent
Hackle: Brown, palmer over thorax, bottom fibers trimmed

Tan Mayfly Spinner

Tied by: Henry Hoffman, Warrenton, OR
Hook: TMC 5210, Mustad 94840, #14-#18
Thread: Gray
Tail: White feather fibers
Abdomen: Brown biot, from rooster wing feather
Hackle/Wing: White, top and bottom fibers trimmed
Thorax: Tan beaver dubbing

Bead-Butt Peeking Caddis

Tied by: Richard Murphy, Manitou Springs, CO
Hook: TMC 200R, #14-#18
Thread: Black, 6/0
Rib: Copper wire, counter wrapped
Case: Pheasant tail feather fibers
Body: Chartreuse dubbing
Head: Peacock herl
Legs: Back hackle, sparse

Ben's Bead-Head Caddis

Tied by: Benjamin Turton, Marquette, MI
Hook: Mustad 80250BR, #12-#16
Thread: Brown
Abdomen: Brown Larva Lace
Thorax: Peacock herl
Head: Gold cone

Body Glass Caddis Larva

Tied by: Edward Caposele, Forked River, NJ
Hook: Orvis 889, #12
Thread: Black, 6/0
Rib: Clear Orvis Body Glass, V-Rib or Larva Lace
Body: Gray fox squirrel dubbing
Thorax: Charcoal Mottled Nymph Blend dubbing
Head: Black 1/8 bead

Bouks' Green Caddis Larva

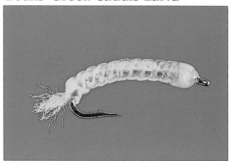

Tied by: Oleg Bouks, Philadelphia, PA
Hook: TMC 200R, #20
Thread: Fluorescent Chartreuse, 8/0
Tail: Small tuft of fluorescent chartreuse Danville Stretch
    Nylon
Body: Chartreuse V-Rib, small
Comments: While this pattern represents a green caddisfly
larva, it can also be taken for a midge larva. Fish it
upstream, dead drifted, anytime of the year.

Brachycentrus Larva

Tied by: Neil J. Selbicky, Talent, OR
Hook: TMC 3761 or Mustad 3906B, #14
Thread: Black, 6/0
Underbody: 2 strips of flat lead, cut in triangular shapes
    and secured to each side of hook, with Super Glue
    or 5-minute epoxy
Case: 4 or 5 bleached and stripped peacock herl strands
    wrapped around lead foundation then covered with a
    coat of head cement
Legs: Grouse or partridge feather fibers

Bright Green Caddis Larva

Tied by: Todd Turner, Ft. Lauderdale, FL
Hook: Daiichi 1140, #18
Thread: Dark brown, 8/0
Body: Chartreuse latex tubing, furled
Head: Dark olive Antron dubbing

Caddis "Caboose"

Tied by: Ted Lawrence, Delta, BC
Hook: Mustad 9672, #14, weighted, cut off at bend after completing body
Thread: Gray, 6/0
Body: Mixed grizzly and brown hackle, trimmed short (optional: sticks and Deep Soft Lead formed into balls and glued to body with Zap-A-Gap)
Front Tandem Hook
Hook: TMC 200, #14
Thread: Black, 6/0
Underbody: Yellow floss
Body: Yellow Crystal Chenille
Head: Black Ostrich herl
Comments: Hooks joined by a single strand of 6lb. monofilament mounted to the hook shanks before starting bodies.

Casino's Caddis Larva

Tied by: Nino Casino, Alatri, Frosinone, Italy
Hook: TMC 5262, #6
Thread: Brown or black, 6/0
Underbody: Lead wire, wrapped to shape
Case: Real case from caddis, glued in place, or cover underbody wire with 5-minute epoxy and roll in clean sand-and-small-pebble mixture
Body: Transparent Body Gum, or epoxy
Legs: Black seal fur
Head: Black Swiss straw

DD Plus

Tied by: Brandon Fessler, North Ogden, UT
Hook: TMC 206BL, #14-#16
Thread: Black, 6/0 or 8/0
Body: Dark green vernille, or color to match the natural
Head: Black hare's ear dubbing

Deer Iridescent

Tied by: Ronn Lucas, Sr., Milwaukie, OR
Hook: 2 or 3XL, #10-#14, weighted
Thread: Black, 6/0
Case: Chopped deer and natural rabbit hair or other "spiky" fur with pine needles and twigs, blended and wrapped in a dubbing loop, then picked out very shaggy
Body: Medium olive Iridescent Dubbing, trim short
Head/Legs: Black Iridescent Dubbing, picked out
Comments: This cased caddis pattern can be tied in any color dubbing or deer hair to match naturals.

Dunsmuir Rockworm

Tied by: Jay Kaneshige, Hayward, CA
Hook: Daiichi 1130, #10-#14, weighted
Thread: Black, 8/0
Tail: 2 pheasant tail feather fibers, cut short
Rib: Fine gold tinsel
Body: 50/50 mix of gold Buggy Nymph dubbing and light olive-brown Hare-Tron dubbing
Legs/Head: Black marabou feather fibers cut into 1/2 inch pieces, mixed and loosely dubbed
Comments: This pattern imitates the October caddis larva. The natural—called a "rockworm" by Uncle George—was the local bait of choice, before I started fly fishing.

Eby's Cased Larva

Tied by: Gord Eby, Fort St. John, BC
Hook: Mustad 9672, #6, bent to shape
Thread: Black, 6/0
Case: Closed-cell foam, covered with Sparkle Chenille and ribbed with clipped olive and brown hackle
Body: Cream latex strip
Head: Black thread
Comments: This fly was developed for traveling sedge caddis larvae.

Electra Larva

Tied by: Mike Lanzone, North Chili, NY
Hook: Daiichi 1150, #12-#16
Thread: Olive, 8/0
Underbody: Green communication wire, stripped using outer shell; if a weighted fly is desired, do not strip the wire
Overbody: Sparsely dubbed clear Scintilla dubbing
Legs: Partridge feather fibers
Head: Woodchuck or brown rabbit dubbing

Free Living Larva

Tied by: Scott Roth, Andover, NJ
Hook: TMC 2457, #10
Thread: Olive, 6/0
Tail/Gills: CDC feather fibers
Abdomen: Tan sheet foam, cut into 1/4 inch strip, wrapped, top colored with brown waterproof marker, coated with Softex
Thorax: Peacock herl
Head: Brass bead

Free Living Net Spinner Larva

Tied by: Charles Robbins, Tracy, CA
Hook: TMC 200R, #12
Thread: Brown, 6/0
Body: Green Larva Lace and white Antron yarn woven with an overhand weave, Antron yarn pick out to suggest gills
Legs: Magic Dub stands, hair singed and bend to shape
Thorax: Brown seed beads
Head: Brown thread

Glass Bead Larva

Tied by: Corey Wiggins, West Linn, OR
Hook: Mustad 3906 or TMC 3761, #12-#16
Thread: Black
Body: Green Antron dubbing with clear glass beads
Thorax: Black rabbit dubbing
Head: Clear glass bead

Holey Head Cased Caddis

Tied by: Vladimir Markov, Irkusk, Russia
Hook: Silver Holey Head Hook, #12
Thread: Cream
Case: 4 sections of sand, amber, brown and black Antron yarn or Mouline (made in Germany), crocheted
Legs: Deer hair
Comments: This pattern looks like a bead head fly, but because the hook rides up it doesn't catch the bottom. The hook is homemade. Its design was developed on the basis of Mormyshka and old Russian lyre created for ice fishing. I take the natural to the craft store to match the colors of the case. (See Fall 2001 *Flyfishing & Tying Journal* for directions on making Holey hooks.)

Jelly Larva

Tied by: Brad Cunningham, Yakima, WA
Hook: TMC 200R, #6-#14
Thread: Olive, 8/0
Body: Olive Jelly Rope on larger hooks, olive V-Rib on smaller hooks
Legs: Black goose biots
Head: Black Ostrich herl

Killer Caddis Larva

Tied by: Raymond Martinez, Hayward, CA
Hook: Daiichi 1710, #6-#16
Thread: Brown
Abdomen: Natural chamois strip
Legs: Horsetail hair
Thorax: Peacock herl
Comments: The chamois, when wet, looks and feels like a caddis larva.

Kim's Cased Caddis

Tied by: Kim Jensen, Ogden, UT
Hook: Mustad 80150 BR, #14
Thread: Olive, 6/0
Case: Micro chenille underbody, coated with 5-minute epoxy, covered with sand and pebbles
Body: Olive Larva Lace strands, woven with an overhand weave
Legs: Black pheasant tail feather fibers
Head: Black dubbing

King's Caddis Larva

Tied by: Matt King, Victoria, BC
Hook: Daiichi 1150, #12-#18
Thread: Brown or color to match the natural, 6/0
Shellback: Mottled Thin Skin
Head/Legs: Natural red squirrel dubbing
Rib/Gills: White ostrich herl and 2lb. mono, spun and wrapped
Body: SLF caddis green or color to match the natural

Kopp's Cased Caddis

Tied by: Bob Kopp, Williams Lake, BC
Hook: Mustad 79580 or TMC 300, #6-#10, weighted
Thread: Dark Brown, 6/0
Case: Olive chenille or yarn, coated with 5-minute epoxy and coated with sand and small sticks
Legs: Black floss
Head: Brass bead

Krystal Caddis Larva

Tied by: Don Heyden, Bozeman, MT
Hook: Mustad 3906B, #12-#16
Thread: Black 6/0
Abdomen: Peacock Krystal Flash, 2-4 strands twisted and wrapped
Thorax: Light green dubbing
Hackle: Black starling

Leptoceridae Caddis Larva

Tied by: Steve Potter, Tracy, CA
Hook: Barbless caddis hook, #6-#8, weighted
Thread: Black, 6/0 or 8/0
Underbody: Floss or dubbing shaped to a firm cigar shape
Case: Small pieces of cork cut by using rasp on a red wine cork, and placed on underbody with Dave's Flexament,
Legs: 6 Emu feathers, cut short
Thorax: Peacock herl twisted with fine copper wire

Lively Caddis Larva-Cased

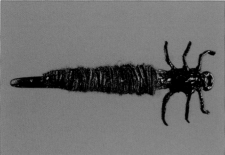

Tied by: Wayne Freeman, Lexington, SC
Hook: Any straight, limerick bend, tuned-down eye streamer hook, #8
Thread: Black 8/0
Case Underbody: Hot glue cut to a tapered form, getting larger towards the hook eye
Case: Light brown to brown pheasant tail feather fibers
Underbody: Iron Gray 6/0 thread
Abdomen: Olive medium size V-Rib
Wing Case: Black Swiss straw
Legs: Black plastic bristle from hairbrush, bent to shape
Thorax: Extra fine black dubbing wrapped through legs
Comments: Coat abdomen, thorax and legs with Softex or a similar product in several thin layers to give shape and translucent quality, let dry. Paint thorax and hook eye with black Pantone marker.

Lively Caddis Larva-Free Swimming

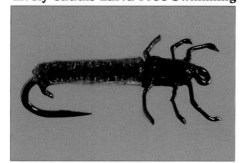

Tied by: Wayne Freeman, Lexington, SC
Hook: Any fine wire, straight, round bend, turned-down eye hook, #10
Thread: Black, 8/0
Anal Claws: Black plastic bristles from hairbrush, bent to shape
Underbody: Iron Gray 6/0 thread
Overbody: Olive medium V-Rib
Wing Case: Black Swiss straw
Legs: Black plastic bristles form hairbrush, bent to shape
Thorax: Extra fine black dubbing
Comments: Coat fly with Softex or similar product in several thin layers and let dry. Paint the thorax and hook eye with a black Pantone marker.

"Mad" Caddis Larva-Bead Head

Tied by: Glenn Weisner, Toledo, OH
Hook: TMC 2487, #10-#14
Thread: Olive, 6/0
Underbody: Electric green synthetic dubbing
Overbody: Green holographic tubing, end melted
Wing: Light Z-lon fibers
Head: Fluorescent green rabbit dubbing, peacock herl, and brass bead

McConville's Caddis Larva

Tied by: Tim McConville, Salt Lake City, UT
Hook: TMC 2457, #12
Thread: Olive
Body: Green vinyl rib
Collar: Peacock herl
Head: Copper bead

Peeping Caddis

Tied by: Ron Pettey, Elie, Man.
Hook: Mustad 9672, #10-#14, weighted
Thread: Brown
Head: Cream Antron yarn, tag end melted
Legs: Partridge feather, 1 wrap
Body: Brown and olive dubbing

Rubber Band Caddis Larva

Tied by: Henry Hoffman, Warrenton, OR
Hook: Mustad 3366, #10-#16
Thread: Tan 6/0
Body: Cream or tan rubber band, wrapped and coated with water based head cement
Hackle: Tuft of barred brown chickabou from base of rooster flank feather
Head: Black brass bead

Rubber Band Green Rock Worm

Tied by: Henry Hoffman, Warrenton, OR
Hook: Mustad 3366, #10-#16
Thread: Olive, 6/0
Body: Green rubber band, wrapped and coated with water based head cement
Hackle: Black knee hackle from hen or rooster
Head: Black brass bead

Schreiner's Bead Head Caddis Larva

Tied by: Robert H. Schreiner, Jr., Southampton, PA
Hook: Partridge K2B, #14
Thread: Olive, 8/0
Rib: Stripped peacock herl, backed with fine gold wire
Shellback: Olive latex strip
Body: Green SLF dubbing
Bead topping: Pheasant tail feather fibers
Thorax: Brass bead
Legs: Pheasant tail feather fibers, tips form bead topping

Stick Boy

Tied by: Kyle Hicks, Berwick, NS
Hook: Mustad 3906, #14-#16, weighted
Thread: Black, 8/0
Case: Deer hair, cut tips off hair, mounted along shank to form case
Head: Peacock herl

Stick Caddis

Tied by: Floyd Franke, Roscoe, NY
Hook: Daiichi 1270, #12, weighted
Thread: Brown, 6/0
Larva: Craft foam, cut to shape, end melted to form head
Legs: Partridge feather fibers
Case: Turkey tail feather fibers, applied overlapping like shingles over squirrel hair dubbing brush

Todd's Caddis Larva

Tied by: Todd Turner, Fort Lauderdale, FL
Hook: Daiichi 1140, #16-#22
Thread: Dark brown 8/0
Abdomen: Bright green Scud Back, thin strip twisted and furled, tied extended, (optional colors: tan and brown)
Shellback: Brown Scud Back
Thorax: Peacock herl

Tuma's Cased Caddis

Tied by: Adam Tuma, Lebanon, OR
Hook: TMC 5263, #8-#12, weighted
Thread: Black, 6/0
Case: Blend of red, black, and natural deer hair spun and clipped to shape
Body: Cream rabbit dubbing
Hackle: Black

Uncased Larva

Tied by: Clifford Sullivan, Sr., Tracy, CA
Hook: TMC 2487, #12-#14
Thread: Green
Underbody: 2 pieces of lead wire mounted to the sides of the hook, trimmed to a taper
Body: Tan and cream embroidery thread strands, woven using the overhand weave
Legs: Horsetail hairs
Head: Peacock herl

Wayne's Caddisfly Larva

Tied by: Andrew Wayne, San Francisco, CA
Hook: Mustad 3906B or TMC 3762, #16, weighted
Thread: Brown, 6/0
Head: Yellow Antron yarn, end melted
Hackle: Partridge
Body: Rabbit hair, clipped

Woven Caddis Larva

Tied by: Walt Lawson, Red Cliff, Alta.
Hook: Mustad 9671 or TMC 5262, #10, weighted
Thread: Olive or brown, 6/0
Body: Olive and yellow Antron yarn strands, woven with an overhand weave
Hackle: Mallard, dyed wood duck
Head: Brown dubbing

Caddisfly Pupae

Antron Caddis

Tied by: Walt Lawson, Red Cliff, Alta.
Hook: Mustad 3906, #8, weighted
Thread: Olive, 6/0
Rib: Green wire
Shellback/Wing Case: Green Antron yarn
Abdomen: Amber Antron dubbing
Thorax: Olive-brown squirrel dubbing

Bead Head Caddis Pupa

Tied by: Adam Tuma, Lebanon, OR
Hook: TMC 2457, #12-#16, weighted
Thread: Black, 6/0
Rib: Yellow floss
Abdomen: Cream rabbit dubbing
Thorax: Black rabbit dubbing
Head: Bass bead

Beamoc Caddis

Tied by: Floyd Franke, Roscoe, NY
Hook: Daiichi 1270, #12
Thread: Olive, 8/0
Body: Insect green chenille
Wings: Gray poly yarn, pulled to sides of body
Legs: Pheasant tail feather fibers
Head: Black bead-chain eyes, 2mm

Bright Green Caddis Pupa

Tied by: Todd Turner, Ft. Lauderdale, FL
Hook: Daiichi 1140, #18
Thread: Dark Brown, 8/0
Body: Chartreuse latex tubing and pale-olive Antron dubbing, furled
Wings/Legs: Partridge feather fibers
Head: Dark brown Antron dubbing

Casino's Caddis Pupa

Tied by: Nino Casino, Alatri, Frosinone, Italy
Hook: TMC 2457, #8, weighted
Thread: Brown or black, 6/0
Underbody: Golden yellow Antron yarn
Rib: Black Antron yarn
Body: Transparent Body Gum, or epoxy
Wings: Tan Swiss straw, cut to shape
Thorax: Black Antron yarn, topped with black Swiss straw
Legs: Deer hair
Antennae: Moose hair

Cowlitz Caddis Emerger

Tied by: Lee Wheeler, Winloch, WA
Hook: TMC 200, #8, weighted
Thread: Black 6/0
Rib: Orange yarn, 1 strand from 3 strand yarn
Abdomen: Yellow chenille, medium
Thorax: Brown chenille, medium
Hackle: Golden pheasant body feather

Deep Caddis Pupa-Olive

Tied by: Neil J. Selbicky, Talent, OR
Hook: Partridge Nymph Emerger, #10
Thread: Olive, 8/0
Abdomen: Olive vernille, end melted to a taper
Thorax: Olive dubbing
Legs: Brown grouse or partridge feather fibers
Wing: White poly yarn fibers
Head: Olive-brown dubbing

Eby's Caddis Pupa

Tied by: Gord Eby, Fort St. John, BC
Hook: Mustad 9671, #8, weight optional
Thread: Black, 6/0
Underbody: Yellow foam
Body: Light green Larva Lace
Shellback: Brown Antron yarn
Wings: Olive Swiss straw, cut to shape
Legs: Pheasant tail feather fibers
Head: Peacock herl
Comments: This pattern was developed for the traveling sedge.

Emerging Sedge Pupa

Tied by: Robert Schreiner, Southampton, PA
Hook: TMC 947BL, #10-#16, weight optional
Thread: Black
Underbody: Thread to shape
Abdomen: Tan Nymph Skin strip, colored with brown permanent marker
Shellback: Brown Flexibody
Wings: Brown Swiss straw, cut to shape and coated with Flexibody
Thorax/Head: Brown CDC dubbing
Legs: Amherst pheasant tail feather fibers, 2 fibers glued together for each leg
Antennae: Amherst pheasant tail feather fibers

Floating Bead Head Pupa

Tied by: Scott Roth, Andover, NJ
Hook: TMC 206BL, #10
Thread: Tan, 6/0
Body: Tan sheet foam, cut into 1/4 inch strip, wrapped, top colored brown with waterproof marker and coated with Softex
Wings: Tan sheet foam, cut to shape
Legs: Emu feather fibers
Thorax: Tan Crystal dubbing
Head: Plastic gold bead

Green Head Breadcrust

Tied by: Gerry Bauer, Littleton, CO
Hook: TMC 3761, #12-#18, weight optional
Thread: Tan, 8/0
Underbody: Tan yarn
Body: Grouse tail feather (red phase is traditional), fibers cut short and stripped from shaft, wrapped
Legs: Partridge or grouse feather, 1 or 2 wraps
Head: Fluorescent green dubbing
Comments: I tied this version of the Breadcrust to match a Mother's Day caddis pupa.

Gold Rush

Tied by: Brandon Fessler, North Ogden, UT
Hook: TMC 3769 or Mustad 3906, #14-#16, weighted
Thread: Black, 6/0 or 8/0
Body: Gold Antron dubbing
Head: Black hare's ear dubbing
Comments: Add fly floatant to the fly, not to float the fly, but for catching little air bubble to make it look realistic.

Holey Head Woolly Pupa

Tied by: Vladimir Markov, Irkusk, Russia
Hook: Silver Holey Head Hook, #12
Thread: Fluorescent Yellow, 6/0
Body: Amber/black fringe tape
Hackle: Brown hen hackle
Comments: Fringe tape made from the mesh of a nylon fish net was created by Siberian anglers seven years ago for winter flies for ice fishing, it is also homemade. The hook is homemade. (See Fall 2001 *Flyfishing & Tying Journal* for directions on making hook.)

Halloween Caddis

Tied by: Don Joslyn, Eagle Point, OR
Hook: Alec Jackson River Dee Low Water, gold, #9, weight optional
Thread: Black 6/0
Tail: Gold Spirit River holographic tinsel strands, short
Rib: Gold Spirit River holographic tinsel
Abdomen: Ardent orange Scintilla Caliente, top colored with olive permanent marker
Wing: CDC feather fibers
Legs: Partridge feather fibers
Antennae: Ginger pheasant tail feather fibers
Thorax: Peacock herl
Head: Gold bead

Iacoletti's Caddis Pupa

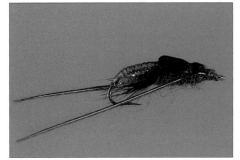

Tied by: Fred Iacoletti, Albuquerque, NM
Hook: TMC 200R, #14, weighted
Thread: Olive, 6/0
Underbody: Green floss
Abdomen: Clear Larva Lace
Legs: Brown hen feather fibers
Wings: Black duck quill
Thorax: Olive-brown dubbing
Shellback/Head: Brown latex over a thin white foam strip
Antennae: Pheasant tail feather fibers

Interior Sedge

Tied by: Ron Pettey, Elir, Man.
Hook: Mustad 3399, #10-#14
Thread: Green, 6/0
Body: Medium to light olive seal dubbing, between 4 green glass beads
Wing: Mallard flank feather fibers
Legs: Golden pheasant crest feather fibers
Head: Light brown seal

Killer Caddis Pupa

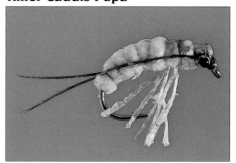

Tied by: Raymond Martinez, Hayward, CA
Hook: Daiichi 1710, #6-#16, weighted
Thread: Brown
Body: Natural chamois, top of thorax colored yellow-tan with waterproof marker
Legs: Horsehair
Antenna: Pheasant tail feather fibers
Eyes: Mono
Comments: Coat top of body and legs with Dave's Flexament.

King's Caddis Pupa

Tied by: Matt King, Victoria, BC
Hook: Daiichi 1150, #6-#18, weighted
Thread: Black 6/0 or color to match the natural
Shellback: Mottled Thin Skin strip
Rib/Gills: White ostrich herl and 2lb. mono, spun and wrapped
Body: SLF caddis green dubbing, or color to match the natural
Wings: Mottled Thin Skin, cut to shape
Legs: Brown CDC feather wrapped, top fibers folded down
Head: Black dubbing
Antennae: Bronze mallard feather fibers

Lawrence's Caddis Pupa

Tied by: Ted Lawrence, Delta, BC
Hook: TMC 200, #12-#14
Thread: Olive, 6/0
Tail: 2 strands of pearl Krystal Flash and olive Antron yarn fibers
Body: Olive Swannundaze, wrapped over tapered thread underbody
Head: Olive dyed ostrich herl and gold bead
Hackle: Olive dyed mallard flank feather

Lumini Caddis Pupa

Tied by: Giuseppe Nova, Bollate, Italy
Hook: TMC 206BL, #8-#14, weighted
Thread: Black 8/0
Rib: Copper wire
Abdomen: Rust Antron dubbing
Wings: Grizzly feathers, delta style
Thorax: Natural Hare-Tron dubbing
Legs: Pheasant tail feather fibers

Micro-Cable Fur Pupa

Tied by: Edward Caposele, Forked River, NJ
Hook: TMC 205BL, #12
Thread: Green, 6/0
Underbody: Thread built up around thorax
Body: Tarnished gold Micro-Cable
Thorax/Legs: Green rabbit fur with guard hairs, used in a dubbing loop and wrapped toward hook eye, top fibers trimmed

October Caddis Pupa

Tied by: Henry Hoffman, Warrenton, OR
Hook: TMC 200, #10, weight optional
Thread: Light Gray, 6/0
Tail: Light barred gray chickabou feather fibers
Rib: Fine gold wire, counter wrapped
Body: Dark barred olive chickabou feather, wrapped
Hackle: Tan barred rooster soft hackle flank feather, 1 wrap
Eyes: Dyed brown mono
Head: Gray chickabou plume, tied in by tips and figure-eight around eyes

Pooper Pupa

Tied by: Kyle Hicks, Berwick, NS
Hook: Mustad 94840, #16, weight optional
Thread: Black, 8/0
Underbody: Brown dubbing
Overbody: Brown turkey feather fibers
Legs: Mallard flank feather fibers
Head: Black hackle, cut to shape

Potter's Caddis Pupa

Tied by: Steve Potter, Tracy, CA
Hook: Mustad 3716 or TMC 205BL, #6-#8, weighted
Thread: Black 6/0 or 8/0
Abdomen: Olive ostrich and gold French tinsel, twisted together to make a rope
Thorax: Black ostrich and gold French tinsel, twisted together to make a rope
Wings: Gray mallard quill sections, inserted after 2 wraps of back ostrich
Hackle: Brown partridge

VR Caddis Pupa

Tied by: Brad Cunningham, Yakima, WA
Hook: TMC 200R, #10-#16
Thread: Olive, 8/0
Body: Olive V-Rib, formed into a tapered body
Wing: Olive-brown CDC feather fibers, topped with short turkey feather section
Legs: Black goose biots
Head: Peacock herl

Wayne's Caddis Pupa

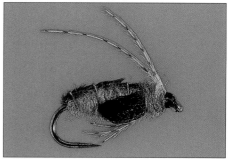

Tied by: Andrew Wayne, San Francisco, CA
Hook: TMC 3761BL, #16, weighted
Thread: Black, 8/0
Rib: Copper wire, counterwrapped
Shellback: Pheasant tail feather fibers
Body: Tan dubbing
Wing pads: Black Antron
Legs: Woodduck flank feather fibers
Head: Tan dubbing
Antennae: Woodduck flank feather fibers

Woven Caddis Pupa

Tied by: Chris French, East Brunswick, NJ
Hook: Mustad 37160, #16, weighted
Thread: Camel
Underbody: 2 strands of .015 wire tied to sides of hook shank
Abdomen: 2 strands of gold glow yarn, woven with an overhand weave
Thorax: Yellow rabbit dubbing
Wings: Duck quill
Hackle: Partridge, 1 wrap

Caddisfly Emergers

Bead-Belly Caddis Emerger

Tied by: Glenn Weisner, Toledo, OH

Hook: TMC 2487, #10-#14
Thread: Brown, 6/0
Tail: Muskrat guard hairs, tips from overbody
Overbody: Muskrat guard hairs topped with pearl Mylar tinsel strand cut short
Body: Iridescent beads
Shuck: Cream Z-lon fibers
Head: Fluorescent green rabbit dubbing, peacock herl

Bright Green Caddis Emerger

Tied by: Todd Turner, Ft. Lauderdale, FL
Hook: Daiichi 1140, #18
Thread: Dark brown, 8/0
Body: Chartreuse latex tubing with olive Antron dubbing, furled
Wing: Dark gray deer hair
Head: Dark green Antron dubbing

Casino's Caddis Emerger

Tied by: Nino Casino, Alatri, Frosinone, Italy
Hook: TMC 2487, #12
Thread: Brown, 0/6
Rib: Peccary hair, colored with yellow Pantone marker
Body: Olive dubbing
Wing: Female pheasant wing feather, backed with tape, folded and cut to shape
Legs: Deer hair
Hackle: CDC, top fibers trimmed
Antennae: Pheasant tail feather fibers

CDC Caddis Emergent

Tied by: John Roper, Jasper, GA
Hook: TMC 2487, #12-#18, weighted
Thread: Black, 6/0
Body: Light hare's ear/Antron dubbing
Collar: Dark dun CDC feather
Head: Black ostrich herl

Chickabou Caddis Emerger

Tied by: Henry Hoffman, Warrenton, OR
Hook: Mustad 37161 or 37160, #10-#16
Thread: Brown, 8/0
Tip: Plastic pearl bead with mono core
Butt: Chartreuse chickabou feather, wrapped
Abdomen: Black chickabou feather, wrapped
Thorax: Brown beaver dubbing
Wing/Post: Brown feather, reversed hackle style
Hackle: Brown

Colleen's Caddis

Tied by: Robert H. Schreiner, Jr., Southampton, PA
Hook: Partridge K2B, #12
Thread: Tan, 8/0
Body: Tan ostrich herl
Wings: Tan Swiss straw, cut to shape
Legs: Partridge feather fibers
Eyes: Mono
Head: Tan ostrich herl, trimmed to shape
Antennae: Woodduck feather fibers
Comments: Can be fished as an emerger or as an egg-laying diving adult.

Crystal Caddis

Tied by: Ted Lawrence, Delta, BC
Hook: TMC 200, #14-#16
Thread: Olive, 8/0
Tail: Pearl Z-lon fibers
Body: Electric green Antron yarn
Overbody: Pearl Krystal Flash strands
Wing: Deer hair

Cutter's E/C Caddis

Tied by: Ron Pettey, Elie, Man.
Hook: Mustad 94840 or TMC 5210, #12-#20
Thread: Brown
Tail: Cream or ginger Antron or Z-lon fibers
Abdomen: Cinnamon or rust Antron dubbing
Thorax: Green dubbing
Wing/Post: Deer or Elk hair
Hackle: Grizzly

Eby's Caddis Emerger

Tied by: Gory Eby, Fort St. John, BC
Hook: Mustad 9671, #8
Thread: Black, 6/0
Tailing Shuck: Olive Swiss straw and Antron yarn fibers
Rib: Pale green Larva Lace
Body: Olive-brown synthetic seal fur
Wing: Deer hair topped with black foam
Legs: Olive hackle
Comments: This fly was developed for the traveling sedge.

Emerger Master

Tied by: Kyle Hicks, Berwick, NS
Hook: Mustad 94840, #16
Thread: Black, 8/0
Tail: White duck feather fibers
Rib: Turkey biot
Body: Brown dubbing, bushed out
Wing/Post: Deer hair
Hackle: Grizzly hackle

French's Caddis Emerger

Tied by: Chris French, East Brunswick, NJ
Hook: Mustad 94831 or TMC 5212, #12-#16
Thread: Red
Tail: Cream Antron fibers
Body: Tan Spectra blend dubbing
Hackle: Ginger, palmered
Wing: Light elk hair

Jay's Marabou Caddis Emerger

Tied by: Jay Kaneshige, Hayward, CA
Hook: Daiichi 1130, #10-#14
Thread: Dark brown, 8/0
Underbody: Light olive-brown Hare-Tron, loosely dubbed
Rib: Fine oval gold tinsel
Body: Olive ultra chenille, top colored with gray waterproof marker
Wings: Duck wing feather sections
Legs/Head: Dark olive-brown marabou feather fibers, cut in short pieces and loosely dubbed

King's Emerging Caddis

Tied by: Matt King, Victoria, BC
Hook: Daiichi 1150, #6-#18
Thread: Black or color to match the natural, 6/0
Trailing Shuck: Pearl Krystal Flash and white Antron fibers
Shellback: Mottled Thin Skin strip
Rib: 2lb. mono
Body: SLF caddis green dubbing, or color to match the natural
Wings: Mottled Thin Skin, cut to shape
Pupa Shuck: White Antron collar
Legs: Brown CDC feather fibers
Head: Black dubbing

McConville's Caddis Emerger

Tied by: Tim McConville, Salt Lake City, UT
Hook: TMC 2957, #12
Thread: Olive
Rib: Fine gold wire
Body: Green rabbit dubbing
Wing: Tan Z-lon fibers
Head: Peacock herl

Poly Emerger

Tied by: Edward Caposele, Forked River, NJ
Hook: TMC 3761, #14
Thread: Black, 6/0
Rib: Pearl Krystal Flash
Body: Olive Hareline Dubbing
Legs: Cree hen hackle
Underwing: Light dun poly yarn
Overwing: Pheasant tail feather fibers
Head: Peacock herl

Shaggy Caddis

Tied by: Brandon Fessler, North Ogden, UT
Hook: TMC 5212 or Mustad 94831, #10-#16
Thread: Black
Body: Dark green Antron dubbing
Wing: Deer hair
Hackle: Grizzly

Show Time Caddis

Tied by: Brad Cunningham, Yakima, WA
Hook: TMC 400T, #12-#16
Thread: Tan, 8/0
Tail: Tan Krystal Flash, 3 strands
Tag: Tan Krystal Flash, use butt ends of tail
Rib: Gold wire
Abdomen: Olive tan Hare-Tron dubbing
Thorax: Golden brown Scintilla dubbing
Wing Post: Orange Bailey's Hi-Vis yarn
Hackle: Dun

Teardrop October Caddis Emerger

Tied by: Mark Hoeser, Stockton, CA
Hook: TMC 2457, #6
Thread: Rust brown, 6/0
Rib: Brown, size G thread
Abdomen: Blend of hot orange, fiery yellow and fluorescent pink SLF dubbing
Shuck: Brown Antron yarn fibers
Wing Case/Wing: Natural deer hair
Thorax: Dubbing as abdomen
Legs: Brown partridge feather
Head: Natural deer hair

Todd's Caddis Pupa

Tied by: Todd Turner, Fort Lauderdale, FL
Hook: Daiichi 1140, #16-#20
Thread: Dark brown 8/0
Tail: Olive Z-lon
Abdomen: Bright green Scud Back, thin strip, touch dubbed with brown Touch Dub dubbing, dubbed strip is then furled and wrapped
Wing Buds: Dark brown Scud Back strips, cut to shape
Thorax: Peacock colored Antron dubbing
Legs: Dark olive grizzly feather marabou fibers

Vulnerable Caddis

Tied by: Vladimir Markov, Irkusk, Russia
Hook: Mustad 94840, #10-#18, bend to shape
Thread: Olive, 6/0
Tail: Tan Antron yarn fibers and 1 strand of pearlescent Flashabou
Rib: Olive monofilament
Body: Olive/clear fringed tape
Hackle: Olive badger hackle
Wing: Deer hair
Comments: Fringe tape, homemade from the mesh of a nylon fish net, was created by Siberian anglers seven years ago for winter flies for ice fishing. The tape—with its olive underbody and clear hair—imitates a caddis pupa's air bubble.

Wayne's Caddisfly Emerger

Tied by: Andrew Wayne, San Francisco, CA
Hook: Mustad 39060 or TMC 3761, #16
Thread: Tan, 8/0
Tail: Olive Antron yarn fibers
Rib: Copper wire, counter wrapped
Body: Olive-brown dubbing
Wing: Dun CDC, topped with light dun Antron yarn fibers
Legs/Antennae: Woodduck flank feather fibers
Head: Olive-brown dubbing

Wiggle Pupa

Tied by: Mike Lanzone, North Chili, NY
Hook: TMC 206 #20
Thread: Camel 8/0
Extended Body: Olive Antron and 3 beads (2 green, 1 yellow)
Underbody: Rust colored dubbing
Overbody: Peacock herl
Wing: Partridge feather fibers
Head: Medium brown dubbing
Comments: For extended body, thread the beads onto a 3-inch piece of Antron, tie on end at rear of hook, then bring remaining Antron forward over beads and form the bubble. This fly is best fished on the swing with, or without, short twitches. The extended body will wiggle in the current imparting a very life-like action to the fly.

Winged Biot Emerger-Caddis

Tied by: Neil J. Selbickly, Talent, OR
Hook: Partridge Nymph Emerger, #10
Thread: Black, 8/0
Rib: Light brown turkey biot
Body: Brown dubbing
Wings: Small grizzly hackle tips
Legs: Brown grouse or partridge feather fibers
Head: Black marabou feather fibers, wrapped

Caddisfly Adults

Attractive Caddis

Tied by: Vladimir Markov, Irkusk, Russia
Hook: Mustad 94840, #12
Thread: Red, 6/0
Body: Rust dubbing
Wings: Clear plastic, painted and cut to shape
Hackle: Deer hair or rooster hackle
Antennae/Legs: Golden pheasant tail feather fibers

BJ's Angel

Tied by: Brandon Fessler, North Ogden, UT
Hook: TMC 5210 or Mustad 94840, #14-#16
Thread: Black, 6/0 or 8/0
Body: Peacock herl
Wing: Deer hair, over 2 grizzly hackle tips tied delta style
Antennae: 2 black saddle feather fibers

Black Caddis

Tied by: Chuck Laftis, Bismarck, ND
Hook: Dry fly hook, #10-#18
Thread: Black
Body: Black thread
Wings: Window tint plastic folded and cut to shape
Hackle: Grizzly
Comments: To form the wing, cut a rectangular piece of window tint to match the hook size. Fold in half and cut an elongated heart shape. For a lifetime supply of window tint, go to any autobody shop. This fly was developed for the black caddis hatches that occur in the West.

Caddie

Tied by: Roy D. Powell, Danville, CA
Hook: TMC 2302, #16-#18
Thread: Iron gray, 8/0
Abdomen: Olive-brown Magic Dub
Thorax: Dark hare's ear dubbing
Wings: Gray or tan Buggy Wing and a small strip of wing material, coated with Dave's Flexament, dried, then folded and cut to shape
Hackle: Brown, top and bottom clipped
Antennae: Tan mallard flank feather fibers

Cajun Caddis

Tied by: Ronn Lucas, Sr., Milwaukie, OR
Hook: Daiichi 1720, #8-#12
Thread: Black, 6/0
Body: Rust Iridescent Dubbing
Rib: Fine red copper wire
Hackle: Black, slightly longer the usual
Antennae: Stripped black hackle stems
Wing: Deer hair

Casino's Caddis Adult

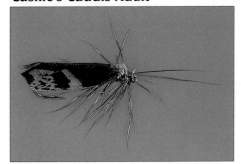

Tied by: Nino Casino, Alatri, Frosinone, Italy
Hook: TMC 100, #8
Thread: Brown, 8/0
Rib: Peccary hair
Abdomen: Olive-gray dubbing
Wing: Female pheasant wing feather, backed with tape, folded and cut to shape
Legs: Deer hair
Thorax: Clipped deer hair from legs
Antennae: Moose hair

CDC Caddisfly

Tied by: Bernard Byng, Tracy, CA
Hook: TMC 900BL, #14-#16
Thread: Olive, 8/0
Body: Yellow CDC feather, twisted and wrapped
Legs: Tan CDC feather fibers
Wing: 2 light dun CDC feathers, tied with natural curve down
Head: Red CDC feather fibers, twisted and wrapped

Cunningham's Swimming Caddis

Tied by: Brad Cunningham, Yakima, WA
Hook: Dai-Riki 305, #16-#12
Thread: Tan, 8/0
Rib: Small gold wire
Body: Tan Krystal Flash, 4 strands
Thorax: Tan Hare-Tron dubbing, behind gold bead
Wings: Olive-gold CDC feather, topped by pheasant feathers, burnt to caddisfly wing shape then lacquered
Antennae: Dark dun micro fibetts

David's Peacock Caddis

Tied by: David Williams, Bloomington, IN
Hook: Mustad 94840, #14-#18
Thread: Black
Rib: Gold tinsel, fine
Body: Peacock herl strands
Wing: Elk hair
Hackle: Grizzly

Diving Caddis

Tied by: Clifford Sullivan Sr., Tracy, CA
Hook: TMC 205BL, #10-#18
Thread: Green, 6/0
Rib: Pearlescent Krystal Flash
Body: Tan Scintilla dubbing
Hackle: 2 Brown mottled hen
Wings: Brown mottled hen feathers
Head: Peacock herl

Dry Fly Caddis

Tied by: Henry Hoffman, Warrenton, OR
Hook: TMC 100, #10-#16
Thread: Olive, 8/0
Rib: Fine gold wire
Body: Olive beaver dubbing
Body Hackle: Ginger grizzly, undersized
Wings: 2 olive grizzly rooster flank feathers, 1 side of each feather trimmed, back fibers preened, mounted and cut to size
Hackle: Ginger grizzly

Eby's Traveling Sedge

Tied by: Gord Eby, Fort St. John, BC
Hook: Mustad 9671, #10
Thread: Black, 6/0
Tail: Deer hair
Wings: Deer hair, tied in 3 bunches along top of hook
Body: Olive-brown synthetic seal dubbing, wrapped between wings
Hackle: Brown
Antennae: Stripped brown hackle stems

Featherstone October Caddis

Tied by: Jeff Lingenfelter, Browns Valley, CA
Hook: TMC 2312, #8-#12
Thread: Black 8/0
Abdomen: Fire cinnamon grizzly saddle feather, wrapped and trimmed to shape
Thorax: Brown grizzly saddle feather, wrapped and trimmed on bottom
Wing: 3-4 CDC feathers, matched and tied flat over body, topped with light elk hair
Head: Butt ends from elk hair wing

Giant Crippled Caddis

Tied by: Scott Roth, Andover, NJ
Hook: TMC 206BL, #10
Thread: Rust, 6/0
Body: Tan sheet foam, cut into 1/4 inch strip, wrapped, colored brown with waterproof marker and coated with Softex
Wing: Coastal deer hair
Legs: Emu feather fibers
Thorax: Tan Crystal dubbing

Goddard's October Caddis

Tied by: Mark Hoeser, Stockton, CA
Hook: TMC 5212, #6
Thread: Brown, 6/0
Legs: Peccary, splayed by dubbed ball of rusty orange Hare-Tron
Body: Natural and orange dyed deer hair, stacked and trimmed to shape
Hackle: Brown
Antennae: Black micro round rubber

Hare's Ear Sparkle Caddis

Tied by: Steve Potter, Tracy, CA
Hook: Mustad 94840 or TMC 5210, #12-#16
Thread: Yellow, 6/0
Tail: 3 pheasant tail feather fibers
Body: Natural hare's ear dubbing
Wing: Pearl Krystal Flash, 3 strands looped
Hackle: Brown

Iridescent Sedge

Tied by: Ronn Lucas, Sr., Milwaukie, OR
Hook: TMC 100BL, #10-#16
Thread: Brown, 8/0
Body: Iridescent Dubbing, color to suit
Hackle: Brown, sparse, top and bottom trimmed
Antennae: Woodduck flank feather fibers
Wing: Flashback, thin slice glued with fabric glue to a feather of choice, dried, cut or burnt to shape
Head: Tan fabric paint

Killer Caddis Adult

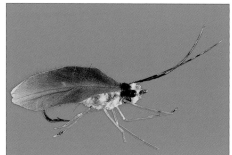

Tied by: Raymond Martinez, Hayward, CA
Hook: Daiichi 1710, #6-#16
Thread: Brown
Body: Natural chamois
Legs: Horsehair, coated with Dave's Flexament
Wings: 2 ginger hen feathers per side, coated with Flexament and trimmed to shape
Antennae: Pheasant tail feather fibers
Eyes: Mono

King's Adult Caddis

Tied by: Matt King, Victoria, BC
Hook: TMC 100, #6-#18
Thread: Brown or color to match the natural, 6/0
Tail: Pearl Krystal Flash strand
Body: Tan Thin Skin strip, wrapped
Underwing: White CDC feather fibers
Wing: Speckled Perfect Cut Wings
Legs: Brown CDC feather fibers
Head: Black dubbing
Antennae: Bronze mallard feather fibers

Light Caddis

Tied by: Robert Martin, Rock Hill, SC
Hook: Mustad 94840, #12-#14
Thread: Gray, 8/0
Body: Light colored fox fur dubbing
Wing: Woodduck feather, pulled back
Hackle: Ginger
Head: Woodduck feather fibers

Main Attraction

Tied by: Ted Lawrence, Delta, BC
Hook: Mustad 94840, #10-#12
Thread: Yellow, 8/0
Tag: Red Flashabou strand
Hackle: Black
Body: Gold Fly Foam
Wing: Black Krystal Flash strands
Head: Yellow Hard Head Finish

Mother's Day Caddis

Tied by: Doug Duvall, Sardis, OH
Hook: TMC 103Y, #11-#17
Thread: Black 8/0
Body: Peacock herl, 2-4 strands
Wing: Partridge feather fibers
Head: Mole dubbing

Mr. Caddis

Tied by: Kyle Hicks, Berwick, NS
Hook: Mustad 94840, #14
Thread: Black, 8/0
Body: Brown CDC feather, wrapped
Wing: White pheasant feather
Hackle: Grizzly, palmered over front 2/3 of body
Antennae: Pheasant tail feather fibers

Orange Caddis

Tied by: Tim McConville, Salt Lake City, UT
Hook: Daiichi, 1279, #8
Thread: Black
Tail: Orange elk hair
Body: Orange Furry Foam
Hackle: Brown saddle, palmered
Wing: Orange elk hair
Head: Tan dubbing

Paper Cloth Caddis

Tied by: Floyd Franke, Roscoe, NY
Hook: TMC 100, #10
Thread: Brown, 8/0
Body: Fine olive chenille
Legs: Partridge feather fibers
Wing: Paper cloth, cut to shape, and colored with a water proof marker
Hackle: Furnace

Robbins' Adult Caddis

Tied by: Charles Robbins, Tracy, CA
Hook: TMC 5210, #10
Thread: Brown, 6/0
Body: Brown olive dubbing
Wings: 2 brown furnace feathers, stripped 1 side of each feather, folded to shape, coated with glue after mounting
Hackle: Brown furnace, tied parachute style on stretched Super Floss on bottom, floss cut 1/4 inch from end after wrapping and tying off feather, drop of CA glue added to end
Antennae: Woodduck feather fibers

Rockwell Caddis

Tied by: Glenn Weisner, Toledo, OH
Hook: TMC 200R, #10-#14
Thread: Tan, 6/0
Rib: Fine gold wire
Body: SLF dubbing, match color of natural
Wing: Dark hen feather, backed with tape, folded and cut to shape
Post: White Hi-Vis yarn
Hackle: Grizzly
Antenna: Badger hairs

Rump Wing Caddis

Tied by: Robert H. Schreiner, Jr., Southampton, PA
Hook: Mustad 9671, #12
Thread: Brown, 8/0
Body: Tan dubbing
Body Hackle: Brown
Wing: Pheasant rump feather, coated with Flexament, dried, folded, and cut to shape
Antennae: Stripped brown hackle stems
Head: Tan ostrich herl, trimmed short

Tent Wing Caddis

Tied by: John Roper, Jasper, GA
Hook: Mustad 94840, #12-#18
Thread: Rust, 6/0
Body: Rust dubbing
Rib: Rust thread
Body Hackle: Medium ginger, wrapped Al Troth style, top fibers trimmed
Wing: Turkey feather fibers, trimmed to a "V" shape
Antennae: Stripped ginger hackle stems

Tied Down Caddis, Orange

Tied by: Neil J. Selbicky, Talent, OR
Hook: TMC 3761 or Mustad 3906B, #10
Thread: Orange, 6/0
Tail: Brown deer hair, tips from body shellback
Body: Orange dubbing
Hackle: Brown, palmered from tail, taking 2 extra wraps at front for collar
Shellback: Brown deer hair

Upland Caddis

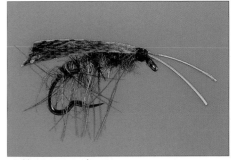

Tied by: Ron Pettey, Elie, Man.
Hook: TMC 101, #12-#18
Thread: Red, 0/8
Body: Olive dubbing
Hackle: Brown, palmered
Wing: 2 grouse or partridge feathers coated with Flexament and trimmed to shape
Antennae: Stems from stripped wing feathers

Wet Caddis

Tied by: Corey Wiggins, West Linn, OR
Hook: TMC 200R, #12-#18
Thread: Tan
Rib: Brown V-Rib
Body: Tan rabbit dubbing
Wings: 2 partridge feathers
Hackle: Grizzly
Head: Black marabou feather fibers, wrapped

X-Wing Caddis

Tied by: Mike Lanzone, North Chili, NY
Hook: TMC 100, #14
Thread: Camel, 8/0
Body: Brown dubbing
Wings: Elk or coastal deer hair

A.J.'s Nymph

Tied by: A.J. Courteau, Erie, PA
Hook: TMC 300, #2-#12, weighted
Thread: Brown
Tails: Brown goose biots
Abdomen: Dark brown Bugskin strip, wrapped, and coated with epoxy
Thorax: Brown Antron dubbing
Wing Case: Brown Bugskin, cut to shape, and coated with head cement
Legs: Brown round rubber
Eyes: Mono
Antennae: Pheasant tail feather fibers

BB Stone

Tied by: Adam Tuma, Lebanon, OR
Hook: Mustad 9672, #10
Thread: Black 3/0
Tail: Pheasant tail feather fibers
Rib: Copper wire
Abdomen: Tan rabbit dubbing
Wing Case: Pheasant tail feather fibers
Legs: Ginger hackle
Thorax/Head: Brass beads

Bead Head Knotted Royal Stone

Tied by: Don Joslyn, Eagle Point, OR
Hook: Alec Jackson Daiichi 2051, black, #3
Thread: Black 3/0
Tails: Black goose biots
Tag: Gold tinsel
Butt: Peacock herl
Abdomen Underbody: Red floss
Abdomen: Black and amber V-Rib strands, woven with an overhand weave
Thorax: Black Krystal dubbing
Legs: Black round rubber
Head: Gold bead

Bead Head Royal Stone

Tied by: Don Joslyn, Eagle Point, OR
Hook: Alec Jackson Daiichi 2051 black, #3
Thread: Black 3/0
Tails: Black goose biots
Tag: Gold tinsel
Butt: Peacock herl
Abdomen: Red floss
Thorax: Black Krystal dubbing
Legs: Black round rubber
Head: Gold bead

Behemoth

Tied by: Fred Iacoletti, Albuquerque, NM
Hook: Daiichi 2340, #8, bent in 2 places for swimming shape
Weight: .025 lead wire, shank coated with CA glue and wire wrapped tightly over hook shank, double wrapped thorax, flattened with pliers
Thread: Yellow "A"
Tails: Hen saddle feather fibers coated with Flexament
Abdomen: Yellow Mottled Nymph Blend dubbing
Abdomen Overbody: Brown Thin Skin strip, wrapped
Thorax: Yellow Mottled Nymph Blend dubbing
Wing Case/Head: Brown Thin Skin cut to shape
Legs/Antennae: Same as tail

Berge's Black Stone

Tied by: Dick Berge, Iron River, WI
Hook: TMC 200R, #4-#8, weighted on sides of hook shank with .030 on #4 and .025 on #6-#8
Thread: Black 6/0
Tails/Antennae: Black goose biots
Rib: Dark brown or black Swannundaze
Body: Brown Furry Foam
Wing Case/Head: Black Swiss straw
Legs: Pheasant church window feather, coated with Flexament, tip tied behind hook eye with concave side up, folded back, legs separated and tied down with 2 wraps. Swiss straw folded over leg and tied down. (Separating legs and folding Swiss straw repeated 2 more times.)

B. K's Golden Stone

Tied by: Bahman Khadivi, Cupertino, CA
Hook: TMC 200R, #6-#8, weighted
Thread: Brown 8/0
Tails: Brown goose biots
Rib: Brown Larva Lace
Shellback/Wing Case: Turkey feather section coated with Softex
Body: Golden-orange squirrel dubbing
Antennae: Brown goose biots

Bob's *Pteronarcys* Stone

Tied by: Bob Churchill, Lakewood, CO
Hook: Mustad 3665A or TMC 300, #4-#8, weighted with lead tape
Thread: Black 6/0
Tails: Black goose biots
Underbody: Brown yarn
Abdomen: Brown dubbing
Rib: Clear Larva Lace and 1 brown ostrich herl
Wing Case: Dark gray goose wing feather, sprayed with Liquid Varathane then cut out a 1/4 inch section
Legs: Brown hen feather
Thorax: Rust/orange Fury Foam, ribbed with 1 tan ostrich herl
Eyes: Mono
Antennae: Black goose biots

Braided Golden Stone

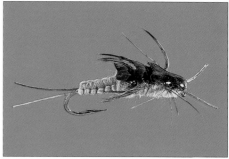

Tied by: Mark Defrank, Chalkhill, PA
Hook: Mustad 79580, #8
Thread: Tan
Tails: Stripped amber hackle stems
Abdomen: Amber and creamy yellow embroidery floss strands, woven with an overhand weave
Thorax: Creamy yellow or golden yellow dubbing
Wing Case: Mottled turkey tail feather sections, cut to shape and coated with epoxy
Legs: Grouse or hen feather fibers
Antennae: Stripped amber hackle stems

C Stone

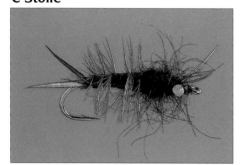

Tied by: Harvey Cormier, Sandy Lake, Ont.
Hook: TMC 200R, #4-#12, weighted
Thread: Brown
Tails: Brown goose biots
Rib: Brown hackle
Underbody: Brown dubbing
Abdomen: Brown Swannundaze
Thorax: Brown dubbing
Eyes: Mono
Antennae: Brown goose biots

CDC Knotted Black Stone

Tied by: Don Joslyn, Eagle Point, OR
Hook: Alec Jackson Daiichi 2051 black, #3, weighted
Thread: Black 3/0
Tails: Blue pheasant tail feather fibers
Underbody: Orange thread
Abdomen: Black and amber V-Rib strands, woven with an overhand weave
Wing Case: Spinner Wing Film
Thorax: Black CDC dubbing
Legs: Blue pheasant tail feather fibers

CDC Knotted Yellow Sally

Tied by: Don Joslyn, Eagle Point, OR
Hook: Dai-Riki 270, #6, weighted with .025 lead wire
Thread: Yellow 3/0
Tails: Yellow goose biots
Underbody: Yellow thread
Abdomen: Small amber V-Rib strands, woven with an over hand weave
Wing Case: Peacock wing feather fibers
Thorax: Yellow CDC dubbing
Legs: Brown round rubber

Chain-Stitched Stone

Tied by: Robert Williamson, Roy, UT
Hook: TMC 200R, #8, weighted
Thread: Brown
Tails: Brown goose biots
Abdomen: Black, olive, brown, gray, and rust nylon threads chain-stitched
Wing Case: Pheasant tail feather fibers, lacquered
Thorax: Brown Antron dubbing
Hackle: Brown

Chris's Real Stone

Tied by: Chris Kazulen, Uniontown, PA
Hook: Mustad 9575, #8, weighted
Thread: Black 6/0
Tails: Stripped pheasant feather stems, darkened with marker and coated with head cement
Rib: Gold oval tinsel
Abdomen: Black and orange Fine & Dry dubbing
Thorax: Black and orange squirrel dubbing
Wing Case: Turkey tail feather sections, cut to shape and coated with head cement
Legs: Pheasant wing feather biots, bent to shape and coated with head cement
Antennae: Stripped pheasant feather stems, darkened with marker and coat with head cement

Cliff's Golden Stone

Tied by: Cliff Stringer, Nampa, ID
Hook: Mustad 79307, #4-#6, weighted
Thread: Black
Tails: Dark brown goose biots
Rib: Goose feather-stem quill strip
Abdomen: Tan poly yarn wrapped to shape then flattened with pliers
Wing Case: Goose feather section
Legs: Pheasant back feather, drawn feather style
Thorax: Tan dubbing
Head: Black ostrich herl
Antennae: Elk or moose hairs

Cliff's Golden Stone Nymph

Tied by: Clifford Sullivan, Tracy, CA
Hook: TMC 205, #6-#8, weighted
Thread: Gold 8/0
Tails: Gold turkey biots
Underbody/Thorax: Golden brown or dubbing to match the natural
Abdomen/Overbody: Brown on top and clear on bottom (Larva Lace strands), woven with an overhand weave
Legs: Brown turkey biots, knotted
Wing Case: Brown hen feathers, burnt or cut to shape and coated with Flexament
Antennae: Gold turkey biots

Cone-Stone

Tied by: Edward Caposele, Forked River, NJ
Hook: Daiichi 2X, #10
Thread: Camel 8/0 UNI-Thread
Tails: Tan goose biots
Rib: Brown V-Rib
Body: Mix of gold and yellow Mottled Nymph Blend
Wing Case: Turkey feather fibers
Legs: Pheasant tail feather fibers
Head: Small gold Conehead
Comments: Tail and wing case are coated with pearl Alien Juice, a flexible sparkle epoxy.

Deep Creek Stone

Tied by: Jess Potter, Fairbanks, AK
Hook: Mustad 9671, #12, weighted
Thread: Black 8/0
Tails: Black goose biots
Abdomen: Black micro chenille
Thorax: Black wool yarn
Hackle: Black saddle hackle, palmered over thorax
Antennae: Black goose biots

Cliff's Salmonfly Nymph

Tied by: Clifford Sullivan, Tracy, CA
Hook: TMC 205, #4-#8, weighted with 2 strands of .030 lead wire mounted to sides of hook shank
Thread: Black 6/0
Tails: Black biots
Rib: Brite penny Fast Eddies Micro Cable
Shellback/Wing Case: Black Swiss straw
Abdomen: Black dubbing mixed with Light Brite
Thorax: Burnt orange dubbing
Legs: Black hen feather, drawn feather style
Eyes: Yellow mono with black dot
Antennae: Black biots

Copper Stone Nymph

Tied by: Robert Williamson, Roy, UT
Hook: TMC 200R, #8, weighted
Thread: Black
Tails: Brown goose biots
Underbody: Brown Mohair Leach yarn
Abdomen: Copper wire strands, woven with an overhand weave
Wing Case: Pheasant feather, lacquered
Thorax: Brown Mohair Leach yarn, picked out
Antennae: Black horsehair

Diamondback Black Stone

Tied by: Don Joslyn, Eagle Point, OR
Hook: Dai-Riki 270, #4, weighted with .025 lead wire
Thread: Black 6/0
Tails: Black goose biots
Rib: Green Krystal Flash, 2 strands, 1 wrapped clockwise and the other counterclockwise
Abdomen: Black CDC dubbing
Wing Case: Spinner Wing Film
Thorax: Black ostrich herl
Legs: Pearl Krystal Flash strands
Head: Peacock herl, gold bead

Creepy Crawly

Tied by: Adam Tuma, Lebanon, OR
Hook: TMC 200R, #8, weighted
Thread: Black 3/0
Tail: Black hackle fibers
Rib: Brown Vinyl Rib
Body: Black rabbit dubbing
Gills: Whit poly yarn strands, pulled along the sides of abdomen
Legs: Black hackle fibers

Dan's Stonefly Nymph

Tied by: Dan Ward, Jr., Clarksville, AR
Hook: TMC 5212, #6-#10, weighted
Thread: Black 6/0
Tails: Stripped brown hackle stems, colored with dark brown marker
Rib: Small gold oval French tinsel
Body: Rusty brown Antron dubbing
Wing Case: Mottled oak Thin Skin
Legs: Pheasant rump feather, trimmed
Antennae: Same as tail

Don's Salmonfly Nymph

Tied by: Don Joslyn, Eagle Point, OR
Hook: Alec Jackson Daiichi 2055 gold, #1.5, weighted with .035 lead wire
Thread: Orange 3/0
Tails: Black goose biots
Underbody: Orange thread
Abdomen: Large brown and amber V-Rib strands, woven with an overhand weave
Wing Case: Peacock Krystal Flash strands, topped with peacock wing feather sections cut to shape and coated with Flexament
Thorax: Golden stone dubbing, picked out
Legs: Brown round rubber
Antennae: Black goose biots

Don's Yellow Sally Nymph

Tied by: Don Joslyn, Eagle Point, OR
Hook: Dai-Riki 270, #6, weighted
Thread: Yellow 3/0
Tails: Brown round rubber
Rib: Gold French tinsel
Abdomen: Golden stone dubbing
Wing Case: Peacock wing feather section, coated with Flexament
Thorax: Yellow CDC dubbing
Legs: Brown round rubber

Drifting Stone Nymph

Tied by: Larry Larsen, Pocatello, ID
Hook: Mustad 37160, #4, weighted
Thread: Black
Tails: Black round rubber
Body: Dark brown nylon yarn, twisted over underbody of untwisted yarn
Wing Case: Black Swiss straw
Hackle: Black
Antennae: Black rubber legs
Comments: Various types of yarn maybe used to create different textures.

Early Brown Copper Stonefly Nymph

Tied by: Chris French, East Brunswick, NJ
Hook: Mustad 9671, #10-#12, weighted
Thread: Brown
Tails: Brown goose biots
Abdomen: Bill's Copper Body Braid
Wing Case/Head: Bill's Copper Body Braid
Thorax: Brown Antron and rabbit dubbing mixed
Legs: Brown goose biots

Eastern Golden Stonefly Nymph

Tied by: Chris French, East Brunswick, NJ
Hook: Mustad 9671, #8-#10, weighted with .015 lead wire strips on sides of hook shank
Thread: Brown
Tails: Light brown goose biots
Rib: Clear Larva Lace
Abdomen: Light rust opossum dubbing
Wing Case: Pheasant back feather coated with head cement
Thorax: Kaufmann's Yellow Stone dubbing
Legs: Thick ends of stripped yellow grizzly hackle stems, shaped and cemented
Antennae: Thin ends of stripped yellow grizzly hackle stems

Erik's Golden Stone Nymph

Tied by: Erik Budwill, Red Deer, AB
Hook: Mustad 3906B, #14, weighted
Thread: Brown
Butt: Black dubbing
Tails: Dark brown goose biots
Rib: Gold oval tinsel and olive V-Rib
Shellback: 2 dark brown goose biots
Body: Golden yellow dubbing
Wing Case: Brown feathers, reversed-hackle style
Legs: Dark brown goose biots, knotted
Collar/Head: Black dubbing, gold bead

Featherback Stone Nymph

Tied by: Harry Gross, Salem, OR
Hook: Alec Jackson, #5-#7
Thread: Black 8/0
Tails: Pheasant tail feather fibers, 2 per side
Underbody: Yellow floss over 2 straight pins cut to size and mounted on the sides of the hook shank
Overbody: Game bird feather cemented, over-wrapped with clear, flat 30lb. mono
Thorax: Yellow orange dubbing
Hackle: Elk neck hair

Flatulent Stone

Tied by: Don Joslyn, Eagle Point, OR
Hook: Alec Jackson 2051, black, #7, weighted
Thread: Black 6/0
Tails: Black goose biots, over back dubbing ball
Abdomen: Black and brown V-Rib strands, woven with an overhand weave
Thorax: Black Hairline Krystal dubbing
Wing Cases: Turkey feather sections, cut to shape and coated with head cement, over pearl Krystal Flash strands cut short
Antennae: Black goose biots

Flexibody Golden Stone

Tied by: Jeff Lingenfelter, Browns Valley, CA
Hook: Daiichi 2055, #3-#7, weighted
Thread: Olive 8/0
Tails: Ginger goose biots
Underbody: Golden olive SLF squirrel dubbing
Abdomen Overbody: Pale yellow Flexibody, top colored brown with permanent marker
Wing Cases: Turkey feather sections, cut to shape and coated with Flexament
Thorax: Golden olive SLF squirrel dubbing
Legs: Yellow pheasant tail feather, coated with Flexament
Eyes: Black glass beads with mono core
Head/Pronotum: Body dubbing and Flexibody colored body
Antennae: Stripped yellow grizzly hackle stems

Freeman's Stonefly Nymph

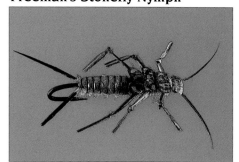

Tied by: Wayne Freeman, Lexington, SC
Hook: Varivas 973, #8, weighted
Thread: Brown 8/0
Tails: Porcupine quills
Rib: Brown horsehair
Shellback: Light brown Swiss straw
Body: Light brown dubbing
Wing Case/Head: Swiss straw, backed with shipping tape and colored with brown Pantone marker
Legs: Turkey biots, knotted
Antennae: Brown turkey biots
Comments: Coat legs and abdomen with Softex or similar product in thin layers to give shape and translucent quality.

Fuzzy Weaving Stony

Tied by: Boyd Elder, Spiro, OK
Hook: Mustad 9872, #8, weighted
Thread: Brown, 6/0
Tails: Brown goose biots
Abdomen: Root beer Krystal Flash strands, twisted into 2 cords and woven with an overhand weave with squirrel dubbing added to the bottom cord during weaving
Thorax: Brown squirrel dubbing
Wing Case: Turkey tail feather sections, cut to shape and coated with Flexament
Legs: Partridge feather fibers

Golden Sarastone

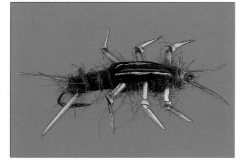

Tied by: Darin Hedley, Fort Macleod, AB
Hook: TMC 200R, #2-#10, weighted
Thread: Pale orange, 3/0
Tails: Ginger goose biots
Rib: Amber Swannundaze
Body: Golden stone dubbing
Wing Case: Pheasant church window feather, lacquered
Legs: Ginger goose biots knotted
Antennae: Ginger goose biots
Comments: This fly was named after my dog Sara who supply the original dubbing.

Hank's Chicken Stone Nymph

Tied by: Henry Hoffman, Warrenton, OR
Hook: Mustad 9672, #6
Weight: 2 strands of .035 lead wire, twisted into a rope and slashed onto each side of hook shank, (this will give the body a flatter shape)
Thread: Brown 6/0
Tails: Dark brown chicken biots
Rib: Medium copper wire
Body: Brown chickabou feather tied on by tips and wrapped
Hackle: Barred brown, bottom trimmed
Wing Case: Barred brown rooster breast hackle coated in Flexament and cut to shape
Eyes: Black mono
Antennae: Dark brown chicken biots

Harry's Golden Stone Nymph

Tied by: Harry Gross, Salem, OR
Hook: Mustad 3665A, #4-#6
Thread: Gray 12/0
Tails: Pheasant tail feather fibers, 2 per side
Underbody: Yellow floss over 2 straight pins cut to size and mounted on sides of hook shank
Overbody: Partridge feather cemented and over-wrapped with 20lb. mono
Thorax: Gold dubbing
Legs: Gold goose biots
Wing Case: Partridge feathers, burnt or cut to shape and coated with head cement
Eyes: Mono
Antennae: Mallard feather fibers

Hoff's Black Stone

Tied by: Scott Hoff, Concord, CA
Hook: Orvis 1510, #8, weighted with .025 lead wire strips mounted on sides of hook shank
Thread: Black 8/0
Tails: Brown goose biots
Rib: DMC Braided Thread (found in craft stores)
Shellback/Wing Case: Black Swiss straw coated with Revlon *Hard as Nails*
Abdomen: Black Antron dubbing mixed with Lite Bright
Thorax: Burnt orange Antron dubbing mixed with Lite Bright
Legs: Black square rubber
Antennae: Brown goose biots

Hoff's Golden Stone

Tied by: Scott Hoff, Concord, CA
Hook: Orvis 1512, #10, weighted with .025 lead wire strips mounted on sides of hook shank
Thread: Tan 10/0
Tails: Tan goose biots
Rib: Fine red wire
Shellback: Glad Sandwich bag strip
Abdomen: Tan Hare-Tron dubbing mixed with Lite Brite
Wing Case: Turkey feather fibers coated with Flexament
Thorax: Burnt orange fox dubbing
Legs: Pheasant tail feather fibers
Antennae: Brown goose biots

Ipsen's Brown Stone

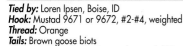

Tied by: Loren Ipsen, Boise, ID
Hook: Mustad 9671 or 9672, #2-#4, weighted
Thread: Orange
Tails: Brown goose biots
Abdomen Underbody: Orange-brown dubbing
Abdomen: Orange-brown heavy latex strip, wrapped
Wing Case: Latex strip, butt end from abdomen
Legs: Partridge or hen pheasant feather, coated with Dave's Flexament, then separated into legs
Thorax: Burnt orange chenille

Iridescent Flashback Black Stone Nymph

Tied by: Ronn Lucas, Sr., Milwaukie, OR
Hook: Daiichi 2340 or Mustad 3665A, #2-#8, weighted
Thread: Black 6/0
Tails: Black goose biots
Rib: Transparent smoke Swannundaze
Underbody: Black yarn
Body: Black Iridescent Dubbing, picked out after ribbing
Wing Case/Head: Blue marlin Flashback
Legs: Black or dark brown hen saddle feather, wrapped over thorax
Eyes: Iridescent black beads and mono
Antennae: Stripped grizzly hackle stems

Iridescent Flashback Gold Stone Nymph

Tied by: Ronn Lucas, Sr., Milwaukie, OR
Hook: Daiichi 2340 or Mustad 3665A, #4-#8, weighted
Thread: Orange 6/0
Tails: Orange goose biots
Rib: Red Swannundaze
Underbody: Brown yarn, form a tapered body
Body: Gold stone Iridescent Dubbing, after ribbing, dubbing picked out and trimmed to around 3/16 inch
Wing Case/Head: Chili powder Flashback
Legs: Brown saddle hackle, wrapped over thorax
Eyes: Iridescent back beads with mono core
Antennae: Stripped grizzly hackle stems

Jack's Golden Stone

Tied by: Jack Johnson, Concord, CA
Hook: TMC 200R or Mustad 9674, #6-#8, weighted
Thread: Dark brown 6/0
Tails: Brown goose biots
Underbody: Brown yarn
Rib: Gold Mylar tinsel
Body: Gold dubbing mix: 6 parts gold, 3 parts rust, and 1 part brown dubbing, top of abdomen darkened with dark brown marker
Wing Case/Head: Dark mottled turkey section, coated with Flexament
Hackle: Furnace, top fibers trimmed
Eyes: Black plastic

Jack's Yellow Stonefly

Tied by: Dick Allebach, Phoenixville, PA
Hook: Mustad 9672, #10, front 2/3 of hook shank weighted with lead wire and flattened with pliers
Thread: Brown 8/0
Tails: Peccary hairs
Abdomen Underbody: Pale yellow dubbing
Abdomen: Stripped mallard primary feather stem
Thorax: Yellow chenille
Wing Case/Head: Brown mottled turkey feather section, coated with Flexament and cut to shape
Legs: Brown hen feather, divided into legs and coated with head cement
Eyes: Black chenille

Comments: To form head and eyes; after pulling the wing case forward and tying off behind the hook eye, lay a 1-inch piece of black chenille across the hook on top behind the eye. Use a bodkin to hold the chenille in place and fold back the butt end of the wing case and tie off behind the chenille. Shape the wing case and cut off the excess chenille. Put head cement on the ends of the trimmed chenille and shape the eyes.

Jan's Black Stone

Tied by: Jan Pickel, New Park, PA
Hook: Daiichi 1730, #12, weighted
Thread: Black
Tails: Black goose biots
Rib: Stripped brown hackle stem
Body: Black-orange Scintilla dubbing
Wing Case: Mottled black Thin Skin, cut to shape
Legs: Black rubber strands
Head: Black brass bead
Antennae: Black goose biots

Jan's Golden Stone Nymph

Tied by: Jan Pickel, New Park, PA
Hook: Daiichi 1730, #12, weighted
Thread: Yellow 8/0
Tails: Rusty or yellow goose biots
Rib: Yellow-brown stripped hackle stem
Body: Golden stone dubbing
Wing Case: Mottled golden stone Thin Skin, cut to shape
Legs: Fluorescent yellow round rubber, colored with brown marker
Head: Gold bead
Antennae: Rusty or yellow goose biots

King's "Thin Skin" Black Stone

Tied by: Matt King, Victoria, BC
Hook: Drennan UV longbelly, #6, weighted
Thread: Black 6/0 Danville
Tails: Black goose biots
Rib: Amber Vinyl Rib
Shellback: Black Thin Skin
Body: Black Wapsi Super Bright Dubbing
Legs: Black CDC feather, pulled of top of thorax
Wing Case/Head: Black Thin Skin, cut to shape
Eyes: Black 20lb. mono, melted to shape
Antennae: Black goose biots

King's "Thin Skin" Brown Stone

Tied by: Matt King, Victoria, BC
Hook: Drennan UV longbelly, #6, weighted
Thread: Brown 6/0
Tails: Tan goose biots
Rib: Small amber Vinyl Rib
Shellback: Mottled bustard Thin Skin
Body: Mixed orange and brown Wapsi Super Bright Dubbing
Legs: Tan CDC feather, drawn feather style
Wing Case: Mottled mustard Thin Skin, cut to shape
Eyes: Black 20lb mono, melted to shape
Antennae: Tan goose biots

King's "Thin Skin" Golden Stone

Tied by: Matt King, Victoria, BC
Hook: Drennan UV longbelly, #10, weighted
Thread: Danville, golden olive 6/0
Tails: Tan goose biots
Rib: Small olive Vinyl Rib
Shellback: Mottled mustard Thin Skin
Body: Golden stone Wapsi Super Bright Dubbing
Legs: Light yellow CDC feather, drawn feather style
Wing Case: Mottled mustard Thin Skin, cut to shape
Eyes: 20lb black mono, melted to shape
Antennae: Tan goose biots

Knotted Golden Stone

Tied by: Don Joslyn, Eagle Point, OR
Hook: Alec Jackson Daiichi 2055 gold, #3, weighted
Thread: Black 3/0
Tails: Yellow goose biots
Abdomen: Gold craft vinyl cord strands, woven with an overhand weave
Thorax: Golden stone dubbing
Wing Case: Peacock wing feather section
Legs: Brown round rubber

Large Yellow Stonefly Nymph

Tied by: A. W. Longacre, Juneau, AK
Hook: Mustad 94720, #6, weighted
Thread: Brown 8/0
Tails: Black goose biots
Rib: Brown Swannundaze
Abdomen: Tan rabbit dubbing
Wing Case: Ring-neck pheasant feathers
Thorax: Yellow dubbing
Legs: Black round rubber
Head: Brown yarn
Antennae: Black goose biots

Larva Lace Golden Stone Nymph

Tied by: Robert Williamson, Roy, UT
Hook: TMC 200R, #8
Thread: Brown
Tails: Brown round rubber
Abdomen: Brown and yellow Larva Lace strands, woven with an overhand weave
Wing Case: Pheasant feather, lacquered
Thorax: Yellow Antron dubbing
Legs/Antennae: Brown round rubber

Lavery's Stonefly Nymph

Tied by: Mike Lavery, Surrey, BC
Hook: TMC 200R, #6-#12, weighted
Thread: Black 8/0
Tails: Black goose biots
Rib: Black V-Rib
Body: Black superfine dubbing
Wing Case: Black Thin Skin, cut to shape
Legs: Hen hackle fibers
Eyes: Black mono
Antenna: Stripped black hackle stems

Little Black Stone

Tied by: Edward Caposele, Forked River, NJ
Hook: TMC 2302, #12, weighted
Thread: Black 6/0
Tails: Black goose biots
Rib: Black V-Rib
Body: Black Mottled Nymph Blend dubbing
Wing Case: Turkey feather section, lacquered
Legs: Black pheasant tail feather fibers
Antennae: Black goose biots

Lost Stone

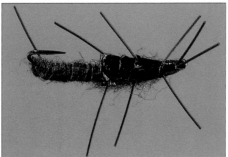

Tied by: Doug Fullerton, Menominee, MI
Hook: Mustad 9575, #6, weighted with .035 over front half of hook shank, tied hook-up
Thread: Black 6/0
Tails: Extra-small black round rubber
Rib: Fine copper wire
Body: Brown-gold dubbing, thorax picked out
Wing Case: Yellow Swiss straw, colored with brown marker
Antennae/Legs: Extra-small black round rubber

Marabou Stonefly Nymph

Tied by: Scott Zadroga, San Diego, CA
Hook: TMC 5212, #12
Thread: Black 6/0
Tails: Black round rubber
Body: Black marabou dubbing
Wing Case/Head: Black Swiss straw
Eyes: Mono
Comments: The body is formed by using chopped marabou feather fibers in a dubbing loop that is wrapped and trimmed to shape. The thorax is trimmed on the bottom, and the legs are trimmed by pinching at the correct length and breaking off the excess.

Mike's Small Brown Stone

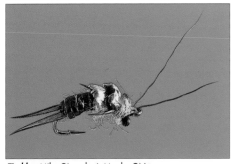

Tied by: Mike Giavedoni, Maple, ON
Hook: Scud hook, #14-#16, weighted with strips of lead lashed to the sides of the hook shank
Thread: Brown
Tails: Small brown biots
Abdomen Underbody: Ginger dubbing
Abdomen: Brown Swannundaze, wrapped
Wing Cases: Brown Swiss straw
Legs: Small brown biots
Thorax: Ginger dubbing
Eyes: Black mono
Antennae: Black moose mane hair

Moss's Salmonfly Nymph

Tied by: L.K. Moss, Draper, MT
Hook: Daiichi 1730, #6
Thread: Black 6/0
Tails: Brown round rubber
Abdomen: Kreinik, colors #011 and #127 strands, woven with an overhand weave
Wing Case: Brown Raffia
Thorax: Dark olive beads with brown dubbing
Legs/Antennae: Brown round rubber

Nino's Stonefly Nymph

Tied by: Nino Casino, Alatri, Italy
Hook: TMC 300, #8, weighted
Thread: Brown 6/0
Tails: Stripped brown feather stems
Abdomen: Latex strip, colored with brown Pantone marker, coated with CA glue
Thorax: Brown Deer Dubbing, (by Palu, an Italian fly fishing product distributor)
Wing Cases/Head: Pheasant feather section, folded and coated with head cement
Eyes: Black beads with mono core

No Frill Bead Head Golden Stone

Tied by: Don Joslyn, Eagle Point, OR
Hook: Dai-Riki 270, #4, weighted
Thread: Black 3/0
Tail: Elk hair
Rib: Copper wire, wrapped over whole body
Abdomen: Yellow Lite Brite dubbing
Thorax: Black ostrich herl
Hackle: Cree
Legs: Brown round rubber
Head: Gold bead

Orange V-Rib Stone

Tied by: Don Joslyn, Eagle Point, OR
Hook: Alec Jackson Daiichi 2051 black, #3, weighted
Thread: Black 3/0
Tails: Black round rubber
Abdomen: Amber V-Rib
Thorax: Black CDC dubbing
Legs: Black round rubber
Head: Gold bead

Pete's Reel Black Stonefly

Tied by: Pete Toscani, Bristol, CT
Hook: Orvis 1524-00, #6, weighted
Thread: Black 3/0
Tails: Tan goose biots
Underbody/Thorax: Black dubbing
Abdomen/Overbody: Fly Skin, colored with back marker
Wing Case: Woodduck feathers, burnt to shape and marked with black marker
Legs: Tan goose biots
Eyes: Mono
Antennae: Black Crazy Hair fibers

Pete's Reel Stonefly

Tied by: Pete Toscani, Bristol, CT
Hook: Orvis 1524-00, #6, weighted
Thread: Black 3/0
Tails: Black goose biots
Abdomen: Black Nymph Glass
Thorax: Fly Skin over black dubbing
Hackle: Black, palmered over thorax
Antennae: Black Crazy Hair fibers

Pete's Reel Stonefly Nymph

Tied by: Pete Toscani, Bristol, CT
Hook: TMC 200R, #6, weighted, wire flattened with pliers
Thread: Brown 6/0
Tails: Brown goose biots
Underbody: Brown dubbing
Body: Brown Nymph Skin strip, wrapped
Wing Cases: Grouse feather, cut to shape, coated with Flexament
Legs: Brown feathers, trimmed and bent to shape
Eyes: Mono
Head: Brown dubbing
Antennae: Brown goose biots

Plastic Back Stonefly Nymph

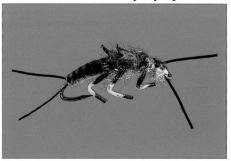

Tied by: James Pierce, Sweet Home, OR
Hook: Mustad 80050 BR, #8
Thread: Gold
Weight: Front half of hook shank, 14 turns of .030 lead wire; rear half, about 30 turns of .010 lead wire, flattened with pliers
Tails: Dark brown small Spanflex
Rib: Gold Spanflex or Super Floss
Body: Golden yellow dubbing
Shellback: Yellow Thin Skin strip, colored with brown water proof maker
Legs: 30lb. Micron Backing, colored with waterproof marks, kink heated to shape
Wing Case/Head: Same as shellback, cut to shape
Antennae: Dark brown small Spanflex

Poxy Rubber Legs Stone

Tied by: Michael Taylor, Etna, CA
Hook: Mustad 9672, #6-#10, bent down 20-30 degrees at the center, weighted at the thorax area with flattened wire
Thread: Black 6/0
Tails/Legs: Black round rubber
Body: Kaufmann's Black Stone dubbing
Wing Case: Top of thorax coated with epoxy
Antennae: Black round rubber

Real Epoxy Stone

Tied by: Chris Kazulen, Uniontown, PA
Hook: Mustad 9575, #8, front half weighted with lead wire and flattened with pliers
Thread: Black 6/0
Tails: Stripped pheasant feather stems, darkened with marker and coated with epoxy
Rib: Gold oval tinsel
Abdomen: Black and orange Fine & Dry dubbing
Thorax: Black and orange squirrel dubbing
Wing Case: Turkey tail feather sections, cut to shape and coated with epoxy
Legs/Antennae: Stripped pheasant feather stems, darkened with marker and coated with epoxy

Ritter's Dark Stone

Tied by: Carl Ritter, Sedona, AZ
Hook: Orvis 8808, #4, weighted with 2 lead wire strands secured to sides of hook shank
Thread: Dark brown 6/0
Tails: Dark brown goose biots
Rib: Gold wire
Shellback: Orange Larva Lace
Body: Black dubbing
Wing Case: Dull side of turkey feather sections, coated with Flexament
Legs: Mallard body feather fibers tied in segments at thorax
Antennae: Horsetail hairs, marked with dark brown water proof marker

Ritter's Golden Stone Nymph

Tied by: Carl Ritter, Sedona, AZ
Hook: Orvis 8808, #8, weighted with 2 lead wire strands mounted to the sides of hook shank
Thread: Dark brown 6/0
Tails: Brown goose biots
Rib: Orange Larva Lace
Abdomen: Yellow/gold floss
Thorax: Rust dubbing
Wing Case: Turkey feather, treated with Flexament, folded over
Legs: Golden pheasant feather fibers
Antennae: Horsetail hairs, marked with dark brown water proof pen

Roth's Brown Stone

Tied by: Scott Roth, Newton, NJ
Hook: TMC 200R, #6-#10, weighted
Thread: Dark brown
Tails: Brown biots
Underbody: Orvis Flat Body Nymph form
Abdomen: Brown foam strip, ironed flat, wrapped and colored with brown marker
Thorax: Brown Sparkle dubbing
Wing Cases: Turkey feather sections, cut to shape and coated with Flexament
Legs: Brown emu feather herl, crimped to shape
Eyes: Black plastic bead chain
Antennae: Brown turkey flat feather fibers

Rod's Beady Stonefly

Tied by: Rod Powell, Gypsum, CO
Hook: TMC 200, #8, weighted thorax area
Thread: Tan 8/0
Tails: Brown goose biots
Abdomen: 2 black craft beads, 1 brass bead, and 1 cut brown-orange craft bead
Thorax: Hare's ear dubbing
Wing Case: Pheasant tail feather fibers
Legs: Mallard hen breast feather fibers
Eyes: Mono, painted black
Antennae: Pheasant tail feather fibers

Romeo's Black Stone

Tied by: Romeo Rancourt, Thunder Bay, ON
Hook: TMC 5263 or Daiichi 1720, #6-#12, weighted
Thread: Black UNI-Thread 8/0
Tails: Black goose biots
Rib: Black Larva Lace Nymph Rib
Body: Black Kaufmann's Nymph Blend dubbing
Wing Case: Dark brown Swiss straw, coated with epoxy
Legs: Black braided line strands, top halves dubbed and ends melted
Antennae: Black goose biots

Romeo's Brown Stone

Tied by: Romeo Rancourt, Thunder Bay, ON
Hook: TMC 5253 or Daiichi 1720, #6-#16, weighted
Thread: Brown UNI-Thread 8/0
Tail: Brown goose biots
Rib: Brown Larva Lace Nymph Rib
Body: Brown stone Kaufmann's Nymph Blend dubbing
Wing Case: Dark brown Swiss straw, coated with epoxy
Legs: Cream braided line strands, top halves dubbed and ends melt
Antennae: Brown goose biots

Romeo's Golden Stone

Tied by: Romeo Rancourt, Thunder Bay, ON
Hook: TMC 5263 or Daiichi 1720, #6-#16, weighted
Thread: Brown UNI-Thread 8/0
Tails: Brown goose biots
Rib: Brown Larva Lace Nymph Rib
Body: Golden stone Kaufmann's Nymph Blend dubbing
Wing Case: Rusty brown Swiss straw, coated with epoxy
Legs: Cream braided line strands, top halves dubbed and ends melt
Antennae: Goose biots

RP'S Golden Stone

Tied by: Roy D. Powell, Danville, CA
Hook: TMC 200R, #2-#8, weighted
Thread: Yellow UNI-Thread 8/0
Tails: Black goose biots
Abdomen: Olive brown and pale yellow Magic Dub strands, woven using overhand weave
Legs: Olive brown Magic Dub strands, spotted with a black marker
Thorax: Golden brown Hare-Tron dubbing
Wing Case/Head: Mallard flank feathers, coated with Softex
Eyes: Mini Umpqua monofilament eyes
Antennae: Black goose biots

Rubber-Legged Krystal Stone

Tied by: Richard Murphy, Sr., Manitou Springs, CO
Hook: 4X long streamer hook, #6-#12, weighted
Thread: Tan, 8/0
Tail: Black round rubber
Rib: Gold wire, counter wrapped
Abdomen: Peacock herl
Wing Case: Turkey feather sections, coated with Flexament
Thorax: Medium ginger Krystal Dub dubbing
Legs: Black round rubber, and partridge feather, drawn feather style

Snagless Creeping Stonefly

Tied by: Wade Malwitz, Portland, OR
Hook: Mustad 32760, #1/0, weighted with .035 lead wire, tied hook-up
Thread: Black 3/0
Tails: Black turkey biots
Rib: Black Vinyl Rib, large, or silver tinsel
Body: Black dubbing
Legs: Black round rubber
Wing cases: Black Swiss straw

Sparkle Stone

Tied by: Jay Kaneshige, Castro Valley, CA
Hook: Daiichi 1270, #6-#8, weighted with 2 lead wire
strips mounted on each side of the hook shank
Thread: Pale orange
Tails: Ginger hackle tips
Rib: Gold oval tinsel
Body: Gold Hare-Tron mixed with Burnt Orange Pseudo
Seal, picked out
Shellback/Wing Case: Brown Swiss straw
Legs: Partridge feather fibers

S.U. Gold Stone

Tied by: Mike Bell, St. George, UT
Hook: TMC 8089, #6, bent up at thorax, weighted, wire
flattened with pliers
Thread: Brown 6/0
Tails: Ginger turkey feather fibers, coated with Flexament
Rib: Black wire
Shellback: Peacock herl strands
Body: Kaufmann's Golden Stone dubbing mixed with
Awesome Possum orange dubbing, picked out thorax
Wing Case: Ginger turkey feather section, cut to shape, and
coated with Flexament
Antennae: Ginger turkey feather fibers, coated with Flexament

Steve's Stone

Tied by: Steve Potter, Tracy, CA
Hook: Streamer hook, #4-#6, weighted
Thread: Brown
Tail: Emu feather fibers
Rib: Brown V-Rib
Body: Blue dun Mohair J. Fair Rope
Shellback/Wing Case/Head: Badger feather, coated with
Softex
Thorax: Same as body with Holographic dubbing added
Legs: Emu feather, drawn feather style
Eyes: Brass bead on mono, glued with Zap-a-Gap

S.U. Super Stone Nymph

Tied by: Wes Atkin, St. George, UT
Hook: Mustad 37160, #8, weighted
Thread: Brown 6/0
Tails: Stripped brown hackle stems, over orange dubbing ball
Rib: Brown Vinyl Rib
Body: Golden brown dubbing
Wing Case/Head: Partridge feather, cut to shape and coated
with Flexament
Legs: Tan Micro Dubb
Eyes: Plastic nymph eyes
Antennae: Stripped brown hackle stems

Shawn's Stone

Tied by: Shawn Poole, Littleton, CO
Hook: Partridge H3ST, #6-#14, weighted
Thread: Tan 6/0
Tails: Gold biots, colored with brown marker
Rib: Yellow UNI-floss
Body: Awesome Possum Golden Stone dubbing
Abdomen: Clear Orvis Body Glass, colored with brown marker
Wing Case: Tyvek, colored with brown and yellow markers
and coated with Softex
Legs: PMD colored Magic Dub, bent to shape and
highlighted with a brown marker
Eyes: X-small mono eyes
Antennae: Gold biots color with a brown marker

Sheldon's Black Stonefly Nymph

Tied by: Sheldon Fedder II, Millville, Pa
Hook: TMC 200R, #6-#10, weighted
Thread: Black
Tails: Black paint brush fibers
Rib: Black Larva Lace
Body: 50% black rabbit dubbing, 50% claret, amber,
orange, rust, black, brow, blue, purple, and ginger goat
fur, mixed
Wing Case: Black Swiss straw
Legs: Black dubbing brush strands, bent to shape and
ends cemented
Eyes: Mono
Antennae: Black Micro Fibetts

Soft Mite

Tied by: Vladimir Markov, Irkutsk, Russia
Hook: Mustad 3906B, #6-#12, weighted
Thread: Brown
Tails: Stripped brown hackle stems
Abdomen Underbody: Brown synthetic dubbing
Abdomen: Black Scud Back, wrapped
Thorax: Golden synthetic dubbing
Wing Case/Head: Black Scud Back, cut to shape and
colored with brown mark
Legs: Black Scud Back, cut to shape
Antennae: Stripped brown hackle stems

Stone Cutter

Tied by: Troy Kelly, Puyallup, WA
Hook: TMC 200R, #10, weighted
Thread: Black
Tails: Black round rubber
Abdomen: Brown Larval Lace
Wing Case: Brown goose biots, coated with Flexament
Thorax: Olive rabbit dubbing
Legs: Black round rubber
Head: Black metal bead

Stony Fillet

Tied by: Sharie Sinclaire, Bowen Island, BC
Hook: Limerick, #6, weighted
Thread: Black 6/0
Tails: Black goose biots
Underbody: Black Antron dubbing
Body: Black yarn
Wing Case: Plastic sheeting, cut to shape and painted black
Legs: Black round rubber, knotted
Eyes: Black mono, medium
Head: Black bead
Antennae: Black goose biots
Comments: After tying fly, coat wing case and top of body
with pearl nail polish.

Stunning Stone

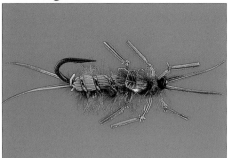

Tied by: Kyle Hicks, Berwick, N.S.
Hook: Mustad 9671, #12, tied hook point-up, weighted
Thread: Black 6/0
Tails: Brown goose biots
Rib: Gold oval tinsel
Shellback: Deer hair
Body: Tan dubbing
Wing Case: Brown hen feather, placed on clear packing tape, then folded and cut to shape
Legs/Antennae: Brown goose flight feather fibers, legs knotted

Swiss Straw Stone

Tied by: Ben Teves, Duluth, GA
Hook: Mustad 36890, #2-#8, weighted
Thread: Olive or black 6/0
Tail: Black, brown or burgundy goose biots
Rib: Stripped ginger hackle stem
Body: Black rabbit and brown opossum dubbing, mixed
Wing Case: Light tan Swiss straw
Legs: Black saddle hackle, wrapped over thorax, top fibers trimmed
Eyes: Small black bead chain

Tarcher Stonefly

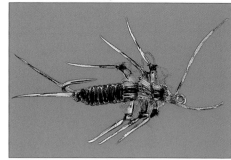

Tied by: Jay Hartman, Eagle, CO
Hook: TMC 200R, #6-#8, weighted with .025 lead wire or for wider profile .010 lead wire wrapped around shank with .035 lead wire strands tied to sides of hook shank
Thread: Tan 6/0
Tails: Tan goose biots
Abdomen: Larva Lace, color #58, top of thread wraps colored with black or brown waterproof marker before wrapping
Thorax: Ginger or golden stone Awesome Possum Nymph Dubbing
Wing Case: Dyed olive speckled turkey feather sections
Legs: Natural or dyed olive turkey biots
Antennae: Natural or dyed olive turkey feather fibers
Comments: Spot legs, tails, and antennae with black marker.

Thera Black Stone

Tied by: Romeo Rancourt, Thunder Bay, ON
Hook: TMC 5263 or Daiichi 1720, #8-#16, weighted
Thread: Black 8/0
Tails: Black round rubber
Abdomen: Black Thera band
Wing Case: Remains of abdomen
Legs: Grouse feather
Thorax: Dark claret (a mix of 50% claret seal, 50% black Hare-Tron dubbing)
Antennae: Black round rubber

Thera Golden Stone

Tied by: Romeo Rancourt, Thunder Bay, ON
Hook: TMC 5263 or Daiichi 1720, #8-#16, weighted
Thread: Yellow UNI-Thread 8/0
Tails: Cream round rubber
Abdomen: Yellow Thera band
Wing Case: Thera band, tag end of abdomen material
Legs: Grouse feather, placed on top of thorax
Thorax: Dubbing mixture of 25% cream seal, 25% brown seal, and 50% gold rabbit
Antennae: Cream round rubber
Comments: Color fly with brown marker.

Tupper's Black Stone

Tied by: Perry Tupper, Salem, OR
Hook: TMC 200R or TMC 5262, #6-#12, weighted
Thread: Black
Tails: Black goose biots
Rib: Copper wire
Body: 2/3 Black and 1/3 Chocolate brown Hare-Tron dubbing mixed
Wing Case: Pheasant tail feather fibers
Legs: Brown hackle, top fibers trimmed
Head: Black metal bead

Ugly Stone

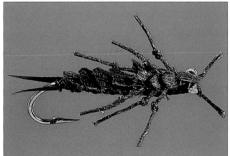

Tied by: Joe Pantell, Greenville, PA
Hook: Mustad 79580, #8, weighted with lead strands lashed to the sides of the hook shank
Thread: Black 6/0
Tails: Black goose biots
Body: Brown and black Antron yarn strands, woven with an overhand weave
Overbody/Wing Case: Dark turkey tail feather, coated with Flexament, shaped and mounted between every other weave
Thorax: Black thread
Legs/Antennae: Heavy black thread, knotted and coated with Flexament
Eyes: Small green beads with mono core

Wayne's Golden Stone

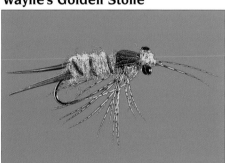

Tied by: Andy Wayne, San Francisco, CA
Hook: TMC 200R, #8-#12, weighted
Thread: Yellow 6/0
Tails: Brown goose biots
Rib: Olive micro-lace
Body: Golden stone Antron dubbing
Wing Case: Turkey feather section, coated with Flexament
Legs: Partridge feather pulled over the top of the thorax
Eyes: Mono
Antennae: Partridge feather fibers

Weaving Stony

Tied by: Boyd Elder, Spiro, OK
Hook: Mustad 9872, #8, weighted
Thread: Brown, 6/0
Tails: Brown goose biots
Abdomen: Root beer Krystal Flash strands, furled into 2 cords and woven with an overhand weave
Thorax: Brown squirrel dubbing
Wing Case: Turkey tail feather sections, cut to shape and coated with Flexament
Legs: Partridge feather, drawn feather style

Wiggler

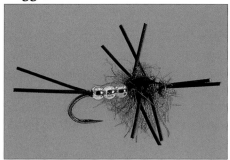

Tied by: Troy Kelly, Puyallup, WA
Hook: TMC 200R, #10, weight thorax area
Thread: Brown
Tails: Black round rubber
Abdomen: Clear glass beads
Thorax: Brown dubbing
Wing Case: Black Scud Back, darkened with black marker
Legs/Antennae: Black round rubber

Woven K.F. Nymph

Tied by: Boyd Elder, Spiro, OK
Hook: Mustad 9672, #8-#3, weighted
Thread: Black 6/0
Tail: Black marabou feather fibers
Abdomen Underbody: Black yarn, form a tapered body
Abdomen: Black and Peacock Krystal Flash strands, furled into 2 cords and woven using overhand weave
Wing Case: Turkey tail feather section, coated with Flexament
Thorax: Peacock herl
Hackle: Black, top fibers trimmed

Woven Prince Stonefly Nymph

Tied by: Chris French, East Brunswick, NJ
Hook: Daiichi 1270, #8, weighted on hook shank sides with .015 lead wire
Thread: Rust
Tails: Light brown goose biots
Body: Black and green small Kreinik Braid Flat Ribbon strands, woven using overhand weave with black ribbon on top
Wings: White goose biots
Hackle: Ginger hen

Stonefly Adults

Barron

Tied by: Adam Tuma, Lebanon, OR
Hook: TMC 200R, #8
Thread: Black 3/0
Tail: Black deer hair
Rib: Black and grizzly hackle
Body: Orange floss
Wing: Coastal or black deer hair
Legs: Black round rubber
Head/Collar: Black deer hair, trimmed to shape

Beaverkill Foam Stone

Tied by: Floyd Franke, Roscoe, NY
Hook: Mustad 3399D, #10
Thread: Brown 6/0
Rib: Tying thread
Abdomen: Brown Craft Foam strip, a needle used to form a folded extension body
Thorax: Brown rabbit dubbing
Legs: Turkey tail feather fibers, knotted
Wing/Head: Brown bucktail

Big Stone

Tied by: Vladimir Markov, Irkutsk, Russia
Hook: Mustad 94831, #4-#8
Thread: Black
Tails: Brown goose biots
Abdomen: Dark brown dubbing
Thorax: Orange dubbing
Wing: Deer hair, tied in 3 clumps
Hackle: Brown, top fibers trimmed
Head/Collar: Deer hair, bullet style
Antennae: Stripped brown hackle stems

Black CDC Gold Butt

Tied by: Don Joslyn, Eagle Point, OR
Hook: Alec Jackson Daiichi 2051 black, #5
Thread: Black 3/0
Tails: Paint brush fibers
Butt: Gold tinsel
Body: Black CDC dubbing
Wing: 2 CDC feathers, tied delta style
Hackle: Black
Head: Black ostrich herl

Black Moose Stone

Tied by: Don Joslyn, Eagle Point, OR
Hook: Alec Jackson Daiichi 2051 black, #3
Thread: Black 3/0
Tails: Black goose biots
Rib: Black V-Rib
Abdomen: Gray hare's ear dubbing
Wing: Moose mane hair
Legs: Black hackle, top fibers trimmed
Thorax/Head: Black ostrich herl

Bow Stone

Tied by: Phil Sheepy, Cochran, AB
Hook: Mustad 9671, #4-#10
Thread: Carmel
Tails: Paint brush bristles
Abdomen: Elk hair, reverse-tied extension style
Legs: Black round rubber
Thorax: Peacock herl
Wing: White calf tail hair, over mallard feather fibers
Head: Elk hair, over peacock herl
Antennae: Paint brush bristles

Bullet Head Golden Stone

Tied by: Mark Defrank, Chalkhill, PA
Hook: TMC 200R, #8
Thread: Tan
Tail: Golden yellow elk hair
Rib: Brown hackle, trimmed short
Body: Amber dubbing
Wing: Light tan Elk hair
Head/Collar: Golden yellow elk hair, bullet style, trimmed bottom collar hair

CDC Black Stone

Tied by: Don Joslyn, Eagle Point, OR
Hook: Alec Jackson Daiichi 2051 black, #3
Thread: Black 3/0
Tails: Black goose biots
Rib: Black V-Rib
Body: Black ostrich herl
Wing: 2 CDC feathers, delta style
Legs: Black round rubber

Cliff's Adult Stonefly

Tied by: Clifford Sullivan, Tracy, CA
Hook: TMC 200, #8
Thread: Gold 8/0
Tag: Red dubbing
Tails: Yellow goose biots
Rib: Cree saddle feather
Body: Yellow foam, wrapped
Wing: Wooduck feather, pulled back and coated with Flexament, then folded over thorax and eyes
Hackle: Cree saddle feather, top fibers trimmed
Eyes: Yellow mono with black dot
Antennae: Yellow goose biots

Crippled Stone

Tied by: Chris Kazulen, Uniontown, PA
Hook: Mustad 9575, #8
Thread: Dark brown 6/0
Tails: Moose body hairs, 2 per side glued together
Rib: Gold oval tinsel
Underbody: Closed-cell foam, wrapped on the thorax area
Body: March brown Fine & Dry dubbing
Hackle: Cree, bottom fibers trimmed
Wing: Elk hair, 2 dun feathers—delta style

Dan's Stonefly

Tied by: Dan Ward, Jr., Clarksville, AR
Hook: TMC 5212, #10-#14
Thread: Black 6/0
Tails: Stripped brown hackle stems
Body: Rusty brown Antron dubbing
Hackle: Cree
Wing: Mottled oak Thin Skin, cut to shape
Antennae: Same as tail

Downwing

Tied by: Tim McConville, Salt Lake City, UT
Hook: TMC 200R, #4-#10
Thread: Brown
Tail: Orange elk hair
Rib: Brown hackle, trimmed short
Abdomen: Orange wool
Wing: Red squirrel tail
Thorax: Peacock herl
Hackle: Grizzly

Elk/CDC Yellow Sally

Tied by: Don Joslyn, Eagle Point, OR
Hook: Dai-Riki 270, #6
Thread: Yellow 3/0
Tails: Tan paint brush fibers
Rib: Gold tinsel
Body: Yellow CDC dubbing, top darkened with brown marker
Wing: Elk hair
Hackle: Cree
Head: Black ostrich herl

E-Z Catching

Tied by: Troy Kelly, Puyallup, WA
Hook: TMC 100, #12-#16
Thread: Black
Body: Gold Antron yarn, furled
Wing: Bleached deer hair
Hackle: Ginger

Fancy Clark Stone

Tied by: Don Joslyn, Eagle Point, OR
Hook: Alec Jackson Daiichi 2055 gold, #3
Thread: Orange 3/0
Tails: Yellow goose biots
Rib: Gold tinsel
Body: Orange thread
Wing: Orange Krystal Flash, orange Aqua Fibers, topped with elk hair
Legs: Brown round rubber
Hackle: Brown saddle, bottom fibers trimmed

Female Golden Stone

Tied by: Jim Riley, Grass Valley, CA
Hook: TMC 5212, #8
Thread: Brown
Egg Sack: Fine black chenille
Tails: Sulfur turkey biots
Rib: Orange grizzly hackle, clipped top and bottom fibers
Body: Golden stone dubbing
Wing: Turkey tail feather section, coated with Flexament, over gray CDC puff
Hackle: Orange grizzly

Flash Biot Stone

Tied by: Tim McConville, Salt Lake City, UT
Hook: TMC 200R, #10-#14
Thread: Black
Tails: Brown goose biots, pearl Krystal Flash strands
Abdomen: Brown goose biot
Thorax: Gray chenille
Wing Case: Clear plastic bag strip, coated with Loon Hard Head cement
Hackle: Black
Legs/Wings: Gray partridge feather fibers
Comments: This fly is meant to imitate a sunken adult stonefly, fish the fly down and across as a wet fly or dead drift.

Fred's Salmon Fly

Tied by: Fred Iacoletti, Albuquerque, NM
Hook: 6XL streamer, #8
Thread: Orange 6/0
Tails: Brown turkey wing feather fibers
Rib: Brown "A" thread
Abdomen: Orange deer hair
Thorax: Orange Mottled Nymph Blend dubbing
Wing: Pearl Krystal Flash, topped by speckled hen saddle feather coated with Flexament and cut to shape
Antennae: Same as tail

Freeman's Adult Stonefly

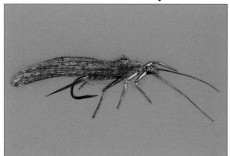

Tied by: Wayne Freeman, Lexington, SC
Hook: Varivas 973 Streamer Hook #8
Thread: Brown 8/0
Tails: Porcupine quills
Rib: Brown horsehair
Abdomen: Light brown dubbing
Wing: Swiss straw, cut to shape, colored with brown Pantone marker and coated with Softex
Legs: Turkey biots, knotted
Thorax: Light brown dubbing
Thorax/Head: Swiss straw, cut to shape and colored with brown and black Pantone markers, coated with Softex

Golden/Skwala Shaving Brush

Tied by: Ed Burke, White Sulphur Springs, MT
Hook: TMC 200R or Dai-Riki 270, #6-#10
Thread: Brown
Butt: Black foam, used to imitate egg sack and float butt of fly
Body: Olive deer or elk hair
Wing: Deer or elk hair
Head: Deer hair, bullet style

Harry's Golden Stone Adult

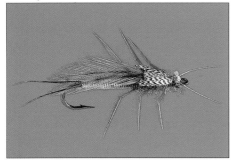

Tied by: Harry Gross, Salem, OR
Hook: Mustad 3665A, #4-#6
Thread: Gray 12/0
Tails: Pheasant tail feather, 2 per side, coated with Flexament
Underbody: Yellow floss, over straight pins cut to size and mounted on sides of hook shank
Overbody: Partridge feather, cemented, topped with 20lb mono
Legs: Gold goose biots
Thorax: Iridescent golden stone dubbing
Wing: 2 light gray hackle feathers
Eyes: 20lb mono melted
Antennae: Mallard feather fibers
Head: Mallard feather, burnt or cut to shape, and cemented

Hoff's Adult Stone

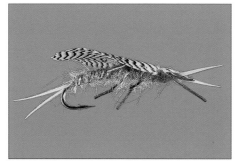

Tied by: Scott Hoff, Concord, CA
Hook: Orvis 1510, #8
Thread: Tan 10/0
Tails: Tan goose biots
Rib: DMC Braided Thread (found in craft stores)
Abdomen: Ginger Hare-Tron dubbing
Thorax: Burnt orange fox dubbing
Wing: Woodduck feather, coated with Flexament
Legs: Black small round rubber, knotted
Antennae: Tan goose biots

Horse Tail

Tied by: Daniel Sternhager, Billings, MT
Hook: 2X long, #8-#12
Thread: Tan
Tail: Horsehair
Body: Brown to tan yarn
Wing: White bucktail hair
Hackle: Brown, bottom fibers trimmed

Ipsen's Salmon Fly

Tied by: Loren Ipsen, Boise, ID
Hook: Mustad 94831, #2-#8
Thread: Orange
Tail: Dark orange Z-lon (represents extruded eggs)
Rib: Orange grizzly hackle, trimmed short
Abdomen: Dark brown dubbing
Wing: Chocolate brown calf hair, orange calf hair, a few strands of orange Krystal Flash, and light elk hair
Head/Collar: Chocolate brown deer hair, bullet style, bottom collar hairs trimmed
Legs: Black round rubber

Iridescent Gold Stone Adult

Tied by: Ronn Lucas, Sr., Milwaukie, OR
Hook: Daiichi 2220, #4-#8
Thread: Rust-orange Mono Cord
Tails: Stripped grizzly hackle stems
Body: Gold stone Iridescent Dubbing #38
Wing: Gray and brown Swiss straw strips, cut to shape, and glued together; option: elk hair
Eyes: Small back glass beads with mono core
Head/Thorax: Gold Flashback #139, tied in behind eye and folded back to cover 1/4 inch of wing
Antennae: Stripped grizzly hackle stems

Iridescent Stone Adult

Tied by: Ronn Lucas, Sr., Milwaukie, OR
Hook: Mustad 9575, #2-#8
Thread: Black
Tails: Brown goose biots
Body: Black Iridescent Dubbing #2
Wing/Head: Gray and brown Swiss straw strips, cut to shape, and glued together
Legs: Brown hackle, wrapped over thorax, top fibers trimmed
Antennae: Stripped grizzly hackle stems

Jan's Little Yellow Stone

Tied by: Jan Pickel, New Park, PA
Hook: Daiichi 1180, #16
Thread: Yellow 8/0
Tails: Yellow turkey biots
Body: Yellow beaver dubbing
Wing: Mottled golden stone Thin Skin, cut to shape, over yellow CDC feather fibers
Hackle: Yellow
Antennae: Yellow turkey biots

King's Giant Salmon Fly

Tied by: Matt King, Victoria, BC
Hook: TMC 2312, #4-#10
Thread: Brown
Tails: Tan goose biots, short
Rib: Single strand of pearl Krystal Flash
Abdomen: Brown/orange Wapsi Super Bright dubbing, mixed
Underwing: Natural CDC feather
Wing: Brown Air Thru Wing material, cut to shape
Thorax Shellback/Head: Natural CDC fibers
Legs: Pearl Krystal Flash strands
Thorax: Orange Wapsi Super Bright Dubbing
Hackle: Grizzly, hackle twisted with 1 strand of pearl Krystal Flash, top fibers trimmed

King's Little Black Stone

Tied by: Matt King, Victoria, BC
Hook: TMC 101, #14-#18
Thread: Black
Tails: Black goose biots, short
Body: Black Wapsi Super Bright Dubbing
Underwing: Natural CDC feather fibers
Wing: Brown Air Thru Wing material, cut to shape
Thorax shellback/Head: Natural CDC feather fibers
Legs: Pearl Krystal Flash strands
Hackle: Grizzly, top fibers trimmed

King's Yellow Sally Stone

Tied by: Matt King, Victoria, BC
Hook: TMC 2312, #10-#16
Thread: Golden olive
Tails: Tan goose biots, short
Rib: Single strand of pearl Krystal Flash
Abdomen: Golden stone Antron dubbing
Wing: Brown Air Thru Wing material, cut to shape
Thorax shellback/Head: Natural CDC feather fibers
Legs: Pearl Krystal Flash strands
Thorax: Golden stone Wapsi Super Bright Dubbing
Hackle: Grizzly, hackle twisted with 1 strand of pearl Krystal Flash, top fibers trimmed

Kulchak's Dry Stone

Tied by: J. Michael Kulchak, Boise, ID
Hook: TMC 5212, #2-#8
Thread: Burnt orange
Tail: Elk hair
Rib: Copper wire, counter wrapped
Body Hackle: Furnace
Body: Orange dubbing
Wing: Elk mane hair, over 2-6 strands of pearl Krystal Flash
Hackle: Furnace

Little Green Foam Stone

Tied by: Floyd Franke, Roscoe, NY
Hook: Eagle Claw L055 or Mustad 80250BR, #16-#18
Thread: Brown 8/0
Abdomen: Bright green Craft Foam, cut to shape
Thorax: Green UNI-Stretch Floss
Wing: White snowshoe hare's foot hairs, tied in by tips
Hackle: Grizzly, bottom fibers trimmed
Comments: When tied in a size 10 hook using yellow foam and matching UNI-Strech, the fly works well imitating yellow stonefly adults.

Little Green Stonefly

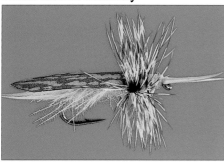

Tied by: Jan Pickel, New Park, PA
Hook: Daiichi 1180, #16
Thread: Green 10/0
Tails: Green turkey biots
Body: Fluorescent lime green SLF dubbing
Wing: Mottled green Thin Skin, cut to shape, over olive yellow CDC feather fibers
Hackle: Green grizzly
Antennae: Green turkey biots

Match Stick

Tied by: Henry Hoffman, Warrenton, OR
Hook: Mustad 9672, #6
Thread: Orange 6/0
Body: Wooden match stick, mounted on top of hook shank and over-wrapped with orange Clark's Yarn
Rib: Brown Vinyl Rib
Wing: Vained plastic wing material, cut to shape
Hackle: Ginger grizzly
Antennae: Brown chicken biots
Comments: Cut a 1-inch section from a match stick, at 1 end round the top corners of a 1 inched section, at the opposite end trim the match down to half of it thickness, this end is mount behind the hook eye. Color the rear end of the stick with a red marker. To keep the stick from shifting, first tie in the yarn on top of the hook shank.

Moss's Little Brown Stone

Tied by: L.K. Moss, Draper, MT
Hook: Mustad 9484, #14
Thread: Black 6/0
Abdomen: Black and brown Micro Tubing strands, woven using the overhand weave
Thorax: Brown dubbing
Legs: Black PVC cord fibers
Wing: Black mottled Thin Skin, cut to shape
Antennae: Black paint brush fibers

Muddler Head Foam

Tied by: Don Joslyn, Eagle Point, OR
Hook: Alec Jackson Daiichi 2055 gold, #3
Thread: Orange 3/0
Body: Orange Larva Lace foam strip, formed into folded extension body using a needle, darkened with brown marker
Wing: Black plastic wing—cut to shape, CDC feather fibers, copper Krystal Flash strands, and elk hair
Head/Collar: Elk hair

Nino's Stonefly Adult

Tied by: Nino Casino, Alatri, Italy
Hook: TMC 100, #8
Thread: Brown, 6/0
Body: Copper wire braided with brown Deer Dubbing, by Palu, an Italian fly fishing product distributor
Wing: Art. 186 Color N 2, by Palu
Hackle: Deer dubbing

No Tail Yellow Sally

Tied by: Don Joslyn, Eagle Point, OR
Hook: Dai-Riki 270, #6
Thread: Yellow 3/0
Rib: Amber V-Rib
Body: Yellow CDC dubbing
Wing: 2 yellow CDC feathers, delta style
Hackle: Cree, bottom fibers trimmed
Head: Black ostrich herl

O2 Air-Filled Stone

Tied by: Robert Williamson, Roy, UT
Hook: TMC 5212, #6
Thread: Orange 6/0
Body: O2 Stonefly preformed body
Wing: Elk hair
Head/Collar: Deer hair, bullet style
Legs: Black round rubber

Para Stone

Tied by: Tim McConville, Salt Lake City, UT
Hook: TMC 200R, #4-#6
Thread: Yellow
Tail: Moose hair
Rib: Yellow thread
Abdomen: Hare's ear dubbing
Wing: Pheasant tail feather fibers, over moose hair
Thorax: Peacock herl, hare's ear dubbing
Post: Yellow foam, folded forward after wrapping hackle
Hackle: Brown, parachute style
Head: Yellow foam from post

Reavis Style Foam Stone

Tied by: Don Joslyn, Eagle Point, OR
Hook: Dai-Riki 710-C, #4
Thread: Orange 3/0
Tail: Moose mane hair
Body: Orange Larva Lace foam strip, colored with brown marker then folded over hook shank and segmented with thread wraps
Wing: CDC feather fibers, topped with Elk hair
Head: Butt end from top half of body material, folded back

Red Butt Timulator

Tied by: Tim McConville, Salt Lake City, UT
Hook: TMC 2312, #8-#16
Thread: Yellow
Tail: White deer hair
Rib: Brown hackle, trimmed short
Abdomen: Red floss, yellow foam strip, wrapped
Thorax: Yellow chenille
Hackle: Brown, wrapped over thorax
Wing: White deer hair and partridge feather fibers

Ronn's Heritage Stone

Tied by: Ronn Lucas, Sr., Milwaukie, OR
Hook: TMC 200, #4
Thread: Black
Tail/Wings: Elk mane hair
Body: Beaver dubbing
Comments: This pattern is derived from an antique fly that I saw but could never find it in a pattern book, so I don't know the original name. I varied the body and wing materials but the overall shape remains the same.

Rubber Legged Half Back

Tied by: J. Mullin, Casper, WY
Hook: Mustad 9671, #6
Thread: Black
Tail: Pheasant tail feather fibers, over 6 strands of green Krystal Flash
Hackle: Brown
Body: Peacock herl
Shellback: Pheasant tail feather fibers—butt ends from tail, over rear half of body
Legs: Yellow mottled brown round rubber

Salmonfly Shaving Brush

Tied by: Ed Burke, White Sulphur Springs, MT
Hook: TMC 200R or Dai-Riki 270, #4
Thread: Thread 6/0
Butt: Black foam, used to imitate egg sack and float butt of fly
Body: Orange deer or elk hair
Wing: Bleached deer or elk hair
Head: Deer hair, bullet style

Salmostone

Tied by: Joe Mullin, Casper, WY
Hook: Mustad 3665A, #1
Thread: Black 6/0
Tails: Black goose biots
Underbody: 2 pieces of Rex Lace, mounted on sides of hook shank 3/16 inch back from hook eye with thread then Super Glued
Body: White floss, wrapped 4 or 5 times over underbody coated with Super Glue, dried then colored with Pantone pens—orange bottom and black for top
Wing: Cloth screen material, cut to shape
Legs: Brown hackle, top fibers trimmed
Head: Orange floss, coated with Super Glue
Antennae: Black horsehair

Scott's Foam Stonefly

Tied by: Scott Zadroga, San Diego, CA
Hook: TMC 5212, #8
Thread: Black 6/0
Body: Gray packing foam, cut to shape
Wing: 2 pieces of white packing foam, cut to shape, and glued to the top of the body with Super Glue
Legs: Black round rubber
Head: Gray packing form, bullet style
Comments: The body is formed like an inverted foam beetle body.

Sheldon's Black Stonefly

Tied by: Sheldon Fedder II, Millville, PA
Hook: TMC 200R, #4-#10
Thread: Black
Tails: Black paint brush fibers
Rib: Black Larva Lace
Body: 50% black rabbit dubbing, 50% claret, amber, orange, rust, black, brow, blue, purple, and ginger goat fur, mixed
Wing: Wing Film, cut to shape
Legs: Black dubbing bush stands, bent to shape, ends cemented
Head: Black Swiss straw
Eyes: Black plastic
Antennae: Black Micro Fibetts
Comments: This fly imitates a sunken adult.

Skipping Stone

Tied by: Larry Larsen, Pocatello, ID
Hook: Mustad 9672, #4
Thread: Orange
Tails: Black Sili-Legs
Rib: Grizzly hackle, clipped short
Body: Orange closed-cell foam1/8-inch strip, wrapped forward
Wing: Moose body hair, over filter screen cut to shape
Legs/Antennae: Black Sili Legs
Head/Collar: Elk hair, bullet style—trim bottom collar hairs, topped with orange foam

Stone Hopper

Tied by: Bahman Khadivi, Cupertino, CA
Hook: TMC 200R, #6-#10
Thread: Yellow 6/0
Tag: Tan dubbing
Tails: Brown goose biots
Body: Tan foam
Wing: Gray foam—cut to shape, over deer hair
Legs: Gray Sili Legs
Head/Collar: Deer hair—bullet style, with orange deer hair staked on top, trim bottom collar hairs

S.U. Super Stone Adult

Tied by: Wes Atkin, St. George, UT
Hook: TMC 200R, #6
Thread: Brown 6/0
Body: Orange foam strip, formed into a folded extension
    body using a needle
Wing: Root beer Krystal Flash, topped with packing foam—
    cut to shape and colored with Pantone brown/yellow
    marker, topped with bleached elk hair
Head/Collar: Gold deer hair, bullet style
Legs: Brown round rubber

Tickler

Tied by: Chuck Peven, Wenatchee, WA
Hook: TMC 2303, #8-#16
Thread: Black or red, 6/0 or 8/0
Tail: Elk hair
Rib: Pearl Flashabou strand
Abdomen: Dark olive dubbing
Wing: Elk hair
Thorax: Dark olive dubbing, teased out
Post: White calf tail hairs
Hackle: Grizzly, parachute style

Troy's Stone

Tied by: Troy Kelly, Puyallup, WA
Hook: Mustad 9672, #10-#14
Thread: Brown
Body: Gold Antron yarn, furled
Head/Collar: Deer hair
Legs: Black round rubber

Twisted Stone Adult

Tied by: Robert Williamson, Roy, UT
Hook: TMC 5212, #12
Thread: Rust
Body: Thin strips of black and rust closed-cell foam, furled
Wing: Elk hair
Legs: Black round rubber
Head: Black foam strip, bullet style

Ultra Stonefly Adult

Tied by: Larry Larsen, Pocatello, ID
Hook: TMC 200R, #6
Thread: Burnt orange
Tails: Stripped grizzly hackle stems
Body: Orange Rainy's Float Foam, top half colored with
    black marker, segment with thread
Wing: Mixed moose body hair and deer hair
Hackle: Brown, black and grizzly
Head/Back: Black foam
Antennae: Russian boar guard hairs

Vegas Stone

Tied by: Don Joslyn, Eagle Point, OR
Hook: Dai-Riki 270, #4
Thread: Orange 3/0
Tail: Pearl Krystal Flash strands
Body: Orange Larva Lace foam strip, colored with brown
    marker, folded and mounted to the top of the hook shank
Thorax: Black ostrich herl
Wing: 2 tan CDC feathers—tied delta style, topped with elk
    hair
Head: Peacock herl

Vulnerable Spent Stonefly

Tied by: Vladimir Markov, Irkutsk, Russia
Hook: TMC 200, #4-#10
Thread: Brown
Tail: Antron yarn strands
Body: Brown and yellow Evazote foam strips, mounted on
    top and bottom of hook shank
Wings: Yellow Swiss straw, cut to shape
Hackle/Legs: Deer hair
Head: Yellow Evazote foam strip, butt end from body
    material

Yellow Feather Stone

Tied by: Jeff Lingerfelter, Browns Valley, CA
Hook: TMC 2312, #6-#16 or TMC 300, #4-#8
Thread: Olive or black 8/0
Rib: Fine gold wire
Abdomen: Black and yellow grizzly saddle hackles, palmered
    and clipped to shape
Wing: 3 or more CDC feathers, topped with cream Z-lon fibers
Eyes: Black plastic
Thorax/Head/Legs: Olive grizzly hackle, palmered and
    clipped to shape
Antennae: Stripped yellow grizzly hackle stems
Comments: The Featherstone is more a style than a specific
    pattern. Varying the size and color enables you to match
    whichever stonefly adult you wish to imitate. This fly is
    designed to ride low in the water and create a realistic sur-
    face impression. These flies are at their best in slightly
    smoother water, such as seams, tailouts and riffle edges.

Yellow Sally Regulator

Tied by: Al Beatty, Delta, CO
Hook: TMC 200R, #14-#20
Thread: Yellow 6/0
Butt: Peacock herl
Abdomen: Yellow floss
Wing: White calf body hair
Thorax: Peacock herl
Hackle: Brown

Yellow Stone

Tied by: Adam Tuma, Lebanon, OR
Hook: Mustad 9672, #10
Thread: Yellow 3/0
Tail: Coastal deer hair
Rib/Hackle: Ginger
Body: Yellow floss
Wing: Coastal deer hair

Youssef's Salmonfly Adult

Tied by: N. Youssef, Pullman, WA
Hook: Mustad AC9672, #4
Thread: Orange 3/0
Tails: Brown Sili Legs
Rib: Orange thread
Abdomen: Orange moose hair, reverse-tied extension
Thorax: Mixed brown, orange and black dubbing
Wings: Tan Swiss straw strips, cut to shape, delta style
Legs: Brown Sili Legs
Eyes: Mono
Head/Collar: Natural deer hair, bullet style

CHAPTER 4

Midge

Larvae

Bates Midge Larva

Tied by: Michael Bates, Steamboat Springs, CO
Hook: Mustad 94840, #20
Thread: Gray 6/0
Tail: Black squirrel tail hairs
Rib: Olive 6/0 thread
Body: Brown/black mohair
Gills: White Fish Hair

B.F. Midget Larva

Tied by: Brandon Fessler, Ogden, UT
Hook: TMC 3761 #12-#20
Thread: Black 8/0
Tail: White CDC feather fibers
Rib: Fine gold wire
Underbody: Brown dubbing
Body: Brown plastic ribbing material
Gills: White CDC feather fibers

Big Red

Tied by: Fred Iacoletti, Albuquerque, NM
Hook: TMC 205BL, #12
Thread: Red 6/0
Rear Pro Legs: Red deer hair
Front Pro Legs: Red micro chenille
Rib: Gold small oval tinsel
Body: Blood red Ultra Lace
Head: Olive brown dubbing

Brown Midge

Tied by: Wayne Noble, Coquitlam, BC
Hook: TMC 100, #14
Thread: Brown 6/0
Tail: Black hackle fibers
Body: Brown dubbing

Copper Chironomid

Tied by: Wayne Noble, Coquitlam, BC
Hook: TMC 2457, #10
Thread: Red 6/0
Tail: Brown hackle fibers
Rib: Red wire
Body: Rust UNI-Floss
Head: Copper glass bead

Eby's Bloodworm

Tied by: Gord Eby, Fort St. John, BC
Hook: Mustad 37160, #10
Thread: Red 6/0
Underbody: Red thread
Overbody: Clear Larva Lace
Gills: Maroon emu hair

Elder's Midge Larva

Tied by: Boyd Elder, Spiro, OK
Hook: TMC 5263, #10-#16
Thread: Brown
Body: Root Beer Krystal Flash, 3 or 4 strands furled, form 2 cords then woven using an overhand weave

Filoplume Midge

Tied by: Henry Hoffman, Warrenton, OR
Hook: TMC 5263, #12-#20
Thread: Red 8/0
Tail: Red aftershaft feather from rooster breast
Rib: Brown mono
Body: Red Bodi Braid
Antennae: Unravelled butt end of body material

Fire Ball Larva

Tied by: Brad Lucy, Coquitlam, BC
Hook: TMC 5262, #12
Thread: Fine monofilament
Gills: Red Micro Fibetts
Body: Red Swannundaze, lashed to hook shank

Gordy's Bloodworm

Tied by: Gordon Mackenzie, Norfolk, England
Hook: TMC 200R, #12, bend front 1/3 upwards 20 degrees and when the fly is completed and still in the vise, bend the hook shank so it curves toward you
Weight: Copper or lead wire
Thread: Black 6/0
Tail: 1 turn of hair hackle made from dyed orange squirrel fur. The fibers of the hackle should be 1/8 inch long. This hackle is surrounded by 1 turn of scarlet squirrel fur hair hackle with fibers half the length of the first hackle
Ribs: Fluorescent red floss, followed by thin gold wire
Abdomen: Mixed red and orange squirrel fur dubbing, pick out and trimmed
Thorax: Short orange squirrel fur hair hackle, followed by bronze peacock herl

Gray Midge Larva

Tied by: Wayne Noble, Coquitlam, BC
Hook: TMC 3769, #10
Thread: Iron gray 8/0
Body: Light gray Antron dubbing
Head: Peacock herl

Hastings Copper Midge

Tied by: Jason Hastings, Reno, NV
Hook: 3906B, #12
Thread: Olive 6/0
Body: Medium copper wire
Head: Olive ostrich herl

JH Beaver Larva

Tied by: Jas Hudlow, Fayetteville, AR
Hook: Mustad 80050BR, #18-#22
Thread: Black 8/0
Underbody: Red copper wire
Overbody: Light gray latex strip

Legged Midge

Tied by: Nadeer Youssef, Pullman, WA
Hook: TMC 2487, #14-#20
Thread: Olive
Tail: Pheasant tail feather fibers
Rib: Rainbow Krystal Flash strand
Body: Pheasant tail feather fibers, wrapped
Legs: Olive marabou feather fibers
Comments: Even though midge larvae do not have legs, they were added to this pattern to give the fly motion.

Little Creeper Larva

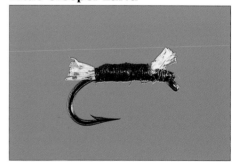

Tied by: Mike Giavedoni, Toronto, ON
Hook: Mustad 3399, #14-#16
Thread: Red 8/0
Tail/Gills: Pearl Krystal Flash strands, lashed to hook shank then trimmed to length after fly is completed
Body: Red fluorescent floss
Head: Red thread

Little Kicky Monster

Tied by: Peter Dunne, Laois, Ireland
Hook: Drenna #12 U.V. Rainbow Trad.
Thread: Red 8/0
Kickers: Datam fluorescent red glo-bright floss
Rib: Red thread
Body: Swift red body rib
Head: Tying thread varnished
Comments: In lakes fish the fly close to the bottom with a sinking line and in rivers use a sink-tip line, with a twitching-pause retrieve, because this causes the fly to twitch like a natural.

Luscious Larva

Tied by: Matt King, Victoria, BC
Hook: TMC 2312, #12-#18
Thread: Black 6/0
Gills: Red ostrich herl
Body: Red Thin Skin strip, wrapped

McConville's Midge #2

Tied by: Tim McConville, Salt Lake City, UT
Hook: TMC 2312, #14
Thread: Black 8/0
Body: Olive Vinyl Rib
Head: Peacock herl

Red

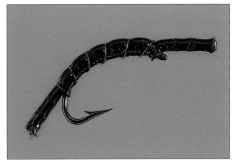

Tied by: Vladimir Markov, Irkutsk, Russia
Hook: Mustad 80200, #12-#20
Thread: Red 6/0
Rib: Red wire
Body: Bloodworm red Larva Lace, extended, ends melted, (to make end segments heat the tips of a pair of fine tweezers and lightly touch the Larva Lace)

Ronn's Bloodworm Larva

Tied by: Ronn Lucas, Sr., Milwaukie, OR
Hook: Daiichi Swimming Nymph 1770, #16
Thread: Brown 8/0
Tail: Red Antron yarn fibers
Underbody: Silver tinsel
Body: Small red Vinyl Rib
Head: Brown thread

Ronn's Skeeter Larva

Tied by: Ronn Lucas, Sr., Milwaukie, OR
Hook: Light wire, #18-#22
Thread: Tan 8/0
Butt: Beaver dubbing
Tail: Elk hair, tag end from body material
Rib: Fine silver wire, counterwrapped
Abdomen: Elk hair, wrapped
Thorax: Beaver dubbing
Head: Black glass bead

Roth's Midge Larva

Tied by: Scott Roth, Andover, NJ
Hook: TMC 206BL, #18-#20
Thread: Red 8/0
Tail: White emu feather, cut short
Underbody: Red thread
Abdomen: Fine red wire
Thorax: Red ostrich herl
Head: Red glass bead

Sullivan's Midge Larva

Tied by: Clifford Sullivan, Tray, CA
Hook: Daiichi 1273, red finish, #16
Thread: Red 12/0
Tail: Lady Amherst pheasant tippet fibers
Rib: Fine silver wire
Abdomen: Red small vinyl rib
Thorax: Fine red dubbing
Head: Red glass bead

Midge Pupae

Argyle Midge

Tied by: Robert Waller, Bay Shore, NY
Hook: Orvis Nymph, #10
Thread: Black 6/0
Tail/Butt: Brown deer hair, spun and clipped to shape
Body: Peacock Crystal Chenille
Hackle: Brown deer hair, sparse

Azz Kicker

Tied by: Kyle Hicks, Berwick, N.S.
Hook: #14 wet fly
Thread: Black
Parachute Post: White foam
Hackle: Grizzly, wrapped on foam post base
Cheeks: 2 strands of orange deer hair per side
Wing Case: Mallard flank feather fibers
Thorax: Peacock herl
Body: Stripped peacock herl
Tail: White marabou feather fibers

Backgammon Chironomid

Tied by: Michael Enns, Abbotsford, BC
Hook: Mustad 3906B, #10-#20
Thread: Black
Rib: Fine silver wire, followed with black thread
Abdomen: Gray fine acetate floss
Thorax: Peacock herl
Gills: White Antron yarn fibers
Head: Small clear glass bead

B.F.D.A.

Tied by: Brandon Fessler, Ogden, UT
Hook: TMC 3761, #14-#18
Thread: Black 8/0
Abdomen: Black plastic ribbing
Gills: White Antron yarn fibers
Thorax: Black dubbing

Biot Midge

Tied by: Mike Giavedoni, Toronto, ON
Hook: Mustad 3399, #14-#18
Thread: Light green, 8/0
Body: White goose biot
Thorax: Peacock herl

Biot Suspender Midge

Tied by: Tim McConville, Salt Lake City, UT
Hook: Mustad 94840, #14
Thread: Black 8/0
Tail/Gills: White packing foam, cut to shape
Rib: Fine copper wire, counterwrapped
Abdomen: Brown turkey biot
Thorax: Peacock herl

Black Midge Pupa

Tied by: Gordon Mackenzie, Norfolk, England
Hook: Partridge K2B, Yorkshire Sedge, #16
Thread: Black 8/0
Tail: White fluorescent floss fibers
Rib: Stripped peacock herl, herl touched with clear varnish for strength before winding
Abdomen: Black pheasant tail feather fibers, wrapped
Wing Pad: Tuft of orange fur
Thorax: Black budding, picked out on underside
Gills: Fluorescent white floss fibers

Blakeston's Buzzer

Tied by: Derek Burwood, Corby, Northants, United Kingdom
Hook: TMC 2457, #10
Thread: Orange 8/0
Rib: Silver wire
Abdomen Shellback: Pearl Mylar tinsel
Body: Black floss
Cheeks: Fluorescent orange floss, tied on sides
Thorax Shellback: Peacock herl

Bloodworm Flashback

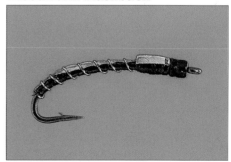

Tied by: Nicholas Norton, Salt Lake City, UT
Hook: TMC 200R, #16-#18
Thread: Red 8/0
Rib: Copper wire, counterwrapped
Body: Red Crystal Splash
Shellback/Wing Case: Pearl Flash Back
Head: Red glass bead

Blue Bead Pupa

Tied by: Jan Pickel, New Park, PA
Hook: TMC 101, #20-#26
Thread: Black 8/0
Tail: Gray CDC feather fibers
Body: Black Krystal Flash
Wing: Gray CDC feather fibers

Blushing Bride

Tied by: Peter Dunne, Laois, Ireland
Hook: TMC 2487, #12
Thread: Black 8/0
Gills: White marabou feather fibers
Rib: Black holographic tinsel
Body: Red fluorescent floss
Thorax: Black Antron dubbing
Cheeks: Fluorescent orange UNI-Yarn
Comments: Coat top of thorax and cheeks with epoxy.

Bree Chironomid

Tied by: Michael Enns, Abbotsford, BC
Hook: Mustad 3906B, #10-#20
Thread: Black
Tail: White Antron yarn fibers
Rib: Red fine wire
Abdomen: Brown Frost Bite strands
Thorax: Peacock herl
Gills: White Antron yarn fibers
Head: Small clear glass bead

Brown Chironomid Pupa

Tied by: Pat Essinger, North Vancouver, BC
Hook: TMC 205BL, #14
Thread: Dark brown, 6/0
Anal Gills: Pearl Krystal Flash strands, short
Rib: Single strand of black floss and small copper wire
Body: 4 strands dark brown floss
Thorax: Peacock herl
Gills: White poly yarn fibers
Head: 3/32 gold bead

Comparable Midge Pupa

Tied by: Vladimir Markov, Irkutsk, Russia
Hook: TMC 2457, #12-#18
Thread: Orange 6/0
Shuck: Zing
Rib: Silver and red fine wires
Body: Black Swiss straw strip, wrapped
Thorax: Orange thread
Wing Buds: Black feathers, reversed hackle style
Head: White ostrich herl

Coquitlam Chironomid

Tied by: Wayne Noble, Coquitlam, BC
Hook: TMC 200R, #8
Thread: Black 6/0
Tag: Silver tinsel
Abdomen: Black Stretch Flex
Thorax: Peacock herl
Head: Amber glass bead

Crooked Pupa

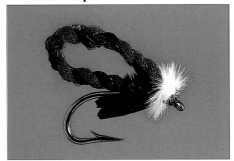

Tied by: Vladimir Markov, Irkutsk, Russia
Hook: Mustad 3399, #12-#20
Thread: Black 6/0
Body: Crocheted red, black, and claret yarn, looped forward after completing wing case
Thorax: Black marabou feather fibers, wrapped
Wing Case: Black Swiss straw, cut to shape, coated with head cement
Head: White marabou feather fibers, wrapped

Don's Black Midge Pupa

Tied by: Don Joslyn, Eagle Point, OR
Hook: Daiichi 1180, #10-#18
Thread: Black 6/0 UNI-Thread
Rib: Copper wire
Body: Small black Vinyl Rib
Wing: Partridge feather fibers

Don's Black Vinyl Pupa

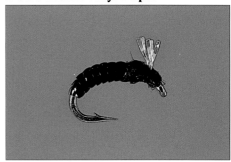

Tied by: Don Joslyn, Eagle Point, OR
Hook: Daiichi 1150, #8-#18
Thread: Black 6/0 UNI-Thread
Body: Small black Vinyl Rib
Wing: Pearl Krystal Flash strands, short

Eby's Midge Pupa

Tied by: Gord Eby, Fort St. John, BC
Hook: Mustad 3906, #10
Thread: Black 6/0
Tag: Red thread
Rib: Fine copper wire
Abdomen: Black thread
Wing Pads: White/gray feather tuffs
Thorax: Peacock herl
Gills: White Antron yarn fibers

Ed's T-n-T

Tied by: Jim Riley, Grass Valley, CA
Hook: TMC 2478, #14
Thread: Brown Monocord
Rib: Fine silver wire, counterwrapped
Body: Brown thread
Head: Tungsten bead, size 3/32
Comments: Fish the T-n-T (Tungsten and Thread) as a
    dropper 9 to 16 inches under anything that floats well.

Fish-On-Nomid

Tied by: Wayne Noble, Coquitlam, BC
Hook: TMC 2487, #10
Thread: Black 6/0
Rib: Gold oval tinsel
Body: Black thread, lacquered
Head: Light gray dubbing

Flash Back Midge

Tied by: Doug Narver, Nanaimo, BC
Hook: TMC 100, #12-#16
Thread: Brown
Tail: Pheasant tail feather fibers
Rib: Copper Krystal Flash strand, wrapped over abdomen
Shellback: Pearl Flashabou, secured with brown thread
Abdomen: Pheasant tail feather fibers, wrapped
Thorax: Peacock herl
Legs: Pheasant tail feather fibers

Green Midge Pupa

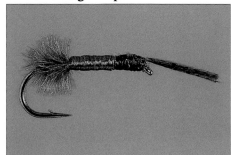

Tied by: Wayne Noble, Coquitlam, BC
Hook: TMC 102Y, #12
Thread: Dark green 8/0
Butt: Green ostrich herl
Body: Green floss
Feelers: Olive wood duck flank feather fibers

Hackle Back Midge

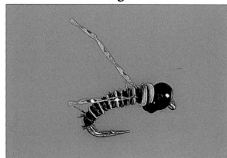

Tied by: Robert Lewis, Yonkers, NY
Hook: TMC 2887, #16-#20
Thread: Black
Rib: Stripped grizzly hackle stem
Body: Black thread
Wings: Peacock Krystal Flash strands
Head: Black glass bead

JH Beaver Pupa

Tied by: Jas Hudlow, Fayetteville, AR
Hook: Mustad 80050BR, #18-#22
Thread: Gray 8/0
Tail: Wood duck flank feather fibers
Underbody: Red copper wire
Overbody: Light gray latex strip
Thorax: Peacock herl

JJ Pupa

Tied by: Jerry Jeffery, Long Beach, CA
Hook: TMC 100BL, #18-#22
Thread: Black 8/0 UNI-Thread
Rib: Black thread
Abdomen: Olive floss
Thorax: Black thread

Joslyn's Black Pupa

Tied by: Don Joslyn, Eagle Point, OR
Hook: Daiichi 1273, #8-#18
Thread: Black 3/0 UNI-Thread
Body: Black thread, wrapped to shape
Wing: Pearl Krystal Flash strands, looped

Joslyn's Copper Pupa

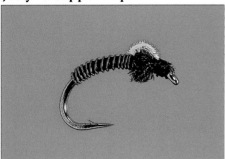

Tied by: Don Joslyn, Eagle Point, OR
Hook: Daiichi 1150, #8-#18
Thread: Black 6/0 UNI-Thread
Rib: Copper wire
Abdomen: Black thread
Wing Case: White CDC feather fibers
Thorax: Peacock herl
Head: Black thread

King's Chironomid Pupa

Tied by: Matt King, Victoria, BC
Hook: TMC 2312, #12-#20
Thread: White 6/0
Tail: White ostrich herl
Abdomen: Light olive Thin Skin strip, wrapped
Wing Case: Mottled Thin Skin strip, butt end from abdomen
Thorax: Peacock herl
Gills: White ostrich herl

Marvelous Midge

Tied by: Troy Kelly, Puyallup, WA
Hook: TMC 3769, #16-#18
Thread: Black 8/0
Abdomen: Gray/olive Antron yarn, furled
Thorax: Gray ostrich herl

McConville's Midge #1

Tied by: Tim McConville, Salt Lake City, UT
Hook: TMC 2312, #14
Thread: Gray 8/0
Tail: Tan CDC feather fibers
Rib: Gold wire, counterwrapped
Abdomen: Gray thread
Wing Case/Tuft: Tan CDC feather fibers
Thorax: Gray dubbing
Head: Gold bead

McConville's Midge #3

Tied by: Tim McConville, Salt Lake City, UT
Hook: TMC 2312, #14
Thread: Brown 6/0
Tail: White poly yarn fibers
Rib: Gold wire
Abdomen: Brown thread
Thorax: Peacock herl
Gills: White poly yarn fibers

McConville Midge #4

Tied by: Tim McConville, Salt Lake City, UT
Hook: TMC 2312, #14
Thread: Red 6/0
Tail: White poly yarn fibers
Rib: Gold wire, counterwrapped
Abdomen: Red thread
Thorax: Hare's ear dubbing
Head: Gold bead

McConville's Midge #5

Tied by: Tim McConville, Salt Lake City, UT
Hook: TMC 2487, #14
Thread: Brown 6/0
Tail: Gray poly yarn fibers
Rib: Pearl Mylar tinsel
Abdomen: Brown micro chenille
Thorax: Peacock herl
Gills: White poly yarn fibers
Head: Gold bead

McConville's Midge #6

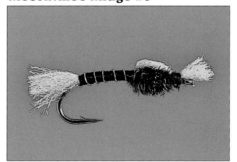

Tied by: Tim McConville, Salt Lake City, UT
Hook: TMC 2312, #14
Thread: Black 8/0
Tail/Gills: Yellow poly yarn
Rib: Gold wire, counterwrapped
Abdomen: Black thread
Wing Case: Yellow poly yarn
Thorax: Peacock herl

Midge Miller

Tied by: Fred Iacoletti, Albuquerque, NM
Hook: TMC 200R, #14
Thread: Black 6/0
Gills: White CDC feather fibers
Rib: Gold small oval tinsel, counterwrapped
Abdomen: Black thread
Thorax: Black fine dubbing
Thorax Shellback: Pheasant tail feather fibers, coated with epoxy
Wings: Yellow turkey biots
Comments: Fish this fly in the surface film; it will sink slowly because of the density of the epoxy.

Midge Supreme

Tied by: Kyle Hicks, Berwick, NS
Hook: #14 wet fly
Thread: Black
Tail: White marabou feather fibers
Abdomen: Brown goose biot
Thorax Shellback: Mallard flank feather fibers
Thorax: Peacock herl
Wing Buds: Micro Web, cut to shape
Cheeks: Orange deer hair, 2 strands per side
Gills: White marabou feather fibers

MPO

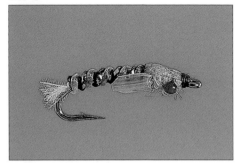

Tied by: Lance Egan, Sandy, UT
Hook: TMC 200R, #18
Thread: Olive 8/0
Tail: White CDC feather fibers
Abdomen: Olive Crystal Splash, twisted with chartreuse Flex-floss
Thorax Shellback: Olive Thin Skin strip
Thorax: Light olive dubbing
Wing Buds: Cream Swiss straw, cut to shape
Eyes: Melted 15lb. Amnesia

Narver's Black Chironomid

Tied by: Doug Narver, Nanaimo, BC
Hook: TMC 100, #14
Thread: Black
Tail/Head: White Antron yarn fibers, tied over hook shank, trimmed to length after completing fly
Rib: Copper wire
Abdomen: Black thread
Thorax: Peacock herl

Red & Peacock Chironomid

Tied by: Henry Hoffman, Warrenton, OR
Hook: Daiichi 1710, #12-#20
Thread: Olive 8/0
Rib: Silver wire, counterwrapped
Abdomen: Red Bodi-Braid (ribbon floss)
Thorax: Peacock herl, (use sword feather herl for a greener look)
Gills: White chickabou feather fibers

Rising Midge Pupa

Tied by: Wayne Noble, Coquitlam, BC
Hook: TMC 101, #12
Thread: Black
Tail: White ostrich herl strands and mallard flank feather fibers
Body: Gray Antron dubbing
Head: White ostrich herl

Ritter's Midge Pupa

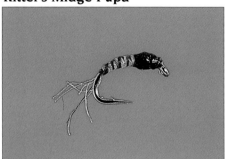

Tied by: Carl Ritter, Sedona, AZ
Hook: Daiichi 1130, #22
Thread: Yellow 8/0
Tail: White Antron yarn fibers
Rib: Brown 8/0 thread
Body: Yellow 8/0 thread
Head: Brown thread

Ronn's Bloodworm Pupa

Tied by: Ronn Lucas, Sr., Milwaukie, OR
Hook: Daiichi 1150, #16-#18
Thread: Brown 8/0
Tail: Red Antron yarn fibers
Underbody: Silver tinsel
Body: Small red Vinyl Rib
Wing Buds: Brown mottled feather sections, tied to sides
Gills: White Wooly Nylon

Roth's Midge Pupa

Tied by: Scott Roth, Andover, NJ
Hook: TMC 206BL, #18-#20
Thread: Gray 8/0
Tail: White Antron yarn fibers
Abdomen: Orange DP quill
Legs: Orange emu feather fibers
Thorax: Gray dubbing

RP's Swimming Pupa

Tied by: Roy Powell, Danville, CA
Hook: Daiichi swimming nymph hook or TMC 947BL, #12-#14
Thread: Red and black 8/0 UNI-Thread
Butt: White ostrich hurl and red thread
Rib: Fine gold wire, counterwrapped
Body: Black floss or waxed thread
Thorax: Creamy olive dubbing
Wing: Brown partridge feather
Gills: White ostrich hurl
Comments: Coat butt thread and body section with 2 or 3 coats of head cement. For wing, pull feather backwards and coat with Softex, continue stroking back until it dries, then cut to shape.

Sullivan's Midge Pupa

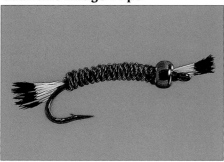

Tied by: Clifford Sullivan, Tracy, CA
Hook: Daiichi 1273, red finish, #16
Thread: Red 12/0
Gills: Lady Amherst pheasant tippet fibers
Body: Peacock Micro Cable, #2
Head: Glass bead

Sunfire Chironomid

Tied by: Wayne Noble, Coquitlam, BC
Hook: TMC 100, #12
Thread: Red 6/0
Rib: Gold oval tinsel
Body: Red thread, lacquered
Head: Red dubbing

Swimming Midge

Tied by: Scott Hoff, Concord, CA
Hook: Daiichi 1770, #12-#16
Thread: Black 8/0
Rib: Fine red wire
Abdomen: Black UNI Nylon Stretch Floss
Legs: Gray ostrich herl strands
Thorax: Peacock herl

Tayo Pupa

Tied by: Brad Lucy, Coquitlam, BC
Hook: TMC 5262, #12
Thread: Black
Tail/Head: Pearl Cactus Chenille, 1 wrap each
Abdomen: Red dubbing
Thorax: Peacock herl
Head: Pearl bead, in front of red bead

Todd's Midge Pupa

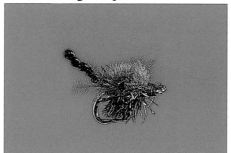

Tied by: Todd Turner, Fort Lauderdale, FL
Hook: Daiichi 1140, #22
Thread: Dark brown 8/0
Abdomen: Red Scud Back, thin strip that is twisted and furled, tied extended, optional colors: tan, olive, gray, and black
Wing Case: Rusty orange CDC feather fibers, fold back front fibers
Thorax: Peacock herl

Tuma's Midge Pupa

Tied by: Adam Tuma, Lebanon, OR
Hook: TMC 2487, #14
Thread: Cream 6/0
Tail: White marabou feather fibers
Rib: Red wire, counterwrapped
Abdomen: Cream thread, lacquered
Thorax: Cream dubbing
Head: Gold bead

Z-Wing Beauty

Tied by: Richard Murphy, Sr., Manitou Springs, CO
Hook: TMC 2487, #18-#22
Thread: Black, 8/0
Rib: Fine copper wire, counterwrapped
Body: Black Frost Bite strand, wrapped
Cheeks: Clear Zing-Wing strips, pulled along each side
Thorax: Black thread, built-up

Midge Emergers

B.F. Emerger

Tied by: Brandon Fessler, Ogden, UT
Hook: TMC 3761, #12-#20
Thread: Black 8/0
Shuck: Dun Antron yarn fibers, ends melted
Rib: Gold wire, counterwrapped
Body: Black plastic ribbing
Hackle: Dun

CDC Emerger-Midge

Tied by: Vladimir Markov, Irkutsk, Russia
Hook: TMC 2387, #12-#20
Thread: Black 6/0
Tail: White CDC feather fibers, pulled forward and tied-in by tips
Thorax: Pheasant tail feather fibers
Wing Case: Black Swiss straw, cut to shape and coated with Flexament
Head: Gray CDC feather fibers

CDC Emerging Midge

Tied by: John Moneyhun, Rapid City, SD
Hook: TMC 2487, #12-#18
Thread: Black
Tail: White round foam
Abdomen: Black Vinyl Rib
Thorax: Gray ostrich herl
Wings: Dun CDC feathers, cut to shape
Head: White round foam

CDC Hatching Midge

Tied by: John Moneyhun, Rapid City, SD
Hook: TMC 2487, #12-#18
Thread: Black
Tail: Rust Z-lon fibers
Abdomen: Black Vinyl Rib
Wing Case: Dun CDC feather
Hackle: Grizzly
Head Tuft: Tips from wing case feather

Designer Blood Midge Emerger

Tied by: Jay Kaneshige, Castro Valley, CA
Hook: Daiichi 1130, #14
Thread: Orange 6/0
Body: Rust Vernille, end melted to a taper
Rib: Red copper wire
Hackle: Brown
Wing: Rust deer hair

Don's K.F. & CDC Emerger

Tied by: Don Joslyn, Eagle Point, OR
Hook: Daiichi 1150, #8-#18
Thread: Black 6/0 UNI-Thread
Tail: Pearl Krystal Flash strands
Body: Black thread
Wing: White CDC feather fibers

Don's Black Rubber Emerger

Tied by: Don Joslyn, Eagle Point, OR
Hook: Daiichi 1180, #10-#18
Thread: Black 6/0 UNI-Thread
Body: Black round rubber strand, over thread base
Wing: Pearl Krystal Flash strands

Eby's Midge Emerger

Tied by: Gord Eby, Fort St. John, BC
Hook: Mustad 3906, #10
Thread: Black 6/0
Tail: Golden Pheasant tippet fibers, lacquered
Tag: Fine red wire
Rib: Fine red wire
Abdomen: Black thread
Thorax: Small foam bead covered with peacock herl
Wings: Turkey feather sections, cut to shape

Foam Midge Emerger

Tied by: John Moneyhun, Rapid City, SD
Hook: TMC 2487, #12-#18
Thread: Black
Tail: White round foam
Abdomen: Black Vinyl Rib
Wing: Elk hair
Legs: Pheasant tail feather fibers
Thorax: Gray ostrich herl
Cheeks: White round foam

GM Midge Emerger

Tied by: Bryan Guy, Chico, CA
Hook: TMC 2487, #18-#22
Thread: Black 8/0
Tail: White CDC feather fibers
Rib: Fine silver wire
Abdomen: Black thread
Thorax: Peacock herl
Head: Gunmetal gray glass bead
Gills: White CDC feather fibers

Hank's Emerger Midge

Tied by: Henry Hoffman, Warrenton, OR
Hook: Daiichi 1710, #12-#20
Thread: Olive 8/0
Tail: White chickabou feather fibers
Rib: Silver wire, counterwrapped
Body: Peacock Krystal Flash strands
Wing Case: White closed-cell foam
Hackle: Grizzly, top fibers trimmed

JJ Emerger

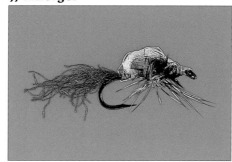

Tied by: Jerry Jeffery, Long Beach, CA
Hook: TMC 100BL, #18-#20
Thread: Tan 8/0
Tail: Orange Antron yarn fibers
Body: Tan thread
Wing Case: White Antron yarn fibers
Hackle: Grizzly, top and bottom fibers clipped

Joslyn's Black Emerger

Tied by: Don Joslyn, Eagle Point, OR
Hook: Daiichi 1150, #8-#18
Thread: Black 6/0
Tail: White CDC feather fibers
Abdomen: Medium or small black Vinyl Rib
Thorax: Black ostrich herl
Gills: White CDC feather fibers
Head: Gold bead

Joslyn's Red Emerger

Tied by: Don Joslyn, Eagle Point, OR
Hook: Daiichi 1150, #8-#18
Thread: Black 3/0 or 6/0
Tail: Fine white calf tail hair
Rib: Black 3/0 UNI-Thread
Abdomen: Orange 3/0 UNI-Thread, twisted to segment
Thorax: Black ostrich herl
Gills: Fine white calf tail hair
Head: Gold bead

King's Midge Emerger

Tied by: Matt King, Victoria, BC
Hook: Daiichi 1150, #12-#18
Thread: White 6/0
Body: Pearl blue Angel Hair
Post: White Rainy's foam
Hackle: Grizzly
Post: Orange CDC feather fibers

Krystal Emerger-Midge

Tied by: Richard Murphy, Sr., Manitou Springs, CO
Hook: TMC 2387, #18 - #22
Thread: Black 8/0
Tail: Lemon wood duck flank feather fibers
Abdomen: Black Krystal Flash strands
Thorax: Gray ostrich herl
Wing Case/Legs: Pearl Krystal Flash strands, pulled over thorax and folded back for legs

Lumini Midge Emerger

Tied by: Giuseppe Nova, Bollate, Italy
Hook: TMC 206BL, #14-#16
Thread: Brown 8/0
Tail: White CDC feather fibers
Underbody: Pearl Krystal Flash strand, wrapped
Abdomen: Red midge plastic tubing
Thorax: Brown CDC dubbing
Wing/Post: White CDC feather fibers

M.M. Emerger

Tied by: Gordon Mackenzie, Norfolk, England
Hook: Partridge K2B, Yorkshire Sedge, #16
Thread: Black 8/0
Tail: Cream fur hair hackle, topped with a longer hackle of sparse olive Antron fibers, pulled back and tied to form a bubble shuck
Rib: Stripped peacock herl
Abdomen: Black pheasant tail feather fibers
Wing: Gray CDC feather fibers
Thorax: Black dubbing, underside picked out
Head: Black thread

Modified RS-2

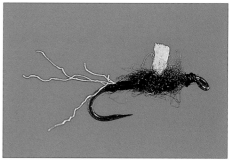

Tied by: Jerry Jeffery, Long Beach, CA
Hook: TMC 100BL, #18-#20
Thread: Black or Gray 8/0
Tail: White Antron yarn fibers
Abdomen: Black thread
Wing: White foam
Thorax: Dark gray dubbing

Pilsner Emerger

Tied by: Brad Lucy, Coquitlam, BC
Hook: TMC 5262, #12
Thread: Red 6/0
Shuck: Gray Scud Back, cut to shape
Rib: Small copper wire
Body: Red dubbing
Hackle: Grizzly, bottom fibers trimmed

Ron's Thread & CDC Emerger

Tied by: Don Joslyn, Eagle Point, OR
Hook: Daiichi 1150, #8-#18
Thread: Black 6/0 UNI-Thread
Tail: White CDC feather fibers, over pearl Krystal Flash strands
Body: Black thread
Wing: White CDC feather fibers, mixed with pearl Krystal Flash strands

Roth's Midge Emerger

Tied by: Scott Roth, Andover, NJ
Hook: TMC 206BL, #18-#20
Thread: Black 8/0
Tail: White Antron yarn fibers
Rib: Fine green wire
Abdomen: Pheasant tail feather fibers, wrapped
Wing: White CDC feather fibers
Thorax: Olive dubbing

Ritter's Midge Emerger

Tied by: Carl Ritter, Sedona, AZ
Hook: TMC 200R, #22
Thread: Brown 8/0
Abdomen: Green Lite Bright
Wing: Lite Bright from body, doubled over
Thorax: Peacock herl

Shuttle Cock Emerger

Tied by: Peter Dunne, Laois, Ireland
Hook: TMC 2487, #12
Thread: Black 8/0
Butt: Red head cement, over thread wraps
Abdomen: Gutterman metallic rainbow thread
Wing Case/Post: 2 natural CDC feathers
Thorax: Tan Hare-Tron dubbing
Head: Bright red Scintilla dubbing

Skokomish Sunset

Tied by: Troy Kelly, Puyallup, WA
Hook: TMC 2487, #14-#18
Thread: Olive 8/0
Abdomen: Olive Antron yarn, furled
Wing: Bleached deer hair, clipped to shape

Sparkle Yarn Midge Emerger

Tied by: A.W. Longacre, Juneau, AK
Hook: Mustad 80000BR, #20-#24
Thread: Black 8/0
Body: Brown Antron yarn, furled
Head: Gray Antron dubbing

Sullivan's Midge Emerger

Tied by: Clifford Sullivan, Tracy, CA
Hook: TMC 2487, #16
Thread: Orange 12/0
Tail: Pearl Krystal Flash strands
Abdomen: Orange Super Floss
Thorax: Orange dubbing
Hackle: Cree, parachute style around tag end of Super Floss, then pulled forward and tied off behind the hook eye

Tuma's Midge Emerger

Tied by: Adam Tuma, Lebanon, OR
Hook: TMC 2487, #14
Thread: Olive 6/0
Tail: White marabou feather fibers
Abdomen: Olive Vinyl Rib
Thorax: Peacock herl
Gills: White marabou feather fibers

Midge Adults

Wade's Emerging Midge

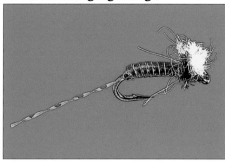

Tied by: Wade Malwitz, Portland, OR
Hook: Mustad 94840, #20
Thread: Green 8/0
Tail: Olive Krystal Flash strand
Rib: Gold wire, fine
Body: Green V-Rib, extra small, optional colors: red, black, and brown
Head: Peacock herl
Wing: White yak hair

B.F. Good Rib

Tied by: Brandon Fessler, Ogden, UT
Hook: TMC 100, #14-#20
Thread: Black 8/0
Body: Black plastic ribbing
Hackle: Dun
Antennae: White Antron yarn fibers

Black Midge Adult

Tied by: Mark Hoeser, Stockton, CA
Hook: Mustad 9479, #16
Thread: Black 12/0
Abdomen: Black micro ultra chenille, end melted to a taper
Wings: Jungle cock feathers, tent style
Wing Case: Iridescent turkey feather fibers
Hackle: Grizzly, top fibers trimmed
Thorax: Black Arizona synthetic dubbing
Antennae: Aftershaft feathers from Lady Amherst pheasant neck tippets

Bob Cat Adams

Tied by: Stephan Lenz, Sequim, WA
Hook: Dry fly hook, #14-#18
Thread: Black 8/0
Tail: Golden pheasant tippet fibers
Body: Gray hair from my cat Bob or muskrat dubbing
Wing: Grizzly hackle tips, divided
Hackle: Grizzly, 3 to 4 wraps

Chironomidge

Tied by: Fred Iacoletti, Albuquerque, NM
Hook: Daiichi 1100, #16
Thread: Black 8/0
Rib: Black thread
Abdomen: Deer hair, reversed pull body style
Wing: Foust's wing material, cut to shape
Legs: Pheasant tail feather fibers, knotted
Thorax Shellback: Black closed-cell foam, coated with epoxy
Thorax: Peacock herl

Cream Midge

Tied by: Jan Pickel, New Park, PA
Hook: TMC 100, #20-#24
Thread: Cream 8/0
Tail: Cream hackle fibers
Body: Cream thread
Hackle: Cream

Cripple Midge

Tied by: Robert Lewis, Yonkers, NY
Hook: TMC 2487, #16-#20
Thread: Gray 8/0
Tail: Gray Antron yarn fibers
Body: Gray thread
Wing: Deer hair

Deer Tail Midge

Tied by: Doug Narver, Nanaimo, BC
Hook: TMC 100, #12-#16
Thread: Black
Tail: Deer hair
Body: Peacock herl
Hackle: Brown, trimmed short

Emerging Adult

Tied by: Jan Pickle, New Park, PA
Hook: TMC 2487, #20
Thread: Black 8/0
Tail: Brown Z-lon fibers
Rib: Fine silver wire
Body: Black thread
Wings: Medium dun hen hackle tips, delta style
Hackle: Brown

Horny Adult Midge

Tied by: Brad Lucy, Coquitlam, BC
Hook: TMC 5262, #12
Thread: Dark red 6/0
Rib: Black thread
Body: Dark red thread
Hackle: Grizzly, bottom fibers trimmed
Legs: Pheasant rump feather fibers

J's Downwing Midge

Tied by: Jay Kaneshige, Castro Valley, CA
Hook: TMC101, #22
Thread: Yellow 8/0
Body: Yellow thread or color to match the natural
Hackle: Light ginger, 2 wraps aft and 2 wraps forward with 1 connecting wrap
Wings: Light ginger hackle tips, delta style

King's Cluster Midge

Tied by: Matt King, Victoria, BC
Hook: TMC 2312, #12-#18
Thread: Black 6/0
Bodies: Black Thin Skin strips
Wings: Gray CDC feather fibers, topped with grizzly hackle tips
Thorax: Peacock herl
Hackle: Grizzly

Low Light Midge

Tied by: Scott Hoff, Concord, CA
Hook: Limerick 1707, #20
Thread: Black 8/0
Tail: Black hackle fibers
Post: Yellow Antron yarn
Body: Black fine dubbing
Hackle: Black
Comments: The yellow Antron makes this a quick sight fly in low light conditions when big fish are feeding on small midge. Body colors of brown, olive and tans will also work.

Mating Midge

Tied by: Nadeer Youssef, Pullman, WA
Hook: TMC 100, #16-#20
Thread: Black
Body: Black and olive dubbing
Wings: Plastic, cut to shape
Hackle: Black

Midge Cluster

Tied by: Carl Ritter, Sedona, AZ
Hook: Daiichi 1273, #18
Thread: Brown 8/0
Tail: White Antron yarn fibers
Body: Peacock herl
Wing: Red Antron yarn fibers
Hackle: Grizzly

Mighty Midge-Olive

Tied by: Peter Dunne, Laois, Ireland
Hook: Mustad 80000BR, #14, floats hook up
Thread: Olive or chartreuse 8/0 UNI-Thread
Abdomen: Olive latex strip, stretched to a neat taper then wrapped
Wing: Scintilla spinner wing material, cut to shape
Thorax Shellback: Olive latex strip
Thorax: Fine olive Antron dubbing
Hackle Post: Olive poly yarn, trimmed short after wrapping hackle
Hackle: Grizzly, parachute style, front fibers trimmed

Ritter's Midge Adult

Tied by: Carl Ritter, Sedona, AZ
Hook: Daiichi 1100, #20
Thread: Brown 8/0
Wing: Gray CDC feather fibers, tied in at bend and looped forward after wrapping body
Body: Stripped peacock herl
Legs: Tips from wing
Hackle: Grizzly

Robert's Midge

Tied by: Robert Lewis, Yonkers, NY
Hook: TMC 100, #18-#22
Thread: Gray
Tails: Clear Antron yarn fibers
Body: Gray dubbing
Wing: Gray CDC feather fibers, compara-dun style

Ronn's Green Midge

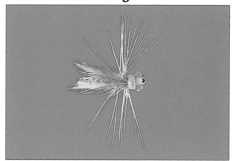

Tied by: Ronn Lucas, Sr., Milwaukie, OR
Hook: Dry light wire, #18-#22
Thread: Bright green 6/0
Underbody: Thread wrapped to body shape
Body: Clear Vinyl Rib
Wings: Cream hen hackle tips, delta style
Hackle: Cream, top and bottom trimmed
Eyes: Green glass beads, with mono core

Roth's Midge Adult

Tied by: Scott Roth, Andover, NJ
Hook: TMC 101, #16-#20
Thread: Black 8/0
Body: DP quill
Wing: White CDC feather fibers
Legs: Emu feather fibers
Head: Black dubbing

RP's Adult Midge

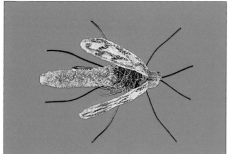

Tied by: Roy Powell, Danville, CA
Hook: TMC 2487, #14-#16
Thread: Light Cahill 8/0 UNI-Thread
Legs: Brown Doug's Bugs Super Hair fibers
Body: Tan micro chenille, end melted to a taper
Thorax: Dark hare's ear dubbing
Wings: Buggy Wing material, cut to shape, coated with
  Flexament
Antennae: Brown Doug's Bugs Super Hair fibers
Head: Thread

Silver Ribbed Midge Adult

Tied by: Nicholas Norton, Salt Lake City, UT
Hook: TMC 100, #18-#22
Thread: Black 8/0 UNI-Thread
Rib: Silver wire
Body: Black thread
Wings: Plastic bag material, cut to shape
Hackle: Grizzly
Head: Black thread
Antennae: Brown CDC feather fibers

Sullivan's Midge Adult

Tied by: Clifford Sullivan, Tracy, CA
Hook: Daiichi 1182, #16
Thread: Gray 8/0
Abdomen: Gray Antron yarn fibers, furled
Thorax: Gray dubbing
Wing: Plastic baggie, cut to shape
Hackle: Light dun, parachute style on Super Floss post that
  is pulled forward and tied off behind hook eye

Trooper

Tied by: Kyle Hicks, Berwick, NS
Hook: #12 dry fly
Thread: Black
Body: Spun black deer hair, clipped to shape
Wings: Micro Web, cut to shape
Hackle: Grizzly
Antennae: Peacock herl strands

Tuma's Adult Midge

Tied by: Adam Tuma, Lebanon, OR
Hook: TMC 100, #16
Thread: Black 6/0
Rib: Stripped grizzly hackle stem
Body: Black thread
Hackles: Grizzly

Wonder Wing Midge

Tied by: Henry Hoffman, Warrenton, OR
Hook: Mustad 94845, #12-#20
Thread: Tan 8/0
Tails: Clear mono strands
Body: Stripped ginger hackle stem
Wings: White feathers, stripped on 1 side, mounted
  reverse-hackle style
Hackle: Barred light and dark ginger

X-Midge

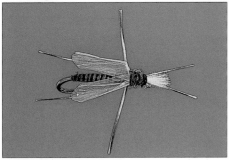

Tied by: Lance Egan, Sandy, UT
Hook: TMC 100, #18
Thread: Black 8/0
Abdomen: Stripped peacock herl
Wings: Cream Swiss straw, cut to shape
Legs: Stripped grizzly hackle stems
Thorax: Fine gray dubbing
Antennae: White CDC feather fibers

CHAPTER 5
Attractor Patterns

Nymphs

52 Buick

Tied by: Henry Hoffman, Warrenton, OR
Hook: Daiichi 1710, #10, weighted with 2 strands of .010 lead wire twisted into a rope, lash 1 piece to each side of hook shank
Thread: Black 6/0
Tail: Golden olive chickabou feather fibers
Rib: Fine bronze wire, counterwrapped
Body: Medium olive chickabou feather, secured by tips and wrapped
Legs: Yellow guinea hen feather fibers
Eyes: Metallic green plastic bead chain
Head: Peacock herl

Alder Larva

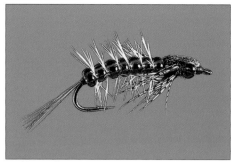

Tied by: Matthias Luenzmann, Jena, Germany
Hook: Mustad 80050BR, #10
Thread: Brown 8/0
Tail: Brown hackle fibers
Gills: Small light ginger hackle; tied in between rear beads, (take 1 wrap, secure, trim excess, then push front against rear bead, repeat with the rest of the abdomen beads)
Abdomen: Small translucent brown glass beads
Thorax Shellback: Brown turkey feather section
Thorax: Brown glass beads, brown Antron dubbing
Legs: Brown partridge feather fibers

Bead Head Attractor

Tied by: Jerry Jeffery, Long Beach, CA
Hook: Nymph, #16
Thread: Red
Abdomen: Turkey biot
Wing: Elk hair
Thorax: Peacock herl, red thread
Head: Brass bead

Black Prince

Tied by: Tom McConville, Salt Lake City, UT
Hook: Dai-Riki 730, #14, weighted
Thread: Black, 8/0
Tails: Black goose biots
Rib: Silver wire
Body: Peacock herl
Wings: Black goose biots, 4 strands of pearl Flashabou
Hackle: Black
Head: Black bead

Bloody Emu

Tied by: Don Joslyn, Eagle Point, OR
Hook: Dai Riki, 135, #6, weighted
Thread: Black 3/0
Tail: Red hackle fibers
Body: Peacock herl
Wings: Yellow goose biots
Hackle: Dun emu
Head: Gold bead

Bloody Mari

Tied by: Jack Pangburn, Westbury, NY
Hook: Mustad 3906B, #10-#16
Thread: Black
Tails: Brown biots
Rib: Peacock herl
Body: Red floss
Hackle: Brown
Head: Brass bead

Brad's Woven Nymph

Tied by: Brad Wilson, Millerton, PA
Hook: Mustad 9672, #4, weighted
Thread: Brown 6/0
Tails: Brown goose biots
Underbody: Tan embroidery floss
Body: Tan and dark brown embroidery floss strands, woven with an overhand weave
Wing Case: Brown Bug Skin
Thorax: Tan rabbit dubbing
Legs: Brown hen hackle
Antennae: Brown goose biots

Breadcrust

Tied by: Jack Pangburn, Westbury, NY
Hook: Mustad 3906B, #8-#16, weighted
Thread: Brown
Rib: Small brown Swannundaze, gold oval tinsel
Underbody: Dental floss on larger hooks
Body: Orange floss
Hackle: Hen grizzly

Brindle Bug

Tied by: J. Mullin, Casper, WY
Hook: Mustad 3906B, #8-#12, weighted
Thread: Black
Tail/Legs: White round rubber strands
Body: Black and white variegated chenille

Bubble Nymph

Tied by: Steve Potter, Tracy, CA
Hook: Scud, #10-#12, weighted with lead wire strands secured to sides of hook shank
Thread: Green 6/0
Underbody: Red and blue wire
Overbody: Epoxy
Hackle: Chartreuse partridge

Bugle Boy

Tied by: Stephen Lopatic, Harrisburg, PA
Hook: Mustad 80050BR, #6-#10, weighted
Thread: Black
Tails: Black goose biots
Rib: Small green copper wire, counterwrapped
Abdomen: Fluorescent chartreuse ostrich herl, 4 strands
Thorax: Chinese red Antron Sparkle dubbing
Throat: Red hackle fibers
Wings: Caddis green turkey biots

Butterfly Nymph

Tied by: Randy Huntley, Sanders, AZ
Hook: Nymph, #12, weight optional
Thread: Black
Tail: Red golden pheasant tippet fibers
Rib: Gold tinsel
Abdomen: Yellow hay bailing cord or floss
Thorax: Peacock herl
Wing: Hen pheasant church window feather
Legs: Golden pheasant tippet and feather fibers

Cliff's Flashback

Tied by: Clifford Sullivan, Tracy, CA
Hook: TMC 3761, #10, weighted
Thread: Olive 8/0
Tail: Olive marabou feather fibers
Rib: Silver wire
Shellback/Wing Case: Gold Mylar tinsel
Body: Olive rabbit dubbing
Legs: Olive marabou feather fibers

Coachman Nymph

Tied by: Don Joslyn, Eagle Point, OR
Hook: Alec Jackson River Dee Low Water, #9
Thread: Black 3/0
Tail: Golden pheasant tippet fibers
Body: Peacock herl, red floss
Hackle: Salmon pink CDC
Head: Peacock herl and gold bead

Craft Lace Nymph

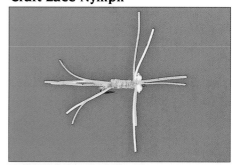

Tied by: Walt Alexander, Gridley, CA
Hook: Mustad 9671, #10, weight optional
Thread: Fluorescent chartreuse 8/0
Tails/Legs: White and chartreuse round rubber
Body: Lemon-lime Craft Lace, from craft store
Eyes: Clear plastic bead chain
Antennae: Chartreuse round rubber

D-Crystal Nymph

Tied by: DuWayne Shaver, Capitan, NM
Hook: Mustad 3399, #10-#16, weighted
Thread: Black
Tail: Pheasant tail feather fibers
Abdomen: Pearl Ice Chenille, or color of choice
Wing Case: Pheasant tail feather fibers
Thorax: Peacock herl
Throat Hackle: Badger hackle fibers

D-Glow Midge Nymph

Tied by: DuWayne Shaver, Capitan, NM
Hook: Mustad 3906B, #16-#20
Thread: Olive 8/0
Tail: Brown hackle fibers
Abdomen: Pearl Mylar tinsel
Wing Case: Yellow feather section
Thorax: Peacock herl
Throat Hackle: Brown hackle fibers

Exemplifly

Tied by: Don Joslyn, Eagle Point, OR
Hook: Alec Jackson River Dee Low Water, #9
Thread: Black 6/0
Tail: Red feather fibers
Body: Opal black Shamrock Extaz Chenille
Wing: White goose biots
Hackle: Black round rubber

Flash Stone

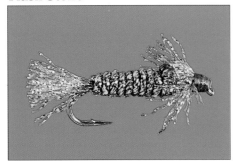

Tied by: Perry Tupper, Salem, OR
Hook: TMC 5263, #10-#14, weighted
Thread: Olive 6/0
Tail: Olive Flashabou Accent fibers
Body: Olive Flashabou Accent
Wing Case: Olive Flashabou Accent fibers
Legs: Olive Flashabou Accent fibers

Flexible Montana Bitch Creek Nymph

Tied by: Curtis Kauer, Salina, KS
Hook: TMC 2488, #8, weighted
Thread: Black 6/0
Tails: Black round rubber
Abdomen: Black and gold felt or Furry Foam, 3 pieces cut to shape and sewn together with black thread, tail mounted and a hinge made from Spirit River Jelly rope attached to the middle section of felt
Thorax: Gold chenille, secure hinged tag end from abdomen to hook shank first
Wing Case: Black Felt or Furry Foam
Hackle: Black
Eyes: Black plastic or metal dumbbell
Antennae: Black round rubber

Foam Fly

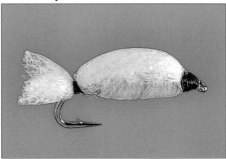

Tied by: Sam de Beer, Cambridge Bay, Nunavut, Canada
Hook: Mustad 9672, #6-#12, weighted
Thread: Red
Tail/Shellback: White packing foam
Body: White floss or thread

Golden Stone (Tolman)

Tied by: Hal Tolman, Riddle, OR
Hook: Mustad 9672, #8-#12, weighted
Thread: Black 6/0
Tails: Black goose biots
Body: Orange Ice Chenille
Wing Case: Orange holographic craft Mylar, cut to shape
Antennae: Black goose biots

Gray's Woolly Bugger

Tied by: Roberto Gray, Puerto Varas, Chile
Hook: Mustad 9672, #8-#12, weighted
Thread: Black
Tail: Olive marabou feather fibers, olive Krystal Flash strands
Shellback: Olive chenille
Body Hackle: Brown
Body: Orange chenille
Legs: White round rubber

Greengo

Tied by: John Raz, Ovilla, TX
Hook: Mustad 79580, #8
Thread: Olive 6/0
Tail: Olive marabou feather fibers
Underbody: Brass wire
Abdomen: Olive and yellow Body Glass strands, woven with an overhand weave
Thorax: Olive marabou feather, wrapped
Wing: Olive marabou feather fibers

Green Sting

Tied by: Dorothy Shorter, 100 Mile House, BC
Hook: Mustad 3906, #10
Thread: Green Mylar tinsel strands
Tail: Dark green pheasant tail feather fibers
Body: Green Mylar tinsel strands, wrapped
Wing: Chartreuse bucktail hairs
Hackle: Green
Head: Green Mylar tinsel

Hare & Peacock

Tied by: Jack Pangburn, Westbury, NY
Hook: Mustad 3906B, #8-#18, weight optional
Thread: Black
Tail: Brown hackle fibers
Rib: Gold oval tinsel
Body: Prism Flash dubbing and SLF peacock Iridescent
   Dubbing, mixed
Wing: Tan rabbit fur

Hot Red Black Prince

Tied by: Tim McConville, Salt Lake City, UT
Hook: Dai-Riki 730, #14, weighted
Thread: Black 8/0
Tails: Black goose biots
Rib: Silver wire, counterwrapped
Body: Peacock Ice Dub dubbing
Wings: Black peacock herl
Hackle: Black
Head: Hot red glass bead

Jack's Marabou Nymph

Tied by: Jack Pangburn, Westbury, NY
Hook: Mustad 3906, #10-#16, weighted
Thread: Brown
Tail: Brown and yellow marabou feather fibers
Body: Tan squirrel dubbing
Wing Case: Peacock herl strands

Jolly Jim

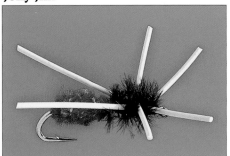

Tied by: Jim Fanoni, Akron, OH
Hook: Nymph, #8-#12, weighted
Thread: Black 6/0
Abdomen: Orange chenille
Thorax: Black ostrich herl
Legs: White round rubber

Krystal Hare's Ear

Tied by: Don Heyden, Bozeman, MT
Hook: Mustad 3906B, #12-#16, weighted
Thread: Brown 6/0
Tail: Mallard flank feather fibers
Rib: Peacock Krystal Flash, twisted and wrapped
Abdomen: Light tan rabbit dubbing
Wing Case: Peacock Krystal Flash strands
Thorax: Dark tan rabbit dubbing, picked out

Krystal Mayfly

Tied by: Don Heyden, Bozeman, MT
Hook: Mustad #12-#16
Thread: Brown 8/0
Tail: Olive mallard flank feather fibers
Abdomen: Peacock Krystal Flash strands
Wing Case: Peacock Krystal Flash strands
Thorax: Medium gray muskrat fur and medium gray Antron
   dubbing, mixed

Mayfly Patriot Nymph

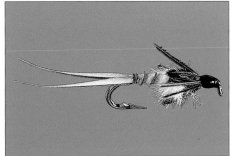

Tied by: Charles Robbins, Tracy, CA
Hook: Mustad 3906B, #12, weighted
Thread: White 8/0
Tails: Macaw parrot biots
Abdomen: Macaw parrot biot
Thorax: White ostrich herl
Wing Case: Macaw parrot feather fibers
Legs: Tips from wing case

Naked Prince

Tied by: Don Joslyn, Eagle Point, OR
Hook: Dai Riki 135, #6, weighted
Thread: Black 3/0
Tails: Black goose biots
Body: Peacock herl, red floss
Hackle: Salmon pink CDC
Head: Peacock herl, gold bead

Newage

Tied by: Dorothy Shorter, 100 Mile House, BC
Hook: Mustad 9672, #8
Thread: Black
Tail: Green pheasant tail feather fibers
Rib: Green thread
Body: Green Metallic Mylar tinsel
Hackle: Green saddle
Wing: Pearl Krystal Flash strands

Nympho

Tied by: Alexandria Kaminski, Victorville, CA
Hook: Gold 3X long ring eye, #10, weight under thorax optional
Thread: Pale yellow 6/0
Tail: Pale yellow hackle fibers
Rib: Fine gold tinsel
Abdomen: Pale yellow, deep yellow, and orange dubbing
Thorax: Rusty brown dubbing
Hackle: Yellow guinea

One Feather Grouse Fly

Tied by: Chris Currie, Bonners Ferry, ID
Hook: Mustad 3906B, #10-#14, weight optional
Thread: Black 8/0
Tail: Grouse marabou feather fibers
Rib: Gold wire, optional
Body: Grouse aftershaft feather, tied in with dubbing loop
Hackle: Grouse

Orange and Green Nymph

Tied by: Randy Huntley, Sanders, AZ
Hook: Nymph, 2X long, weight optional
Thread: Orange
Tail: Yellow and red golden pheasant feather fibers
Rib: Yellow Krystal Flash strand
Abdomen: Orange floss
Wing Case: Hen pheasant feather section
Thorax: Peacock herl
Legs: Hen pheasant feather fibers

Orange Gorbenmac Buggy Nymph

Tied by: Gordon Mackenzie, Syderstone, Norfolk, England
Hook: Nymph, 2X long, #6-#14, weighted
Thread: Orange
Tail: Hot orange woodchuck guard hairs hackle, 1 to 2 turns
Rib: Peacock herl
Body: Orange imitation seal dubbing
Wing Case: Mallard blue wing feather section
Hackle: Blue hair hackle, 1 to 2 turns
Comments: Use dubbing loop to spin hairs into a hair hackle.

Peacock Conehead Nymph

Tied by: Ron Beasley, St. Louis, MS
Hook: Mustad 9672, #12, weight optional
Thread: Black 8/0
Tails: Olive biots, pearl Krystal Flash strands
Rib: Silver wire
Body: Peacock herl, about 8 strands
Wing Case: Flat silver tinsel, over pearl Krystal Flash strands
Legs: Pearl Krystal Flash strands, ends from wing case
Head: Nickel cone head, size 5/32

Pearl Attractor

Tied by: Vladimir Markov, Irkutsk, Russia
Hook: Mustad 3906B, #10-#16
Thread: Black 6/0
Tail: Golden pheasant tippet fibers
Underbody: First 2/3 orange thread, remainder black thread
Overbody: Pearl Ice Dub
Hackle: Furnace

Pete's Reel Nymph

Tied by: Pete Toscani, Bristol, CT
Hook: Nymph, #10
Thread: Black 6/0
Tail: Black hackle fibers
Rib: Gold oval tinsel
Body: Small black Body Glass
Wing Case: Turkey feather section
Thorax: Black dubbing
Legs: Black saddle hackle
Eyes: Small silver dumbbell
Comments: Coat body, wing case, and head with epoxy.

Pheasant Gosling Nymph

Tied by: Randy Huntley, Sanders, AZ
Hook: TMC 200R, #10, weighted
Thread: Black
Tail: Yellow golden pheasant feather fibers
Rib: Gold holographic Mylar tinsel and brown hackle twisted together, use hackle 2 sizes smaller than hook size
Body: Yellow plastic hay bailing cord, or yellow floss
Wing Case: Golden pheasant body feather
Legs: Red golden pheasant and mallard flank feather fibers

Poacher

Tied by: Jack Pangburn, Westbury, NY
Hook: Mustad 3906, #10-#16, weight optional
Thread: Black
Tail: Brown hackle fibers
Body: Rear 1/3 orange dubbing, front 2/3 peacock herl
Hackle: Brown

Red Gorbenmac Nymph

Tied by: Gordon Mackenzie, Syderstone, Norfolk, England
Hook: Nymph, 2X long, #6-#14, weighted
Thread: Black
Tail: Hot orange woodchuck guard hair hackle, 1 to 2 turns
Rib: Red flat Mylar tinsel
Abdomen: Peacock herl
Wing Case: Mallard blue wing feather section
Thorax: Red imitation seal fur dubbing ribbed with peacock herl
Hackle: Blue hair hackle, 1 to 2 turns
Comments: Use a dubbing loop to spin the hairs into a hair hackle.

Red Squirrel Nymph

Tied by: Scott Zadroga, San Diego, CA
Hook: Nymph, 2X long, #12, weighted
Thread: Black 6/0
Tail: Red squirrel body guard hairs
Body: Red squirrel under fur dubbing
Wing: Light colored hairs from red squirrel
Eyes: Brown plastic

RP's Attractor Nymph

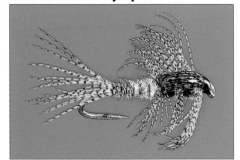

Tied by: Roy Powell, Danville, CA
Hook: TMC 3761, #12
Thread: Black
Tail: Lemon wood duck feather fibers
Rib: Copper wire, counterwrapped
Abdomen: Ginger #8 Hare-Tron dubbing
Wing Case: Lemon wood duck feather fibers, coated with epoxy
Thorax: Brown/pearl glass beads, ginger dubbing
Legs: Lemon wood duck feather fibers

Royal Coachman Clone Nymph

Tied by: Randy Huntley, Sanders, AZ
Hook: Nymph, #14, weighted
Thread: Black
Tail: Red golden pheasant feather fibers
Rib: Peacock herl and gold tinsel
Abdomen: Red floss
Wing Case: Red golden pheasant feather fibers
Hackle: Brown, bottom fibers trimmed
Thorax: Peacock herl, and silver tinsel
Legs: Golden pheasant tippet fibers
Wing: White Antron yarn fibers
Head: Peacock herl

Royal Nymph

Tied by: Don Heyden, Bozeman, MT
Hook: Mustad 3906B, #12-#16
Thread: Dark brown 6/0
Tail: Deer hair
Abdomen: Peacock herl, red floss
Wing Case: Pheasant tail feather fibers
Thorax: Brown rabbit dubbing

Royal Prince Nymph

Tied by: Jason Morin, Olympia, WA
Hook: Nymph 1X long in sizes 14 and larger, 2X long in sizes 16 and smaller
Thread: Red 8/0
Tails: Red goose biots
Body: 1/3 peacock herl, 1/3 red wire, and 1/3 peacock herl
Hackle: Black
Wings: White goose biots
Head: Gold metal bead

Royal Ugly

Tied by: Nadeer Youssef, Pullman, WA
Hook: Mustad 9671, #16
Thread: Red 6/0
Tail: Golden pheasant tippet fibers
Rib: Brass wire
Shellback: Pheasant tail feather fibers
Body: Peacock herl, red ostrich herl
Hackle: Brown grizzly hen saddle, top fibers trimmed
Eyes: Mono
Wing Case/Head: Pheasant tail feather fibers

Silver Death

Tied by: Sam de Beer, Cambridge Bay, Nunavut, Canada
Hook: Mustad 9672, #10, weighted
Thread: Black
Tail: Silver and multi-colored Flashabou strands, ends from body material
Body: Silver and multi-colored Flashabou strands, wrapped
Wing: Silver and multi-colored Flashabou strands, tag ends from body material

Spun Seal Nymph

Tied by: Jeff Lingenfelter, Browns Valley, CA
Hook: TMC 200, #6-#16, weighted
Thread: Black 6/0
Tail: Golden-olive grizzly feather marabou fibers
Abdomen: Brown imitation seal dubbing, spun in dubbing loop and trimmed to shape
Wing Case: Turkey tail feather section, coated with Flexament
Thorax: Medium cinnamon imitation seal, spun in dubbing loop

Sunset Orange

Tied by: Dorothy Shorter, 100 Mile House, BC
Hook: Mustad 9672, #10
Thread: Orange
Tail: Orange bucktail hair
Body: Orange Antron yarn
Hackle: Orange saddle

Tim's Nymph

Tied by: Tim McConville, Salt Lake City, UT
Hook: Dai-Riki 730, #14, weighted
Thread: Red 8/0
Tail: Black pheasant tail feather fibers
Rib: Peacock herl
Body: Red dubbing
Wing: Black pheasant tail feather fibers
Head: Nickel metal bead

Utrera's Purple Woven

Tied by: Lucas Utrera, Cordoba, Argentina
Hook: TMC 200R, #12
Thread: Red 8/0
Tail: Black and red rabbit fur
Abdomen: Black and red floss strands, woven with the parallel weave
Thorax: Black, red, and purple rabbit fur hackles, formed in dubbing loops and wrapped
Head: Peacock herl

What The...?

Tied by: Monte Smith, Brownsville, OR
Hook: Dai-Riki 060, #12
Thread: Black 8/0
Tail: Brown marabou feather fibers
Abdomen: Medium copper wire
Thorax: Peacock herl, 3-4 strands, ribbed with copper wire
Throat: Grouse feather fibers
Wings: 2 tan goose biots

Willow Worm

Tied by: J. Mullin, Casper, WY
Hook: TMC 400T, #8
Thread: Black
Tag: Orange thread
Body: Orange and black plastic tubing, woven with George Grant weave
Head: Purple glass bead

Attractor Dry Flies

American Patriot

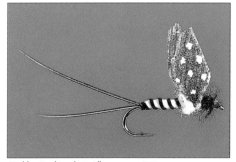

Tied by: Fred Iacoletti, Albuquerque, NM
Hook: Daiichi 1280, #12
Thread: Fine nylon
Tails: African blue parrot tail feather fibers
Rib: Red vinyl
Abdomen: White UNI-Stretch
Wing: Micro Web, cut to shape, colored with permanent markers
Thorax: White beaver dubbing and Wapsi Red Enhancer dubbing

Bear Paw

Tied by: Henry Hoffman, Warrenton, OR
Hook: Mustad 94840, #10-#14
Thread: Black 8/0
Tag: Red floss
Body: Red and yellow floss
Hackle: Grizzly

Bill's Rubber Legged Stimulator

Tied by: Bill Keister, Marlborough, CT
Hook: Mustad 9672, #8
Thread: Brown
Tail: Gold Antron yarn fibers, topped with dark deer hair
Body Hackle: Grizzly
Abdomen: Green Antron yarn
Wing: Dark deer hair
Thorax: Orange Antron dubbing
Legs: Brown round rubber
Hackle: Grizzly

Bi-Visible

Tied by: Jack Pangburn, Westbury, NY
Hook: Mustad 94838, #8-#14
Thread: Black
Tail: Brown hackle fibers
Body: Rear: ginger hackle, front: white hackle

Black Swallow

Tied by: Robert Schreiner, Southampton, PA
Hook: Mustad 94840, #12
Thread: Black
Tail: Amherst pheasant tippet fibers
Rib: Fine black Mylar tinsel
Body: Pearl Krystal Flash strands
Wings: Crested guinea feather sections
Hackle: Black/silver badger

Blackwater Double Wing

Tied by: Carl Ritter, Sedona, AZ
Hook: Dai-Riki 710, #12
Thread: Dark brown 8/0
Tag: Red Mylar tinsel
Abdomen: Peacock herl
Wing: White Antron, golden pheasant tippet fibers, and deer hair
Thorax: Fine ginger dubbing
Hackle: Ginger

Blue Seatrout Stimulator

Tied by: Matthias Luenzmann, Jena, Germany
Hook: Mustad 80050BR, #8-#12
Thread: Black 6/0
Tail: Elk hair
Rib: Fine silver wire
Abdomen: Kingfisher blue seal fur substitute dubbing
Abdomen Hackle: Silver badger
Wing: Elk hair
Thorax: Kingfisher blue seal fur substitute dubbing
Thorax Hackle: Blue grizzly

Blue Wing Adams

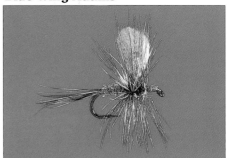

Tied by: Tony Kaminski, Victorville, CA
Hook: Mustad 98480, #12
Thread: Gray 6/0
Tail: Brown and grizzly hackle fibers
Body: Gray muskrat dubbing
Wings: Blue dun hen feathers
Hackle: Brown and grizzly

Bridge Fly

Tied by: Scott Roth, Newton, NJ
Hook: None, tie fly on needle, optional 2X long dry fly hook
Thread: Tan
Eye loop: 3X mono, not used if tied on hook
Underbody: Tan foam strip, ironed flat, coated with Flexament and wrapped
Body: Tan Antron dubbing
Wing: Coastal deer hair
Legs: Emu herl
Eyes: Black plastic
Antennae: Tan turkey flat feather fibers
Comments: Slide body off needle after tying. Without a hook, this is a true attractor fly.

Bubblegum Usual

Tied by: Jack Pangburn, Westbury, NY
Hook: Mustad 94840, #10-#16
Thread: Tan
Tail: Natural snowshoe rabbit foot fur
Body: Pink snowshoe rabbit foot fur dubbing
Wing: Natural snowshoe rabbit foot fur

Butterfly

Tied by: Randy Huntley, Sanders, AZ
Hook: Dry fly, #12
Thread: Black
Tail: Red golden pheasant tippet fibers
Rib: Twisted gold wire
Abdomen: Yellow hay bailing cord, or floss
Thorax: Peacock herl
Legs: Golden pheasant tippet fibers
Hackle: Brown, wrapped over thorax
Wing: White calf tail hairs, over golden pheasant body feather fibers

Charlie's Revenge

Tied by: Chuck Sawyer, Belfast, ME
Hook: Mustad 94831, #10
Thread: Black
Tail: Red squirrel tail hair
Body: Red squirrel body fur dubbing
Wings: Red squirrel tail hair
Hackle: Red

Chartreuse Mocker

Tied by: Don Joslyn, Eagle Point, OR
Hook: Alec Jackson 2051, black, #7
Thread: Black 6/0
Tail: Grizzly hackle fibers
Body: Peacock herl, Alec Jackson chartreuse silk, peacock herl
Hackle: Grizzly

Cliff's Crawler

Tied by: Clifford Sullivan, Tracy, CA
Hook: Daiichi 1130, #10
Thread: Gold 8/0
Tail: Olive Krystal Flash, 6 strands
Underbody: Olive Krystal Flash strands from tail
Abdomen: Medium olive Vinyl Rib
Wing: Deer hair
Legs: Gold Silly Legs
Thorax: Medium olive Antron dubbing
Hackle: Olive grizzly, mounted parachute style on stretched Super Floss strand, then the Super Floss is folded forward and tied off behind the hook eye

Comadreja

Tied by: Lucas Utrera, Cordoba, Argentina
Hook: TMC 200R, #12
Thread: Yellow 8/0
Tail: Deer hair
Body Hackle: Undersized ginger
Body: Black and yellow floss strands, woven with a parallel weave
Wings: Deer hair
Hackle: Brown, 2 feathers

Cream Wulff

Tied by: Jack Pangburn, Westbury, NY
Hook: Mustad 94840, #10-#16
Thread: Red
Tail: Badger or woodchuck hair
Body: Cream dubbing
Wings: White poly yarn fibers
Hackle: Ginger

Deer Hair Indicator

Tied by: Steve Potter, Tracy, CA
Hook: Mustad 9672, #6-#8
Thread: Brown 6/0
Tail: Golden pheasant tippet fibers
Legs: Brown round rubber
Body: Brown and natural deer hair, stacked and trimmed to shape
Wing: White calf tail hair
Head: Same as body

Deer Hair Miller

Tied by: J.E. Mullin, Casper, WY
Hook: Eagle Claw 58, #10
Thread: Black
Tail: Deer hair
Hackle: Brown
Body: Olive wool
Wing: Deer hair

Dreadlocker

Tied by: Don Joslyn, Eagle Point, OR
Hook: Alec Jackson 2051, black, #7
Thread: Black 3/0
Tail: Red calf tail hair
Rib: Gold flat French tinsel
Body: Black CDC dubbing
Wings: White bucktail hair
Hackle: Brown

D-Useagoose Special

Tied by: DuWayne Shaver, Capitan, NM
Hook: Mustad 94840, #12-#18
Thread: Orange
Tail: Golden pheasant tippet fibers
Rib: Peacock herl
Abdomen: White goose biot
Thorax: Peacock herl
Wings: White goose or duck quills
Hackle: Grizzly

Flash Drake

Tied by: Perry Tupper, Salem, OR
Hook: TMC 900BL, #10-#14
Thread: Black 8/0
Tail: Moose body hair
Rib: Olive Flashabou Accent
Body: Chartreuse Sparkle Dub
Wings: Black calf tail hair
Hackle: Olive grizzly

Flight Stimulator

Tied by: Gregory Krause, Coopersburg, PA
Hook: TMC 200R, #8-#12
Thread: Yellow 6/0
Tail: Elk hair, sided with white calf tail hair
Rib: Small silver tinsel
Abdomen: Yellow floss
Wing: Elk hair, sided by white calf tail hair
Hackle: Ginger
Thorax: Orange dubbing

Florida Wulff

Tied by: Al Milano, Bronx, NY
Hook: Mustad 94842, #14
Thread: Black 6/0
Tail: Black moose hair
Body: Peacock herl, orange floss, and peacock herl
Wings: White calf tail hair
Hackle: Dark brown

Foam-back Humpy

Tied by: J. Kulchak, Boise, ID
Hook: Mustad 94840, #10-#14
Thread: Black
Tail: Moose hair
Shellback: Orange foam
Body: Peacock herl
Wings: White Z-lon fibers
Hackle: Brown

Foam H/S

Tied by: Rod Dines, New Meadows, ID
Hook: TMC 2312, #6-#8
Thread: Tan 3/0
Body: Tan and yellow foam strips, cut to shape
Legs: Yellow and brown round rubber
Wing: Light elk hair
Indicator: Orange foam

Foxie

Tied by: Don Joslyn, Eagle Point, OR
Hook: Alec Jackson River Dee Low Water, gold, #9
Thread: Black 6/0
Tail: Red hackle fibers
Body Hackle: Brown grizzly
Body: Red fox tail dubbing
Wing: Moose hair, over rainbow Krystal Flash strands
Hackle: Brown grizzly
Head: Butt ends from wing material

Frosty Coachman

Tied by: Alexandria Kaminski, Victorville, CA
Hook: Mustad 98480, #12
Thread: White 6/0
Tail: Amherst tippet fibers
Body: Peacock herl, white floss, and peacock herl
Wings: White poly yarn fibers
Hackle: White

Go Ducks

Tied by: Ron Raykowski, Jackson Hole, WY
Hook: Dai Riki 200R, #10-#14
Thread: Yellow
Tail: Peacock herl
Rib: Peacock herl
Abdomen: Yellow floss
Wings: Peacock herl strands
Thorax: Black Peacock Ice Dub dubbing
Hackle: Light olive grizzly

H&L Water Walker

Tied by: Ronn Lucas, Sr., Milwaukie, OR
Hook: Dry fly, #8-#14
Thread: Black
Tail: White calf body hair
Body: Barbary sheep hair, peacock herl
Wings: White calf body hair
Hackles: Brown, tied Water Walker style (parachute style around each wing)

Ice-O-Lator

Tied by: Ron Raykowski, Jackson Hole, WY
Hook: TMC 200R, #10-#14
Thread: Green
Tail: Elk hair
Rib: Green thread
Body: Hare-Tron Caddis Green Ice Dubbing
Wing: Elk hair
Hackle: Grizzly
Comments: Silver or gold Ice Dubbing are color body options.

Iridescent Ausable Wulff

Tied by: Ronn Lucas, Sr., Milwaukie, OR
Hook: Dry fly, #8-#14
Thread: Bright orange
Tail: Wolf guard hair
Body: Rust Iridescent Dubbing
Wings: White calf tail hair
Hackle: Brown

Iridescent Picket Pin

Tied by: Ronn Lucas, Sr., Milwaukie, OR
Hook: Any long shank dry fly hook
Thread: Olive
Tail: Red hackle fibers
Rib: Gold oval tinsel
Body: Bronze Peacock Iridescent Dubbing
Wing: Gray squirrel tail hair
Eyes: Black iridescent glass beads, with mono core

Jack's Patriot

Tied by: Jack Pangburn, Westbury, NY
Hook: Mustad 94840, #10-#16
Thread: Red
Tail: Brown hackle fibers
Body: Pearlescent Mylar tinsel, with red thread bands
Wings: White poly yarn fibers
Hackle: Brown

John's Woodchuck

Tied by: John Peterson, Waldport, OR
Hook: Mustad 94840, #10-#16
Thread: Black
Tail: Woodchuck guard hairs
Body: Woodchuck under fur dubbing
Wings: Woodchuck guard hairs
Hackle: Cree

Leggy Spider

Tied by: Sam de Beer, Cambridge Bay, Nunavut, Canada
Hook: Mustad 9671, #12-#16
Thread: Black
Tail: Brown hackle fibers
Legs: Goose primary feather fibers
Body: Red floss
Hackle: Brown and white

Looped Wing Adams

Tied by: Mike Giavedoni, Maple, ON
Hook: Mustad 94840, #12
Thread: Black
Tail: Moose hair
Body: Gray dubbing
Wings: Brown feathers, reverse-hackle style
Hackle: Grizzly

Mayfly Patriot Adult

Tied by: Charles Robbins, Tracy, CA
Hook: Mustad 94840, #12
Thread: White 8/0
Tails: Macaw parrot biots
Body: Macaw parrot biot
Wings: 4 red and 4 blue mallard flank feather fibers for each wing, looped
Hackle: White, tied parachute style on the bottom of the hook shank, use 1 strand of stretched Super Floss for the post, when the Super Floss is relaxed after wrapping the hackle cut the excess leaving a small nub to retain the hackle
Head: Black 8/0 thread

Orange and Green

Tied by: Randy Huntley, Sanders, AZ
Hook: Dry fly, #12
Thread: Orange
Tail: Yellow and red golden pheasant feather fibers
Rib: Yellow Krystal Flash strand twisted with brown hackle, use hackle 2 sizes smaller than hook size
Abdomen: Orange floss
Thorax: Peacock herl
Hackle: Brown wrapped over thorax
Wing: Hen pheasant feather fibers, over golden pheasant tippet fibers

Patriot Stimulator

Tied by: Monte Smith, Brownsville, OR
Hook: TMC 200R, #12
Thread: Black 8/0
Egg Sack: Royal coachman red rabbit dubbing
Tails: Black goose biots
Rib: Black saddle feather, clipped short
Underbody: Black Superfine dubbing
Body: Blue Krystal Flash, 4-5 strands
Wing: White calf tail hairs
Hackle: Grizzly
Thorax: Royal coachman red rabbit dubbing

Pearl

Tied by: Vladimir Markov, Irkutsk, Russia
Hook: TMC 2487, #10-#16
Thread: Red 6/0
Tail: Rust Antron yarn fibers
Body: Red thread
Overbody: Pearl Krystal Flash strands
Thorax: Peacock herl
Post: White foam
Hackle: Grizzly

Peter Ross

Tied by: Greg Mayers, Fredricksberg, VA
Hook: Mustad 94840, #14-#20
Thread: Red
Tail: Golden pheasant tippet fibers
Rib: Extra fine silver oval tinsel
Abdomen: Silver prismatic Mylar tinsel
Thorax: Red dubbing
Wing: Amherst pheasant tail feather fibers
Hackle: Badger

Pete's Reel Patriot Humpy

Tied by: Pete Tozcani, Bristol, CT
Hook: Orvis 1524, #8
Thread: Red 3/0
Tail: White calf body hair
Shellback: Blue deer hair, coated with epoxy
Body: Red thread
Wings: Blue deer hair, tips from shellback material
Hackles: Grizzly, brown

Pheasant Gosling

Tied by: Randy Huntley, Sanders, AZ
Hook: Dry fly, 2X long
Thread: Black
Tail: Red and yellow golden pheasant body feather fibers, mallard flank feather fibers
Rib: Gold holographic Mylar tinsel and brown hackle twisted together, use hackle 2 sizes smaller than hook size
Body: Yellow plastic hay baling cord, or yellow floss
Hackle: Brown
Wing: Red, yellow and tippet feather fibers from golden pheasant, topped with mallard flank feather fibers

Popsicle Parachute

Tied by: Ron Beasley, St. Louis, MS
Hook: Mustad 94840, #12-#16
Thread: Black
Tail: Black hackle fibers
Body: Red floss, optional colors: fluorescent chartreuse, orange, yellow and pink
Wing/Post: White poly yarn fibers
Hackle: Grizzly
Comments: This fly was designed for bluegill, but also works for trout.

Prince Charming

Tied by: Gordon Mackenzie, Syderstone, Norfolk, England
Hook: Dry fly, #10-#16
Thread: Black
Tail: Hot orange woodchuck guard hair hackle, 1 to 2 turns
Body: Peacock herl, silver tinsel, and peacock herl
Wing: Dark blue squirrel tail hair
Hackle: Blue hair hackle, 1 to 2 turns
Comments: Use dubbing loop to spin hairs into a hair hackle.

P.T. Wulff

Tied by: Scott Zadroga, San Diego, CA
Hook: Dry fly, #14
Thread: Brown 6/0
Tail: Moose body hair
Body: Pheasant tail feather fibers, peacock herl
Wings: White calf tail hair
Hackle: Dun

Red Mocker

Tied by: Don Joslyn, Eagle Point, OR
Hook: Alec Jackson River Dee Low Water, gold, #9
Thread: Black 6/0
Tail: Brown hackle fibers
Body: Peacock herl, red floss, peacock herl
Hackle: Brown

Royal Caddis

Tied by: Don Heyden, Bozeman, MT
Hook: Mustad 94840, #10-#16
Thread: Cream 6/0
Tail: Golden pheasant tippet fibers
Body: Peacock herl, red floss, peacock herl
Wing: Bleached elk hair

Royal Coachman Clone

Tied by: Randy Huntley, Sanders, AZ
Hook: Dry, 2X long, #14
Thread: Black
Tag: Red floss
Tail: Red golden pheasant feather fibers
Body: Peacock herl
Body Hackle: Brown
Wing: White Antron yarn fibers, topped with golden pheasant tippet fibers
Hackle: White hen saddle

Royal Pullback

Tied by: Nadeer Youssef, Pullman, WA
Hook: Daiichi 1270, #10
Thread: Red 8/0
Tail: Golden pheasant tippet fibers
Rear Hackle: Brown, 1 size smaller than hook size
Body: Peacock herl, red floss, and peacock herl
Wing/Head: Light deer hair, head pulled back over top, bullet style
Hackle: Light brown

RPX's

Tied by: Roy Powell, Danville, CA
Hook: TMC 2312, #8
Thread: Yellow, black
Tail: Yellow deer hair
Rib: Yellow grizzly hackle, trimmed short
Body: Yellow #9 Hareline dubbing
Wing: Ring-necked pheasant neck feather, trimmed to shape, treated with Softex
Head/Collar: Yellow deer hair, bullet style
Legs: Yellow round rubber secured with black thread, rubber ends colored with black permanent marker

September Stimulator

Tied by: Glenn Weisner, Toledo, OH
Hook: TMC 200R, #8
Thread: White 6/0
Tail: Elk hair
Rib: Fine mono
Body Hackle: Grizzly
Body: Red, white, and blue GB3 Body Thread
Wing: Elk hair
Hackle: Grizzly

Sierra Bright

Tied by: Jerry Jeffery, Long Beach, CA
Hook: Mustad 94840, #12-#16
Thread: Black
Body: Peacock herl, pink fluorescent floss, peacock herl
Hackles: Grizzly

Simplifly

Tied by: Don Joslyn, Eagle Point, OR
Hook: Alec Jackson 2051, black, #5
Thread: Black 3/0
Butt: Intense tangerine Scintilla Caliente Dubbing
Tails: Black goose biots
Abdomen: Gold tinsel
Thorax: Intense tangerine Scintilla Caliente Dubbing
Wing: CDC feather, over moose hair
Hackle: Brown

Supper Wulff

Tied by: A.J. Courteau, Erie, PA
Hook: TMC 900BL, #6-#14
Thread: Brown 6/0
Tail: Moose body hair
Body: Peacock herl, red floss, peacock herl
Rear Wing: White calf body hair, down wing style
Front Wings: White calf body hair, upright and divided
Legs: Brown round rubber
Hackle: Brown

Tennessee Wulff

Tied by: Al Milano, Bronx, NY
Hook: Mustad 94842, #14
Thread: Black 6/0
Tail: Deer hair
Body: Peacock herl, green floss, and peacock herl
Wing: Deer hair
Hackle: Brown

Warhol's Wonder

Tied by: David McCants, Pleasant Hill, CA
Hook: TMC 5210, #14
Thread: White 8/0
Tails: Silver pheasant tail feather fibers
Body: White Angora goat dubbing
Wings: Silver pheasant wing covert feathers
Hackle: Grizzly

Yankee Doodle Dandy

Tied by: Ed Kraft, Lancaster, PA
Hook: Mustad 94833, #12
Thread: Red, white, and blue 6/0, use color to match dubbing
Tails: 3 split tails, 1 red, 1 white and 1 blue from dyed hackle fibers
Body: Blue Arctic fox rear 1/3, white Antron dubbing middle 1/3, and red Antron for the front 1/3
Wing/Post: White Antron yarn fibers
Hackles: Blue for bottom, white for middle, and red for top

Soft Hackles

1906 Night Fly

Tied by: G. Taggart, Hazleton, PA
Hook: Nymph, 4X long, #4-#6, weighted
Thread: Red
Tail: Black marabou feather fibers
Rib: Gold wire, 5 turns at rear of body then wrapped forward
Body Hackle: Black
Body: Black chenille
Wing: Gold Krystal Flash, 2 strands, optional
Hackle: Black blue eared pheasant

Aura Boreal Bead & Partridge

Tied by: Roland Coleman, Tracy, CA
Hook: Dry fly, #12
Thread: Black
Rib: Gold holographic tinsel
Body: Orange silk floss
Overbody: Clear vinyl ribbing
Thorax: Aura boreal clear bead
Hackle: Burnt orange partridge

B.H. Carrot Nymph Special

Tied by: Henry Hoffman, Warrenton, OR
Hook: Daiichi 1710, #12
Thread: Black 8/0
Tail: Black chickabou feather fibers
Rib: Gold wire, optional
Body: Orange chickabou feather, tied in by its tip and wrapped
Hackle: Black knee hackle from chicken
Head: Green glass bead, size 11/0

B.H. Knee Hackle Special, Brown

Tied by: Henry Hoffman, Warrenton, OR
Hook: Daiichi 1710, #12
Thread: Brown 8/0
Tail: Brown chickabou plume feather fibers
Rib: Fine gold wire, counterwrapped
Body: Brown grizzly knee hackle feather, tied in by its tips and wrapped
Hackle: Brown grizzly knee hackle feather
Head: Teal colored glass bead, size 11/0

Black & Blue

Tied by: Calvin Mohney, Boston, MA
Hook: Nymph, #14
Thread: Black 8/0
Rib: Silver oval tinsel
Body: Black floss
Wings: Blue mallard feather sections
Throat Hackle: Black hen feather fibers

Black Flymph

Tied by: Doug Duvall, Sardis, OH
Hook: TMC 9300, #10-#16
Thread: Black 8/0
Tail: Black hen feather fibers
Body: Black Hare-Tron dubbing
Hackle: Black hen saddle

Black Hackle Peacock

Tied by: Malcolm Stark, Northern Fort Providence, NWT
Hook: Mustad 9671, #10-#16
Thread: Black 6/0
Butt: Silver oval tinsel
Rib: Silver oval tinsel
Body: Peacock herl strands
Hackle: Black saddle

Black Max

Tied by: Perry Tupper, Salem, OR
Hook: TMC 5263, #10, weighted
Thread: Black 6/0
Tails: Black goose biots, split with black dubbing ball
Underbody: Black thread
Abdomen: 20lb. brown Maxima strands, woven with an overhand weave
Thorax: Black dubbing
Hackle: Grouse

Blood Worm Soft Hackle

Tied by: Cary Wilson, Newcastle, WY
Hook: Pupa, #14
Thread: Black 6/0
Body: Red wire
Hackle: Grizzly hen

Blue & Green Soft Hackle

Tied by: Scott Roth, Swartswood Lake, NJ
Hook: TMC 206BL, #10
Thread: Green 14/0
Tail: Blue emu feather fibers
Rib: Gold French tinsel
Abdomen: Olive pheasant tail feather fibers, wrapped
Thorax: Blue peacock herl
Hackle: Blue guinea
Head: Peacock herl

Breadcrust Soft Hackle

Tied by: Jack Pangburn, Westbury, NY
Hook: Mustad 3906, #10-#14
Thread: Brown
Underbody: Dental floss, built to a football shape
Ribs: Gold wire, brown V-Rib
Body: Orange floss
Hackle: Grizzly

Brown Hackle Yellow

Tied by: Malcolm Stark, Fort Providence, NWT
Hook: Mustad 9671, #10-#16
Thread: Black 6/0
Butt: Gold oval tinsel
Rib: Gold oval tinsel
Body: Yellow floss
Hackle: Coachman brown saddle

Brown Owl Variant

Tied by: Calvin Mohney, Boston, MA
Hook: Nymph, #16
Thread: Yellow
Body: Yellow Pearsall's Gossamer Silk thread
Hackle: Ginger hen
Head: Peacock herl

Brown Spider

Tied by: Hal Tolman, Riddle, OR
Hook: Nymph
Thread: Black
Tail: Red feather fibers
Body: Gold braid
Hackle: Furnace saddle

Claret Bumble

Tied by: Malcolm Stark, Northern Fort Providence, NWT
Hook: Dry fly, #10-#14
Thread: Black 6/0
Rib: Gold oval tinsel
Body: Claret floss
Hackle: Woodcock breast feather
Head: Black ostrich herl

Copper Cupid

Tied by: Troy Pearse, Boise, ID
Hook: TMC 3761, #14-#18
Thread: Brown
Body: Copper wire, medium
Wings: Medium dun CDC feathers
Hackle: Partridge

Dink

Tied by: Robert Schreiner, Southampton, PA
Hook: Mustad 3906B, #8
Thread: Black 8/0
Tail: Chartreuse hen saddle fibers
Abdomen: Stripped peacock herl, coated with lacquer
Thorax: Peacock herl
Hackles: Orange and chartreuse hen saddle

Dun Deal

Tied by: Steven Wascher, Greenhurst, NY
Hook: TMC 200R
Thread: Gray
Rib: Clear V-Rib
Abdomen: Caddis-green Antron dubbing
Thorax: Brown ostrich herl
Wing: Wood duck feather fibers
Hackle: Dun hen

Glass Bead Extended Body

Tied by: Curtis Kauer, Salina, KS
Hook: Mustad 81001BR, #10-#16
Thread: Black 8/0
Body: Glass beads, color of choice, 1 bead placed on hook
 shank, 4 beads mounted on mono with a melted end for
 extended body
Hackle: Partridge

Golden Soft

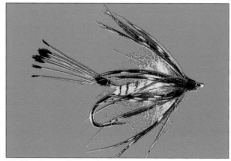

Tied by: Don Joslyn, Eagle Point, OR
Hook: Dai Riki 270, #14
Thread: Tan 6/0
Tail: Golden pheasant tippet fibers
Rib: Copper wire, fine
Abdomen: Yellow silk floss
Thorax: Ardent orange Scintilla Caliente Dubbing
Hackle: Partridge

Gold & White

Tied by: Randy Huntley, Sanders, AZ
Hook: Nymph, #14
Thread: Tan
Ribs: Clear Vinyl rib, white small ostrich herl
Abdomen: Gold holographic Mylar tinsel
Thorax: Golden olive Antron dubbing
Hackle: Golden pheasant tippet, Amherst pheasant tippet,
 Reeves pheasant
Head: Gold paint

Gray Hackle Yellow

Tied by: Malcolm Stark, Northern Fort Providence, NWT
Hook: Mustad 9671, #10-#16
Thread: Black 6/0
Butt: Silver oval tinsel
Rib: Silver oval tinsel
Body: Yellow floss and wool yarn twisted together and
 wrapped
Hackle: Grizzly saddle

Gray Sparkler

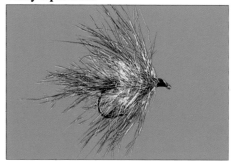

Tied by: Gordon Mackenzie, Syderstone, England
Hook: Nymph, #10-#16
Thread: Black 8/0
Tail: Black squirrel speckled guard hairs
Rib: Silver wire
Body: Gray rabbit fur and pearl/blue Lite Brite fibers,
 mixed, dubbing loop style
Hackle: Black squirrel speckled guard hairs, dubbing loop
 style

Green & Brown

Tied by: Randy Huntley, Sanders, AZ
Hook: Nymph, #14
Thread: Tan
Ribs: Clear Vinyl rib, brown ostrich herl, herl fibers trimmed
 to body
Abdomen: Dark olive Krystal Flash, 4 strands
Thorax: Arizona Peacock Dubbing
Hackle: Amherst pheasant crest, golden pheasant tippet,
 (stripped on 1 side, golden pheasant covert)
Head: Gold paint

Green & Widgeon

Tied by: David Burns, McCall, ID
Hook: TMC 200, #10
Thread: White
Tag: Silver oval tinsel
Rib: Silver oval tinsel
Body Hackle: Light dun
Abdomen: Green silk floss
Thorax: Peacock herl
Hackle: American Widgeon

Guinea Soft Hackle

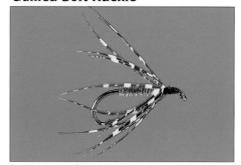

Tied by: Doug Fullerton, Menominee, MI
Hook: Mustad 94840, #12-#16
Thread: Black 6/0
Body: Guinea wing feather fibers, wrapped untwisted
Hackle: Mottled Guinea

Handsome Possum

Tied by: Al Milano, Bronx, NY
Hook: Orvis 1641-00, #10
Thread: Orange Pearsall's Gossamer tying silk
Rib: Copper Orvis Glimmer Thread
Abdomen: Australian possum dubbing, guard hairs removed
Thorax: Australian possum dubbing, with guard hairs
Hackle: Red grouse

Hoff's Partridge B/H Soft Hackle

Tied by: Scott Hoff, Concord, CA
Hook: Orvis 1524, #14
Thread: Tan 8/0
Tail: Gray partridge feather fibers
Rib: Copper wire, fine, counterwrapped
Body: Hare's Ear dubbing
Wing: Brown partridge feather fibers
Hackle: Gray partridge
Head: Copper tungsten bead

Hoff's Partridge & Red B/H

Tied by: Scott Hoff, Concord, CA
Hook: Orvis 1510, #14
Thread: Tan 8/0
Tail: Gray partridge feather fibers
Rib: Copper wire, fine
Body: Peacock herl, red floss, peacock herl
Hackle: Gray partridge
Head: Copper tungsten bead

Ipsen's Soft Hackle

Tied by: Loren Ipsen, Boise, ID
Hook: TMC 5210, #12-#16
Thread: Orange
Butt: Orange thread
Rib: Gold thread, counterwrapped
Body: Red squirrel dubbing, (road kill run over by a 1954 Studebaker)
Hackle: Brown partridge

Jeffery's Soft Hackle

Tied by: Jerry Jeffery, Long Beach, CA
Hook: Mustad 3906B
Thread: Black
Tail: Red marabou feather fibers
Rib: Gold holographic Mylar tinsel
Body: Red floss
Hackle: Partridge

John's Improved Partridge & Green

Tied by: Don Johnson, Shelton, WA
Hook: Daiichi 1560, #10-#14
Thread: Green silk, size A
Abdomen: Green silk, twisted
Thorax: Hare's mask dubbing
Wing: Antron yarn, 6-8 fibers
Hackle: Partridge

L.D.S. Double Hackle Black

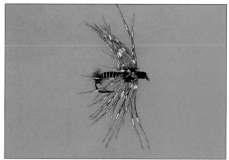

Tied by: Larry Stephens, Kansas City, MO
Hook: Mustad 3906, #14
Thread: Black 6/0
Tail: Red UNI-Stretch
Rib: Copper wire, fine
Abdomen: Black UNI-Stretch
Thorax: Black dubbing
Hackles: Guinea, space left between hackles

Marabou Soft Hackle

Tied by: Ron English, Rescue, CA
Hook: Nymph, #12-#16
Thread: Red 6/0
Tail: Tan marabou feather fibers, tan Z-lon fibers, olive Krystal Flash strands
Rib: Gold wire
Body: Tan dubbing
Wing: Olive Krystal Flash, 4 strands
Hackle: Partridge
Head: Tan dubbing

March Brown Soft Hackle

Tied by: Jack Pangburn, Westbury, NY
Hook: Mustad 3906, #10-#14
Thread: Rust
Rib: Copper wire
Body: Hare's Ear dubbing
Hackle: Grouse or partridge

Montreal

Tied by: Jack Pangburn, Westbury, NY
Hook: Mustad 3906B, #10-#14
Thread: Black
Rib: Gold oval tinsel
Body: Coffee floss
Hackle: Brown

Olive Bead Soft Hackle

Tied by: Michael Taylor, Etna, CA
Hook: TMC 2312
Thread: Olive
Tail: Pearl Krystal Flash, 2 strands
Body: Olive glass beads, 2 small and 2 micro, olive dubbing between beads
Hackle: Olive guinea

Olive Spider

Tied by: Malcolm Stark, Northern Fort Providence, NWT
Hook: Dry fly hook, #10-#16
Thread: Black 6/0
Butt: Gold oval tinsel
Rib: Gold oval tinsel
Body: Olive floss
Hackle: Woodcock breast feather

Orange & Black

Tied by: Hal Tolman, Riddle, OR
Hook: Nymph
Thread: Black
Tail: Black feather fibers
Rib: Gold wire
Body: Light gray floss
Hackles: Orange and black saddle

Partridge & Orange (Duvall)

Tied by: Doug Duvall, Sardis, OH
Hook: TMC 3761, #10-#16
Thread: Orange 8/0
Body: Orange floss
Thorax: Hare's Ear dubbing
Hackle: Partridge

Partridge & Orange (Gritton)

Tied by: Elliott Gritton, Reno, NV
Hook: Dai-Riki 300, #10-#14
Thread: Fire orange 8/0
Rib: Copper wire
Abdomen: Orange UNI-Stretch Nylon
Thorax: Rust Hare-Tron dubbing
Hackle: Partridge

Partridge & Orange Variant

Tied by: Lawson Devery, Fareham, United Kingdom
Hook: TMC 103BL, #15
Thread: Orange
Tail: Rhode Island red rooster hackle fibers
Butt: Gold tinsel
Body: Orange SLF dubbing
Hackles: Orange partridge, gray partridge

Partridge & Yellow Variant

Tied by: Lawson Devery, Fareham, United Kingdom
Hook: TMC 103BL, #15
Thread: Yellow
Tail: Rhode Island red rooster hackle fibers
Butt: Gold tinsel
Body: Yellow SLF dubbing
Hackles: Yellow partridge, gray partridge

Peacock & Lace Soft Hackle

Tied by: Walt Alexander, Gridley, CA
Hook: Cable Model 21, #12
Thread: Fluorescent chartreuse 14/0
Underbody: Tying thread
Abdomen: Clear craft lace, split in half
Thorax: Peacock herl
Hackle: Guinea

Pete's Reel Soft Hackle

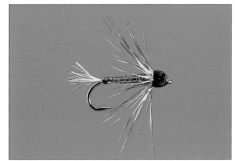

Tied by: Pete Toscani, Bristol, CT
Hook: Nymph, #14
Thread: Black 8/0
Tail: Pearl Lite Brite strands
Body: Peacock Lite Bright strands, wrapped
Hackle: Grizzly
Head: Black thread, coated with epoxy

Pink & Blau

Tied by: Randy Huntley, Sanders, AZ
Hook: Nymph, #12
Thread: Tan
Tail: Blue-gray pheasant rump feather fibers
Rib: Gold oval tinsel
Abdomen: Pink Rayon floss, coated with Hardcoat head cement
Thorax: Muskrat dubbing
Hackles: Blue-gray pheasant rump, white hen
Head: Gold paint

Purple Soft Hackle

Tied by: Roland Coleman, Tracy, CA
Hook: Salmon dry fly, #8
Thread: Black
Tip: Silver oval tinsel, 3 wraps
Tag: Lavender silk floss
Tail: Purple feather fibers
Rib: Silver oval tinsel
Body: Purple silk floss
Hackles: Purple rhea, claret guinea

Quilled Spider

Tied by: Dawn Stevens, Wilmington, DE
Hook: Scud
Thread: Black 8/0
Tail: Teal feather fibers
Abdomen: Moose mane hairs, 2 dark, 1 light
Thorax: White chenille
Hackle: Teal

Red & Brown

Tied by: Randy Huntley, Sanders, AZ
Hook: Nymph, #12
Thread: Red
Tail: Amherst pheasant crest fibers
Ribs: Clear Vinyl rib, brown ostrich herl, gold oval tinsel
Abdomen: Silver holographic tinsel, tinted red with Pantone pen
Hackle: Grouse, wrapped over thorax
Thorax: Brown ostrich herl
Head: Gold paint

Red Cock & Orange

Tied by: Jack Pangburn, Westbury, NY
Hook: Mustad 3906B, #10-#14
Thread: Rust
Abdomen: Orange Antron dubbing
Thorax: Red-brown dubbing
Hackle: Brown

Red Quill Ice

Tied by: Bruce Raymond, Woodridge, IL
Hook: TMC 3769, #8-#16
Thread: Red
Abdomen: Fred Reese red quill turkey biot
Thorax: Golden brown Ice Dub, dark orange and tan squirrel dubbing, mixed
Hackle: Hen pheasant variant

Red Snapper

Tied by: Dorothy Shorter, Williams Lake, BC
Hook: Mustad 3906, #10
Thread: Black
Tail: Red duck feather section
Rib: Gold metallic cord
Body: Red Mylar tinsel
Hackle: Grouse

Red Soft Hackle

Tied by: Ben Byng, Tracy, CA
Hook: TMC 7999, #8-#12
Thread: Black
Tag: Silver tinsel
Rib: Gold oval tinsel
Body: Red silk floss
Hackle: Red
Head: Peacock herl

Rick's Orange

Tied by: Richard Weisend, Bozeman, MT
Hook: TMC 3761, #16
Thread: Orange 8/0
Rib: Hot orange Ultra Wire
Abdomen: Pumpkin UNI-Floss
Thorax: Rusty-brown Antron dubbing
Hackle: Brown hen

Rinaldin Soft Hackle

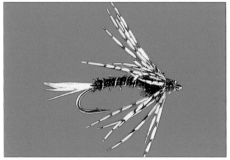

Tied by: Giuseppe Nova, Bollate, Italy
Hook: TMC 200, #16-#20
Thread: Black 8/0
Tail: Gray partridge feather fibers
Rib: Gold wire
Abdomen: Stripped peacock herl
Thorax: Peacock herl
Hackle: Partridge

Snip & Purple

Tied by: Al Milano, Bronx, NY
Hook: Partridge G3A, #14
Thread: Purple Pearsall's Gossamer tying silk
Abdomen: 2 layers of tying silk
Thorax: Mole dubbing
Hackle: Snipe

Soft Hackle Flash

Tied by: Rich Bogardus, Schenectady, NY
Hook: Nymph, #12-#16
Thread: Red 8/0
Butt: Red thread
Abdomen: Pearl Flashabou strand, wrapped flat
Thorax: Pearl blue Lite Brite dubbing
Hackle: Grizzly hen

Soft Hackle Flashback Emerger

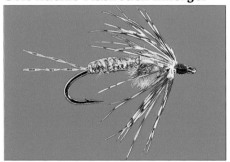

Tied by: Steve Potter, Tracy, CA
Hook: TMC 200R, #8-#16, weighted with 2 pieces of lead mounted on sides of hook shank and secured with CA glue
Thread: Black 8/0
Tail: Olive Krystal Flash strands, optional
Abdomen: Olive Krystal Flash strands, woven with half-hitches
Wing Case: Pearl Flashabou strand
Thorax: Olive ostrich herl
Hackle: Partridge
Comments: Change the colors of the abdomen and thorax materials to match the naturals.

Soft Hackle Stone

Tied by: Gary McConnell, Auburn, CA
Hook: Nymph, 3X long, #10-#16
Thread: Black
Tail: Orange mallard flank feather fibers
Rib: Pearl Krystal Flash strand, counterwrapped
Body: Black dubbing
Hackle: Burnt orange hen, black hen, 1 wrap each

Soft Hackle Valentine

Tied by: Stephen Lopatic, Harrisburg, PA
Hook: Mustad 80050, #16
Thread: Red 8/0
Abdomen: Red Krystal Flash, 2 strands twisted and wrapped
Thorax: Red Antron dubbing
Wing: Red Krystal Flash strands, red Antron dubbing fibers, red marabou feather fibers
Collar: Pink marabou fibers
Head: Red glass bead, mounted on Amnesia mono strand, front end melted to secure bead

Sullivan's Soft Hackle

Tied by: Clifford Sullivan, Tracy, CA
Hook: Orvis 8891, #10-#16
Thread: Green 8/0
Tail: Dark olive Krystal Flash, 6 strands
Underbody: Dark olive Krystal Flash, strands from tail wrapped forward
Abdomen: Light olive V-Rib
Thorax: Olive Antron dubbing
Hackle: Olive hen

Syl's Midge Soft Hackle

Tied by: Jack Pangburn, Westbury, NY
Hook: Nymph, 1X short
Thread: Brown
Body: Peacock herl
Hackle: Grizzly, oversized

Tups Indispensable

Tied by: Doug Duvall, Sardis, OH
Hook: TMC 9300, #10-#16
Thread: Pale yellow 8/0
Tail: Light dun hen feather fibers
Abdomen: Yellow floss, built to a taper
Thorax: Pink dubbing
Hackle: Light dun hen

Twin Tail Tups

Tied by: David McCants, Pleasant Hill, CA
Hook: TMC 5210, #14-#18
Thread: Yellow 8/0
Tail: 2 medium dun hen feathers, tied splayed
Abdomen: Tying thread, tapered
Thorax: Hendrickson pink dubbing
Hackle: Medium dun hen

Wet CDC Brown Bubble

Tied by: Don Joslyn, Eagle Point, OR
Hook: Dai Riki 270, #14
Thread: Tan 6/0
Tail: Wood duck flank feather fibers
Abdomen: Tan thread, top colored with brown marker
Thorax: Scintilla Scintillator Bubble, size 3mm
Hackle: Dun CDC
Head: Tan thread, top colored with brown marker

Wet Drake

Tied by: Gary McConnell, Auburn, CA
Hook: Dry fly, #12-#16
Thread: Tan
Tail: Wood duck flank feather fibers
Rib: Olive Krystal Flash strand, counterwrapped
Shellback: Dark mottled turkey tail feather fibers
Body: Light olive dubbing
Hackle: Honey-dun hen

Wet Green Bubble

Tied by: Don Joslyn, Eagle Point, OR
Hook: Dai Riki 070, #14
Thread: Green 6/0
Tail: Wood duck flank feather fibers
Abdomen: Green thread
Thorax: Scintilla Scintillator Bubble, size 3mm
Hackle: Partridge
Head: Peacock herl

Wet Green Guinea

Tied by: Don Joslyn, Eagle Point, OR
Hook: Dai Riki 270, #14
Thread: Green 6/0
Tail: Black golden pheasant tippet fibers
Rib: Copper wire, fine, counterwrapped
Abdomen: Green silk floss
Thorax: Green guinea marabou dubbing
Hackle: Green guinea

Wet Orange Guinea

Tied by: Don Joslyn, Eagle Point, OR
Hook: Dai Riki 070, #10
Thread: Orange 3/0
Tail: Orange guinea feather fibers
Body: Peacock herl strands, twisted with orange thread
Hackle: Orange guinea

Wet Flies

Woodcock & Orange

Tied by: Malcolm Stark, Northern Fort Providence, NWT
Hook: Dry fly, #10-#16
Thread: Black 6/0
Butt: Gold oval tinsel
Rib: Gold oval tinsel
Body: Orange floss
Hackle: Woodcock breast feather

Alexandria

Tied by: Malcolm Stark, Northern Fort Providence, NWT
Hook: TMC 200R, #8-#12
Thread: Black 6/0
Tail: Peacock sword feather fibers
Rib: Gold oval tinsel
Body: Silver Body Braid
Wing: Peacock sword feather fibers
Shoulders: Red goose feather strips
Throat: Peacock sword feather fibers
Head: Black ostrich herl

Black Dose

Tied by: Dawn Stevens, Wilmington, DE
Hook: Mustad 3906
Thread: Black 8/0
Tag: Silver tinsel
Tail: Golden pheasant crest fibers
Butt: Yellow floss
Rib: Silver tinsel
Body: Black floss
Throat: Black feather fibers
Wing: Peacock secondary, Kenya crested guinea, and bronze mallard feather fibers, married

Black Pearl

Tied by: Robert Schreiner, Southampton, PA
Hook: 3906B, #10
Thread: Black 8/0
Tail: Amherst tippet fibers
Rib: Black Mylar tinsel
Body: Pearl Krystal Flash strands, wrapped flat
Throat: Amherst tippet fibers
Wing: Married feather fibers, 2 black goose shoulder, 3 crested guinea, 2 hot pink goose shoulder, 3 crested guinea, 2 hot pink goose shoulder, 3 crested guinea

Blae & Black

Tied by: Roland Coleman, Tracy, CA
Hook: Dry fly, #12
Thread: Black
Tail: Orange golden pheasant tippet fibers
Rib: Silver oval tinsel
Body: Black silk floss
Wing: Gray mallard primary feather sections
Throat: Black feather fibers

Chartreuse & Blue Wet Fly

Tied by: Roy Powell, Danville, CA
Hook: TMC 5263, #8
Thread: White, black 8/0
Tag: Silver tinsel
Rib: Silver tinsel
Body: Chartreuse Depth Ray 4-strand nylon floss
Hackle: Chartreuse
Wing: Married goose shoulder feather fibers, 7 yellow, 6 blue, and 5 yellow

Classic Copper Cutthroat Killer

Tied by: David Burns, McCall, ID
Hook: Nymph
Thread: Orange
Tag: Bronze micro tinsel, crimson silk floss
Tail: Barred wood duck feather section
Butt: Orange wool dubbing
Rib: Silver oval tinsel
Body: Copper tinsel
Throat: Orange grizzly and American widgeon feather fibers
Underwing: Golden pheasant tippet fibers, peacock strands
Wing: Mottled turkey tail feather and red goose shoulder feather sections married, veiled with wood duck feather

Coachman

Tied by: Malcolm Stark, Northern Fort Providence, NWT
Hook: TMC 200R, #10-#16
Thread: Black 6/0
Butt: Gold wire
Rib: Gold wire, counterwrapped
Body: Peacock herl strands
Hackle: Coachman brown saddle
Wing: White fox body hair

Conglomeration

Tied by: Jack Pangburn, Westbury, NY
Hook: Streamer
Thread: Black
Tag: Silver tinsel
Tail: Brown feather fibers
Butt: Peacock herl
Body Hackle: Grizzly
Body: Light blue floss
Throat: Orange feather fibers
Wing: Pheasant church window feathers, small blue feather fibers
Hackle: Grizzly

Dark Montreal

Tied by: Malcolm Stark, Northern Fort Providence, NWT
Hook: Mustad 9671, #10-#14
Thread: Black 6/0
Tail: Claret feather fibers
Rib: Gold oval tinsel
Body: Claret floss
Wing: Dark brown mottled turkey tail feather sections
Hackle: Claret saddle

Divine Caddis

Tied by: Clifford Sullivan, Tracy, CA
Hook: Orvis 8891, #10-#18
Thread: Olive 8/0
Tail: Pearlescent Krystal Flash, 4 strands
Underbody: Pearlescent Krystal Flash end strands from tail, wrapped forward
Abdomen: Light olive V-Rib
Wings: Black mottled hen feathers
Hackle: Black mottled hen

Golden Wet Fly

Tied by: Stephen Lopatic, Harrisburg, PA
Hook: Mustad 36890, #10
Thread: Brown 6/0
Tail: Brown mottled duck flank feather fibers
Rib: Brown ostrich herl
Body: Gold floss
Throat: Brown mottled duck flank feather fibers
Wing: Brown mottled duck flank feather, coated with Flex-Seal, dried, then split in half and cut to shape

Gorbenmac Wet Fly

Tied by: Gordon Mackenzie, Syderstone, England
Hook: Nymph, #8-#14
Thread: Black
Tail: Golden pheasant tippet fibers
Rib: Red fur hackle, dubbing loop style, sparse
Body: Peacock herl strands
Hackle: Blue variegated feather fibers, dubbing loop style
Wings: Mallard wing feather blue sections

Go Ducks Wet Fly

Tied by: Ron Raykowski, Jackson Hole, WY
Hook: TMC 5263, #10
Thread: Yellow 8/0
Tail: Brown partridge feathers, 2 tips tied vertical fishtail style
Rib: Green wire
Body: Fluorescent green dubbing
Throat: Olive grizzly feather fibers
Head: Brown dubbing
Wing: Pearl Krystal Flash strands, olive grizzly feather, tied flat

Golden Brown Wet May

Tied by: Randy Huntley, Sanders, AZ
Hook: Nymph, #12
Thread: Yellow
Tail: Golden pheasant crest fibers
Butt: Red ostrich herl
Rib: Yellow thread
Body: Gold marabou feather fibers, wrapped
Hackle: Reeves pheasant body feather
Wings: Golden pheasant yellow body feather, wood duck flank feather fibers, topped with Reeves pheasant tail feather sections

Grandpa Hill

Tied by: Wade Malwitz, Portland, OR
Hook: TMC 5262, #10
Thread: Green 6/0
Tail: Moose mane hairs
Rib: Olive V-Rib, extra small
Body: Green Antron dubbing
Wing: Olive marabou feather fibers
Hackle: Pheasant rump

Hairy Mary Wet

Tied by: Jack Pangburn, Westbury, NY
Hook: Salmon
Thread: Black
Tag: Gold oval tinsel
Tail: Golden pheasant tippet fibers
Rib: Gold oval tinsel
Body: Black floss
Throat: Blue feather fibers
Wing: Red squirrel tail hairs

Hannah's Woolly

Tied by: Ron Beasley, St. Louis, MO
Hook: Mustad 3906B, #10-#16, weighted
Thread: Black
Tail: Pearl Krystal Flash, 3 strands
Shellback: Silver Mylar tinsel
Body Hackle: Grizzly
Body: Peacock herl, 3-4 strands

Hare's Ear Wet

Tied by: Curtis Kauer, Salina, KS
Hook: Dry fly, #16
Thread: Orange 8/0
Tail: Partridge feather fibers
Rib: Gold wire
Body: Hare's mask dubbing
Wing: Dun hen feathers

H&L Variant Wet

Tied by: Rich Bogardus, Schenectady, NY
Hook: Nymph, #12-#16
Thread: Black 8/0
Tail: White calf tail hairs
Abdomen: Stripped peacock herl
Thorax: Peacock herl
Hackle: Ginger
Wings: White duck quill sections

Hoff's Partridge Wet Fly

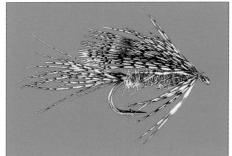

Tied by: Scott Hoff, Concord, CA
Hook: Orvis 1524, #14
Thread: Tan 8/0
Tail: Gray partridge feather fibers
Rib: Copper wire, fine
Body: Hare's Ear dubbing
Wing: Brown partridge feather fibers
Hackle: Gray partridge

Ipsen's Wet Fly

Tied by: Loren Ipsen, Boise, ID
Hook: Mustad 3906B, #10-#14
Thread: Black
Tail: Dun feather fibers
Rib: Black thread, counterwrapped
Body: Muskrat dubbing
Wings: Grizzly hen feathers, splayed
Hackle: Grizzly hen

Killer Brown

Tied by: Hal Tolman, Riddle, OR
Hook: Nymph, 3X long
Thread: Black
Tail: Orange bucktail hairs
Rib: Gold wire
Body: Orange floss
Wing: Orange bucktail hairs, brown saddle feathers
Hackle: Brown saddle

Lady-D Wet Fly

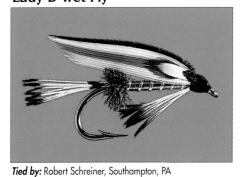

Tied by: Robert Schreiner, Southampton, PA
Hook: Mustad 3906B, #10
Thread: Black 6/0
Tail: Amherst pheasant tippet fibers
Butt: Peacock herl
Rib: Fine gold oval tinsel
Body: Copper tinsel
Wing: White, green, white, and black married goose feather fibers
Cheeks: Jungle cock eye feathers
Throat: Amherst tippet fibers

L.D.S. Special

Tied by: Larry Stephens, Kansas City, MO
Hook: Mustad 9671, #14
Thread: Gray 6/0
Tail: Brown feather fibers
Body: Light olive chenille, fine
Hackle: Light dun mallard flank
Wings: Light dun hen feathers, splayed

Little Brown Job

Tied by: Gary McConnell, Auburn, CA
Hook: Nymph, #14-#18
Thread: Red-brown
Body: Pheasant tail feather fibers
Wings: Light dun hen feathers
Hackle: Light dun hen

Much Improved Governor

Tied by: Michael Taylor, Etna, CA
Hook: TMC 2312
Thread: Black
Tail: Gadwall flank feather fibers
Butt: Red glass bead
Body: Peacock herl
Hackle: Mottled brown hen
Wing: Gadwall black feather fibers

Murdoch

Tied by: Carl Ritter, Sedona, AZ
Hook: Orvis 1526, #16
Thread: Brown, 8/0
Tag: Silver wire
Tail: Dark pheasant body feather fibers
Body: Brown and chocolate Antron dubbing, mixed, dubbing loop style, ruff trimmed
Throat: Red hen feather fibers
Wing: Pheasant church window feather

October Hare

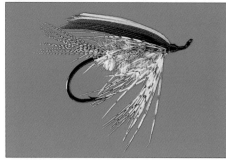

Tied by: Steven Wascher, Greenhurst, NY
Hook: Daiichi 2421
Thread: Red
Tag: Gold tinsel
Tail: Wood duck flank feather fibers
Rib: Gold tinsel
Body: Hare's mask dubbing
Hackle: Partridge
Wing: Married goose shoulder feather fibers, 6 natural, 3 orange, 2 yellow

Peacock & Lace Wet Fly

Tied by: Walt Alexander, Gridley, CA
Hook: Cabela Model 21, #12
Thread: Fluorescent chartreuse 14/0
Tail: Wood duck flank feather fibers
Underbody: Tying thread
Abdomen: Clear craft lace, split in half
Thorax: Peacock herl
Wing: Wood duck flank feather fibers
Hackle: Grizzly saddle

Pete's Reel Hornberg

Tied by: Pete Toscani, Bristol, CT
Hook: Nymph, #6
Thread: White 8/0
Wing: Copper Lite Brite strands
Cheeks: Artificial jungle cock eye feather
Hackle: Grizzly

Pete's Reel Wet Fly

Tied by: Pete Toscani, Bristol, CT
Hook: Nymph, #12
Thread: White 8/0
Tail: Golden pheasant tippet fibers
Body: Green, red, and green Krystal Flash strands, wrapped, coated with epoxy
Wing: White marabou feather fibers
Head: Red bead

Por Pavo Real

Tied by: Doug Fullerton, Menominee, MI
Hook: Partridge 22A, #10
Thread: Camel 6/0
Tail: Peacock herl, 6 strands
Body: Butt ends from tail material, wrapped untwisted
Throat: Peacock herl strands
Wing: Turkey feather section, cut to shape, coated with head cement

Professor (Stark)

Tied by: Malcolm Stark, Northern Fort Providence, NWT
Hook: Mustad 9671, #8-#14
Thread: Black 6/0
Tail: Red feather fibers
Rib: Silver oval tinsel
Body: Yellow yarn
Wing: Barred mallard breast feather fibers
Hackle: Coachman brown saddle

Red Chickabou Special

Tied by: Henry Hoffman, Warrenton, OR
Hook: Daiichi 1560, #6-#10
Thread: Red 6/0
Tail: Red chickabou feather fibers
Rib: Red copper wire, optional
Underbody: 30lb. flat mono, 1 strand lashed to each side of the hook shank, coated with CA glue
Body: Red chickabou feather, tied in by its tip and wrapped
Hackle: Red
Eyes: Gold Spirit River Real Eyes
Head: Red dubbing

Red, White & Black Wet Fly

Tied by: Roy Powell, Danville, CA
Hook: TMC 5263, #10
Thread: Black 8/0
Tag: Silver tinsel
Tail: Married fibers from goose shoulder feathers, 3 black, 3 white, and 3 red
Rib: Silver tinsel
Body: Red UNI-Floss
Body Hackle: Black, top fibers trimmed
Wing: Married fibers from goose shoulder feathers, 5 black, 5 white, and 5 red

Red, White, & Blue Wet Fly

Tied by: Roy Powell, Danville, CA
Hook: TMC 5263, #10
Thread: Black 8/0
Tag: Silver tinsel
Rib: Silver tinsel
Body: Blue Depth Ray 4-strand nylon floss
Wing: Married fibers from goose shoulder feathers, 3 white, 3 red, 4 white, and 7 red
Hackle: Blue chickabou

Rio Grand Queen

Tied by: John Peterson, Waldport, OR
Hook: Nymph, 3X long
Thread: Black
Tail: French partridge feather fibers
Body: Black peacock herl, pearl Mylar tinsel, black peacock herl
Wing: Pintail flank feather fibers
Hackle: Dark dun

Royal Coachman Wet Fly

Tied by: Jack Pangburn, Westbury, NY
Hook: Nymph
Thread: Black
Tail: Golden pheasant tippet fibers
Body: Peacock herl, red floss, peacock herl
Wing: White poly yarn fibers
Throat: Brown feather fibers

Rube Wood

Tied by: Jack Pangburn, Westbury, NY
Hook: Mustad 3906B, #8-#12
Thread: Black
Tail: Red and light gray poly yarn fibers
Body: White chenille
Wing: Light gray, white, and black poly yarn fibers, mixed
Throat: Brown feather fibers

Scott's Quill Gordon

Tied by: Scott Roth, Swartswood Lake, NJ
Hook: TMC 206BL, #12
Thread: Brown 14/0
Tails: Brown biots
Abdomen: Fred Reese's amber D/P stone fly quill material
Wings: Dun hen feathers
Hackle: Emu, wrapped over thorax, top fibers trimmed
Thorax: Brown dubbing

Silver Doctor

Tied by: Malcolm Stark, Northern Fort Providence, NWT
Hook: Mustad 9671, #8-#12
Thread: Black 6/0
Tail: Red feather fibers
Body: Silver Body Braid
Hackle: Blue saddle
Wing: Barred mallard breast feather fibers, 6-8 strands of peacock herl

Sir Robert

Tied by: Robert Schreiner, Southampton, PA
Hook: Mustad 3906B, #10
Thread: Black 8/0
Tail: Amherst pheasant tippet fibers
Butt: Black ostrich herl
Rib: Embossed silver flat tinsel
Body: Fine copper Mylar tinsel
Wing: Silver pheasant quills
Throat: Amherst tippet fibers

Skip Jack

Tied by: Richard Wager, Gloversville, NY
Hook: Nymph, #8-#16
Thread: Black
Tail: Red squirrel tail hairs
Rib: Black thread
Body: Orange UNI-Stretch Floss
Wing: Red squirrel tail hairs

Tan Crystal Caddis

Tied by: Elliott Gritton, Reno, NV
Hook: Mustad 3906, #10-#14
Thread: Tan 6/0
Rib: Root beer Krystal Flash strand, counterwrapped
Body: Natural Hare-Tron dubbing
Wing: Hen pheasant wing feather sections, 1 strand of root beer Krystal Flash per side
Hackle: Ginger hen

Vel-Crow Hilty

Tied by: Paul Smith, Manteca, CA
Hook: Dai-Riki 899, #6, weighted
Thread: Black
Tag: Gold oval tinsel, medium
Tail: Pearl Spectra Mylar Motion fibers
Body: Chartreuse chenille, 2 wraps, black Velcro loop strip 1/8-inch wide, wrapped
Wing: Light gray poly yarn fibers, pearl Spectra Mylar Motion fibers, sided by grizzly hen saddle feathers
Hackle: Grizzly saddle

Viceroy

Tied by: Jack Pangburn, Westbury, NY
Hook: Salmon or nymph
Thread: Black
Tail: Orange feather fibers
Rib: Gold oval tinsel
Body: Black floss
Throat: Orange feather fibers
Wing: 2 golden pheasant tippet feathers

Wager's Wet Fly

Tied by: Richard Wager, Gloversville, NY
Hook: Nymph, #10-#16
Thread: Black
Rib: Gold oval tinsel
Body: Arizona Peacock Dubbing
Wing: Peacock sword feather fibers
Hackle: Cree saddle

Wet Moose Head

Tied by: Don Joslyn, Eagle Point, OR
Hook: Dai Riki 270, #4
Thread: Black 6/0
Tails: Gold goose biots
Body: Olive-brown Hareline Krystal Dubbing
Hackle: Ring-necked pheasant
Wings: Ring-necked pheasant feathers
Head: Olive-brown Hareline Krystal Dubbing

Wide Eyed Fox

Tied by: Don Joslyn, Eagle Point, OR
Hook: Alec Jackson River Dee Low Water, #9
Thread: Black 6/0
Body: Medium brown Hareline Krystal Dubbing
Wing: Fire orange Krystal Flash strands, red fox tail hairs
Cheeks: Jungle cock eye feathers
Head: Peacock herl

CHAPTER 7

Damselflies and Dragonflies

Damselfly Nymphs

Anorexic Damsel Nymph

Tied by: Sam de Beer, Alberta, AB
Hook: Nymph or swimming nymph, #8-#14
Thread: Brown 6/0
Tail: Brown marabou feather fibers
Rib: Olive nylon
Shellback: Clear plastic strip
Body: Brown dubbing
Eyes: Black plastic

Beaded Damsel

Tied by: Bill Peters, Pine Top, AZ
Hook: TMC 200RBL, #10-#12
Thread: Black
Tail: White Antron yarn fibers
Abdomen: 10 small blue beads, (green beads may be used)
Wing Case: Pearl Flashabou, 3 strands
Thorax: Ostrich herl, 2 strands
Hackle: Black, top fibers trimmed
Eyes: Mono

Beady Damsel

Tied by: Jerry Jeffery, Long Beach, CA
Hook: Mustad 3906, #8
Thread: Olive
Tail: Olive Swiss straw, secured with abdomen mono core
Abdomen: Root beer glass beads, with mono core
Wing Case: Olive Swiss straw
Thorax: Olive marabou feather fibers
Head: Brass bead

B.H. Chenille Damsel

Tied by: Jack Pangburn, Westbury, NY
Hook: Mustad 79580, #8-#12
Thread: Black 6/0
Tail: Cree hackle fibers
Body: Tan and black variegated chenille
Hackle: Cree
Head: Brass bead

Black Eyed Booger

Tied by: Jerry Gardner, Lethbridge, AB
Hook: TMC 200R, #12-#16
Thread: Yellow
Tail: Olive marabou feather fibers
Body: Green Krystal Flash strands, wrapped
Wing: Green marabou feather fibers and green Krystal Flash strands
Head: Olive dubbing

Bou-Chen Damsel

Tied by: Jack Pangburn, Westbury, NY
Hook: Mustad 79580, #4
Thread: Tan 6/0
Tail: Rust marabou feather fibers, with a few strands of root beer Krystal Flash
Body: Rust and ochre variegated chenille
Hackle: Light brown
Eyes: Black plastic
Comments: Treat the fly with floatant and fish it on the surface, manipulating it to imitate a struggling nymph.

Coleman's Damsel Nymph

Tied by: Roland Coleman, Tracy, CA
Hook: Nymph, 3X long, #12
Thread: Tan
Tail: Golden-olive marabou feather fibers
Rib: Lime tinsel
Body: Golden-olive marabou feather fibers, wrapped
Wing Case: Golden-olive biots
Legs: Burnt orange Lure Flash
Eyes: Olive glass beads, with mono core painted black
Comments: Coat the eyes, wing case, and legs with epoxy.

Dalton's Damsel

Tied by: Brooke Dalton, Castlegar, BC
Hook: Mustad 79580, #10-#14
Thread: Olive
Tail: Grizzly feather marabou fibers
Rib: Fine gold tinsel
Body: Olive dubbing, thorax picked out
Wing Case/Head: Olive deer hair
Eyes: Olive vinyl ribbing, ends melted

Damsel Lite

Tied by: Ben Bying, Tracy, CA
Hook: Dai-Riki 270, #10
Thread: Olive
Rib: Chartreuse Flashabou
Tail/Body: Golden/olive marabou feather fibers
Wing Case: Pheasant tail feather fibers
Eyes: Mono
Legs: Tips from wing case fibers

Deadly Damsel

Tied by: Steven Dolley, Arlington, WA
Hook: Swimming nymph, #14
Thread: Olive
Tail: Golden-olive marabou feather fibers
Rib: Fine copper wire
Body: Light-olive New Dub
Wing Case: Grouse feather, cut to shape, coated with Flexament
Legs: Light-olive New Dub strands, bent to shape, ends melted
Eyes: Brown or gold glass beads, with mono core

Dewy Damsel Nymph

Tied by: Neil Dumont, Burnaby, BC
Hook: Mustad 3906, #10
Thread: Olive 6/0
Tail: Olive marabou feather fibers
Rib: Fine silver wire, counterwrapped
Body: Olive dubbing
Wing Case: Green mallard flank feather fibers
Legs: Tips from wing case
Eyes: Black plastic

Dole Side Weave Damsel

Tied by: Gordon Hsu Olson, Three Hills, AB
Hook: Swimming nymph hook, #8
Thread: Olive
Tail: Golden olive marabou feather fibers
Body: Blue and olive braid strands, woven with an overhand weave
Wing Case: Olive Swiss straw strip
Legs: Golden olive marabou feather, drawn feather style
Eyes: Gold bead chain

Doug's Olive Damsel

Tied by: Doug Narver, Nanaimo, BC
Hook: Mustad 9671, #10
Thread: Olive
Tail: Olive Antron yarn fibers
Rib: Copper wire, counterwrapped
Abdomen: Small green chenille
Thorax: Olive dubbing
Wing Case: Olive Swiss straw
Legs: Olive marabou feather fibers
Eyes: Black plastic

Eby's Damsel

Tied by: Gord Eby, Fort St. John, BC
Hook: Scud, #8
Thread: Black
Tail: Green Swiss straw, secured with mono core from abdomen
Abdomen: Green glass beads, extended over mono core
Thorax: Green dubbing
Wing Case: Green Swiss straw strip
Legs: Green pheasant tail feather fibers
Eyes: Black plastic

Electric Lady Damsel

Tied by: Bill Peters, Pine Top, AZ
Hook: TMC 200RBL, #10-#12
Thread: Black
Tail: Blue hackle fibers
Underbody: Royal blue Flashabou strands, wrapped
Abdomen: Blue or clear 8lb. mono, wrapped
Wing Case: Clear Scud Back strip, over 3 strands of pearl Flashabou
Thorax: Black ostrich herl, 2 strands
Hackle: Black, top fibers trimmed
Eyes: Mono

Floating Damsel Nymph

Tied by: Jerry Jeffery, Long Beach, CA
Hook: Mustad 3906, #8-#12
Thread: Olive
Tail: Olive marabou feather fibers mixed with white Antron yarn fibers
Underbody: Closed-cell foam strip, wrapped
Body: Olive dubbing
Hackle: Grouse

G.M. Damsel

Tied by: Greg Mayers, Fredricksberg, VA
Hook: Mustad 3906, #12, weighted
Thread: Brown
Tail/Abdomen: Stalcup's Damsel
Thorax: Brown marabou feather fibers, spun in dubbing loop and wrapped, followed with brown dubbing
Wing Case: Gold pheasant tail feather fibers, coated with Flexament
Hackle: Brown hen saddle hackle, top and bottom fibers trimmed
Eyes: Mono

Green Darner

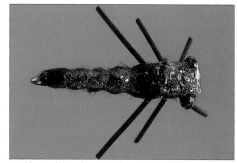

Tied by: Jack Pangburn, Westbury, NY
Hook: Mustad 79580, #8
Thread: Brown
Shellback: Brown foam, coated with head cement
Rib: Brown thread
Abdomen: Brown and black variegated chenille
Thorax: Peacock herl
Legs: Black round rubber
Eyes: Black plastic

Green Hornet

Tied by: Jerry Gardner, Lethbridge, AB
Hook: TMC 200R, #12-#16
Thread: Chartreuse
Tail: Chartreuse partridge feather fibers, green Krystal Flash strands
Body: Green glass beads
Wing: Olive Swiss straw
Head: Olive dubbing
Eyes: Black plastic

Grizzly Green Damsel

Tied by: Boyd Elder, Spiro, OK
Hook: Mustad 9672, #8-#12
Thread: Black
Tail: Black marabou feather fibers
Body: Green chenille
Wing Case: Turkey feather section, coated with Flexament
Hackle: Grizzly

Henry's Damsel Nymph

Tied by: Henry Hoffman, Warrenton, OR
Hook: Mustad 80150BR, swimming nymph hook, #6-#10, front 1/3 of hook shank weighted
Thread: Olive
Tail: Olive chickabou feather fibers
Rib: Fine gold wire, counterwrapped
Body: Olive chickabou plume, tied in by tips and wrapped
Wing Case: Olive knee hackle feather, colored with brown marker
Legs: Olive chickabou feather fibers
Eyes: Black plastic, colored with blue marker
Head: Olive beaver dubbing

Hosmer Damsel Nymph

Tied by: Wade Malwitz, Portland, OR
Hook: Mustad 3906, #12-#16
Thread: Olive
Tail: Olive marabou feather fibers
Abdomen: Green Vinyl rib, wrapped around 25lb. mono core
Thorax: Olive Antron dubbing
Wing Case: Olive Swiss straw strip, folded
Legs: Mallard flank feather fibers
Eyes: Mono

Iridescent Flashback Damsel Nymph

Tied by: Ronn Lucas, Sr., Milwaukie, OR
Hook: Daiichi 1270
Thread: Olive
Tail: Olive grizzly feather marabou fibers
Rib: Mono
Shellback: Thin Ice Flashback
Abdomen: Medium olive Iridescent Dubbing, trimmed short
Thorax: Dark olive Iridescent Dubbing
Legs: Olive grizzly feather fibers
Eyes: Iridescent blue glass beads, with mono core

Joe's Damselfly

Tied by: Joseph Bergel, Kitchener, ON
Hook: Nymph hook 1 XL, #8
Thread: Olive
Tails: Ostrich herl strands, trimmed to shape
Rib: Olive tubing, stretched
Body: Olive dubbing
Wing Case: Olive Thin Skin
Legs: Olive ostrich herl
Eyes: Mono

Knotted Olive Damsel

Tied by: Wayne Wallace, Victoria, BC
Hook: TMC 2457, #10
Thread: Olive
Abdomen: Olive Antron yarn, knotted, end tail fibers brushed out
Thorax: Olive Antron dubbing
Legs: Olive pheasant tail feather fibers
Wing Case: Pheasant tail feather fiber
Eyes: Black plastic

KR Damsel Nymph

Tied by: Ed Kraft, Lancaster, PA
Hook: Mustad 38941, #6, weighted with .035 lead wire strands lashed to the hook shank sides, tied hook point-up
Thread: Olive 6/0
Tail: Olive marabou feather fibers
Body: Olive chenille and 2 strands of peacock Krystal Flash, twisted and wrapped
Wing Case: Brown hen feather, coated with Flexament, cut to shape, and mounted on bottom of hook shank
Hackle: Olive
Eyes: Small lead eyes, covered with pearl salt water tinsel, and mounted on the top of the hook shank

Locatelli's Damsel Nymph

Tied by: Ron Locatelli, Castro Valley, CA
Hook: TMC 3761, #12
Thread: Tan
Tail: Gray marabou feather fibers
Abdomen: Tan Ultra Chenille, colored dark brown with waterproof marker
Thorax: Tan dubbing
Wing Case: Pheasant tail feather fibers
Eyes: Maxima Chameleon 30lb. mono, melted to shape
Legs: Tips from wing case

Marabou Damsel Nymph

Tied by: Jack Pangburn, Westbury, NY
Hook: Mustad 3906B, #10-#14
Thread: Olive 6/0
Tail: Stacked 4-6 brown, 6-8 olive and 6-8 brown marabou feather fibers
Abdomen: Tail fiber butt ends, wrapped
Wing Case: Peacock herl stands
Thorax: Tan dubbing
Legs: Brown craft fur

Millenium Damsel

Tied by: Mark Hoffart, Lethbridge, AB
Hook: TMC 5263, #12
Thread: Gray
Tail: Olive marabou feather fibers, green Krystal Flash strands
Abdomen: Green glass beads, extended on mono core
Thorax/Head: Olive dubbing
Wing Case: Olive duck feather section, cut to shape, coated with Flexament
Legs: Olive and gray marabou feather strands, and strands of green Krystal Flash, mixed
Eyes: Green glass beads with mono core, mono ends colored with black waterproof marker

MPT

Tied by: Jeff Lingenfelter, Browns Valley, CA
Hook: TMC 5262, #14
Thread: Olive 8/0
Tail: Olive marabou feather tips
Rib: Copper wire
Abdomen: Olive marabou feather from tail, wrapped
Wing Case/Head: Olive pheasant tail feather fibers
Thorax: Olive Antron dubbing
Legs: Tips from wing case
Eyes: Mono

Ostrich Damsel

Tied by: Jack Pangburn, Westbury, NY
Hook: Mustad 3906B, #8-#12, weighted
Thread: Black 6/0
Tail: 3 ostrich herl tips
Rib: Fine gold wire, counterwrapped
Body: Olive ostrich herl
Wing Case: Mottled turkey feather section, coated with head cement
Legs: Pheasant rump feather fibers
Eyes: Black plastic

P. T. Damsel

Tied by: Brad Cunningham, Yakima, WA
Hook: TMC 200R, #12, weighted
Thread: Black 8/0
Tail: Dyed green pheasant tail feather fibers
Rib: Fine copper wire
Abdomen: Dyed green pheasant tail feather fibers, wrapped
Wing Case: Dyed green pheasant tail feather fibers
Thorax: Dark olive dubbing
Legs: Pheasant tail feather section, over top of thorax
Eyes: Small gold beads, with mono core

Ralph Damselfly Nymph

Tied by: Ralph D'Errico, Jr., Tucson, AZ
Hook: TMC 947BL, #12
Thread: Yellow-green
Tail: Olive marabou and olive partridge feather fibers, topped with 3 blue-green pheasant rump feather fibers
Abdomen Underbody: Gold Antron dubbing
Abdomen: Stripped yellow peacock herl
Wing Case/Shellback: Hopper olive Stalcup Medallion strip
Thorax/Head: Gold Antron dubbing
Legs: Gold-olive grizzly feather fibers
Eyes: Olive Stalcup Damselfly Eyes, "drooped" downward
Antennae: Moose body hair

Roth's Damsel Nymph

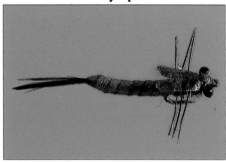

Tied by: Scott Roth, Newton, NJ
Hook: Scud
Thread: Brown
Tail: 2 brown hackle tips
Abdomen: Sheet foam strip, ironed flat, tied extended on a
   mono core, and colored with waterproof marker
Thorax: Brown dubbing
Wing Case: Packing foam, ironed flat, cut to shape, colored
   with waterproof marker
Legs: Emu feather fibers
Eyes: Black plastic

Rubber Damsel

Tied by: Curtis Kauer, Salina, KS
Hook: Scud hook, #6-#14
Thread: Olive
Tail: Olive marabou feather fibers
Abdomen: Olive round rubber leg material
Thorax: Olive dubbing
Eyes: Green plastic

Shaver's Jointed Damsel

Tied by: DuWayne Shaver, Capitan, NM
Abdomen Hook: Mustad 3399, #8-#12, weighted, cut off at
   bend after tying
Thorax Hook: Mustad 3399, #10-#14, mono loop joint
Thread: Brown
Tail: Brown marabou feather fibers
Abdomen: Brown vinyl ribbing
Thorax: Brown marabou feather fibers, followed by tan
   dubbing
Wing Case: Turkey feather sections, coated with Flexament
Legs: Brown feather stems, barbs trimmed short, bent to shape
Eyes: Mono

Spell's Wiggle Damsel

Tied by: Koshoni Spell, Provo, UT
Abdomen Hook: Mustad 3906, 12-16, cut off at bend
Thorax Hook: Daiichi 1560, #12-16, weighted, 6lb. mono
   loop connection
Thread: Olive
Tail: Olive marabou feather tips
Abdomen: Olive marabou feather from tail, wrapped
Thorax: Olive marabou feather, tied in with tips extended
   then wrapped
Wing/Head: Olive marabou feather tied in with tips
   extended then wrapped
Eyes: Gold chain eyes, small or extra small

Stan's Damsel Nymph

Tied by: Stan Gredes, Three Hills, AB
Hook: Scud hook, #12
Thread: Olive 8/0
Tail: Olive marabou feather fibers, threaded through
   abdomen tube
Abdomen: Olive Larva Lace
Wing Case: Olive Scud Skin
Thorax: Olive dubbing
Eyes: Mono

Stan's Swimming Damsel

Tied by: Stan Gredes, Three Hills, AB
Hook: Swimming nymph, #12, tied hook point-up
Thread: Olive 8/0
Tail: Olive marabou feather fibers
Rib: Copper wire
Shellback: Olive Scud Skin
Body: Olive dubbing
Wing Case: Olive Scud Skin
Legs: Pheasant feather tail fibers
Eyes: Black plastic

TP's Damsel Nymph

Tied by: Tim Andries, Three Hills, AB
Hook: TMC 400T, #10, tied hook point-up
Thread: Olive 8/0
Tail: Olive marabou feather fibers
Rib: Fine copper wire
Shellback: Plastic bag strip
Abdomen: Olive marabou feather fibers, counterwrapped
Wing Case: Plastic bag strip
Thorax: Olive Antron dubbing, picked out
Legs: Pheasant tail feather fibers
Eyes: Black plastic

U.S.D. Swimming Damsel

Tied by: Jack Pangburn, Westbury, NY
Hook: Mustad 94838, #10-#12, weight optional, tied hook
   point-up
Thread: Olive 6/0
Tail: Olive ostrich herl
Rib: Fine copper wire
Body: Olive poly yarn
Wing Case: Gray Swiss straw
Eyes: Black plastic
Legs: Olive hen hackle fibers
Head: Olive dubbing

Wiggle Damsel

Tied by: Jack Pangburn, Westbury, NY
Abdomen: Mustad 3906B, #10-#14
Thorax: Mustad 94840, #10-#14, mono loop connection,
   hook cut at bend after tying
Thread: Olive 6/0
Tail: Tan Swannundaze, 3 strands cut to length
Rib: Mono
Shellback: Brown Bugskin strip
Abdomen/Thorax: Olive dubbing
Wing Case: Brown Bugskin strip
Legs: Partridge feather fibers
Eyes: Black mono

Wiggle Damsel Nymph

Tied by: Steve Potter, Tracy, CA
Abdomen Hook: Eagle Claw L052, #10, cut off at bend after tying
Thorax Hook: Mustad 3256B, #12, 10lb. mono connection loop
Thread: Brown
Tail: 3 emu feather fibers
Abdomen: Pearsall's Marabou Silk twisted with fine silver wire, followed by olive Krystal Dub dubbing
Wing Case: Mottled turkey feather section
Thorax: Olive Krystal Dubbing
Legs: Gray partridge feather, drawn feather style

Wilson's Damselfly Nymph

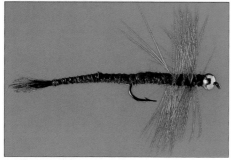

Tied by: Cary Wilson, Newcastle, NY
Hook: Streamer, #6-#8
Thread: Brown 6/0
Body: Green deer hair, extended
Hackle: Olive grizzly
Head: Gold bead

Damselfly Adults

BC Debris Emerging Damsel

Tied by: Wade Malwitz, Portland, OR
Hook: Mustad 94840, #10
Thread: Green 6/0
Tail/Abdomen: Olive marabou feather over-wrapped with green V-Rib, extended over a 20lb. mono core
Legs: Pheasant rump feather fibers
Wing Case: Olive Swiss straw, folded
Thorax/Head: Olive dubbing
Debris: Wood twig

Blue Damsel Adult

Tied by: Jack Pangburn, Westbury, NY
Hook: Mustad 94840, #10-#14
Thread: Black 6/0
Abdomen: Heavy mono, colored with blue and black permanent markers
Thorax: Peacock dubbing
Wing: White Antron yarn fibers
Legs: Silver badger hackle, top fibers trimmed
Eyes: Black plastic

Bright Eyes

Tied by: Henry Hoffman, Warrenton, OR
Hook: Mustad 80000BR, #12
Thread: Blue
Abdomen: Braided mono, colored with blue and black waterproof markers
Thorax: Light blue dubbing
Wings: Light blue grizzly hackle, top and bottom trimmed
Thorax Topping: Metallic blue ribbon floss
Eyes: Black plastic, colored with blue marker

Coleman's Damsel Adult

Tied by: Roland Coleman, Tracy, CA
Hook: Dry fly hook, #12
Thread: Gray
Abdomen: Braided mono, colored blue and black with waterproof markers
Rib: Fine black tinsel
Thorax: Blue dubbing
Shellback: Blue poly yarn fibers
Wings: Clear Wing Film, cut to shape
Eyes: Small black plastic
Legs: Plastic broom fibers, bent to shape

Currie Damsel

Tied by: Chris Currie, Bonners Ferry, ID
Hook: Mustad 94840, #12
Thread: Black 8/0
Abdomen: Blue foam strip, colored with black waterproof marker
Thorax/Head: Blue dubbing
Wings: Black hackle tips
Hackle: Light dun
Eyes: Black plastic

Dew Damsel Adult

Tied by: Neil Dumont, Burnaby, BC
Hook: TMC 109BL, #12
Thread: Black 6/0
Abdomen: Blue grizzly feather
Thorax: Blue dubbing
Wings: Dark dun feathers
Legs: Peacock herl strands, trimmed short
Hackle: Grizzly
Eyes: Black plastic

Doug's Adult Damsel

Tied by: Doug Narver, Nanaimo, BC
Hook: Mustad 3906B, #10
Thread: Black
Tail: Blue bucktail hair, with 30lb. mono core
Rib: Black thread
Body: Blue dubbing
Wings: Mottled light blue dun Wing Film, cut to shape
Eyes: Dark deer hair

Drown'd Zel

Tied by: James Vatter, Latrobe, PA
Hook: Mustad 9672, #14
Thread: Blue 6/0
Extended Body: Blue Antron yarn and black UNI-Stretch Floss strands, twisted and furled
Body: Blue Antron dubbing
Wings: Cream hen saddle feathers
Hackle: Grizzly, top fibers trimmed
Head: Black metal bead

Dun Wing Bluet

Tied by: Jack Pangburn, Westbury, NY
Hook: Mustad 94840, #10-#12
Thread: Black 6/0
Abdomen: Braided mono, furled, colored with waterproof blue and black markers and coated with Soft Body
Wings: Dun hen saddle feathers, spotted with waterproof marker
Eyes: Black plastic
Head: Peacock herl
Hackle: Dun

Extended Body Damsel

Tied by: Wade Malwitz, Portland, OR
Hook: Mustad 80000BR, #10-#14
Thread: Olive
Tail: Olive saddle feather fibers
Abdomen: Olive Antron dubbing, extended over 25lb. mono core
Wings: Paint brush fibers, delta style
Post: Fluorescent chartreuse Flashabou strands
Thorax: Olive Antron dubbing
Hackle: Grizzly, parachute style
Head: Mono

Iridescent Damsel Adult

Tied by: Ronn Lucas, Sr., Milwaukie, OR
Hook: Mustad 94720, #8
Thread: Brown
Tail: Elk mane hair
Body: Blue Iridescent Dubbing
Hackle: Dun saddle, trim to fibers
Wings: Elk mane hairs
Eyes: Blue Iridescent glass beads, with mono core
Antennae: Dun hackle fibers

Joe's Parachute Damsel

Tied by: Joseph Bergel, Kitchener, ON
Hook: Dry fly hook, #14
Thread: Black
Abdomen: Olive micro chenille, end melted to a taper
Thorax: Olive dubbing
Wing Post: White Antron, top colored with green waterproof marker
Hackle: Cree

KR Blue Damsel

Tied by: Ed Kraft, Lancaster, PA
Hook: Mustad 94840, #8
Thread: Blue 6/0
Abdomen: Blue poly yarn, with strands of light and dark blue Krystal Flash, furled together
Shellback: Light blue foam
Thorax: Blue Krystal Flash strands, wrapped
Wings: Blue squirrel tail hairs
Eyes: Black plastic

KR Dark Blue Damsel

Tied by: Ed Kraft, Lancaster, PA
Hook: Mustad 94840, #8
Thread: Blue 6/0
Abdomen: Dark blue tinsel strands, furled
Shellback: Dark blue foam
Thorax: Blue glitter mixed with Zap-a-Gap
Wings: Blue squirrel tail hairs
Eyes: Black plastic

Krystal Damsel

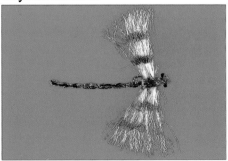

Tied by: Jeff Lingenfelter, Browns Valley, CA
Hook: TMC 2487, #14
Thread: Olive 8/0
Abdomen: 6-8 strands of root beer Krystal Flash and 2 strands of black Krystal Flash, furled
Shellback: Tag ends of abdomen material
Thorax: Tan Antron dubbing
Wings: White Antron yarn, spotted with black waterproof marker
Eyes: Mono

Nadeer's Damsel

Tied by: Nadeer Youssef, Pullman, WA
Hook: TMC 2487, #14
Thread: Black 3/0
Rib: Black thread
Abdomen: Blue bucktail hair
Thorax: Light blue dubbing
Wings: Deer hair
Eyes: Mono

Pete's Reel Dragonfly

Tied by: Pete Toscani, Bristol, CT
Hook: Orvis 1524, #10
Thread: Chartreuse
Rib: Chartreuse thread
Body: Chartreuse bucktail hair
Wings: Black feathers
Legs: Copper wire, bent to shape, painted black
Eyes: Black plastic bead chain

Roth's Damsel Adult

Tied by: Scott Roth, Newton, NJ
Hook: Scud
Thread: Olive
Tail: Blue biot
Abdomen: Sheet foam strip, ironed flat, tied extended over a mono core, colored with waterproof marker
Wings: Air duct filter strips, ironed flat, cut to shape, colored with waterproof marker
Thorax: Ostrich herl, topped with ironed flat packing foam, colored with waterproof marker
Legs: Emu father, drawn feather style
Eyes: Orange glass beads, with mono core

RP's I'll-Be-Dam-sel

Tied by: Roy Powell, Danville, CA
Hook: TMC 2487, #14
Thread: Blue
Abdomen: Hareline blue Adult Damsel Body
Thorax/Eyes: Blue packing foam strip, pulled forward over bottom of hook shank and folded back to form eye, color with blue waterproof marker
Wings: Grizzly feathers
Hackle Post: Flexi Floss strand
Hackle: Blue grizzly, folded-post parachute style

Shaver's Damsel

Tied by: DuWayne Shaver, Capitan, NM
Hook: Mustad 94840, #10-#14
Thread: Black
Underbody: 10lb. mono core, with 1/8-inch foam strip wrapped over it
Body: Light and dark blue strands of embroidery floss, woven with an overhand weave
Wings/Post: Antron yarn
Hackle: Brown, parachute style

Dragonfly Nymphs

Abbies Crooked Dragon

Tied by: Wade Malwitz, Portland, OR
Hook: Mustad 3906, #6-#12, weighted
Thread: Brown
Tail: Olive feather fibers
Rib: Small oval silver tinsel
Body: Brown dubbing
Wing Case: Brown Swiss straw
Legs: Mallard flank feather fibers
Eyes: Black glass beads, with mono core

Bead-Chain Dragon

Tied by: Chuck Rondeau, Port Angeles, WA
Hook: Dai-Riki 060, #8
Thread: Black
Tail: Barred turkey feather fibers
Rib: 17lb. mono
Abdomen: Hairline olive STS Trilobal dubbing
Legs: Barred turkey feather fibers
Thorax: Hairline peacock Ice Dubbing
Eyes: Black bead chain

Big Eyed Dragon Nymph

Tied by: Sam de Beer, Calgary, AB
Hook: Nymph or swimming nymph hook, #4-#12
Thread: Brown 6/0
Tail: Brown marabou feather fibers
Rib: Copper wire, counterwrapped
Body: Brown dubbing
Wing Case: Molted turkey feather section, cut to shape
Legs: Hen feather fibers
Eyes: Black plastic

Cone Head Dragon

Tied by: Boyd Elder, Spiro, OK
Hook: Mustad 9672, #6-#10
Thread: Black
Tail: Black marabou feather fibers
Body: Black chenille
Wing Case: Turkey feather section, coated with Flexament
Hackle: Black
Head: Brass cone

Chickabou Dragon Nymph

Tied by: Henry Hoffman, Warrenton, OR
Hook: Daiichi 2340, #6
Thread: Olive
Tail: Olive/tan chickabou feather fibers
Body: Alternating olive and light brown chickabou feathers, wrapped and trimmed to shape, flat on the bottom and oval on the top
Wing Case: Barred tan hen feather, trimmed to shape, coated with Flexament
Legs: Barred tan hen feather fibers
Eyes: Black mono
Head: Olive chickabou plumes, wrapped and trimmed to shape

Craft Fur Dragon

Tied by: Jack Pangburn, Westbury, NY
Hook: Mustad 79580, #2-#8, weighted
Thread: Brown 6/0
Body: Dark brown craft fur
Hackle: Pheasant rump feather

Dalton's Dragon

Tied by: Brooke Dalton, Castlegar, BC
Hook: TMC 300, #6-#10
Thread: Black
Tail/Underbody: Olive deer hair
Rib: Green vinyl ribbing
Abdomen Underbody: Light olive dubbing
Abdomen: Sparkle Peacock Chenille
Wing Case: Olive Thin Skin strip
Legs: Brown rubber, colored with black marker
Thorax: Peacock herl
Eyes: Round foam

Dave's Dragon

Tied by: Dave McCants, Pheasant Hill, CA
Hook: Nymph 2Xl, #4
Thread: Black 6/0
Tail: Pheasant tail feather fibers
Body: Variegated peacock Flash Chenille
Wing Case: Pheasant tail feather fibers, butt ends from tail
Legs: Pheasant tail feather fibers
Eyes: Black plastic

Dragon Bugger

Tied by: Jack Pangburn, Westbury, NY
Hook: Mustad 3906B, #6-#10, weighted
Thread: Olive 6/0
Body: Brown craft fur
Wing Case: Peacock herl
Eyes: Black mono
Head: Dubbed craft fur, trimmed to shape

Dragonfly Naiad

Tied by: Floyd Franke, Roscoe, NY
Hook: Mustad 94833, #10
Thread: Black 8/0
Rib: Brown thread
Abdomen: Black foam, folded and cut to shape, extended
Thorax Shellback: Black foam, end from top of abdomen
Thorax: Dark brown dubbing
Legs: Pheasant tail feather fibers, knotted
Eyes: Black bead chain

Emu Dragonfly Nymph

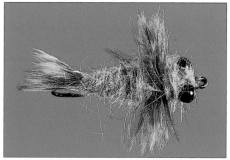

Tied by: Brad Bireley, Galeton, PA
Hook: Partridge H 3 ST, #10
Thread: Olive 6/0
Tail: Olive grizzly feather marabou fibers
Body: Olive #91 Dave Whitlock Plus SLF dubbing
Legs: Olive emu feather fibers
Eyes: Black bead chain

Felt Dragon

Tied by: Curtis Kauer, Salina, KS
Hook: Scud hook, #6-#10
Thread: Black
Body: Olive and dark brown felt cut to shape and sewn together, stuffed with small scraps of felt
Legs: Brown marabou feather fibers
Eyes: Black bead chain, coated between eyes with epoxy

Generic Dragon Nymph

Tied by: Tim Andries, Three Hills, AB
Hook: TMC 5263, #6, weighted
Thread: Olive 6/0
Underbody: Green yarn
Rib: Medium copper wire
Shellback: Olive Swiss straw, colored with brown water proof marker
Body: Olive Antron dubbing
Wing Case/Head: Olive Swiss straw, colored with brown waterproof marker
Legs: Pheasant tail feather fibers
Eyes: Gunmetal glass beads, with mono core

Glass Bead Dragon

Tied by: Carl Ritter, Sedona, AZ
Hook: Dai-Riki 710, #10
Thread: Olive 8/0
Tail/Shellback: Pheasant tail feather fibers
Body: Green glass beads
Legs: Brown horsetail hair, knotted
Antennae: Butt ends from legs
Eyes: Dark brown plastic bead chain
Comments: Spot legs and antennae with black marker.

Just Molted Dragon

Tied by: Gord Eby, Fort St. John, BC
Hook: Mustad 3906B, #6
Thread: Black
Tail: Pheasant tail feather fibers
Underbody: Foam strip, wrapped
Rib: Copper wire, counterwrapped
Body: Pale green chenille
Wing Case: Green pheasant tail feather fibers, trimmed to shape
Legs: Green pheasant tail feather fibers
Eyes: Black plastic

Lake Dragon

Tied by: Stan Gredes, Three Hills, AB
Hook: Steamer, #8
Thread: Olive
Shellback: Olive Swiss straw
Rib: Copper wire
Body: Olive dubbing
Wing Case: Olive Swiss straw
Legs: Pheasant tail feather fibers
Eyes: Black plastic

Midnight Dragon

Tied by: Boyd Elder, Spiro, OK
Hook: Mustad 9672, #6, weighted
Thread: Black
Tails: Brown goose biots
Abdomen: Black Holographic Flashabou strands, twisted into 2 cords and woven with an overhand weave
Wing Case: Turkey tail feather section, coated with Flexament
Thorax: Peacock herl
Hackle: Black

Montana Dragonfly

Tied by: Jack Pangburn, Westbury, NY
Hook: Mustad 70580, #8-#12, weighted
Thread: Black 6/0
Tail: Black feather fibers
Abdomen: Black chenille
Thorax: Green chenille
Wing Case: Black chenille
Hackle: Black
Head: Red head cement

Mosquito Hawk

Tied by: Jack Pangburn, Westbury, NY
Hook: Mustad 79580, #8, weighted
Thread: Black 6/0
Tails: Brown goose biots
Rib: Fluorescent green silk
Body: Brown and green dubbing, mixed
Hackle: Brown partridge
Head: Peacock herl

Pearl Eyed Dragon

Tied by: J. M. Jackson, Salt Spring Island, BC
Hook: 4X long, #2-#8
Thread: Black 6/0
Tail: Olive marabou feather fibers
Rib: Copper wire
Body: Green and black chenille, woven using moss back method
Wing Case: Black Swiss straw
Hackle: Olive
Eyes: Plastic pearl necklace, 2 beads melted into barrel shape

Red-Phire Dragon

Tied by: Joseph Bergel, Kitchener, ON
Hook: Nymph, #10
Thread: Black 8/0
Tail: Red bucktail hair
Rib: Red wire, counterwrapped
Shellback: Green Crinkle Flash
Body: Brown/olive chenille
Legs: Red bucktail hair and red dubbing
Eyes: Silver bead chain

Roth's Dragon Nymph

Tied by: Scott Roth, Newton, NJ
Hook: Scud
Thread: Olive
Tails: Olive biots
Abdomen: Packing foam, ironed flat, tied extended on mono core, and colored with waterproof marker
Thorax: Green dubbing
Wing Case: Packing foam strip, ironed flat, cut to shape and colored with waterproof marker
Legs: Emu feather fibers
Eyes: Myuki Drops
Antennae: Brown biots

RP's Dragon Nymph

Tied by: Roy Powell, Danville, CA
Hook: TMC 3761, #6-#10
Thread: Olive 8/0
Tail: Olive wood duck flank feather fibers
Abdomen: Olive partridge filoplume feather, wrapped
Legs: Olive marabou feathers fibers
Wing Case: Mallard flank feather cut to shape and coated with Flexament
Eyes: Black mono
Thorax/Head: Peacock herl

Schneider's Dragon Nymph

Tied by: Alan Schneider, Penticton, BC
Hook: TMC 300, #6-#10, weighted
Thread: Black 6/0
Tails: Olive biots
Rib: Blue/green thread
Abdomen: Olive/brown dubbing
Legs: Pheasant tail feather fibers
Thorax/Head: Peacock herl
Eyes: Mono

Shaver's Jointed Dragon

Tied by: DuWayne Shaver, Capitan, NM
Abdomen Hook: Mustad 3399, #6-#10, cut at bend after tying
Thorax Hook: Mustad 3399, #10-#14, mono loop joint
Thread: Olive
Tail: Olive marabou feather fibers
Abdomen Underbody: Lead wire, flattened
Abdomen: Olive vinyl ribbing
Thorax: Olive marabou, followed by olive dubbing
Wing Case: Olive turkey feather sections, coated with Flexament
Legs: Olive feather stems, barbs trimmed short, bent to shape
Eyes: Mono

Stan's Dragon Nymph

Tied by: Stan Gredes, Three Hills, AB
Hook: Streamer, #8
Thread: Olive 6/0
Rib: Copper wire
Shellback: Brown Scud Skin
Body: Olive dubbing
Wing Case: Brown Scud Skin
Legs: Pheasant tail feather fibers
Eyes: Black plastic

Stringer's Dragon

Tied by: Clifford Stringer, Nampa, ID
Hook: Mustad 9672, #8
Thread: Black
Tail: Grouse feathers fibers
Body: Dark olive chenille
Legs: Pheasant tail feather fibers
Eyes: Black bead chain
Head: Black ostrich herl

Swimming Dragon Nymph

Tied by: Roland Coleman, Tracy, CA
Hook: Dry salmon fly hook, #6, weighted
Thread: Black
Rib: Brown Swannundaze
Body: Mixed olive, black, and brown dubbing
Wing Case: Turkey tail feather section, cut to shape, coated with Flexament
Legs: Golden pheasant tail feather fiber
Eyes: Black plastic

T.S. Olive Dragon

Tied by: Wayne Wallace, Victoria, BC
Hook: TMC 200R, #6-#10, tie hook point-up
Thread: Olive
Tails: Olive goose biots
Shellback: Mottled olive Thin Skin
Rib: Olive Arizona Crystal Possum dubbing, dubbed tight on thread
Body: Olive Arizona Crystal Possum dubbing
Wing Case: Olive pheasant rump feather, coated with Flexament
Legs: Spanflex stands, colored yellow/brown with waterproof markers, knotted
Eyes: Lead barbell, colored black with marker, mounted on top of hook shank

Ultimate Dragon

Tied by: Brad Cunningham, Yakima, WA
Hook: Alec Jackson Spey, #7
Thread: Olive 8/0
Rib: Fine copper wire, counterwrapped
Shellback: Turkey feather section, coated with Flexament
Body: Dark olive-brown dubbing
Wing Case: Turkey feather sections, cut to shape, coated with Flexament
Legs: Pheasant tail feather fibers
Eyes: Black medium bead chain

Dragonfly Adults

Woolly Dragon

Tied by: Jeff Lingenfelter, Browns Valley, CA
Hook: TMC 5263, #8-#10
Thread: Olive 8/0
Tails: Olive goose biots
Abdomen: Dark olive wool, stacked, clipped to shape
Wing Case: Turkey tail feather section, coated with Flexament, trimmed to shape
Thorax/Head: Olive-brown Antron dubbing
Legs: Olive marabou feather fibers, trimmed short
Eyes: Mono

Woven Dragon

Tied by: Stan Gredes, Three Hills, AB
Hook: Streamer, #8
Thread: Olive 6/0
Abdomen: Olive and black chenille strands, woven with an overhand weave
Legs: Black hen feather fibers
Thorax: Olive dubbing
Eyes: Black plastic

Blue Dragonfly

Tied by: Louis Stolarchuk, Vancouver, BC
Hook: Mustad 94840, #6
Thread: Black 6/0
Rib: Black thread
Abdomen: Blue floss, extended over toothpick core
Thorax: Blue floss, over black dubbing
Wings: Medium dun Umpqua Medallion Sheeting, cut to shape
Eyes: Black Styrofoam, epoxy to hook
Comments: Coat body with epoxy.

Colby's Flash Dragon

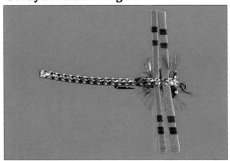

Tied by: Colby Sorrells, Mansfield, TX
Hook: Mustad 3366, #2-#8
Thread: Olive
Abdomen/Overbody: Nylon Metallic cord, (Mylar or waxed shoelace), cement ends
Thorax: Blue chenille
Wing: 2mm Blue foam strippers, colored with black water proof marker
Hackle: Grizzly
Eyes: Plastic bead chain

Coleman's Adult Dragon

Tied by: Roland Coleman, Tracy, CA
Hook: Dry salmon fly hook, #6
Thread: Gray
Rib: Black tinsel
Body: Blue foam strip, folded foam extension style
Wings: Tan Wing Film, cut to shape
Legs: Plastic broom fibers, bent to shape
Head: Blue dubbing
Eyes: Glass eyes

Dam Dragon

Tied by: Dave McCants, Pheasant Hill, CA
Hook: TMC 2487, #10
Thread: Blue
Body: Blue packing foam, trimmed to shape, colored with black waterproof marker
Wings: Large jungle cock nails
Post/Head: Foam from body folded back
Hackle: Badger
Eyes: Black plastic

Generic Dragonfly

Tied by: Doyle Bartsch, Mayville, WI
Hook: TMC 2488, #12
Thread: Black 6/0
Abdomen: Olive buck tail, extended, thread wraps coated with Flexament
Wings: White Z-lon fibers and pearl Krystal Flash strands, mixed
Thorax: Olive dubbing
Hackle: Olive

Little Dragon

Tied by: Jesse Goodwin, Auburn, ME
Hook: Streamer hook, #6
Thread: Black
Tail: Strips from blue and black goose shoulder feathers, married
Body: Electric blue SLF dubbing
Wings: Plastic bag strips, cut to shape, scratched with needle, colored with black marker
Head: Black-claret SLF dubbing

Little Red Dragon

Tied by: Thomas Peterson, Aberdeen, MD
Hook: Mustad 94840, #12-#14
Thread: Black
Abdomen: Red Micro Chenille strand, furled
Thorax: Peacock herl
Wings: Clear wrapping ribbons, cut to shape
Hackle: Grizzly
Eyes: Mono

Quill Dragon

Tied by: Ronn Lucas, Sr., Milwaukie, OR
Hook: Mustad 9575, #8
Thread: Black
Abdomen: Large feather quill, split and CA glued to hook shank, secured with thread at front, rear, and middle, coat with head cement
Wings: Elk mane hairs, colored with black marker
Thorax: Brown dubbing
Eyes: Brown glass beads, with mono core

Red Dragon Fly

Tied by: Henry Hoffman, Warrenton, OR
Hook: Daiichi 1280, #12
Thread: Red thread
Body: Red foam, extended, wrapped, colored with black marker
Wings: Grizzly feathers
Hackle: Badger

Rusty Dragonfly

Tied by: Joseph Bergel, Kitchener, ON
Hook: Scud, #12
Thread: Black
Rib: Black thread
Body: Deer hair
Post: White Antron yarn fibers
Hackle: Brown, bottom fibers trimmed

Schneider's Dragonfly

Tied by: Alan Schneider, Penticton, BC
Hook: Mustad 94845, #12
Thread: Black
Abdomen: Green yarn and strand of green Krystal Flash, furled, extended
Wings: Mylar sheet, cut to shape
Thorax: Green yarn
Legs: Pheasant tail feather fibers
Eyes: Mono

Spotted Dragon

Tied by: Jack Pangburn, Westbury, NY
Hook: Mustad 94840, #10
Thread: Black 6/0
Abdomen: Peacock eyed feather, trimmed to shape
Thorax: Olive dubbing
Wings: Fabric interfacing material, cut to shape, colored with waterproof markers
Eyes: Black plastic

Squirrel Winged KR Dragon

Tied by: Ed Kraft, Lancaster, PA
Hook: Mustad 94840, #8
Thread: Fluorescent orange 6/0
Abdomen: Orange poly yarn and 1 strand of copper Krystal Flash, furled
Thorax Shellback: Orange foam
Thorax: Copper Krystal Flash strands, wrapped
Wings: Orange squirrel tail hairs
Eyes: Black plastic

Swiss Straw Winged Dragon

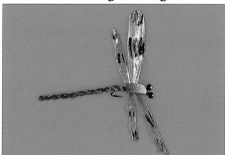

Tied by: Ed Kraft, Lancaster, PA
Hook: Mustad 94840 #8
Thread: Fluorescent orange 6/0
Abdomen: Orange poly yarn and copper Krystal Flash strand, furled
Thorax Shellback: Orange foam
Thorax: Copper Krystal Flash strands, wrapped
Wings: Orange Swiss straw, cut to shape, spotted with black waterproof marker
Eyes: Black plastic

Wet Dragon

Tied by: R. Waller, Bay Shore, NY
Hook: Mustad 9672, #8
Thread: Black
Tail: Pheasant tail feather tip
Body: Green Ice Chenille
Wings: Tan wing material, cut to shape
Eyes: Yellow/black plastic
Head: Black dubbing

CHAPTER 8

Scuds, Sow Bugs, Freshwater Shrimp, Snails, Water Boatmen

Scuds

Big Horn Scud

Tied by: Mike Giavedoni, Maple, ON
Hook: Scud, #12-#18
Thread: Orange
Tail/Antennae: Red squirrel tail hair
Shellback: Orange Scud Back
Rib: 12lb. mono
Body: Olive dubbing, bottom fibers picked out

Buggin

Tied by: Boyd Elder, Spiro, OK
Hook: TMC 2457, #14
Thread: Orange 6/0
Body: Burnt orange squirrel dubbing, mixed with 6-8 strands of root beer and pearl Krystal Flash, furled into 2 cords, and woven with an overhand weave. Dubbing trimmed from top and sides.

Caught in the Act

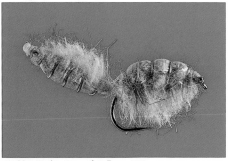

Tied by: Nadeer Youssef, Pullman, WA
   Male
Rear Hook: None, fly is tied on mono, ends melted
Thread: Olive 8/0
Rib: Brass wire
Shellback: Clear plastic
Body: Light olive rabbit dubbing, picked out
Eyes: Black mono
   Female
Hook: Daiichi 1130, #12
Thread: Olive 8/0
Rib: Brass wire
Shellback: Clear plastic
Body: Light olive rabbit and orange Antron dubbing mixed, picked out
Eyes: Black mono
Comments: Flatten bodies with non-serrated pliers.

Bionic Scud

Tied by: Jay Kaneshige, Castro Valley, CA
Hook: TMC 200R, #14-#18
Thread: Olive
Rib: Copper wire
Shellback: Pearl Sophisti-Shred strip, found in craft stores
Body: Green caddis Hare-Tron dubbing
Head: Brass bead

Caliente Scud

Tied by: Jeff Lingenfelter, Browns Valley, CA
Hook: TMC 2457, #10-#18
Thread: Tan 8/0
Tail/Antennae: Wood duck flank feather fibers
Rib: 5X tippet
Shellback: Tan 1/8-inch Scud Back
Body: Tan Scintilla Caliente Dubbing, bottom fibers picked out
Throat: Wood duck flank feather fibers

C&F Scud

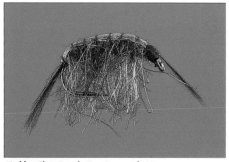

Tied by: Chris French, East Brunswick, NJ
Hook: Mustad #14-#18
Thread: Red
Tail/Feelers: Red hackle fibers
Rib: Red wire
Shellbacks: Clear Scud Back
Back: Fire-red and yellow SLF dubbing mixed, bottom fibers picked out

Deschutes Blue

Tied by: John Jones, Lyons, OR
Hook: Mustad 3906B, #12, weight optional
Thread: Dark blue
Shellback: Clear plastic strip
Rib: Green wire
Body: Light blue hare's mask and Crystal Seal King Fisher Blue dubbing mixed 50/50, bottom fibers picked out

Emu Scud

Tied by: Don Joslyn, Eagle Point, OR
Hook: Mustad 37160, #6
Thread: Black 3/0
Tail: Pheasant tail feather fibers
Rib: Fine copper wire
Shellback: Pheasant tail feather fibers
Body: Black and gold New Age Chenille
Hackle: Emu, top fibers trimmed
Head: Peacock herl
Feelers: Tips from shellback

Epoxy Scud

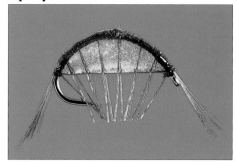

Tied by: Vladimir Markov, Irkutsk, Russia
Hook: Scud, #14-#16
Thread: Brown 8/0
Tail/Antennae: Brown hackle fibers
Legs: Brown thread
Body: Epoxy, mixed with finely chopped yellow Antron yarn fibers

Fly-Rite Scud

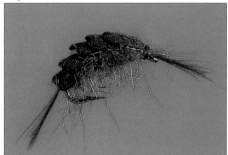

Tied by: Vladimir Markov, Irkutsk, Russia
Hook: Scud, #12-#14
Thread: Brown 8/0
Tail/Antennae: Red hackle fibers
Underbody: Brown and orange squirrel dubbing, picked out
Shellback: Brown Poly II sheeting, burned to shape

Frazzle-N-Dazzle Scud

Tied by: Boyd Elder, Spire, OK
Hook: TMC 2457, #14
Thread: Dark green, 6/0
Shellback/Body: Pearl Krystal Flash, formed into 2 cords, each cord formed from 5 strands that are furled, overhand weave used to form the shellback. Hare's Ear dubbing added to the underside of the weave knot. Dubbing trimmed from top and sides.
Head: Black glass bead

Fred's Scud

Tied by: Fred Iacoletti, Albuquerque, NM
Hook: TMC 205BL, #18, weighted
Thread: Olive 8/0
Antennae: Mallard flank feather fibers
Rib: Fine copper wire, counter wrapped
Shellback: Gray 1/4 inch Scud Back
Body: Olive Estaz chenille

Glass Bead Scud

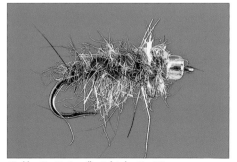

Tied by: Tim McConville, Salt Lake City, UT
Hook: TMC 200R, #16, weighted
Thread: Gray 6/0
Rib: Tan V-Rib
Body: Hare's Ear dubbing
Head: Pearl glass bead

Gold Back Olive Scud

Tied by: Don Joslyn, Eagle Point, OR
Hook: Dai-Riki 135, #8, weighted
Thread: Black 6/0
Rib: Fine copper wire
Shellback: Gold Flashabou strands
Body: Olive Antron dubbing, bottom fibers picked out
Head: Peacock herl

Green Back Brown CDC Scud

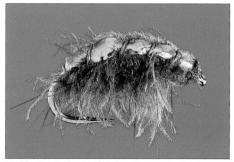

Tied by: Don Joslyn, Eagle Point, OR
Hook: Dai-Riki 135, #6, weighted
Thread: Black 3/0
Rib: Fine copper wire
Shellback: Green Mylar craft tape stripe
Body: Brown CDC dubbing

Green KF Back Emu Scud

Tied by: Don Joslyn, Eagle Point, OR
Hook: TMC 205BL, #8
Thread: Black 3/0
Tail: Pheasant tail feather fibers
Rib: Fine copper wire
Shellback: Green Krystal Flash strands
Body: Olive Antron dubbing, bottom fibers picked out
Hackle: Emu

Jerry's Scud

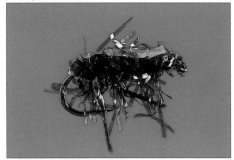

Tied by: Jerry Jeffery, Long Beach, CA
Hook: Mustad 94845, #12-#16, weighted
Thread: Orange
Rib: Mono
Shellback: Pearl Flashabou strand
Body: Rust Crystal Chenille

K.L. Scud

Tied by: Kip Lowric, Okemos, MI
Hook: Mustad 80200BR, #6-#8, weighted
Thread: White
Shellback: Plastic strip
Rib: Fine gold wire
Body: Gray dubbing
Hackle: Emu

Lee's Ferry Scud

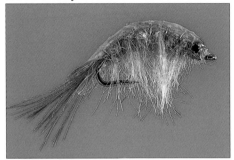

Tied by: Carl Ritter, Sedona, AZ
Hook: Scud, #18
Thread: Orange 8/0
Tail: Orange feather fibers
Rib: Fine gold wire
Shellback: Orange Scud Back, coated with epoxy
Body: Orange Antron dubbing, bottom fibers picked out
Eyes: Black mono

Mustard Pearl Back Scud

Tied by: Don Joslyn, Eagle Point, OR
Hook: Dai-Riki 135, #8, weighted
Thread: Black 6/0
Rib: Fine copper wire
Shellback: Pearl Flashabou strands
Body: Orange/yellow Antron dubbing, bottom fibers picked out
Hackle: Black, fibers trimmed on the top and sides
Feelers: Tag ends from shellback

Nickel Bead Ostrich Scud

Tied by: Tim McConville, Salt Lake City, UT
Hook: TMC 200R, #16
Thread: Gray 8/0
Tail: Mallard flank feather fibers
Shellback: Black ostrich herl
Body: Rust dubbing
Head: Ostrich herl, nickel bead

Nickel Bead Scud

Tied by: Tim McConville, Salt Lake City, UT
Hook: TMC 200R, #16
Thread: Gray 6/0
Shellback: Dark dun Antron yarn fibers
Body: Amber Hare's Ear dubbing
Feelers: Mallard flank feather fibers
Head: Nickel bead

OHBGO Scud-Gold

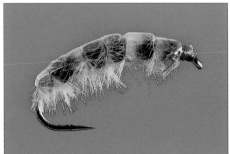

Tied by: Dave McCants, Pleasant Hill, CA
Hook: TMC 5263, #12
Thread: Tan 8/0
Rib: Mono, counter wrapped
Shellback: Clear plastic
Body: Olive/white Heche beads
Legs: Gold ostrich herl, wrapped between beads

OHBOO Scud-White

Tied by: Dave McCants, Pleasant Hill, CA
Hook: TMC 5263, #12
Thread: Olive 6/0
Rib: Mono, counter wrapped
Shellback: Clear plastic
Body: Olive/white Heche beads
Legs: Light olive ostrich herl, wrapped between beads

Ollie Scud

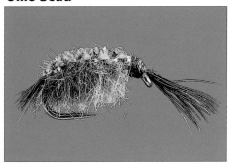

Tied by: Boyd Elder, Spiro, OK
Hook: TMC 2457, #14
Thread: Olive 6/0
Tail/Antennae: Pheasant back feather fibers
Body: Olive squirrel dubbing, mixed with 6-8 strands of olive and pearl Krystal Flash, furled into 2 cords, and woven with an overhand weave. Trim dubbing from top and sides.

Orange CDC Flash Back Scud

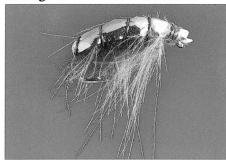

Tied by: Don Joslyn, Eagle Point, OR
Hook: Dai-Riki 135, #6, weighted
Thread: Clear mono
Rib: Copper wire
Shellback: Pearl Mylar craft tape strip
Body: Orange Antron dubbing
Hackle: White CDC
Head: Butt end from shellback

Orange Scud

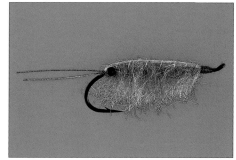

Tied by: John Moneyhun, Rapid City, SD
Hook: TMC 7989, #2-#8
Thread: Red
Feelers: Stripped brown feather stems
Rib: Silver wire
Shellback: Plastic strip
Eyes: Black mono
Body: Orange dubbing, bottom fibers picked out

Pantall's Scud

Tied by: Joe Pantall, Greenville, PA
Hook: Mustad 80200BR, #10, weighted
Thread: Black 6/0
Tail: Dark turkey feather fibers
Rib: 4lb. mono, tied in half-hitches, (helps hold shellback in position)
Shellback: Mottled natural oak Thin Skin strip
Body: Gray rabbit and Antron dubbing, bottom fibers picked out

Pete's Reel Copper Bead Scud

Tied by: Pete Toscani, Bristol, CT
Hook: Scud, #14
Thread: Black
Tail: Brown feather fibers
Body: Peacock herl
Hackle: Grizzly, top fibers trimmed
Head: Copper bead
Shellback: Epoxy

Pete's Reel Glass Bead Scud

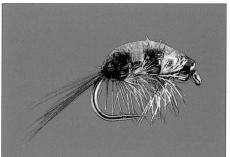

Tied by: Pete Toscani, Bristol, CT
Hook: Scud, #14
Thread: Black
Tail: Brown feather fibers
Body: 3 dark and 2 clear glass beads
Hackle: Grizzly, top fibers trimmed
Shellback: Epoxy

Pete's Reel Scud

Tied by: Pete Toscani, Bristol, CT
Hook: Scud, #16
Thread: Black
Tail: Brown feather fibers
Rib: Orange Krystal Flash
Body: Peacock herl
Legs: Grizzly hackle, top fibers trimmed
Shellback: Epoxy

Rabbit Scud

Tied by: Jack Pangburn, Westbury, NY
Hook: Mustad 3906B, #12-#18, weighted
Thread: Gray
Tail: Tan Antron yarn fibers
Rib: Fine gold tinsel
Body: Tan Antron dubbing
Wing: Gray rabbit fur

Red Back Scud

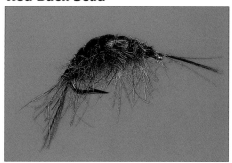

Tied by: Valia Markova, Irkkutsk, Russia
Hook: Scud, #12-#14, weighted
Thread: Black 8/0
Tail/Antennae: Red feather fibers
Rib: Mono
Shellback: Dark feather fibers, with red floss down center
Body: Squirrel dubbing, fibers picked out

Red Egg Scud

Tied by: Henry Hoffman, Warrenton, OR
Hook: Daiichi 1560, #12-#18
Thread: Olive 8/0
Tail: Barred olive chickabou feather fibers
Shellback: Green Body Braid
Body: Olive chickabou feather, twisted and wrapped
Egg: Red glass bead
Head: Green glass bead

Scooter Scud

Tied by: Robert Waller, Bay Shore, NY
Hook: Scud, #6, weighted
Thread: Brown 6/0
Tail: Red saddle feather
Body: Brown dubbing
Eyes: Self-adhesive eyes

Scuddley

Tied by: Boyd Elder, Spiro, OK
Hook: TMC 2457, #14
Thread: Orange 6/0
Tail/Antennae: Orange feather fibers
Body: Burnt orange squirrel dubbing, mixed with 6-8 strands of root beer and pearl Krystal Flash, furled into 2 cords, and woven with an overhand weave. Dubbing trimmed from top and sides.

Shaver's Peacock Scud

Tied by: DuWayne Shaver, Capitan, NM
Hook: Mustad 3906B, #10-#18
Thread: Brown
Tail/Antennae: Pheasant tail fibers
Rib: Fine copper wire, counter wrapped
Shellback: Clear plastic strip
Body: Peacock herl
Legs: White ostrich herl

Sheldon's Olive Scud

Tied by: Sheldon G. Fedder II, Millville, PA
Hook: Mustad 80250BR, #12-#16, weighted
Thread: Tan
Tail/Feelers: Dark dun feather fibers
Rib: Tan thread
Shellback: Olive Scud Back, topped with 4 strands of olive Krystal Flash
Body: Dark olive and gray Hare-Tron dubbing, mixed

Sparkle Scud

Tied by: Vladimir Markov, Irkutsk, Russia
Hook: Scud, #12-#14
Thread: Brown 8/0
Tail/Antennae: Brown feather fibers
Rib: Brown hackle, top and side fibers trimmed to shape
Body: Gold V-Rib

Stringer's Scud

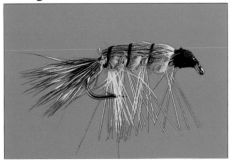

Tied by: Clifford Stringer, Nampa, ID
Hook: Mustad 3906B, #10, weighted
Thread: Black 6/0
Tail/Shellback: Deer hair
Rib: Black thread
Hackle: Ginger, top fibers trimmed
Body: Tan yarn
Head: Black thread, coated with black fabric paint
Eyes: Red fabric paint

Todd's Scud

Tied by: Todd Turner, Fort Lauderdale, FL
Hook: TMC 200R, #20
Thread: Tan 8/0
Shellback: Tan Scud Back
Body: Thin strip of clear Scud Back, touch dubbed with chopped dubbing mix of snowshoe hare's foot pad, and tan, gray, orange or pink Antron dubbing. The dubbed strip is twisted tightly and wrapped.
Head: Tag end of shellback

Wood Duck Green Scud

Tied by: Don Joslyn, Eagle Point, OR
Hook: TMC 295BL, #8, weighted
Thread: Black 6/0
Rib: Fine copper wire
Shellback: Green wood duck flank feather fibers
Body: Medium-brown Krystal Dubbing, bottom fibers picked out
Feelers: Tips from shellback

Freshwater Shrimp

Angel Shrimp

Tied by: Don Joslyn, Eagle Point, OR
Hook: Alec Jackson 2055, #7
Thread: Clear mono
Rib: Mono
Shellback: Pink CDC feather
Body: Pink Antron dubbing
Hackle: Pink
Head: Peacock herl

Boyd's Freshwater Shrimp

Tied by: Boyd Elder, Spiro, OK
Hook: Mustad 9672, #10-#14, tied hook point-up
Thread: White 6/0
Tail: White body feather tip
Hackle: White
Shellback: White Swiss straw
Body: White Sparkle Chenille
Eyes: Black plastic

Brown Bead Shrimp

Tied by: Jack Pangburn, Westbury, NY
Hook: Mustad 94840, #16-#18
Thread: Tan
Body: Tan/gray dubbing, top darken with brown marker
Legs: Brown hackle fibers
Head: Small brown bead

Brown Legged Pearl Flash Back

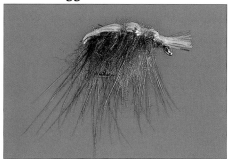

Tied by: Don Joslyn, Eagle Point, OR
Hook: Dai-Riki 135, #8
Thread: Clear mono
Rib: Mono
Shellback: Pearl Flashabou strands
Body: Pink Antron dubbing, bottom fibers picked out
Hackle: Brown
Head: Butt ends from shellback

Cabaret Shrimp

Tied by: Don Joslyn, Eagle Point, OR
Hook: Alec Jackson 2055, #5
Thread: Black 3/0
Shellback: Pink craft film stripe
Body: Hot pink Lite Brite dubbing
Hackle: Black
Legs: Multi-color Krystal Flash strands
Head: Black ostrich herl

Candy Cane Shrimp

Tied by: Don Joslyn, Eagle Point, OR
Hook: Alec Jackson 2055, #7
Thread: Clear mono
Tail: Pearl Krystal Flash strands
Rib: Pink Floss
Body: Pearl Krystal Flash strands, twisted and wrapped
Hackle: Light dun CDC, pink hackle
Head: Peacock herl

Carl's Mysis Shrimp

Tied by: Carl Ritter, Sedona, AZ
Hook: TMC 200R, #20
Thread: Clear mono sewing thread
Tail/Antennae: Clear Antron yarn fibers
Shellback: Clear Antron yarn fibers, from tail material
Body: White ostrich herl
Eyes: Black mono

Chartreuse Shrimp

Tied by: Ed Kraft, Lancaster, PA
Hook: Mustad 80250BR, #12, weighted, wrapped to form a hump at mid shank
Thread: Chartreuse 6/0
Tail: Chartreuse marabou feather fibers, split style
Rib: Fine gold wire
Shellback: Pearl tinsel
Body: Chartreuse dubbing
Legs: Chartreuse grizzly, top fibers trimmed
Eyes: Mono, with glued-on glitter
Antennae: Chartreuse Antron yarn fibers

Chinese Shrimp

Tied by: Don Joslyn, Eagle Point, OR
Hook: Alec Jackson 2055, #7
Thread: Clear mono
Rib: Mono
Shellback: Pink Flashabou strands
Body: Pink dubbing
Hackle: Pink
Head: Butt ends from shellback

Dubbing Shrimp

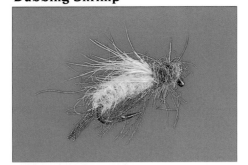

Tied by: Jack Pangburn, Westbury, NY
Hook: Mustad 80250, #14-#20, weighted
Thread: Gray
Tail: Very fine stranded copper wire strands
Body: Tan dubbing
Legs: Light tan CDC feather fibers
Wing: Light dun feather fibers
Head: Light brown dubbing

Estuary Shrimp

Tied by: Don Joslyn, Eagle Point, OR
Hook: Alec Jackson 2055, #7
Thread: Clear mono
Rib: Mono
Shellback: Orange goose feather section
Body: Polar shrimp New Age Chenille, fuchsia dubbing
Head: Butt ends from shellback

Fred's Mysis Shrimp

Tied by: Fred Iacoletti, Albuquerque, NM
Hook: Daiichi 1770, #16, bent to shape
Thread: Green 8/0
Tail/Feelers: Olive Stalcup's Damsel Legs
Abdomen: Small clear glass beads
Thorax: Light dun Hi Vis yarn fibers
Eyes: Black mono
Antennae: Brown Micro Fibetts
Comments: Coat head and top of thorax with epoxy.

Glass Shrimp

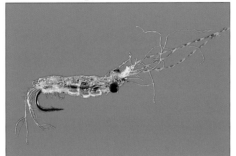

Tied by: Carl Ritter, Sedona, AZ
Hook: Swimming nymph, #18
Thread: Clear mono sewing thread
Tail: Clear Antron yarn fibers
Shellback: Clear Antron yarn fibers, pearl Krystal Flash strands
Body: Clear Antron dubbing, clear glass beads
Eyes: Black mono
Antennae/Feelers: Clear Antron yarn fibers, pearl Krystal Flash

Gray Shrimp

Tied by: D.W. Finch, Orem, UT
Hook: TMC 2457, #10-#18
Thread: White 8/0
Tail/Antenna: Partridge feather fibers
Rib: Mono
Shellback: Clear Flexibody
Body: Gray dubbing
Hackle: Partridge

Grizzly Freshwater Shrimp

Tied by: Henry Hoffman, Warrenton, OR
Hook: Daiichi 1710, #8-#14
Thread: Gray 8/0
Feelers: Light grizzly breast feather fibers
Rib: Clear mono thread
Shellback: Clear plastic, over pearl body braid
Body: Light grizzly chickabou feather, twisted and wrapped
Tail: 2 light grizzly saddle feathers trimmed to shape
Hackle: Light grizzly saddle
Eyes: Mono

Jack's Olive Shrimp

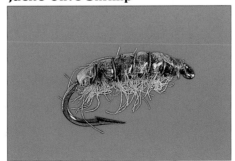

Tied by: Jack Pangburn, Westbury, NY
Hook: Mustad 80250, #12-#18
Thread: Tan
Rib: Copper wire
Shellback: Clear plastic strip
Body: Light olive dubbing, bottom fibers picked out

Krystal Shrimp

Tied by: Boyd Elder, Spiro, OK
Hook: Mustad 9672, #8, tied hook point-up
Thread: White 6/0
Eyes: Mono
Tail/Antennae: White feather fibers
Head: Gray dubbing
Hackle: White, top fibers trimmed
Underbody: White yarn
Body: 6-8 strands of pearl Krystal Flash, furled into 2 cords, woven with an overhand weave, (hackle fibers pulled to bottom)

Low Light Shrimp

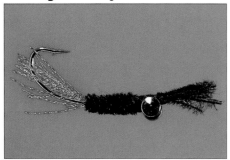

Tied by: Don Joslyn, Eagle Point, OR
Hook: Alec Jackson 2055, #3
Thread: Black 3/0
Tail: Orange Krystal Flash strands
Body: Peacock herl
Eyes: Gold 3/16 Dazl-Eyes
Feelers: Butt ends from body

Metal Bead Chain Grass Shrimp

Tied by: Thomas Peterson, Aberdeen, MD
Hook: Streamer, #8, tied hook point-up
Thread: White 8/0
Feelers: White calf tail hair
Antennae: Gold Krystal Flash, 2 strands
Eyes: Medium silver bead chain
Body: Small silver bead chain, 4 beads per side
Rib: 12lb. green mono
Shellback: Large pearl Flashabou
Legs: Pearl Estaz chenille, 3 wraps

Mini Shrimp

Tied by: Mike Giavedoni, Maple, ON
Hook: Mustad 9671, #12-#14
Thread: Yellow
Feelers: Gold Z-lon fibers
Rib: 12lb. silver mono thread
Shellback: Gray Scud Back
Body: Gold dubbing, fibers picked out
Eyes: Black plastic

Mono Mysis

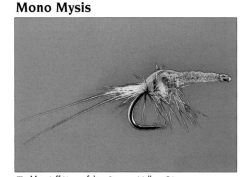

Tied by: Jeff Lingenfelter, Browns Valley, CA
Hook: Partridge K14ST, #10-#12
Thread: Fine UNI-Mono
Tail: White kid goat hair
Antennae: Polar bear guard hair
Eyes: Red 20lb. Amnesia
Thorax: Polar bear underfur
Legs: Grizzly hackle
Shellback: Clear Scud Back
Abdomen: Fine UNI-Mono, wrapped

Naked Lady

Tied by: Don Joslyn, Eagle Point, OR
Hook: Alec Jackson 2055, #7
Thread: Clear mono
Tail: Pink feather fibers
Body: Pink Flex Floss
Hackle: Pink CDC
Head: Peacock herl

Olive Shrimp

Tied by: John Moneyhun, Rapid City, SD
Hook: TMC 7989, #2-#8
Thread: Olive
Feelers: Orange squirrel tail hair
Antennae: Stripped brown feather stems
Rib: Silver wire
Shellback: Flexibody
Hackle: Brown
Body: Olive chenille
Head: Olive dubbing
Eyes: Black mono

Olson's Freshwater Shrimp

Tied by: Gordon Hsu Olson, Three Hills, AB
Hook: Gold scud, #8, weighted
Thread: Black
Tail: Chartreuse CDC feather fibers
Rib: Red wire
Shellback: Olive Scud Back
Body: Chartreuse CDC feathers, wrapped

Pale Olive Shrimp

Tied by: Jack Pangburn, Westbury, NY
Hook: Mustad, #12-#18, weighted
Thread: Pale olive
Body: Light olive Ultra Vernille, top darkened with dark olive
   marker
Legs: Brown feather fibers
Head: Tan dubbing

Pantall's Freshwater Shrimp

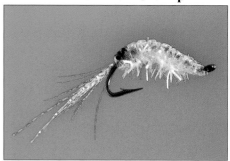

Tied by: Joe Pantall, Greenville, PA
Hook: Mustad 37160, #10
Thread: White 6/0
Antennae/Feelers: Pearl Krystal Flash, 2 strands, mallard
   flank feather fibers
Rib: Clear Swannundaze
Body: Pearl Crystal Chenille
Eyes: Black dots, painted
Comments: The chenille is wrapped around the
Swannundaze and pulled under to form body.

Rob's Mysis Shrimp

Tied by: Robert Lewis, Yonkers, NY
Hook: Eagle Claw L144, #12
Thread: Gray 6/0
Antennae/Feelers: 2 strands of Polar Fiber, mallard flank feather fibers
Eyes: Black mono
Rib: Gray mono
Shellback: Gray Raffia (option: coated with epoxy)
Body: Gray dubbing
Tail: Butt end from shellback

RP's Mysis Shrimp

Tied by: Roy D. Powell, Danville, CA
Hook: Daiichi 1770, #12-#16
Thread: White 8/0
Tail/Feelers: Silver-gray Antron yarn fibers
Rib: Orvis Super Strong 7X mono
Shellback: Silver gray Antron yarn fibers
Underbody: Silver tinsel
Body: White UNI-Floss
Legs: White Antron dubbing
Eyes: Black mono

Salmon Scud

Tied by: Bruce Raymond, Woodridge, IL
Hook: Dai Riki 135, #6
Thread: Red
Shellback: Fluorescent red poly yarn
Body: Pink Estaz chenille

Sheldon's Pink Shrimp

Tied by: Sheldon G. Fedder II, Millville, PA
Hook: Mustad 80250BR, #12-#16, weighted
Thread: White
Tail/Antennae: Feather fibers picked
Rib: White thread
Shellback: Pink Scud Back, topped with 4 strand of pink Krystal Flash
Body: Pink Shrimp Hare-Tron dubbing

Steely Shrimp

Tied by: Don Joslyn, Eagle Point, OR
Hook: Mustad 37160, #6, weighted
Thread: Clear mono
Rib: Mono
Shellback: Pink Mylar craft film stripe
Body: Pink Antron dubbing
Legs: Pink Krystal Flash strands

Tina's Shrimp

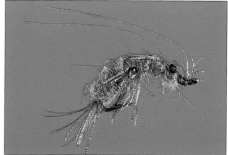

Tied by: Tina Stalker, Vulcan, AB
Hook: Mustad 37168, #12
Thread: Olive 6/0
Tail/Feelers: Olive Comes Alive strands
Rib: 7X tippet
Body: Olive dubbing, bottom fibers picked out
Legs: Olive Comes Alive strands
Eyes: Black mono
Antennae: 7X mono

Woolly Shrimp

Tied by: Tom Berry, Bay St. Louis, MS
Hook: Nymph, #6
Thread: Olive 6/0
Head: Gold bead
Antennae/Feelers: Badger hair, 3-4 strands of copper, 2 strands of pearl Krystal Flash, and 2 partridge feathers cut to claw shape and mounted on sides
Hackle: Olive and brown chickabou feathers wrapped to mid shank, thread tied off and then the gold bead pushed over the hackles to form a cone
Eyes/Weed Guard: Mono, ends melted and formed to bend while warm
Body: Olive ostrich herl, olive-brown micro chenille

Snails

Braided Snail

Tied by: Henry Hoffman, Warrenton, OR
Hook: Mustad 3906, #8
Thread: Brown 6/0
Body: Brown parachute cord, knotted, end melted
Eyes: Mono

Chickabou Snail

Tied by: Henry Hoffman, Warrenton, OR
Hook: Daiichi 1530, #10
Thread: Brown 8/0
Body: Brown chickabou feathers, wrapped and clipped to shape, then colored with black marker
Eyes: Mono

George's Snail

Tied by: George Kosmicki, Martin, SD
Hook: Scud, #14-#16
Thread: Black
Tail: Black marabou feather fibers, and 2 strands of pearl Flashabou
Body: Peacock herl, coated with 5-minute epoxy
Eyes: Butt ends from body herl

Hard Shell Creeper

Tied by: J.E. Mullin, Casper, WY
Hook: Mustad 36890, #6
Thread: Black 6/0
Tail: Horsetail or moose mane hairs, 2 fibers divided
Underbody: White floss
Overbody: 25lb. Flat Cobra fishing line or clear Larva Lace, colored with markers
Hackle: Black hair hackle, woven George Grant style

Hot Glue Snail

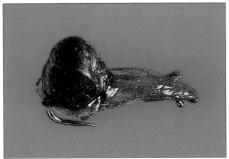

Tied by: Ronn Lucas, Sr., Milwaukie, OR
Hook: Small light wire
Thread: Brown 8/0
Underbody: Brown thread
Overbody: Hot glue to shape, coated with black and brown fabric paints

Iridescent Daphnia

Tied by: Ronn Lucas, Sr., Milwaukie, OR
Hook: Small light wire
Thread: Olive, red, or orange 8/0
Body: Olive, red, or orange Iridescent Dubbing, some long fibers brushed out and lightly painted with green, red or orange fingernail polish, (the polish will naturally clump on the dubbing strands)
Comments: Daphnia are small, 1.1 to 3.2mm. They clump together while mating in the shallow waters of lakes.

Mullin's Snail

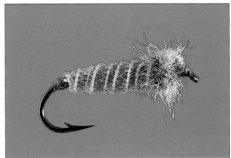

Tied by: J.E. Mullin, Casper, WY
Hook: Mustad 9671, #8
Thread: Gray 6/0
Underbody: Gray floss
Overbody: White and clear mono strands, woven in a figure-eight pattern into a cord, wrapped
Collar: Gray Antron dubbing

Pond Snail

Tied by: Dave McCants, Pleasant Hill, CA
Hook: TMC 2457, #12
Thread: Brown 8/0
Body: Olive Magic Dub, (bottom colored with brown marker)
Head: Brown dubbing
Eyes: Brown broom bristle, melted, tips colored with black marker

Ramshorn Snail

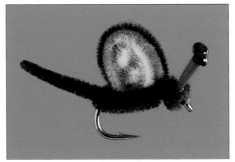

Tied by: Dave McCants, Pleasant Hill, CA
Hook: TMC 2457, #10
Thread: Dark brown 6/0
Tail/Shell/Head: Light olive Vernille, head, tail and top of shell colored with brown marker. Shell is formed over a double 30lb. mono at 45-degree angles 1/3-inch above hook shank, mono clipped short after forming body.
Eyes: Brown broom bristle, ends melted, ends colored with black marker

Sparkle Snail

Tied by: Jack Pangburn, Westbury, NY
Hook: Mustad 94840, #12-#20
Thread: Olive
Underbody: Olive dubbing
Overbody: Brown Antron yarn strands, tied in at the rear and pulled forward
Foot: Partridge feather, coated with Flexament

Sow Bugs

Stanek's Escargot

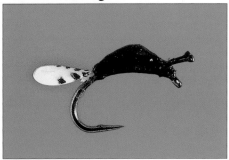

Tied by: Earl Stanek, Cotter, AR
Hook: TMC 2457, #14-#16
Thread: Black 8/0
Foot and Eye Stalks: 1X tippet, loop formed for foot, and melted tag ends used for eyes. Mix 5-minute epoxy with a small amount of gray craft fabric paint. With a tooth pick, swipe the epoxy over the loop to fill it in. Let it dry.
Body: 4 strand black floss, tied on top of hook shank then folded 4 times, each layer secured with thread wraps, forming a tapered hump on top of the hook shank. Mix 5-minute epoxy with a small amount of gray craft fabric paint and coat body.

Bead Head Sow Bug

Tied by: Jack Pangburn, Westbury, NY
Hook: Mustad 80250, #12-#18
Thread: Tan
Tail: Tan dubbing brush, extended
Body: Tan dubbing brush from tail, wrapped forward
Hackle: Brown
Head: Brass bead

Brown & Green CDC Sow Bug

Tied by: Don Joslyn, Eagle Point, OR
Hook: Dai-Riki 135, #6
Thread: Black 3/0
Rib: Dark dun CDC feather, top fibers trimmed
Body: Black & green New Age Chenille

Chickabou Sow Bug

Tied by: Henry Hoffman, Warrenton, OR
Hook: TMC 9300, #12-#18, weighted, .010 lead wire twisted into a rope lashed to sides
Thread: Gray 8/0
Tails/Antennae: Gray chicken biots
Rib: Clear mono
Shellback: Clear plastic strip
Body: Gray chickabou feather, twisted and wrapped

Egg Sack Sow Bug

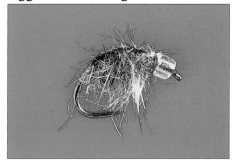

Tied by: Tim McConville, Salt Lake City, UT
Hook: TMC 2487, #14
Thread: Gray 6/0
Tag: Pink Antron yarn fibers
Shellback: Dark gray Antron yarn fibers
Body: Hare's Ear, or Antron dubbing
Head: Pearl glass bead

Emu Peacock Sow Bug

Tied by: Don Joslyn, Eagle Point, OR
Hook: Dai-Riki 135, #6
Thread: Black 3/0
Tail: Emu feather fibers, peacock herl strands
Rib: Fine gold round tinsel
Shellback: Peacock herl strands from tail
Body: Black dubbing, bottom fibers picked out

Foam Sow Bug

Tied by: Don Joslyn, Eagle Point, OR
Hook: Dai-Riki 135, #6
Thread: Black 6/0
Tail: Golden pheasant tippet fibers
Hackle: Black, top and side fibers trimmed
Body: Black foam

Glass Bead Sow Bug

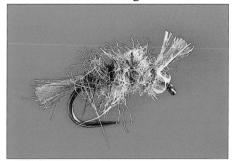

Tied by: Tim McConville, Salt Lake City, UT
Hook: TMC 2487, #16
Thread: Gray 8/0
Tail/Feelers: Gray Antron yarn fibers
Rib: Gray V-Rib
Body: Hare's Ear, or Antron dubbing
Head: Clear glass bead

Gold Backed Ostrich Sow Bug

Tied by: Don Joslyn, Eagle Point, OR
Hook: Dai-Riki 135, #10, weighted
Thread: Clear mono
Tail: Pheasant tail feather fibers
Rib: Clear mono
Shellback: Gold Flashabou strands
Body: Black ostrich herl

Gold & Black Sow Bug

Tied by: Don Joslyn, Eagle Point, OR
Hook: TMC 205BL, #8, weighted
Thread: Black 3/0
Rib: Fine copper wire
Shellback: Gold Flashabou strands
Body: Brown & black New Age Chenille
Hackle: Black, top fibers trimmed
Feelers: Gold Flashabou strands from shellback

Gray Sow Bug

Tied by: Jack Pangburn, Westbury, NY
Hook: #12-#18
Thread: Black
Body: Gray dubbing
Wing: Mallard wing feather section
Legs: Light yellow, olive feather fibers

McConville's Sow Bug

Tied by: Tim McConville, Salt Lake City, UT
Hook: TMC 2487, #14
Thread: Gray 6/0
Shellback: Pear Flashabou strands
Body: Hare's Ear, or Antron dubbing
Feelers: Brown feather fibers

Metolius Green Sow Bug

Tied by: Coleen Jones, Lyons, OR
Hook: TMC 200R, #18, weight optional
Thread: Dark olive 8/0
Body: Insect green and olive brown Hare's Ear Plus dubbing
    mixed 50/50, top trimmed, sides and bottom fibers
    tapered, top colored with a black waterproof marker

Midnight Pearl Sow Bug

Tied by: Don Joslyn, Eagle Point, OR
Hook: TMC 205BL, #8
Thread: Clear mono
Tail: Pheasant tail feather fibers
Rib: Mono
Shellback: Pearl Flashabou strands
Body: Midnight Fire New Age Chenille
Feelers: Butt ends from shellback

Ostrich & Peacock Sow Bug

Tied by: Don Joslyn, Eagle Point, OR
Hook: Dai-Riki 700B, #10
Thread: Brown 6/0
Rib: Fine gold tinsel
Shellback: Pheasant tail feather fibers
Abdomen: Black and brown ostrich herl strands
Thorax/Head: Peacock herl
Legs: Fine gold and pearl Flashabou strands
Feelers: Tip ends from shellback

Ostrich & Pheasant Sow Bug

Tied by: Don Joslyn, Eagle Point, OR
Hook: Dai-Riki 135, #12
Thread: Brown 6/0
Tail/Feelers: Pheasant tail feather fibers
Rib: Brown thread
Shellback: Pheasant tail feather fibers from tail
Body: Black ostrich herl

Ostrich Sow Bug

Tied by: Jeff Lingenfelter, Browns Valley, CA
Hook: TMC 2457, #10-#14
Thread: Gray 8/0
Tail: Gray goose biots
Rib: 5X tippet
Shellback: Gray 1/8-inch Scud Back
Body: Gray dubbing
Legs: Gray ostrich herl, pulled along each side

Peacock Back Sow Bug

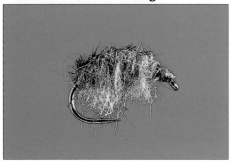

Tied by: Tim McConville, Salt Lake City, UT
Hook: TMC 2487 #16
Thread: Gray 8/0
Rib: Gold wire
Shellback: Peacock herl strands
Body: Hare's Ear dubbing, bottom fibers picked out

Red Tail Sow Bug

Tied by: Don Joslyn, Eagle Point, OR
Hook: Dai-Riki 135, #12
Thread: Black 6/0
Tail: Red feather fibers
Rib: Fine copper wire
Shellback: Peacock herl strands
Body: Black dubbing, bottom fibers picked out

Shaver's Sow Bug

Tied by: DuWayne Shaver, Capitan, NM
Hook: Mustad 3906B, #10-#18
Thread: Black
Tails: Gray goose biots
Rib: Copper wire, counter wrapped
Shellback: Goose wing feather section
Body: Gray Hare's Ear dubbing, bottom fibers picked out

Shenk's Cress Bug

Tied by: Ed Shenk, Carlisle, PA
Hook: TMC 5262 #12-#18
Thread: Gray 6/0
Body: Muskrat belly fur or mink fur
Comments: Use the dubbing loop technique to form a dubbing brush and wrap the brush over the hook shank. Cut the top and bottom short and then trim the side into an oval shape. You should end up with a thin oval body. Optional: add a dark center line down the back of the fly with marker.

Tim's Sow Bug

Tied by: Tim McConville, Salt Lake City, UT
Hook: TMC 2487, #14
Thread: Gray 8/0
Shellback: Gray Antron yarn strands
Body: Hare's Ear, or Antron dubbing

Todd's Sow Bug

Tied by: Todd Turner, Fort Lauderdale, FL
Hook: TMC 3761, #18-#22
Thread: Gray 8/0
Tail: Tan marabou feather fibers
Shellback: Tan Scud Back strip
Dorsal stripe: Thin strip of dark Scud Back
Body: Thin strip of clear Scud Back touch dubbed with chopped dubbing mix of snowshoe hare's foot pad, tan and gray Antron dubbing (the dubbed strip is twisted tightly and wrapped)
Head: Tag end of shellback
Comments: Snowshoe hare dubbing collects air bubbles and the flared Scud Back adds to its translucency.

Water Boatmen

Down's Water Boatman

Tied by: Neville Downs
Hook: TMC 2457, #12-#14, weighted
Thread: Black 3/0
Shellback: Gray Foust Wing-back, cut to shape
Rib: Tying thread
Butt: Silver thread
Body: Black embroidery thread
Legs: Brown round rubber

Iridescent Flashback Boatmen

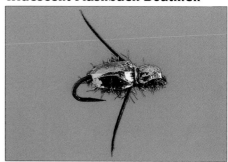

Tied by: Ronn Lucas, Sr., Milwaukie, OR
Hook: Daiichi 1560, #12-#14, weighted
Thread: Brown 6/0
Shellback: Thin Ice Flashback strip
Body: Brown Iridescent Dubbing
Legs: Brown goose biots

Sam's Water Boatmen

Tied by: Sam de Beer, Calgary, AB
Hook: Nymph, #10-#14, weighted
Thread: Black
Butt: Clear glass bead
Shellback: Black foam strip
Body: Peacock herl
Legs: Black round rubber

CHAPTER 9

Terrestrials

Ants

Baker's Black Ant

Tied by: Brennan Baker, Powell River, BC
Hook: Mustad 94840, #10-#12
Thread: Olive 6/0
Body: Black dubbing
Indicators: Yellow foam
Hackle: Black

Bead Ant (Wet)

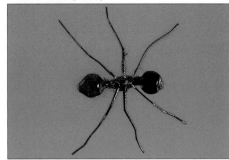

Tied by: Floyd Franke, Roscoe, NY
Hook: Mustad AC 80100, #20
Thread: Rust brown
Body: Red and black 2mm plastic beads, mounted on mono
   core, and coated with Loon Soft Head Fly Finish
Legs: Stripped brown hackle stems, bent to shape

Black Carpenter Ant

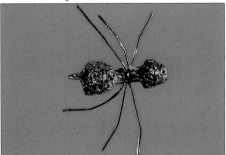

Tied by: Jack Pangburn, Westbury, NY
Hook: Mustad 94840, #14-#18
Thread: Black 8/0
Body: Black closed-cell foam
Legs: Black thread strands, coated with head cement

Black Fur Ant

Tied by: Floyd Franke, Roscoe, NY
Hook: Mustad 94840, #18
Thread: Black
Body: Black beaver fur dubbing
Legs: Black hackle
Wing: Dun hackle tips, delta style

Carpenter

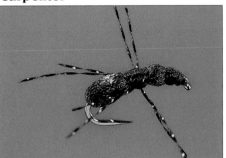

Tied by: Don Joslyn, Eagle Point, OR
Hook: Dai Riki 135, #12
Thread: Black 3/0
Body: Black 1/8-inch foam, cut to shape
Legs: Black Krystal Flash strands

Carpenter Ant

Tied by: Phil Joest, Salinas, CA
Hook: TMC 101, #14-#16
Thread: Black
Body: Black Superfine or Sparkle dubbing
Wing Post: Black round foam, cut short after tying in hackle
Hackle: Black

Epoxy/Foam Black Ant

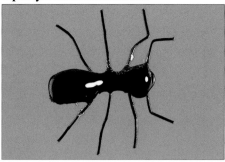

Tied by: Fred Iacoletti, Albuquerque, NM
Hook: Daiichi 1100, #16
Thread: Black 6/0
Body: Black closed-cell foam, cut to shape
Legs/Antennae: Black poly rope fibers, bent to shape with heated forceps
Comments: Coat top of body and head with epoxy and paint with black gloss enamel.

Flying Carpenter

Tied by: Don Joslyn, Eagle Point, OR
Hook: Dai Riki 305, #14
Thread: Black 3/0
Rib: Copper wire
Underbody: Black thread
Shellback: Black 1/8-inch foam strip
Wing: Black Krystal Flash strands
Thorax: Black ostrich herl

Flying ICU Carpenter Ant

Tied by: Richard Pilatzke, Little, CO
Hook: TMC 100BL, #10
Thread: Black 8/0
Body: Black sheet foam, cut to shape
Wings: Metallic Twist, burnt to shape with caddis wing burner
Legs: Black deer hair
Post: Yellow foam

Foam Loop Parachute Ant

Tied by: Jim Riley, Grass Valley, CA
Hook: TMC 101, #10-#18
Thread: Black
Body: Fine black chenille
Wing Post: White foam noodle, looped
Hackle: Black

Jess's Flying Ant

Tied by: Jess Potter, Fairbanks, AK
Hook: Mustad 3096, #10
Thread: Black 6/0
Body: Black chenille
Wings: Mallard feather sections, delta style

Little Black Ant

Tied by: Don Joslyn, Eagle Point, OR
Hook: Dai Riki 101, #20
Thread: Black 8/0
Body: Black foam
Legs/Antennae: Turkey feather fibers

Mike's Flying Ant

Tied by: Mike Giavedoni, Maple, ONT
Hook: Mustad 94840, #16
Thread: Black
Body: Black and yellow dubbing
Wings: Grizzly hackle tips, delta style
Hackle: Grizzly

My Favorite Foam Ant

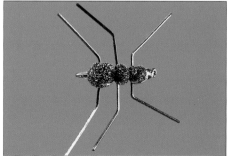

Tied by: Tom Peterson, Aberdeen, MD
Hook: TMC 100, #12-#18
Thread: Black
Body: Black foam strip
Legs: Paint brush fibers, bent to shape

Nino's Ant

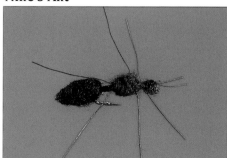

Tied by: Nino Casino, Alatri, Italy
Hook: TMC 246Z, #16
Thread: Brown
Body: Brown dubbing, copper wire used for core of extension
Legs: Weasel guard hair

Nino's Flying Ant

Tied by: Nino Casino, Alatri, Italy
Hook: TMC 246Z, #16
Thread: Black
Body: Black dubbing, copper wire used for core of extension
Wing: Cartene (cold cuts wrapping film), cut to shape
Legs: Black seal dubbing

Parachute Fur Ant

Tied by: Rod Dines, New Meadows, ID
Hook: TMC 100, #8-#16
Thread: Black
Body: Black dubbing
Wing Post: White poly yarn fibers
Hackle: Black

Perfect Ant

Tied by: Bahman Khadivi, Cupertino, CA
Hook: Mustad 94840, #14-#20
Thread: Black 8/0
Shellback/Post: Fine moose hair, pulled over the abdomen and posted
Body: Black dubbing
Hackle: Brown

Pete's Reel Ant

Tied by: Pete Toscani, Bristol, CT
Hook: Orvis Dry, #12
Thread: Black 8/0
Body: Black beads, coated with epoxy
Post: White calf body hair
Hackle: Black, top fibers trimmed

Realistic Black Foam Ant

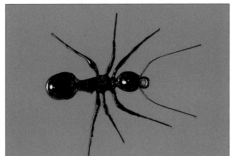

Tied by: Floyd Franke, Roscoe, NY
Hook: Mustad 94840, #18
Thread: Black
Body: Black foam, coated with Loon Soft Head Fly Finish
Legs: Stripped black hackle stems, coated with Loon Soft Head Fly Finish
Antennae: Stripped black hackle stems

Red Hot Ant

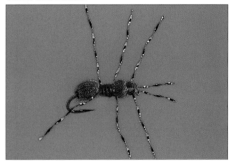

Tied by: Don Joslyn, Eagle Point, OR
Hook: Dai Riki 305, #14
Thread: Red 3/0
Body: Red 1/8-inch foam
Legs/Antennae: Red Krystal Flash strands

Royal Carpenter

Tied by: Don Joslyn, Eagle Point, OR
Hook: Dai Riki 305, #14
Thread: Black 3/0
Body: Peacock herl, with Alec Jackson Red Silk center
Legs/Antennae: Black Krystal Flash strands

RP's Flying Ant

Tied by: Roy Powell, Danville, CA
Hook: Mustad 94831, #12
Thread: Black 8/0
Body: Black open-cell foam, 1/16-inch strip wrapped, red Flashabou tinsel in center
Wings: Brown hackle tips, delta style
Hackle: Grizzly

RP's In and Out Ant

Tied by: Roy Powell, Danville, CA
Hook: TMC 2487, #12-#16
Thread: Black 8/0
Body: Black open-cell foam, 1/16-inch strip wrapped, with red Flashabou tinsel in center
Wings: Grizzly hackle tips, delta style
Hackle Post: Black Super Floss strand
Hackle: Black, folded post parachute style

Simple Ant

Tied by: Don Joslyn, Eagle Point, OR
Hook: Daiichi 1270, #16
Thread: Black 8/0
Body: Black 1/8-inch foam strip, cut to shape, red dubbing in center
Legs/Antennae: Turkey feather fibers

Steve's Winged Ant

Tied by: Steve Potter, Tracy, CA
Hook: TMC 102Y, #17
Thread: Black 8/0
Body: Black thread, coated with EZ Shape Sparkle Body
Wings: Grizzly hackle tips, delta style
Hackle: Grizzly, 2 turns

Super Ant

Tied by: Kyle Hicks, Berwick, NS
Hook: Mustad 3906, #14
Thread: Black 8/0
Body: Red preformed foam ant body
Hackle: Brown
Antennae: Red Krystal Flash strands

Velvet Ant

Tied by: Henry Hoffman, Warrenton, OR
Hook: Galmakatsu 31, #14
Thread: Tan 8/0
Body: Rust Seal-Lite dubbing, colored with brown marker
Legs/Antennae: Fine peacock strands, bent to shape

Wayne's Ant

Tied by: Andy Wayne, San Francisco
Hook: TMC 100, #12
Thread: Black
Body/Head: Small red glass beads, coated with epoxy
Legs: Black hackle

Winged Cinnamon Ant

Tied by: Carl Ritter, Sedona, AZ
Hook: TMC 100, #18
Thread: Rust
Body: Rust dubbing
Wing: 3 moose hairs, over brown hackle tips, delta style
Hackle: Brown, clipped bottom and top fibers

Beetles

Beamoc Orange Spot Beetle

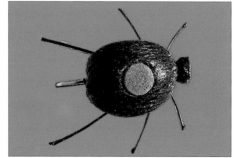

Tied by: Floyd Franke, Roscoe, NY
Hook: Mustad 94840, #12
Thread: Black
Body: Black foam
Legs: Size A Monocord strands, coated with Loon Soft Head Fly Finish
Comments: The orange dot on the back is an inlay of orange foam. A hole is punched in the foam body and the filled with a similar size plug of orange foam and glued in place.

Beefy Beetle

Tied by: Ralph D'Errico, Jr., Tucson, AZ
Hook: TMC 5210, #10
Thread: Black
Shellback: Black goose feather section, dull side coated with Flexament, tied in shiny side up
Underbody: Foam 1/8-inch strip, wrapped, coat with Flexament
Body: Peacock herl
Hackle: Black, 2 feathers
Overbody: Peacock herl

Black May Beetle

Tied by: Jack Pangburn, Westbury, NY
Hook: Mustad 94840, #14-#18
Thread: Black 6/0
Body: Peacock herl
Shellback/Head: Black Swiss straw

Coffee Bean Beetle

Tied by: Vic Flagello, New Fairfield, CT
Hook: Mustad 94840, #12-#16
Thread: Black 6/0
Tail/Legs: Black saddle feather, drawn feather style, legs trimmed to desired length
Underbody: Fine black chenille and peacock herl, twisted and wrapped
Overbody: Coffee bean, with groove filed in underside and Super Glued on top of underbody, colored to imitate natural or for indicator

Easy Beetle

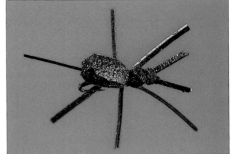

Tied by: Don Joslyn, Eagle Point, OR
Hook: Daiichi 1270, #16
Thread: Black 3/0
Body: Black 1/8-inch foam, cut to shape
Legs: Black/red silicone rubber

Epoxy/Foam Leaf Beetle

Tied by: Fred Iacoletti, Albuquerque, NM
Hook: Daiichi 1280, #12
Thread: Brown 6/0
Body: Brown closed-cell foam strip, cut to shape, CA glue used to attach hook shank
Legs: Red nylon fibers, cut from a paintbrush, bent with heated forceps
Antennae: Black poly rope fibers
Comments: Paint with Testor's enamel, coat carapace and head with epoxy.

Flash-Back Beetle

Tied by: Henry Hoffman, Warrenton, OR
Hook: Mustad 94833, #12
Thread: Black 8/0
Shellback: Peacock Ribbon Floss, 2 strands
Rib: Fine gold wire
Body: Black deer hair, pulled body style
Hackle: Black saddle feather

Fire Beetle

Tied by: Joe Borkowski, Firestone, CO
Hook: Mustad 37160, #8-#12
Thread: Red
Body: Orange and pink egg yarn
Legs: Red rubber band strands

High Vis Foam Beetle

Tied by: Rod Dines, New Meadows, ID
Hook: TMC 100, #8-#16
Thread: Black
Body: Peacock herl
Shellback: Black foam
Indicator: Yellow foam
Legs: Black round rubber

Iridescent Flashback Beetle

Tied by: Ronn Lucas, Sr., Milwaukie, OR
Hook: Daiichi 1150, #12-#16
Thread: Black
Shellback: Flashback color to suit, over Foamback, color to suit
Body: Black Iridescent Dubbing #2 or color to suit, picked out and trimmed

Iridescent Foamback Lady Bug

Tied by: Ronn Lucas, Sr., Milwaukie, OR
Hook: Daiichi 1640, #12-#16
Thread: Black
Shellback/Head: Red Foamback #211
Body/Legs: Black Iridescent Dubbing #2, picked out and trimmed
Mouth Parts: Body fibers, pulled forward
Comments: Color shell spots and head with a black waterproof marker and make eyes with a bright yellow fabric paint.

Japanese Beetle

Tied by: Jack Pangburn, Westbury, NY
Hook: Mustad 94840, #14-#16
Thread: Black 6/0
Legs: Black mono strands, coated with varnish
Body: Peacock herl
Shellback: Copper Swiss straw

Nino's Beetle

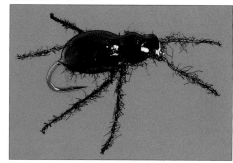

Tied by: Nino Casino, Alatri, Italy
Hook: TMC 100, #10
Thread: Black
Abdomen: Rust/black dubbing
Thorax: Black seal fur dubbing
Legs: Black seal fur, twisted over glue coated thread strands
Shellback: Painted foam, coated with epoxy

One Clump Beetle

Tied by: Vladimir Markov, Irkutsk, Russia
Hook: Dry fly
Thread: Brown
Tail: Brown Antron yarn fibers
Body: Deer hair, pulled body and bullet head styles, bottom collar hairs trimmed, body formed from 1 clump of hair

Polka Dot Ladybird

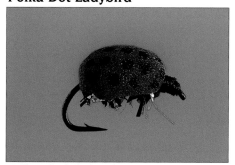

Tied by: Richard Pilatzke, Littleton, CO
Hook: TMC 102Y, #15
Thread: Black 8/0
Shellback: Orange/red Wapsi Bug Body, size 12, spots added with fine tipped black marker
Body: Peacock Kreinik Micro Ice Chenille

Ritter's Beetle

Tied by: Carl Ritter, Sedona, AZ
Hook: TMC 100, #12
Thread: Black
Tail: Black squirrel
Shellback: Black foam
Body: Black and orange dubbing, mixed
Hackle: Black
Indicator: White poly yarn fibers

Royal Beetle

Tied by: Don Joslyn, Eagle Point, OR
Hook: TMC 207BL, #8
Thread: Black 3/0
Body: Peacock herl, with Alec Jackson Red Silk in middle
Legs: Black turkey feather fibers, coated with Flexament, rear legs knotted
Antennae: Black turkey feather fibers

Spider Beetle

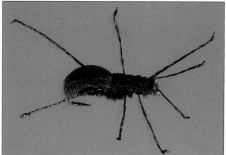

Tied by: Don Joslyn, Eagle Point, OR
Hook: TMC 5212, #10
Thread: Black 3/0
Shellback: Black 1/8-inch foam, cut to shape
Body: Black/silver chenille
Legs/Antennae: 2 black Krystal Flash strands, glued together

Stacked Hair Beetle

Tied by: Jeff Lingerfelter, Browns Valley, CA
Hook: TMC 900BL, #10-#14 or TMC 22487, #16-#18
Thread: Black Kevlar and black UNI 6/0 or 8/0
Underbody: Peacock Angel Hair, dubbed in 2-3 layers
Overbody: Black deer hair, stacked, trimmed to shape
Head: Ball of dubbed peacock Angel Hair, with 12-15 coarse elk hairs pulled over
Legs: Elk hair from head, 3 to each side
Indicator: Yellow deer hair
Comments: A thick, shaggy body of Angel Hair helps to hide the wraps used to tie in the hair. Tie off the Kevlar thread after stacking the last bunch of hair and cut it off. Gather all the hair and pull firmly upward. Make a curving cut about a 1/4-inch above the hook shank on a size 10 hook. Preen the remaining hair outwards and backwards with your fingers then clip to desired shape. This pattern is durable with good flotation and excellent profile.

Tight Black Beetle

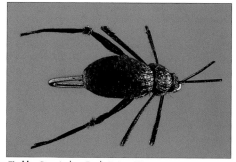

Tied by: Don Joslyn, Eagle Point, OR
Hook: TMC 207BL, #8
Thread: Black 3/0
Body: Peacock herl
Shellback: Black 1/8-inch foam, cut to shape
Legs/Antennae: Black turkey feather fibers, coated with Flexament

Grasshoppers

American Grasshopper

Tied by: Jack Pangburn, Westbury, NY
Hook: Mustad 79580, #12
Thread: Tan 6/0
Body: Yellow closed-cell foam
Wing: Partridge feather, deer hair
Legs: Brown Swannundaze, knotted
Head: Deer hair, spun and trimmed

Baker's Hopper

Tied by: Brennan Baker, Powell River, BC
Hook: Mustad 94833, #6
Thread: Olive 6/0
Tail: Red feather fibers
Body: Bright olive dubbing
Wings: Plastic strips, cut from "waffle" section of Glad bag
Legs: White round rubber, knotted
Hackle: Olive and grizzly
Head: Thread, coated with glitter nail polish
Eyes: White nail polish, with black marker spot

Banjo Hopper

Tied by: Wes Atkin, St. George, UT
Hook: Mustad 94831, #6
Thread: Tan
Body: Tan foam, cut to shape
Legs: Grizzly feathers, trimmed and knotted
Wing: Cream Air-Thru Fly Wing material, cut to shape, over 4-5 pearl Krystal Flash strands
Post: White foam
Hackle: Cream and light brown

Blonde Royal Hopper

Tied by: Don Joslyn, Eagle Point, OR
Hook: Alec Jackson, #3
Thread: Yellow 3/0
Tail: Red silk, blonde Aqua Fibers, looped
Body: Peacock her, red silk
Legs: Turkey feather fibers, knotted
Wing: Blonde Aqua Fibers, brown hen feather, light deer hair
Hackle: Brown
Head: Deer hair, butt end from wing

Bright Yellow Hopper

Tied by: Don Joslyn, Eagle Point, OR
Hook: Alec Jackson, #7
Thread: Yellow 3/0
Tail: Alec Jackson Red Silk
Body: Yellow 1/8-inch foam strip, tied extended
Wing: Gold Krystal Flash strands, orange Aqua Fiber, pheasant feather, elk hair
Legs: Cree feathers, trimmed and knotted
Hackles: Cree, brown
Head: Yellow thread, colored with brown marker

Bullet Head Hopper

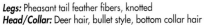

Tied by: Doyle Bartsch, Mayville, WI
Hook: Daiichi 1270, #14
Thread: Yellow 6/0
Tail: Red calf tail hair
Body: Yellow foam strip
Wing: Pearl Flashabou strands, pheasant body feather, coated with Flexament
Legs: Pheasant tail feather fibers, knotted
Head/Collar: Deer hair, bullet style, bottom collar hair clipped

Bushy's Foam Hopper

Tied by: B. Bughman, Murray, UT
Hook: Mustad 9672, #10
Thread: Yellow Flymaster A
Shellback/Head: Tan foam strip, folded back for head
Body: Yellow foam strip, folded over sides of hook shank
Rib: Yellow thread
Rear Legs: Yellow grizzly feathers, trimmed to shape, knotted
Wing: Mottled Thin Skin, cut to shape
Front Legs: Yellow grizzly feather stems, trimmed to shape
Antennae: Deer hair
Eyes: Black permanent marker spots

Byng's Hopper

Tied by: Ben Byng, Tracy, CA
Hook: Mustad 94831, #6-#10
Thread: Yellow
Tail: Red feather fibers
Rib: Brown hackle
Body: Yellow poly yarn
Wing: Yellow turkey tail feather section, cut to shape
Post: White Antron yarn fibers
Hackle: Yellow grizzly

Chenille and Peacock Hopper

Tied by: Don Joslyn, Eagle Point, OR
Hook: Alec Jackson, #7
Thread: Black 3/0
Tail: Red silk
Body: Brown and gold chenille, extended over mono core
Wing: Pearl Krystal Flash strands, blonde Aqua Fibers, pheasant feather
Legs: Cree feathers, trimmed and knotted
Head: Peacock herl

Cicada Hopper

Tied by: Robert Lewis, Yonkers, NY
Hook: Mustad 5262,
Thread: Black
Tail: Salmon pink poly yarn fibers
Body: Deer hair, spun, clipped to shape
Legs: Pheasant tail feather fibers, knotted
Wing: Yellow deer hair
Eyes: Mono
Antennae: Pheasant tail feather fibers

Deer Hair Steelhead Hopper

Tied by: Don Joslyn, Eagle Point, OR
Hook: Alec Jackson, #3
Thread: Black 3/0
Body: Coastal deer hair, spun, trimmed to shape
Legs: Golden pheasant feathers, trimmed and knotted
Wing: Pearl Krystal Flash strands, orange Aqua Fibers, pheasant feather
Hackle: Gold pheasant tippet
Head/Collar: Coastal deer hair, bullet style

Don's Bullet Head Hopper

Tied by: Don Joslyn, Eagle Point, OR
Hook: TMC 5212, #10
Thread: Yellow 3/0
Tail: Natural Aqua Fiber, looped, over red silk
Body: Yellow Aqua Fiber
Legs: Turkey feather fibers, knotted
Wing: Deer hair, wood duck feather, and deer hair tips from head
Hackle: Cree, trimmed
Head: Deer hair, bullet style

Doyle's Parachute Hopper

Tied by: Doyle Dartsch, Mayville, WI
Hook: Daiichi 1270, #14
Thread: Green 6/0
Post: White calf tail hair
Rib: Orange floss
Body: Yellow/green dubbing
Legs: Pheasant tail feather fibers, knotted
Wing: Bleached elk hair, turkey feather section, cut to shape, coated with Flexament
Hackle: Olive grizzly

Easy Hopper

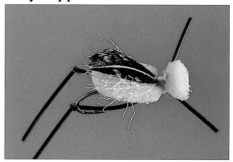

Tied by: Don Joslyn, Eagle Point, OR
Hook: TMC 5212, #10
Thread: Yellow 3/0
Underbody: Gold tinsel
Body: Yellow 1/8-inch foam strip, cut to shape
Legs: Brown round rubber, rear legs knotted
Wing: Blonde Aqua Fiber, and brown hen feather, coated with Flexament

Eby's Hopper

Tied by: Gord Eby, Fort St. John, BC
Hook: Mustad 9672, #8
Thread: Black
Body: Yellow foam, cut to shape
Wing: Turkey feather section, deer hair, coated with Flexament
Legs: Brown Ultra Chenille, twisted with copper wire
Head: Deer hair, spun, trimmed to shape

E-Z Hopper

Tied by: Don Brown, Riga, MI
Hook: Mustad 9671, #4-#10
Thread: Brown 8/0
Body: Olive deer hair, extended, pulled body style
Wing: Olive Micro Web Wing material, cut to shape, colored with green marker
Legs: Brown round rubber, knot rear legs
Eyes: Medium green plastic, mounted with Zap-a-Gap glue

Flying Hopper

Tied by: Ed Kraft, Lancaster, PA
Hook: Mustad 79580, #6
Thread: Brown
Tail: Tips of 2 orange saddle hackles, split
Abdomen: Chartreuse deer body hair, spun, cut to shape
Rib: 2 chartreuse grizzly hackles, trimmed short
Hind Legs: Chartreuse grizzly hackles, front half formed by stroking fibers back with vinyl cement until fixed, aft section clipped and bent to shape
Front Legs/Antennae: Stripped chartreuse feather stems
Thorax: Chartreuse dubbing
Wings: Swiss straw, cut to shape, using 3 different colors, spread out and separated
Thorax Shellback: Brown hen back feather, coated with Flexament
Head: Caribou body hair, spun, cut to shape
Eyes: Melted mono, attached to head with Zap-a-Gap glue, colored with red marker

Grass Hopper

Tied by: Mike Giavedoni, Maple, ONT
Hook: Mustad 9672, #10
Thread: Yellow
Body: Sulphur dubbing
Wing: Goose wing feather section, cut to shape, coated with Flexament
Legs: Hackle stems, knotted, trimmed to shape
Head/Collar: Yellow and natural deer hair, spun, trimmed to shape

Green CDC Hopper

Tied by: Don Joslyn, Eagle Point, OR
Hook: TMC 5212, #10
Thread: Black
Tail: Orange yarn
Body: Green CDC dubbing, extended over orange yarn core
Legs: Peacock herl, 3 strands per leg, knotted, lower legs coated with Flexament
Wing: Multi-color Krystal Flash strands, orange Aqua Fiber, pheasant body feather
Hackle: Cree, bottom fibers trimmed

Green Fuzzy Hopper

Tied by: Don Joslyn, Eagle Point, OR
Hook: TMC 5212, #10
Thread: Brown 6/0
Tail: Red silk
Rib: Cree hackle, trimmed short
Body: Green CDC dubbing
Wing: Brown saddle feather, coated with Flexament and trimmed to shape, green deer hair
Legs: Brown round rubber legs, rear legs knotted
Head: Green deer hair, spun, trim to shape

Hank's Hopper

Tied by: Henry Hoffman, Warrenton, OR
Hook: TMC 200, #6
Thread: Tan 6/0
Tail: Elk hair, tips from body
Rib: Fine gold wire, counterwrapped
Body: Elk hair
Hackle: Ginger grizzly saddle
Wings: Coastal deer hair, turkey feather section, coated with Flexament
Legs: Olive Super Floss, knotted
Head/Collar: Coastal deer hair, bullet style

High Banks Hopper

Tied by: Bruce Raymond, Woodridge, IL
Hook: TMC 100 or 101, #12
Thread: Green 8/0
Body: Cream Variant, #26 Fly-Rite Extra Fine Ploy dubbing
Wing: Golden pheasant tippet fibers, olive deer hair
Hackle: Brown

Lil'Dull Hopper

Tied by: Jay Kaneshige, Castro Valley, CA
Hook: TMC 5310, #10
Thread: Orange
Rib: Orange thread
Body: Deer belly hair, extended
Legs: Grizzly feathers, trimmed to shape and knotted
Wing: Partridge feather, grizzly feather fibers
Head/Collar: Elk hair, spun, trimmed to shape

Little Yellow Grasshopper

Tied by: Fred Iacoletti, Albuquerque, NM
Hook: Mustad 94831, #14
Thread: Brown 6/0
Rib: Olive-green thread
Body: Yellow deer hair, pulled body style
Wing: Green deer hair, hen saddle feather, coated with Flexament
Legs: Pheasant tail feather fibers, knotted
Head/Collar: Deer hair, spun, trimmed to shape

Ma's Hopper

Tied by: Vladimir Markov, Irkutsk, Russia
Hook: Mustad 948331, #12
Thread: Rust
Body: Closed-cell foam, cut to shape, coated with epoxy, painted
Rear Legs: Green feathers, clipped to shape, knotted
Front Legs: Moose hair
Wing: Turkey tail feather section, cut to shape, coated with Flexament
Antennae: Badger hair

Orange Foam Steelhead Hopper

Tied by: Don Joslyn, Eagle Point, OR
Hook: Alec Jackson, #1.5
Thread: Orange 3/0
Tail: Golden pheasant tippet
Abdomen: Orange foam strip, folded extension style
Thorax: Purple dubbing
Collar/Hackle: Golden pheasant tippet, wood duck, and brown hackle
Beard: Multi color Krystal Flash strands
Legs: Black feathers, trimmed to shape, knotted
Head: Salmon dubbing

Pantall's Hopper

Tied by: Joe Pantall, Greenville, PA
Hook: Mustad 7958, #8-#12
Thread: Olive 6/0
Tail: Red feather fibers
Rib: Copper wire
Shellback: Yellow foam
Body: Gold dubbing
Wing: Turkey feather section, cut to shape, coated with Flexament
Hackle: Olive
Eyes: Mono
Head: Yellow foam, butt end from shellback

Pantall's Parachute Hopper

Tied by: Joe Pantall, Greenville, PA
Hook: Mustad 7958, #8-#12
Thread: Pale yellow 6/0
Tail: Red feather fibers
Rib: Fine copper wire
Abdomen: Gold and tan dubbing, mixed
Wings: Gray squirrel hair, molted turkey feather sections, cut to shape and coated with Flexament
Legs: Pheasant tail feather fibers, knotted
Post: Bright orange Antron yarn fibers
Hackle: Grizzly
Thorax: Yellow dubbing

Para Vis Hopper

Tied by: Rod Dines, New Meadows, ID
Hook: TMC 5212, #8-#12
Thread: Tan
Body: Brown-olive dubbing
Wing: Molted turkey feather sections, cut to shape, coated with Flexament
Legs: Pheasant tail feather fibers, knotted
Wing Post: Yellow poly yarn fibers
Hackle: Grizzly

Red & Yellow Parachute Hopper

Tied by: Mark Hoeser, Stockton, CA
Hook: Daiichi 1720, #10
Thread: Yellow 6/0
Wing Post: Fluorescent yellow calf body hair
Rib: Brown 3/0 thread
Body: Yellow dubbing
Wing: Yellow mottled turkey wing feather section, cut to shape, coated with Flexament
Legs: Red pheasant feather tail fibers, knotted
Hackle: Yellow grizzly
Antennae: Small red Life-Flex strands

Ritter's Hopper

Tied by: Carl Ritter, Sedona, AZ
Hook: Mustad 9672, #12
Thread: Brown
Tail: Coastal deer hair, tips from body
Rib: Brown thread
Body: Coastal deer hair
Wing: Clear Antron fibers, turkey feather section, deer hair
Legs: Yellow round rubber, spotted with brown marker
Head: Peacock herl, pheasant tail feather fibers, pulled back

Scott's Hopper

Tied by: Scott Zadroga, San Diego, CA
Hook: Mustad 94831, #10
Thread: Tan 6/0
Rib: Brown hackle, trimmed short
Body: Yellow foam
Wing: Deer hair
Legs: Yellow round rubber
Head: Yellow foam, bullet style

Steve's Wet Grasshopper

Tied by: Steve Potter, Tracy, CA
Hook: Eagle Claw live hopper hook, #6-#8
Thread: Black
Rib: Grizzly hackle
Body: Burnt orange Sparkle Chenille
Wing: Wood duck feather, coated with head cement, folded
Hackle: Brown hen

Ultimate Hopper

Tied by: Brad Cunningham, Yakima, WA
Hook: TMC 5212, #8-#10
Thread: Yellow 6/0
Rib: Fine copper wire
Body: Yellow elk hair
Wing: Brown Swiss straw, cut to shape, turkey feather section, cut to shape, coated with Flexament
Legs: Grizzly feathers, trimmed to shape, knotted
Head/Collar: Elk hair, bullet style

Ultra Hopper

Tied by: Bahman Khadivi, Cupertino, CA
Hook: Mustad 9672, #6
Thread: Tan
Tails: Brown goose biots
Rib: Tan thread
Body: Tan foam
Wing: Brown Swiss straw, elk hair, turkey feather section
Rear Legs: Brown Ultra Chenille, knotted, tips melted
Head: Brown deer hair, bullet style, trimmed bottom collar hairs
Front Legs: Black round rubber

Verde Good Hopper

Tied by: Don Joslyn, Eagle Point, OR
Hook: Alec Jackson, #7
Thread: Brown 6/0
Tag: Red silk
Tail: Black Krystal Flash strands
Rib: Brown thread
Body: Green foam strip, folded extension style
Wing: Green Krystal Flash strands, pheasant feather, coated with Flexament and cut to shape, green deer hair
Hackle: Brown
Head: Butt ends from wing

Williams Creek Hopper

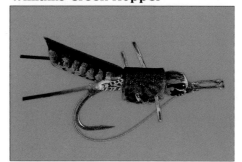

Tied by: Nick Norton, Salt Lake City, UT
Hook: TMC 8089, #10
Thread: Olive 6/0
Weed Guard: Mono
Abdomen: Yellow Rainy's Round Foam
Legs: Yellow round rubber, rear legs knotted
Thorax: Tan foam strip, CA glued around hook shank
Eyes: Mono
Head: Yellow foam strip, pulled over eyes
Antennae: Yellow cord strands
Comments: Color body with waterproof markers.

Yellow Royal Hopper

Tied by: Don Joslyn, Eagle Point, OR
Hook: Alec Jackson, #7
Thread: Yellow 3/0
Tail: Deer hair
Abdomen: Yellow 1/8-inch foam strip, folded extension style, colored with brown marker
Body: Peacock herl, Alec Jackson Red Silk
Wing: Pearl Krystal Flash strands, pheasant feather
Legs: Cree feathers, trimmed to shape, knotted
Hackle: Brown
Head: Yellow foam, folded back, colored with brown marker

Yellow Rubber Legged Hopper

Tied by: Don Joslyn, Eagle Point, OR
Hook: TMC 5212, #10
Thread: Yellow 3/0
Tail: Red silk
Tag: Gold tinsel
Rib: Yellow thread
Body: Yellow foam stripe, folded extension style, colored with brown marker
Legs: Brown round rubber strands, rear legs knotted
Wing: Pearl Krystal Flash strands, orange Aqua Fiber, pheasant feather, deer hair
Head: Butts from deer hair wing

Miscellaneous Terrestrials

Annual Cicada

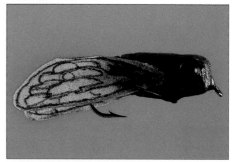

Tied by: Jack Pangburn, Westbury, NY
Hook: Mustad 79580, #6
Body: White hi-density popper body foam, carved to shape, epoxied to hook, coated with black acrylic paint
Wing: Fabric liner material, cut to shape, painted
Legs: Black round rubber

Black Peafowl

Tied by: Darrell Edwards, Erwin, TN
Hook: TMC 200, #10
Thread: Black
Tail: Blue bucktail hair, trimmed short
Rib: Green copper wire
Body: Black Vinyl rib
Head: Peacock herl

Black Widow

Tied by: Jim Riley, Grass Valley, CA
Hook: TMC 2487, #10
Thread: Black 6/0
Shellback: Black foam
Body: Red floss
Hackle: Black

Brown Tree Hopper

Tied by: Jack Pangburn, Westbury, NY
Hook: Mustad 94840, #10
Thread: Black 6/0
Body: Silver tinsel
Wings: Matched hen pheasant wing feathers
Hackle: Brown, cree

Byng's Cricket

Tied by: Ben Byng, Tracy, CA
Hook: Mustad 94831, #8-#10
Thread: Black
Tail: Black feather fibers
Rib: Dark brown hackle
Body: Black poly yarn
Wing: Black turkey tail feather section, cut to shape
Legs: Black turkey tail feather fibers, knotted, butt ends pulled forward over head, coated with Flexament, bent to shape
Post: Yellow Antron yarn
Hackle: Dark brown

Housefly

Tied by: Robert Schreiner, Southampton, PA
Hook: Mustad 3906, #12-#14
Thread: Black 8/0
Shellback/Head: Black closed-cell foam
Body: Peacock herl
Wings: Mallard quill sections, cut to shape
Legs: Black hackle, top fibers trimmed

Iridescent Black Cricket

Tied by: Ronn Lucas, Sr., Milwaukie, OR
Hook: TMC
Thread: Black
Ovipositor: Stripped black feather stem, end fibers trimmed to arrowhead shape (for female cricket only)
Tails: Stripped black feather stems
Antennae: Stripped grizzly feather stems
Eyes: Iridescent black beads, with mono core
Body: Black Foamback, wrapped
Rear Legs: Black pheasant tail feather fibers, knotted, coated with head cement
Wing/Thorax Shellback: Black turkey feather sections, cut to shape, coated with head cement
Thorax: Black Iridescent Dubbing, picked out
Front Legs: Black soft hackle, trimmed short

Jonny Bee Good

Tied by: Richard Pilatzke, Littleton, CO
Hook: TMC 100, #12
Thread: Black 8/0
Body: Rainy's Bumble Bee Popper foam
Wings: Metallic Twist, burned to shape with caddis wing burner
Legs: Black deer hair

Live Bait Floating Cricket

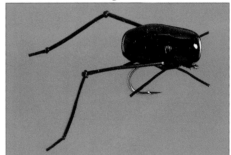

Tied by: Curtis Kauer, Salina, KS
Hook: TMC 2488, #10
Thread: Black
Legs: Black round rubber, rear legs knotted
Body: Live Bait Float, available at bass tackle shops, mounted to hook shank with epoxy, painted black, coated with epoxy

Mud Dauber

Tied by: Darrell Edwards, Erwin, TN
Hook: Mustad 3906, #6-#8
Thread: Black
Tail: Pheasant tail feather fibers
Body: Black thread, coated with head cement
Wings: Black feathers
Hackle: Brown

One Clump Wasp

Tied by: Vladimir Markov, Irkutsk, Russia
Hook: Any dry-fly hook
Thread: Yellow
Rib: Black silk
Body: Yellow deer hair, pulled body, bullet style head, bottom collar hairs trimmed (body formed from 1 clump of hair)
Wings: Zing, cut to shape

Sierra Catakiller

Tied by: Jay Kaneshige, Castro Valley, CA
Hook: TMC 200R, #8
Thread: Black 8/0
Rib: Light brown hackle, trimmed short, wrapped over middle of body
Body: Black ostrich herl front and rear, rust Hair-Tron dubbing in middle

Sloe Bug

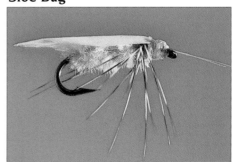

Tied by: Jack Pangburn, Westbury, NY
Hook: Mustad 94840, #14-#16
Thread: Pale yellow 8/0
Body: Yellow mini chenille
Wing: Yellow feather tip
Hackle: Grizzly, V-cut on bottom
Antennae: Mono strands

Wooly Bear

Tied by: Jack Pangburn, Westbury, NY
Hook: Mustad 79580, #8
Thread: Black 6/0
Body: Black and orange chenille
Hackle: Light dun

Abbies Sparkle

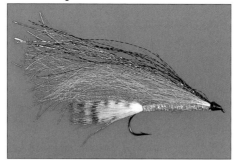

Tied by: Wade Malwitz, Portland, OR
Hook: Mustad 38941, #2
Thread: Black 4/0
Tail: White marabou feather, striped with black marker
Body: Pearl braided
Wing: Pearl Krystal Flash strands, white yak hair, pearl holographic Flashabou strands, black Krystal Flash strands
Head: Red thread stripe

A.J.'s Fishy

Tied by: Larry Howard, Roy, UT
Hook: Up eyed salmon
Thread: White
Tail: Gold and silver Flashabou strands
Rib: Clear mono
Body: Pearl Braid
Wing: White Rabbit strip, mounted Matuka style
Throat: Red and pearl Krystal Flash strands
Eyes: Stick-on
Head: White thread; after eyes are mounted, wrap over with clear mono and coat with epoxy

A.J.'s Minnow

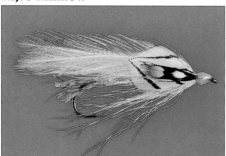

Tied by: A.J. Courteau, Erie, PA
Hook: TMC 300
Thread: Clear mono
Tail: Butt ends from body material
Body: Pearl Mylar tubing
Wing: 4 white saddle feathers
Throat: White bucktail hairs
Cheeks: Silver pheasant feather, jungle cock eye feather

Alaskan Deceiver

Tied by: Mark Broer, Issaquah, WA
Hook: Mustad 3407, #10
Thread: White Monocord
Wing: White bucktail hair, 4 white saddle feathers, silver Flashabou strands, blue bucktail hair, 10 peacock herl strands
Eyes: Black and white flat enamel paint, coated with head cement

Articulated Sculpin

Tied by: Earl Stanek, Cotter, AR
Hook: Mustad 34007, #4, weighted with lead tape cut to shape
Thread: Olive
Hinge: .013 Dead Soft craft wire
Tail: Olive grizzly feather marabou fibers, tied to short section of an Aberdeen hook, hook shank cut behind thread wraps after tying in tail, then mounted to hinge
Dorsal Fin: Deer hair
Body: Olive wool rope, trimmed to shape, colored with permanent marks
Pectoral Fins: Brown speckled hen feathers, coated with Flexament
Eyes: Black mono

Baby Bluegill

Tied by: Brian Machado, Cambria, CA
Hook: Eagle Claw LO52S, #6
Thread: Red
Body: Flat pearl Diamond Braid
Wing: White fox hair, green, gold, and blue Flashabou strands, blue Krystal Flash strands, 2 strands of peacock herl, olive arctic foxtail hair
Head: .011 wire looped through hook eye and twisted, twisted wire covered with dental floss and coated with CA glue, white thread topped with peacock herl and blue Krystal Flash strand butt ends from wing, head coated with epoxy
Eyes: Plastic

CHAPTER 10: STREAMERS • 147

Barred Sculpin (bottom view)

Tied by: Jeff Lingenfelter, Browns Valley, CA
Hook: TMC 300, #6
Thread: Dark Brown 6/0, weighted
Rib: Copper wire
Body: Tan Diamond Braid
Wing: Brown/yellow barred rabbit strip, Matuka style
Fins: Golden-olive grizzly feather marabou fibers
Collar: Coastal deer hair, trimmed to shape
Head: Mottled brown jumbo chenille, trimmed to shape
Eyes: Black bead chain

Bead Head Blue

Tied by: Doug Fullerton, Menominee, MI
Hook: Mustad 3261, #4
Thread: Black 6/0
Body: 10-12 blue phase ring-necked pheasant feathers, wrapped
Head: Gold bead

Black Maraai

Tied by: Sam de Beer, Cambridge Bay, Nunavut, Canada
Hook: Mustad 3906, #6-#14
Thread: Black
Rib: Gold oval tinsel
Body: Peacock herl
Hackle: Black
Eyes: Silver bead chain

Bates Brown Marabou

Tied by: Michael Bates, Steamboat Springs, CO
Hook: Streamer hook, weighted
Thread: Brown
Tail: Brown marabou feather fibers, root beer Krystal Flash strands
Lateral Line: Root beer Krystal Flash, 2-4 strands on each side
Body: Brown dubbing
Wing: Brown marabou feather fibers, black ostrich herl strands, alternated clumps tied Aztec style
Head: Black ostrich herl, over brown dubbing

Big Mike's Copper Smelt

Tied by: Steve Potter, Tracy, CA
Hook: Martinek Rangeley Streamer Hook by Gaelic Supreme, 8X long, #1
Thread: Black 6/0
Rib: Copper wire, 4 strands twisted
Body: Copper Mylar
Beard: White bucktail hair
Wing: 2 brown and 1 black saddle feathers per side, mounted concave side in
Cheeks: Wood duck flank feather, jungle cock eye feather
Head: Black lacquer

Bladed Minnow

Tied by: Wade Malwitz, Portland, OR
Hook: Mustad 9672, #8
Thread: Black 4/0
Tail: White yak hair, striped with permanent marker
Body: Pearl Mylar braid
Blade: Formed from copper sheet, cut to shape with hole drilled, attached to hook with Kevlar thread loop
Wing: White yak hair, pearl holographic Flashabou strands, black Krystal Flash strands
Eyes: Silver bead chain

Bates Olive Marabou Streamer

Tied by: Mickael Bates, Steamboat Springs, CO
Hook: Streamer hook, weighted
Thread: Olive
Tail: Olive marabou feather fibers, peacock Krystal Flash strands
Lateral Line: Peacock Krystal Flash, 2-4 strands on each side
Body: Olive dubbing
Wing: Olive marabou feather fibers, gray ostrich herl strands, alternated clumps tied Aztec style
Head: Gray ostrich herl, over olive dubbing

Big Ugly

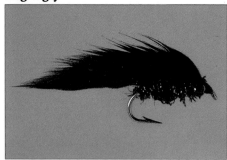

Tied by: David McCants, Pleasant Hill, CA
Hook: Mustad 3399A, #6, weighted
Thread: Black 6/0
Body: Large black Ice Chenille, trimmed on top fibers
Wing: Black rabbit strip, tied in at rear body and in front of eyes
Eyes: Black plastic bead chain, colored blue with permanent marker

Braided Carp Minnow

Tied by: Henry Hoffman, Warrenton, OR
Hook: Daiichi X472 or TMC 9395, #2-#6, weighted with 2 strands of .025 lead wire twisted into a rope and lashed to the underside of the hook shank
Thread: Clear mono and orange 6/0
Tail: Tan grizzly chickabou feather fibers
Rib: Clear mono
Body: Orange nylon parachute cord
Backstrap: Brown chenille
Wing: 2 tan grizzly saddle feathers, mounted Matuka style
Gills: Red chickabou feather fibers
Hackle: Tan grizzly
Eyes: Plastic stick-on
Head: Orange thread, top colored with brown waterproof marker, coated with epoxy

Bristol Bay Smolt

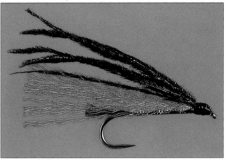

Tied by: Mark Broer, Issaquah, WA
Hook: TMC 5263, #6
Thread: Black
Tail: Red floss
Body: Silver tinsel
Wing: White and olive Super Hair, 6-8 peacock herl strands

Bunny Streamer

Tied by: Rod Powell, Gypsum, CO
Hook: Streamer, weighted, 25lb. weed guard
Thread: White
Body: White and yellow rabbit strips glued together with contact cement
Gills: Red Krystal Flash strands
Head: White thread
Eyes: Stick-on, coated with epoxy

Chartreuse Black Lace

Tied by: Christopher Helm, Toledo, OH
Hook: Partridge CS17, 6X long
Thread: Black
Body: Peacock and red Lite Brite dubbing
Wing: 2 Whiting black lace hen feathers, lower fibers stripped to hook bend, glued to top of body
Hackle: Yellow black lace hen feather

Chartreuse Candy

Tied by: Curtis Kauer, Salina, KS
Hook: Gamakatsu SS15, #10-#12
Thread: Chartreuse
Tail: Chartreuse round rubber, tuft of rabbit fur tied to end, secured with CA glue
Body: Pearl Mylar braid, thread, colored with permanent markers, coated with epoxy

Cher Minnow

Tied by: Don Joslyn, Eagle Point, OR
Hook: Alec Jackson Daiichi River Dee Low Water, #3
Thread: Black 3/0
Tails: Black goose biots, pearl Rad Floss, hot pink Fluorofiber
Body: Black Hareline Krystal dubbing
Fins: Black goose biots
Wing/Throat: Pearl Rad Floss, hot pink Fluorofiber

Chickabou Golden Shiner

Tied by: Henry Hoffman, Warrenton, Or
Hook: Daiichi X472 or TMC 9395, #2-#6, weighted with 2 strands of .025 lead twisted into a rope and lashed to the bottom of the hook shank
Thread: Clear mono and orange 6/0
Tail: Tan grizzly feather marabou fibers, green Krystal Flash strands
Topping: 3 strands of olive green braided Mylar tinsel
Body: Gold Mylar tubing
Gills: Red chickabou feather fibers
Hackle: Tan grizzly chickabou
Head: Orange thread
Eyes: Stick-on, coated with epoxy

Chris's Fresh Water Baitfish

Tied by: Chris French, East Brunswick, NJ
Hook: Mustad 3407, #8
Thread: Clear mono
Body: White and chartreuse Poly Bear Fibers, trimmed to shape
Eyes: Stick-on #2

Cinnamon Low Rider

Tied by: Don Joslyn, Eagle Point, OR
Hook: Alec Jackson Daiichi 2051, #3
Thread: Black 3/0
Tail: Peacock herl strands
Body: Rust Hareline Krystal dubbing
Wing: Brown grizzly feather, hen ring-necked pheasant tail feather
Hackle: Ginger, top fibers trimmed
Head: Orange 3/0 thread

Clouser Perch Fly

Tied by: Jack Pangburn, Westbury, NY
Hook: Mustad 79580, #8, hoop point up
Thread: Black, red
Belly: White and yellow bucktail hairs
Wing: Yellow Super Hair, orange Krystal Flash strands, bait fish Poly Bear, black bucktail hair
Eyes: Painted lead barbell

Clouser Pinhead Minnow

Tied by: Jack Pangburn, Westbury, NY
Hook: Streamer, hoop point up
Thread: Red and brown
Body/Wing: White bucktail hair, gold Krystal Flash strands, natural bucktail hair, flanked by 2 strands of pearl Flashabou
Eyes: Painted lead barbell

Cone-Head Foxy Brook Trout

Tied by: Bruce Raymond, Woodridge, IL
Hook: Dai-Riki 700, #10
Cone-Head: Small gold cone
Thread: Red 6/0
Tail: Green fox hair, red floss
Rib: Silver oval tinsel, counterwrapped
Body: Pearl Hareline Ice Dubbing
Throat: Orange fox hair
Wing: White, orange, and green fox hair, coyote hair

Cutthroat Streamer

Tied by: Wayne Noble, Coquitlam, BC
Hook: Daiichi 2457, #12
Thread: Black
Tail: Butt ends from body
Body: Silver Mylar tubing, silver tinsel chenille
Wing: Golden Fish Fuss strands
Throat: Red rabbit hair
Head: Black thread

Deer Hair Minnow

Tied by: Steve Potter, Tracy, CA
Hook: Mustad 3366, #1/0
Thread: White Monocord
Tail: 2 olive, black and gray feathers, trimmed to shape
Body: Gray, white, olive and black deer belly hair, stacked, trimmed to shape
Eyes: Plastic doll

Delaware Shiner

Tied by: Robert Lewis, Pound Ridge, NY
Hook: Varivas 990, #8
Thread: Gray
Tail: Grizzly feather, lower fibers stripped from stem and stem slid into body tubing, remaining fibers cut to shape
Body: Pearl Mylar tubing, the rear butt ends coated with CA glue
Wing: White and gray Sea Fibers
Gills: Orange Krystal Flash strands
Eyes: Stick-on, coated with epoxy

Dusty's Alvein Minnow

Tied by: Roger Hub, Abbotsford, BC
Hook: TMC 5263, #8
Thread: White
Rib: Silver wire
Body: Silver Mylar tinsel
Wing: Pearl Lite Brite, and baitfish Angel Hair fibers
Gills: Red dubbing
Head: White thread
Eyes: Prism eyes, coated with Soft Body
Egg Sack: Orange hot glue

Egg Sucking Cactus Leach

Tied by: Bill Keister, Marlborough, CT
Hook: Mustad 9672, weight optional
Thread: Black
Tail: Peacock Krystal Flash strands, black marabou feather fibers
Body: Large black Cactus Chenille
Head: Red/orange egg yarn, trimmed to shape

Epoxy Streamer

Tied by: Scott Zadroga San Diego, CA
Hook: Mustad 9674, #4, weight optional
Thread: Olive
Tail: Olive marabou feather fibers, silver Krystal Flash strands
Body: 2 plastic strips cut to shape and mounted to the top and bottom of the hook shank, gaps filled with epoxy and dried, color added to the epoxy for final coat
Eyes: Formed with colored epoxy

Exeter Grayling Tub Fly

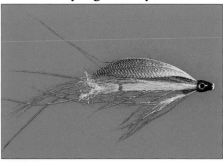

Tied by: Grant Lockhart, Kelowna, BC
Tube: 2-inch long plastic tube
Thread: Red 6/0
Tail: Butt ends from body, Mylar tubing
Body: Pearlescent Mylar tubing
Underwing/Beard: White and purple polar bear hair, or substitute
Wing: Red Flashabou strands, 2 mallard flank feathers
Head: Red thread
Eyes: Plastic stick-on

Fat Fry

Tied by: Jack Pangburn, Westbury, NY
Hook: Streamer, #4-#8
Thread: Tobacco
Tail: Tan yak hair
Underbody: Tan chenille, 2 pearl Flashabou strands
Sides: Tan marabou feathers, brown feathers
Shoulder: Marked eye patch pheasant body feather

Ferdi's Minnow

Tied by: Ferdi Hianes, Abbotsford, BC
Hook: Mustad 9672, #6-#12
Thread: Black
Tail: White Antron dubbing fibers
Lateral Line: Olive Krystal Flash, 2 strands
Body: White Antron dubbing, brushed out, trimmed to shape, top colored with black waterproof marker
Head: Black thread
Eyes: Plastic stick-on

Foam Fry

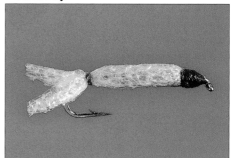

Tied by: Sam de Beer, Cambridge Bay, Nunavut, Canada
Hook: Streamer, 3X-4X long, weight optional
Thread: Red
Tail: Foam from shellback, cut to shape
Underbody: Pearl Mylar tubing, wrapped
Shellback: White foam, cut to shape

Giavedoni's Baitfish

Tied by: M. Giavedoni, Maple, ON
Hook: Streamer, #10
Thread: White
Tail: White marabou feather fibers
Body: White dubbing
Wing: White marabou feather fibers, 4-6 clumps mounted on top of hook shank, Aztec style, 4-6 strands of silver Krystal Flash on each side
Eyes: Silver bead chain

Giavedoni's Streamer

Tied by: M. Giavedoni, Maple, ON
Hook: Streamer, #10
Thread: Red
Body: Silver tinsel
Wing/Head: Brown and yellow bucktail, bullet head style

Golden Darter

Tied by: Jack Pangburn, Westbury, NY
Hook: Streamer
Thread: Black
Tail: Cree feather fibers
Rib: Flat gold tinsel
Body: Cream poly or Antron yarn
Wing: Tan yak hair, 2 golden badger feathers
Shoulders: Marked pheasant feather tips

Golden Shiner

Tied by: Harry Gross, Silverton, OR
Hook: Streamer 6X long, #6-#10
Thread: Black
Tail: Orange feather fibers
Rib: Gold tinsel
Body: White yarn, slightly tapered
Belly: White bucktail hair
Throat: Orange feather fibers
Wing: Yellow bucktail hair, 4-6 strands of peacock herl
Shoulders: Gray/blue dun saddle feathers, 1 per side
Cheeks: Jungle cock eye feathers

Gord's Sculpin

Tied by: Gord Eby, Fort St. John, BC
Hook: Mustad 3665A, #8, weight optional
Thread: Black
Tail: Brown marabou feather fibers, furnace feathers 1 per side
Body: Natural and black deer hair, spun, trimmed to shape
Fins: Pheasant rump feathers, trimmed to shape
Comments: For unweighted fly fishing with a sinking line.

Green Demon

Tied by: J. Mullin, Casper, WY
Hook: Mustad 3906B, #6, weighted
Thread: Green
Tail: Green marabou feather fibers
Body Hackle: Green saddle
Body: Green Estaz chenille

Guinea Hen Streamer

Tied by: Larry Stephens, Kansas City, MO
Hook: TMC 5263, #8
Thread: Black 6/0
Tail: Yellow hen feather fibers
Rib: Copper wire
Body: Black floss
Wing: White calf tail hair, between 2 guinea feathers
Head: Black thread

Holographic Fly

Tied by: Boyd Elder, Spiro, OK
Hook: Mustad 9672, #8, weighted
Thread: Black
Tail: Black marabou feather fibers
Body: Silver holographic tinsel strands twisted into 2 cords
     and woven with an overhand weave
Hackle: Furnace

Jak's Perch

Tied by: Jack Pangburn, Westbury, NY
Hook: Mustad 79580, #2-#6
Thread: Black
Tail: Cree feathers, 2 pair
Underbody: Dental floss
Body: Peacock herl
Wing: Cree feathers, 5 pair, tied Aztec style
Body Apron: Cream/white feather fibers
Beard: Orange feather fibers
Eyes: Jungle cock eye feather

Kootenay Killers

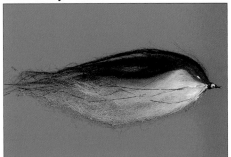

Tied by: Sam de Beer, Cambridge Bay, Nunavut, Canada
Hooks: Stainless steel, #3/0 and #1/0 for stinger, wire
     leader to connect the hooks
Thread: Black
Underbody: Red floss
Body: White, yellow, brown, red, and black Icelandic sheep
     fur
Lateral Line: Silver Flashabou stands
Throat: Red Krystal Flash strands
Eyes: Plastic doll

Lead Fry

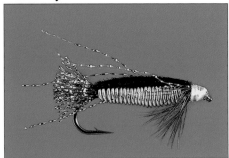

Tied by: Sam de Beer, Cambridge Bay, Nunavut, Canada
Hook: Mustad 9672
Thread: White
Tail: Multi colored Krystal Flash strands
Shellback: Peacock herl strands
Body: Lead-free wire
Lateral line: Multicolored Krystal Flash strands
Throat: Red grizzly feather fibers

Little Brook Trout

Tied by: Sheldon Fedder II, Millville, PA
Hook: Mustad 9575
Thread: Black
Tail: Bright green bucktail hair, red Krystal Flash strands
Rib: Silver oval tinsel
Body: Cream wool yarn
Wing: White, orange, and green bucktail, gray squirrel tail
     hair
Throat: Orange bucktail hair
Cheeks: Jungle cock eye feathers

Little Critter

Tied by: Jesse Goodwin, Auburn, ME
Hook: Mustad 9672, #6, weighted
Thread: White
Tail: Pink rabbit strip, pearl Krystal Flash strands
Body: Pearl and red Ice Dubbing
Wing: Pink rabbit strip
Head: Olive Ice Dubbing

Lockhart Grayling

Tied by: Grant Lockhart, Kelowna, BC
Hook: Mustad 36890, #4
Thread: Red 6/0
Tag: Red thread, coated with epoxy
Body: Silver braid
Wing: Clear and purple Ultra Hair fibers, red Flashabou
     strands and mallard flank feather
Beard: Pink polar bear hair and clear Ultra Hair fibers
Head: Red thread
Eyes: Stick-on, coated with epoxy

Macho Muddler

Tied by: Don Joslyn, Eagle Point, OR
Hook: Alec Jackson Daiichi Steelhead Iron, #5
Thread: Black 3/0
Tag: Gold French tinsel
Tails: Black goose biots
Butt: Black Hareline Krystal dubbing
Abdomen: Gold French tinsel
Thorax: Black Hareline Krystal dubbing
Wing: Bronze turkey tail feather, brown deer hair
Head: Deer hair, butt ends from wing, trimmed to shape

Mad Tom

Tied by: Jack Pangburn, Westbury, NY
Hook: Streamer, #4
Thread: Black
Tail: Black raccoon tail hair
Body: Black raccoon tail hair, white mountain goat hair

Marabou Double Bunny

Tied by: Carl Ritter, Sedona, AZ
Hook: Streamer, #2-#8
Thread: Black 8/0
Wing: Black and brown rabbit strips, glued together, 5 strands of pearl Krystal Flash on each side
Hackle: Black marabou
Head: Black thread coated with black, red, and clear nail polish
Eyes: Prismatic eyes, secured with epoxy

Marabou Muddler

Tied by: Jack Pangburn, Westbury, NY
Hook: Mustad 79580, #2-#8
Thread: Tan
Tail: Red feather fibers
Body: Gold Krinkle tinsel
Wing: Olive-brown marabou feather fibers
Head/Collar: Deer hair, spun, trimmed to shape

May Morning Custom

Tied by: Harry Gross, Silverton, OR
Hook: Streamer
Thread: Black
Rib: Medium silver oval tinsel
Body: Flat silver tinsel
Wing: 6 strands of peacock herl, 1 bright tangerine feather and 1 blue feather per side
Belly: Bright pink and white bucktail hairs, golden pheasant crest
Throat: White schlappen, orange feather fibers
Valings: Orange golden pheasant crest topped with golden pheasant crest, 1 each on top and bottom
Shoulders: Orange golden pheasant body feather
Cheeks: Jungle cock eye feather

Midnight Muddler

Tied by: Mark Hoeser, Stockton, CA
Hook: Daiichi 2271, #1
Thread: Black
Tail: Black turkey feather section
Body: Kreinik medium copper braid
Wing: Golden badger rooster feathers, 2 per side
Shoulder: Golden pheasant tippet feathers
Collar/Head: Natural coastal deer hair and black deer hair, spun, trimmed to shape
Eyes: White solid plastic, 4 1/2mm

Mini Rainbow

Tied by: Gord Eby, Fort St. John, BC
Hook: Mustad 36890, #4, weight optional
Thread: Black 6/0
Tail: Gray marabou feather fibers, silver Krystal Flash strands
Body: Pearl Mylar tubing
Wing: Pearl Flashabou stands, olive Super Hair, olive marabou feather fibers
Gills: Red ostrich herl
Eyes: Stick-on

Money

Tied by: Chris Gerono, State College, PA
Hook: Mustad 9672, #4-#8
Thread: Dark olive
Body: Gold tinsel
Wing: Olive rabbit strip, wood duck flank feather fibers
Collar/Head: Dark olive deer hair, spun, trimmed to shape
Nose: Gold bead

Natal Silver Minnow

Tied by: Gordon Mackenzie, Syderstone, England
Hook: Streamer, 4X long, #2
Thread: Black
Tag: Silver oval tinsel
Tail: Red rabbit guard hair hackle, wrapped around hook shank
Body: Silver Mylar braid
Belly: White bucktail hair
Wing: 4 grizzly saddle feathers, 2 peacock herl strands
Hackle: Grizzly
Shoulders: Teal flank feather
Cheeks: Jungle cock eye feather
Topping: Black golden pheasant crest

Noble's White Streamer

Tied by: Wayne Noble, Coquitlam, BC
Hook: Daiichi 2457, #2
Thread: Black
Tail: White marabou feather fibers, silver, and black Flashabou strands
Body: Roots white Llama fiber and ice blue Flashabou strands used to form a wire core dubbing brush, wrapped
Eyes: Red/black barbell

Olive Polly Wager

Tied by: Keith Stephens, Kansas City, MO
Hook: Mustad 9672, #10-#14, weight optional
Thread: Olive or black 6/0
Tail: Olive marabou feather fibers
Underbody: Olive Antron yarn
Body: Olive ostrich herl
Hackle: Olive hen
Head: Olive chenille

Orange Witch

Tied by: Ed Kraft, Lancaster, PA
Hook: TMC 5263, #8
Thread: Black 6/0
Tail: Orange and black hen feather fibers
Rib: Gold holographic tinsel
Body: Orange Antron yarn
Throat: Orange and black hen feather fibers
Wing: Turkey body feather section, folded
Cheeks: Jungle cock eye feather

Oreo Clouser

Tied by: Boyd Elder, Spiro, OK
Hook: Mustad 9672, #4
Thread: Black
Body: Silver and black Krystal Flash strands, twisted into 2 cords and woven with the overhand weave
Wing: Black bucktail hair
Belly: White Fish Hair fibers, silver Krystal Flash strands
Eyes: Red/black lead barbell

Pancurra Crab

Tied by: Bill Keister, Marlborough, CT
Hook: Mustad 9672, tied hook point-up
Thread: Brown
Tail: Green marabou feather fibers
Legs: Orange Spandex
Shellback: Olive Bugskin, mounted to the bottom of the hook shank, trimmed to shape
Body: Cream Fuzzy Foam
Eyes: Black barbell, mounted to top of hook shank
Feelers: Black Spandex

Perch Fry

Tied by: Jack Pangburn, Westbury, NY
Hook: Mustad 79580, #8
Thread: Black
Tail: Golden pheasant tippet fibers
Rib: Flat gold tinsel, counterwrapped
Body: Yellow poly or Antron yarn
Wing: 2 olive grizzly hen saddle feathers
Beard: Red feather fibers

Pete's Reel Minnow

Tied by: Pete Toscani, Bristol, CT
Hook: Mustad 3665A, #4
Thread: Black
Tail: Pearl holographic Flashabou strands, gray Crazy Hair fibers, gray marabou feather fibers
Body: Silver EZ Body Mylar tubing, waterproof markers used for black lateral line and red gills
Eyes: Stick-on

Pete's Reel Rainbow

Tied by: Pete Toscani, Bristol, CT
Hooks: Mustad 34007, #6, gray Dynacord thread loop used for hook connection
Thread: White flat wax nylon
Tail: Gray marabou feather fibers, holographic Flashabou strands
Body: White deer hair, trimmed to shape and colored with waterproof markers
Eyes: Plastic

Pharaoh

Tied by: Bob Doran, Grand Rapids, MI
Hook: Mustad 79580, #6-#8
Thread: Black
Tail: Olive marabou feather fibers
Body: Gold holographic tinsel
Wing: White and red bucktail hairs, red Krystal Flash strands
Eyes: I-Balz barbell

Piker

Tied by: Don Joslyn, Eagle Point, OR
Hook: Alec Jackson Daiichi Steelhead Iron, #3
Thread: Black 3/0
Tail: Gray Hungarian partridge, 2 feathers
Fins/Wing: Gray Hungarian partridge feathers
Body: Pearl Rad Floss

Pink & Purple Streamer

Tied by: Chris French, East Brunswick, NJ
Hook: Mustad 9672
Thread: Black
Tail: Tag ends from body material
Body: Silver Mylar tubing
Wing: Silver Flashabou strands, purple marabou feather fibers
Belly: Pink marabou feather fibers
Eyes: Plastic, coated with epoxy

Poly Puppy

Tied by: Jack Pangburn, Westbury, NY
Hook: Streamer
Thread: Brown
Tail: Furnace feathers, 2 per side, splayed
Butt Hackle: Cree
Body: Variegated brown/black chenille
Eyes: Brass bead chain

Polystickle

Tied by: Jack Pangburn, Westbury, NY
Hook: Mustad 79580, #6
Thread: Black
Tail/Shellback: Copper Swiss straw
Rib: Thread "X" plamered
Body: White chenille
Gills: Red chenille
Beard: Lemon wood duck feather fibers

Polywog

Tied by: Jack Pangburn, Westbury, NY
Hook: Mustad 79580, #4
Thread: Black
Tail: Black marabou feather, black and pearl Krystal Flash strands
Body: Black Krystal Flash chenille (Estaz), trimmed flat on top and bottom

Rainbow Minnow

Tied by: Henry Hoffman, Warrenton, OR
Hook: Daiichi X472 or TMC 9395, #2-#6, weighted with 2 strands of .025 lead wire twisted into a rope and lashed to the bottom of the hook shank
Thread: Clear mono and gray 6/0
Tail: Grizzly chickabou feather fibers, green Krystal Flash strands, 2 strands of red Flashabou
Underbody: White parachute cord, slid over hook shank and secured
Body: Silver or pearl Mylar tubing, topped with 3 strands of green Rad Floss
Gills: Red chickabou feather fibers
Hackle: Grizzly
Eyes: Plastic stick-on
Head: Gray thread, coated with epoxy

Rainbow Minnow Special

Tied by: Henry Hoffman, Warrenton, OR
Hook: Straight eyed streamer hook
Thread: Clear mono and white 6/0
Tail: Olive grizzly chickabou feather fibers
Body: Silver Mylar tubing, top colored with green marker and sides with red marker, a strand of red Flashabou lashed on each side
Wing: 2 olive grizzly hen saddle feathers mounted Matuka style
Hackle: Olive grizzly
Eyes: Plastic stick-on
Head: White thread, top colored with green marker, coated with epoxy

Rattle Sculpin

Tied by: Curtis Kauer, Salina, KS
Hook: Dai-Riki 810, #2
Thread: Brown Monocord
Tail: Black Spirit River Jelly Rope, with a tuft brown grizzly feather marabou fibers tied in at end
Underbody: Jig rattle
Body: Brown rabbit strip, wrapped
Fins: Fox squirrel tail hairs
Eyes: Black lead barbell

Red Nosed Rascal

Tied by: Koshoni Spell, Provo, UT
Hook: Daiichi 2200, #4-#10, weighted
Thread: Red
Tail: Butt ends of body material
Body: Pearl Mylar tubing, coated with Loon Hard Head epoxy
Wing: Rabbit strip
Eyes: Holographic silver stick-on

Red & White Black Lace

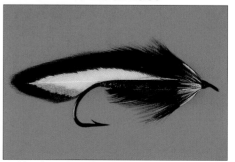

Tied by: Christopher Helm, Toledo, OH
Hook: Partridge CS17, 6X long
Thread: Black
Body: Black Gudebrod Ultra Braid
Wing: 2 Whiting black lace hen saddle feathers, bottom fibers stripped off to hook bend, stems glued to top of body
Belly: 2 red Whiting black lace hen saddle feathers, top fibers stripped off, stems glued to bottom of body
Hackle: Whiting hen black lace

Ring Neck Pheasant Fish

Tied by: Don Joslyn, Eagle Point, OR
Hook: Alec Jackson Daiichi River Dee Low Water, #3
Thread: Orange 3/0
Tail/Fins: Hen ring-necked pheasant body feathers
Abdomen: Orange thread
Thorax: Olive/brown Hareline Krystal dubbing
Wing: Lower section from hen ring-necked pheasant tail feather, bottom fibers stripped off
Head: Black Hareline Krystal dubbing

Roberto's Woolly Bugger

Tied by: Roberto Gray, Puerto Varas, Chile
Hook: TMC 200R, #6-#10, weighted
Thread: Red
Tail: Olive marabou feather fibers, pearl Flashabou strands
Body Hackle: Brown saddle
Shellback: Pearl Flashabou strands, ends from tail material
Body: Olive chenille
Hackle: Dark dun saddle
Head: Peacock herl strands
Eyes: Plastic

Rooster & Rabbit

Tied by: Charlie Moore, Powell, WY
Hook: Streamer, weighted
Thread: Brown
Rib: Red copper wire
Body: Brown Sparkle Chenille
Wing: Yellow rabbit strip, mounted Matuka style, between 2 brown saddle feathers mounted shiny sides out
Hackle: Brown and yellow

RP's Matuka Small Fry

Tied by: Roy Powell, Danville, CA
Hook: TMC 300, #8-#10
Thread: White 6/0
Underbody: Everglow Flash, 2 strands, wrapped
Rib: 4lb. mono
Body: Pearl Re-Flash Mylar tubing
Wing: Badger feather, mounted Matuka style
Gills: Orange guinea feather fibers
Egg Sac: Dark roe hot glue
Head: Epoxy
Eyes: Silver Spirit River 3-D eyes, size 3.0

RP's Small Fry

Tied by: Roy Powell, Danville, CA
Hook: TMC 300, #8-#10
Thread: White 6/0
Tail: Butt ends from body material
Underbody: Everglow Flash, 2 strands, wrapped
Body: Pearl Re-Flash Mylar tubing, overwrapped with 9lb. mono
Wing: Pink Fluorofiber, white SLF Hank fibers, trimmed to shape
Egg Sac: Dark roe hot glue
Head: Epoxy
Eyes: Silver Spirit River 3-D eyes, size 3.0

RP's Super Fry

Tied by: Roy Powell, Danville, CA
Hook: TMC 300, #8-#10
Thread: White 6/0
Tail: Tag ends from body
Underbody: Everglow Flash, 2 strands, wrapped
Body: Re-Flash Mylar tubing, over-wrapped with 9lb. mono
Wing/Belly: White SLF Hank fibers, trimmed to shape
Egg Sac: Dark roe hot glue
Head: Epoxy
Eyes: Silver Spirit River 3-D Molded eyes, size 2.5-3.0

Sam's Choice

Tied by: Chuck Sawyer, Belfast, MA
Hook: Streamer, 8X long, #4-#10
Thread: Red UNI-Stretch
Tail: Red feather section
Rib: Silver tinsel
Body: Red thread
Wing: 6 white, 6 lavender, and 6 black bucktail hairs, flanked by 2 emu feathers
Belly: White bucktail hair
Head: Red thread, coated with epoxy
Eyes: Yellow doll

Sea Fiber Brown Trout

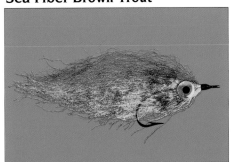

Tied by: Cory Tumolo, Manitou Springs, CO
Hook: Mustad 3366, #1/0-#4
Thread: Black 6/0
Body: Brown, white, and yellow Sea Fiber, colored with black, red, and green permanent markers
Eyes: Stick-on

Sheldon's Shad

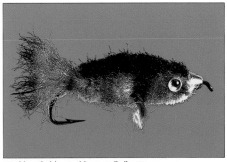

Tied by: Sheldon Fedder II, Millville, PA
Hook: Mustad 9575
Thread: Gray
Body/Tail: Gray Plushille, twisted, wrapped, trimmed to shape
Fins: Gray floss strands
Eyes: 3-D eyes
Nose: Gold cone

Shiner Minnow

Tied by: Jack Pangburn, Westbury, NY
Hook: Mustad 79580, #8
Thread: Red and gray
Tail: Tag ends of body material
Underbody: Dental floss
Body: Pearlescent Mylar tubing
Wing: Rabbit fur strip, Zonker style
Beard: Red feather fibers
Hackle: White
Eyes: Mylar stick-on

Silver Shiner

Tied by: Cory Tumolo, Manitou Springs, CO
Hook: Mustad 9672, #6-#12, weight optional
Thread: White 6/0
Tail: Grizzly marabou feather fibers
Body: Sliver Brite Blend Dubbing
Eyes: Stick-on
Lateral Line: Black permanent marker

Silver Stayner

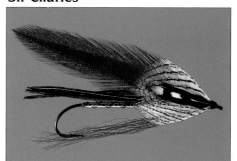

Tied by: Rod Hoston, Reno, NV
Hook: Mustad 9672, #6-#14
Thread: Black 6/0
Tail: Silver Krystal Flash strands
Rib: Gold oval tinsel, counterwrapped
Body: Silver Sparkle Chenille
Wing: Teal flank feather
Beard: Sliver Krystal Flash strands

Simple Squirrel

Tied by: Larry Howard, Roy, UT
Hook: Streamer
Thread: Flame orange
Body: Gold prismatic Mylar tinsel
Wing: Red squirrel tail hair

Sims' Shade

Tied by: A. Ray Sims, Dallas, TX
Hook: Mustad 34011, #1/0
Thread: White
Tail: Yellow bucktail hair, pearl Flashabou strands
Body: White Polar Aire fibers, trimmed to shape
Lateral Line: Olive grizzly saddle feather, 1 per side
Eyes: 3-D eyes
Nose: Gold cone

Sir Charles

Tied by: Robert Schreiner, Southampton, PA
Hook: Gaelic Supreme, 8XL, #1
Thread: Black
Rib: Copper flat tinsel, flanked by red oval tinsel on forward side and green oval tinsel on rear side
Body: Silver flat tinsel
Wing: Peacock herl strands, 2 red feathers, flanked by 2 magenta feathers
Throat: Red bucktail hair
Shoulders: Sliver pheasant body feather
Cheeks: Jungle cock eye feathers

Spawning Kokanee

Tied by: David Burns, McCall, ID
Hook: Streamer
Thread: Black
Tag: Silver twist, green silk
Tail: Orange golden pheasant crest, topped with red golden pheasant tippet fibers
Butt: Red ostrich herl
Rib: Silver oval tinsel
Body: Silver tinsel
Belly: White ostrich herl strands
Throat: Green guinea feather fibers
Underwing: 2 hot pink golden pheasant hackle points, topped with 2 red hackle points
Wing: 2 red golden pheasant sword feathers, topped with 2 green golden pheasant hackle points
Cheeks: Green feather, jungle cock eye feather, and gray jungle cock feather

Splash-N-Dash

Tied by: Boyd Elder, Spiro, OK
Hook: Mustad 9672, #6
Thread: Black
Tail: Black squirrel tail hair
Body: Black and UV Pearl Mylar tubing strands, woven with an overhand weave
Wing: White marabou feather fibers

Spotted Blue & Orange

Tied by: Don Joslyn, Eagle Point, OR
Hook: Alec Jackson Daiichi River Dee Low Water, #5
Thread: Black 3/0
Tag: Gold French tinsel
Tails: Black goose biots
Body: Gray Hareline Krystal dubbing
Hackle: Orange and blue guinea
Wing: Lemon wood duck feather

Spring Smolt

Tied by: Wade Malwitz, Portland, OR
Hook: Mustad 36890, #10
Thread: Black 6/0
Body: Pearl braided Krystal Flash
Yolk: Orange yarn
Wing: 2 grizzly saddle feathers
Eyes: Silver bead chain

Spruce

Tied by: Ronn Lucas, Sr., Milwaukie, OR
Hook: Mustad 90240
Thread: Black
Tail: Peacock herl tips
Body: Red floss, peacock herl
Wing: 2 badger feathers, tied flared
Hackle: Badger

Streaming Nymph

Tied by: Sam de Beer, Cambridge Bay, Nunavut, Canada
Hook: Mustad 9672, #6-#10, weighted
Thread: Black
Butt: Yellow egg yarn
Tail: Black marabou feather fibers
Rib: Gold wire, optional
Body: Black dubbing
Wing Case: Yellow egg yarn
Hackle: Brown
Head: Red thread

Sugar Creek Shad

Tied by: Jeff Schroll, Crawfordsville, IN
Hook: Mustad 9672, #4
Thread: White Monocord
Tail: 2 White marabou feathers, silver holographic Flashabou strands
Body: Dan Bailey white Body Fur, wrapped, trimmed to shape
Eyes: Molded 3-D eyes
Gills: Red waterproof marker
Head: Silver Conehead

Susquehanna Shiner

Tied by: Ed Kraft, Lancaster, PA
Hook: TMC 200R, #6, hook point-up
Thread: Gray 6/0
Eyes: Small lead barbell, painted red/black
Tail/Body: White arctic fox hair
Wing: Blue and gray arctic fox hair, silver and gold Flashabou strands

Thunder Head

Tied by: Grant Lockhart, Kelowna, BC
Hook: Mustad 9672, #2-#8
Thread: Black 6/0
Tail: Silver Krystal Flash strands
Rib: Gold oval tinsel, counterwrapped
Body: Chartreuse Mylar braid
Wing: Chartreuse marabou feather fibers, peacock Krystal Flash strands, and peacock herl strands
Collar/Head: Black elk body hair, bullet style

Trouting Around

Tied by: Boyd Elder, Spiro, OK
Hook: Mustad 9672, #8, weighted
Thread: Black
Tail: Red wool yarn
Body Hackle: Grizzly saddle
Body: Green and black Krystal Flash strands, twisted into 2 cords, woven through body hackle with an overhand weave

Trout Scout

Tied by: Boyd Elder, Spiro, OK
Hook: Mustad 9672, #8, weighted
Thread: Black
Tail: Black marabou feather fibers
Body Hackle: Grizzly saddle
Body: Green and black Krystal Flash strands, twisted into 2 cords, woven through body hackle with an overhand weave

Umpqua River Shad Minnow

Tied by: Henry Hoffman, Warrenton, OR
Hook: Daiichi X472, #4-#8, weighted with 2 strands of .025 lead twisted into a rope and lashed to the bottom of the hook shank
Thread: Clear mono and white 6/0
Tail: Green butt ends of backstrap, between 2 white feathers, cut to shape
Underbody: White parachute cord, threaded over hook shank and secured
Backstrap: Olive green Rad Floss
Body: Silver Mylar tubing
Gills: Fluorescent flame thread
Throat: White feather fibers
Head: White thread
Eyes: Plastic stick-on
Comments: Coat backstrap and head with epoxy.

Undulating Bunny

Tied by: Cory Tumolo, Manitou Springs, CO
Hook: Mustad 9676, #2-#8, hook point-up
Thread: Black 3/0
Tail: Olive rabbit strip, red Krystal Flash strands
Legs: Yellow round rubber
Body: Olive rabbit strip, wrapped
Eyes: Gold barbell
Head: Red dubbing

Wayne's Streamer

Tied by: Wayne Noble, Coquitlam, BC
Hook: Eagle Claw L1197N, #8
Thread: Black
Rib: Copper wire
Body: Silver holographic tinsel
Wing: Red and black calf tail hairs
Eyes: Gold bead chain

White Soft-Hackle Minnow

Tied by: Joe Pantall, Greenville, PA
Hook: Mustad 43077, #4
Thread: Black 3/0
Body: 1 turn of red marabou, 1 turn of brown marabou, 4
 turns of white marabou feathers
Hackle: Light blue, 1 turn
Head: Black thread
Eyes: Yellow/red paint, coated with epoxy

Wool Head Tri-Wing

Tied by: Charlie Moore, Powell, WY
Hook: Streamer, weighted
Thread: Black
Body: Tan/black variegated chenille
Wings: Grizzly feathers, inner feathers shiny sides out,
 outer feather shiny sides in
Head: Tan and black wool, mixed, stacked, trimmed to
 shape, bottom coated with head cement

Woven Splash-N-Dash

Tied by: Boyd Elder, Spiro, OK
Hook: Mustad 9672, weighted
Thread: Black
Tail: Black marabou feather fibers
Body: Green and blue Krystal Flash strands, twisted into 2
 cords, woven with an overhand weave
Wing: Black saddle

Yellow Soft-Hackle Minnow

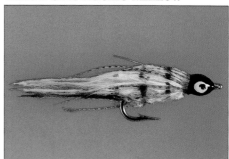

Tied by: Joe Pantall, Greenville, PA
Hook: Mustad 3477, #4
Thread: Black
Wing: 2 turns of red marabou, 4 turns of yellow marabou
 feather, colored with green permanent marker
Hackle: 1 turn of wood duck flank feather
Eyes: Yellow/red paint, coated with epoxy

Yellow Surprise

Tied by: Dorothy Shorter, Williams Lake, BC
Hook: Mustad 9672, #10
Thread: Yellow
Tail: Olive and yellow marabou feather fibers
Body: Yellow chenille
Hackle: Yellow

Bass
Surface
Patterns

A.J.'s Bass Bug

Tied by: A. Courteau, Erie, PA
Hook: Mustad 37187, #2, mono weed guard
Thread: Black
Tail: Black and chartreuse saddle feathers
Hackle: Black saddle
Body: Chartreuse and black deer hair, spun, trimmed to shape
Eyes: 5mm doll eyes, CA glued to hair

Black Magic

Tied by: Don Joslyn, Eagle Point, OR
Hook: Alec Jackson 2051, #3
Thread: Black 3/0
Underbody: Midnight Fire River Born Chenille
Tail: Black Krystal Flash strands, mounted to foam overbody
Overbody: Black foam, extended segments formed on needle
Legs: Black round rubber
Wing: Rainbow Flashabou strands

Diving Foam Frog

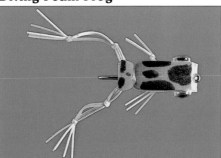

Tied by: Dan Gober, Oswego, NY
Hook: TMC 9394, #2-#8
Thread: White Danville Plus
Legs: White and green round rubber strands, knotted together, 5 strands for rear legs and 3 strands for front legs
Underbody: White marabou feather, twisted and wrapped
Body: Green and white 6mm foam strips, glued together, cut to shape with 45 degree angle at front, spotted with black waterproof marker, hook threaded to the front 1/4 of body, secured at hook bend with thread, rest secured with CA glue.
Eyes: Doll eyes, 4mm
Comments: A strip pause retrieve will allow frog to dive on the strip and return to the surface at the pause.

Bass-Hopper

Tied by: Wade Malwitz, Portland, OR
Hook: Mustad 37187, #7
Thread: Black 6/0
Tail/Underbody: Orange closed-cell foam
Rib: Silver oval tinsel
Body Hackle: Brown, counterwrapped
Body: Red yarn
Wing: Antelope hair
Hackle: Brown

D-Hopper Popper

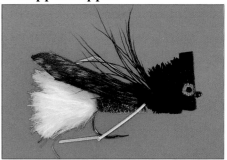

Tied by: DuWayne Shaver, Capitan, NM
Hook: TMC 8089, #1/0-#10
Thread: Black 6/0
Tail: Yellow marabou feather fibers, pearl Krystal Flash strands, mixed
Abdomen: Deer hair, spun, trimmed to shape
Wing: Mottled turkey feather section
Legs: White round rubber strands, knotted
Thorax: Black deer hair, spun, trimmed to shape
Head: Black closed-cell foam, cut to disk shape
Eyes: Yellow/black paint

Diving Frog

Tied by: Steve Potter, Tracy, CA
Hook: Mustad 3366, #1/0-#2/0, mono weed guard, diving lip formed with 20lb. mono loop coated with Softex
Thread: Black Orvis A
Tail: 6 strands of chartreuse rubber legs, pearl Flashabou strands, olive marabou feather fibers, with 4 grizzly saddle feathers on each side, splayed
Hackle: Grizzly
Body: Natural, olive, yellow, and black deer hair, stacked, trimmed to shape
Eyes: White/black doll

Dragon Lady

Tied by: Don Joslyn, Eagle Point, OR
Hook: Alec Jackson 2051, #3
Thread: Black 3/0
Underbody: Midnight Fire River Born Chenille
Tail: Pearl Krystal Flash strands, mounted to foam overbody
Overbody: Blue foam, extended segments formed on needle
Legs: White round rubber strands
Wing: Pearl Krystal Flash strands

Fire Tiger Slider

Tied by: Jeff Lingerfelter, Browns Valley, CA
Hook: TMC 8089, #6-#10, green Amnesia mono weed guard
Thread: Fluorescent fire orange 6/0
Tail: Green over yellow bucktail hair, orange grizzly saddle feathers, yellow, green, and burnt orange chickabou feathers, splayed
Hackle: Green grizzly saddle
Head: Hard foam popper head reversed, painted fluorescent yellow, green, and black with Testors permanent marker
Legs: Orange and chartreuse grizzly silicon legs
Eyes: 3D orange/black

Helm's Deer Hair Mouse

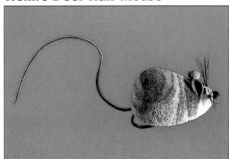

Tied by: Chris Helm, Toledo, OH
Hook: Partridge CS41, #3/0
Thread: Black Gudebrod GX2
Tail: Gray ultra suede strip
Body: Whitetail deer hair, stacked, cut to shape
Ears: Gray ultra suede, cut to shape
Whiskers: Moose body hairs
Eyes: Black plastic beads, 3mm

High-Vis Mouse

Tied by: Stephen Lopatic, Harrisburg, PA
Hook: Long shank bass
Thread: Black 3/0
Tail: Black deer hair
Body: Black deer hair, spun, trimmed to shape
Eyes: Red plastic bead chain

John's Foam Frog

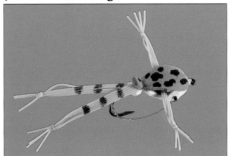

Tied by: John Ridderbos, Kalamazoo, MT
Hook: Bass hook of choice, mono weed guard
Thread: White 6/0
Legs: Green round rubber strands, thread used to secure ends
Body: Green and white 2mm craft foam, cut to shape
Eyes: Plastic doll eyes
Comments: Mark body and rear legs with black waterproof marker.

Leopard Frog

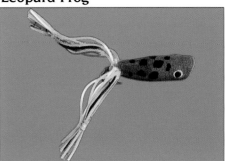

Tied by: Jack Pangburn, Westbury, NY
Hook: Long shank bass hook
Thread: White 6/0
Legs: Round rubber strands, mixed colors, ends secured with thread
Body: Green/white painted foam popper
Eyes: Yellow/black stick-on

Pete's Reel Mouse

Tied by: Pete Toscani, Bristol, CT
Hook: Bass, #2
Thread: Black Dynacord
Tail: Brown rawhide strip
Body: Brown and white deer hair, spun, trimmed to shape
Ears: Tan suede, cut to shape
Whiskers: Black paint brush fibers
Eyes: Black plastic balls

Rat Slider

Tied by: Wade Malwitz, Portland, OR
Hook: Mustad 37187, #6
Thread: Black 6/0
Tail: Deer hide leather strip
Underbody: Closed-cell foam strip, wrapped
Body: Black crosscut rabbit strip, wrapped
Head: Black rabbit dubbing
Ears: Deer hide, cut to shape
Whiskers: Black moose mane hairs

Red & White Popper

Tied by: Jack Pangburn, Westbury, NY
Hook: Long shank, mono weed guard
Thread: White
Tail: White feathers, white Angel Hair fibers
Hackle: White
Body: Red/white foam popper body
Eyes: Yellow/black stick-on

Red Winged Black Bird

Tied by: Henry Hoffman, Warrenton, OR
Hook: Streamer, #1/0 3X long
Thread: Black 3/0
Tail: Black chickabou feather fibers, 2 black rooster breast feathers—mounted flat, 3 black dry fly hackle tips
Body: Black deer hair, spun, trimmed to shape, topped with black rooster soft hackle
Wings: 4 black and 2 red matched rooster soft hackles from breast
Beak: Black pheasant tail quill tip
Head: Black deer hair, spun, trimmed to shape
Eyes: Anglers Choice, glued with CA glue
Legs: Black round rubber strands (optional)

Ty's Tantilizer Diver

Tied by: Chris Helm, Toledo, OH
Hook: Gamakatsu B10S, #2/0
Thread: Tail-black 14/0, body-Gudebrod GX2
Tail: Olive speckled round rubber strands, Mirage Flash strands, olive and red marabou feather fibers, red and olive feathers, splayed
Body: Red and olive deer hair, stacked, trimmed to shape
Eyes: Gold/black plastic

Wayne's Frog

Tied by: Wayne Samson, Perrysburg, OH
Hook: Body—Daiichi 2720, #5/0, Legs—Partridge CS41 #2-#6
Thread: Dynacord
Legs: Dyed deer belly hair, color to suit, stacked, trimmed to shape, excess hook cut off, each leg hook eye attached to the rear of the body hook with 15lb. hard Mason mono loop
Body: Dyed deer belly hair, color to suit, stacked, trimmed to shape
Eyes: Green/black doll eyes

Bass Sinking Patterns

Bass-Bugger

Tied by: Wade Malwitz, Portland, OR
Hook: Mustad 37187, #10
Thread: Black 6/0
Tail: Black marabou feather fibers
Hackle: Black
Body: Black chenille
Legs: Black round rubber strands
Head: Black brass bead

Bass Minnow

Tied by: Scott Hoff, Concord, CA
Hook: Bass bug hook, 2/0, weighted
Thread: White mono cord
Tail: Pearl Krystal Flash strands
Wing: Rabbit strip
Body: Medium Pearl E-Z Braid
Hackle: Pearl Krystal Flash strands
Eyes: Black/white 3-D eyes, coated with 30 minute epoxy

Bead-Eyed Minnow

Tied by: Jack Pangburn, Westbury, NY
Hook: Stream, #6-#10, weighted
Thread: Black 6/0
Underbody: Yellow Antron dubbing
Overbody: Brown and white Sili Legs
Eyes: Gold bead chain
Gills: Red enamel paint
Head: Clear Coat or epoxy

Black & Orange Chickabou Special

Tied by: Henry Hoffman, Warrenton, OR
Hook: Nymph 2X-3X long, #6-#8, weighted
Thread: Black 6/0
Tail: Black chickabou feather fibers, 4 strands of black Krystal Flash
Body: Black and orange chickabou feathers, tied in by tips and wrapped
Hackle: Soft black rooster
Head: Fine black chenille
Eyes: Spirit River Real Eyes
Comments: This fly will fish hook point-up. Great for fishing in rocky streams for smallmouth bass.

Brad's Kinky Fiber Perch

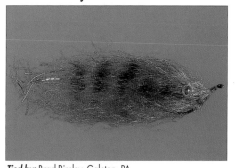

Tied by: Brad Bireley, Galeton, PA
Hook: Eagle Claw L144, #2, weighted
Thread: Mono
Throat: Red Kinky Fiber
Underwing: Orange Kinky Fiber, gold Come's Alive strands
Overwing: Light olive Kinky Fiber
Eyes: 3-D plastic
Comments: Use black marker to add stripes to wing.

Chartreuse Goof

Tied by: Don Joslyn, Eagle Point, OR
Hook: Alex Jackson 2051, #3
Thread: Chartreuse 3/0
Body: White packing foam, folded foam extension style
Wing: Chartreuse egg yarn
Hackle: Black
Legs: Pearl Krystal Flash strands
Head: Awesome Olive Scintilla Caliente Dubbing
Eyes: Gold barbell, mounted on bottom of hook shank

Chartreuse Minnow

Tied by: Scott Hoff, Concord, CA
Hook: Bass bug hook, 2/0, weighted
Thread: Black Monocord
Tail: Red Amherst pheasant tippet fibers
Wing: Chartreuse rabbit strip
Underbody: Peacock herl
Overbody: Pearl medium E-Z Braid
Hackle: Red feather fibers
Eyes: Black/red 3-D eyes, coated with 30 minute epoxy

Chartreuse Mino

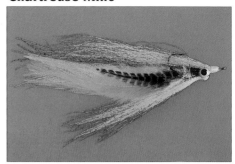

Tied by: Ed Kraft, Lancaster, PA
Hook: Mustad 3400 or 3366, #1/0
Thread: Chartreuse 3/0
Eye: Yellow/black painted barbell eyes
Tail: 6 or more chartreuse saddle feathers, between 2 yellow grizzly saddle feathers
Body: Yellow and red Estaz
Bottom Wing: Yellow deer tail hair
Top Wing: Gold Krystal Flash strands, gold holographic tinsel strands, pearl Flashabou strands, chartreuse deer tail hair

Cher

Tied by: Don Josly, Eagle Point, OR
Hook: Alec Jackson 2051, #3
Thread: Orange 3/0
Body: Spirit River pumpkin Fly Foam, folded foam extension style, with pearl Krystal Flash strands tied in at each segment
Legs: Red Flex Floss strands
Head: Burgundy Lite Brite
Eyes: Spirit River Real Eyes

Chris's Sunfish

Tied by: Chris French, East Brunswick, NJ
Hook: Mustad 3261, #4-#1/0, weighted
Thread: Black 6/0
Body: Sea Fibers, SLF fibers and Angel Hair fibers, colors of choice, mixed
Gills: Red wool
Eyes: Yellow/black stick-on

Cone Head Purple Worm

Tied by: Mark Broer, Steilacoom, WA
Leading Hook: Mustad 36890, #4, cut off at the hook bend
Trailing Hook: Daiichi 2441, #4, connected with a 20lb. mono loop
Thread: Black
Tailing Hook: Purple rabbit strip, extended 1 hook length, wrapped to hook eye and secured
Body: Purple rabbit strip, wrapped
Head: Brass cone head

Croppie

Tied by: Jack Pangburn, Westbury, NY
Hook: Salmon
Thread: White
Tag: Gold tinsel
Tail: Red and yellow feather fibers
Rib: Oval gold tinsel
Body: Silver doctor blue dubbing
Throat: Yellow feather fibers
Wing: 2 mallard breast feathers
Head: Red lacquer
Comments: D.C. Estes wrote to *American Angler* circa 1899 that he finally had a bass fly that would take crappie. He added a split shot to the leader just ahead of the hook eye and fished the fly as a jig.

Dragon Streamer

Tied by: Zachary Worr, Millbrook, ON
Hook: Mustad 3906, #4-#6, weighted
Thread: Olive 6/0
Tail: Black marabou feather fibers
Hackle: Brown
Body: Brown chenille
Eyes: Silver bead chain

D-Split Shot Grubamander

Tied by: DuWayne Shaver, Capitan, NM
Hook: Bass hook, #3/0-#6, weighted with split shot behind hook eye
Thread: Black 6/0
Tail: Black marabou feather fiber, red buck tail hair
Rib: Gold tinsel
Belly: Red buck tail hair, from tail pull forward over body
Body: Gray dubbing
Wing: Black round rubber strands
Hackle: Badger

Elder's Crawdad

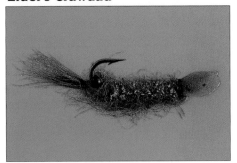

Tied by: Body Elder, Spiro, OK
Hook: Mustad 9672, #8, weighted
Thread: Brown 6/0
Tail: Olive/black Fly Tail cut to shape
Underbody: Burnt orange squirrel dubbing
Body: Root beer and pearl Krystal Flash strand, twisted into 2 cords, woven with an overhand weave
Pinchers: Fox squirrel tail hair
Eyes: Medium black plastic

Flatwing Leech

Tied by: Rich Bogardus, Schenectady, NY
Hook: TMC 300, #6-#8
Thread: Orange 6/0
Tail/Wing: Red/brown pheasant feathers, tied flat
Body: Brown chenille

Flex Crawfish

Tied by: Curtis Kauer, Salina, KS
Hook: Dai-Riki 700-B or 810, #6
Thread: Brown
Tail: Brown marabou feather fibers, 3 brown round rubber strands
Body: Brown Furry Foam, cut to shape
Body Extension: Brown dubbing over 3 strands of brown round rubber
Eyes: 2 lead dumbbell eyes painted brown, 1 mounted behind hook eye and the other at the end of the body

Fly Tail Crawdad

Tied by: Boyd Elder, Spiro, OK
Hook: 2X long, #4, weighted
Thread: Brown
Claws: Speckled brown rubber twisters
Shellback/Tail: Speckled brown Fly Tail, cut to shape
Body: Brown and rust chenille strands, woven with an over hand weave
Legs: Speckle brown rubber legs

Fly Tail Frog

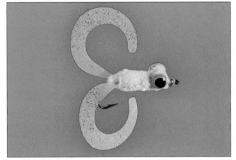

Tied by: Boyd Elders, Spiro, Ok
Hook: Bass hook #2
Thread: White
Legs: Speckled green twisters
Body: Green and white chenille strands, woven with an overhand weave
Eyes: Gold/black plastic barbell
Nose: Olive glass bead

Foam Diver

Tied by: Sam de Beer, Cambridge Bay, Nunavut, Canada
Hook: Mustad 9672, #4-#12,
Thread: White
Tail: Red Krystal Flash strands, red Mylar tinsel strands, 2 pink saddle feathers, splayed
Legs: Red round rubber strands
Body: Pink marabou feather fibers
Head: White round foam

Glass Bead Epoxy Minnow

Tied by: David McCants, Pleasant Hill, CA
Hook: Mustad 3908C, #2, de-barbed
Thread: Gudebrod 6/0 clear mono
Tail: Peacock sword fibers, Mylar tubing strands from body
Underbody: Clear, red, and blue glass beads
Overbody: Silver Mylar tubing, top colored with Pantone mark of choice
Eye: Doll eyes
Comments: Mix 5-minute epoxy so there are some air bubbles, coat body to a slightly round shape, rotate for 3-4 minutes than let set for 24 hours.

Heavy Metal

Tied by: John Raz, Ovilla, TX
Hook: Streamer 3X-4X, #8, weighted, mono weed guard
Thread: Red 6/0
Body: Silver oval tinsel
Wing: Gold Krystal Flash strands
Cheeks: Golden pheasant feathers

Jack's Crawfish

Tied by: Jack Pangburn, Westbury, NY
Hook: Streamer
Thread: Rust
Tail/Shellback: Copper Swiss straw
Rib: Copper wire
Abdomen: Rust/yellow chenille
Legs: Brown round rubber
Thorax: Rust Prism Flash dubbing
Claws: Rust marabou feather fibers and root beer Krystal Flash strands, ends secured with thread
Eyes: Black plastic dumbbell
Antennae: Heavy black thread, coated with head cement

Jak's Yak Bak

Tied by: Jack Pangburn, Westbury, NY
Hook: Bass
Thread: Yellow
Tail: Yak hair, green Krystal Flash strands
Shellback: Green foam strip
Body: Rabbit strip, wrapped

K.J.'s Crayfish

Tied by: Kim Jensen, Ogden, UT
Hook: Dai Riki 700B, #2, hook point-up
Thread: Brown 6/0
Tail: Brown marabou feather fibers
Underbody: Open-cell foam
Abdomen: Brown Larva Lace, 2 strands, overhand weave
Thorax: Brown dubbing
Legs: Brown hackle
Shellback: Brown Thin Skin strip
Eyes: Black plastic
Claws: Brown hen saddle feathers
Antennae: Moose hairs

Krystal Crawdad

Tied by: Boyd Elder, Spiro, OK
Hook: Mustad 9762, #8, weighted
Thread: Olive 6/0
Tail: Olive/black Fly Tail, cut to shape
Underbody: Olive squirrel dubbing
Body: Olive and pearl Krystal Flash strands, twisted into 2 cords, woven with an overhand weave
Pinchers: Green squirrel tail hair
Eyes: Black medium plastic

Little Tease

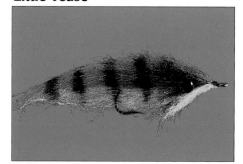

Tied by: Robert Schreiner, Southampton, PA
Hook: Mustad 34011, #1
Thread: Clear mono
Body: Neon-green, sparkle-pearl, olive, and kelly-green EP Silky Fibers, marked with black waterproof pen
Gills: Red EP Silky Fibers
Eyes: Orange/black

Mike's Crawdad

Tied by: Michael Taylor, Etna, CA
Hook: Nymph 3X long, #2-#8, 12lb. weed guard, lead barbell eyes flattened with hammer and mounted behind hook eye
Thread: Brown 6/0
Antennae: Brown Sili Legs
Eyes: Black plastic
Underbody: Packing foam strip, rolled, tied to bottom of hook shank, wrap with thread to shape, coated with Flexament
Body: Rusty dubbing
Legs: Brown Sili Legs
Rib: Copper wire
Shellback/Pinchers: Tan ultra suede, cut to shape, glued to underbody with Pliobond

Mini-Streamer

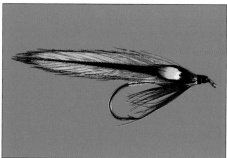

Tied by: David McCants, Pleasant Hill, CA
Hook: Nymph 2X long, #12
Thread: Black 8/0
Body: Silver tinsel
Wing: Coch-y-bondu or Coq De Lean feathers
Throat: Red feather fibers
Cheeks: Jungle cock eye feathers

Nova Scotian Muddler

Tied by: Kyle Hicks, Berwick, Nova Scotia
Hook: Nymph 2X long, #8, weight optional
Thread: Black 6/0
Tail: Gold Flashabou strands, white marabou feather fibers
Body Hackle: Brown, trimmed short
Body: Tan dubbing
Hackle: Orange, trimmed
Head: Deer hair, spun, trimmed to shape

Orange Crayfish

Tied by: Henry Hoffman, Warrenton, OR
Hook: Streamer 6X long, #6-#8, weighted
Thread: Brown 6/0
Tip: Orange floss, used to prop up and separate claws
Claws: Barred orange knee hackle feathers
Antennae: Stripped barred orange quills
Eyes: Black mono
Shellback: Barred orange schlappen, coated with Flexament
Body: Tan chenille
Hackle: Barred orange schlappen
Rib: Copper wire, counterwrapped
Tail: Barred orange knee hackle tips, wedged apart with orange single strand floss

Oreo Woolly Bugger

Tied by: Boyd Elder, Spiro, OK
Hook: 3X long, #6-#8, weighted
Thread: Black
Tail: Grizzly marabou feather fibers
Body: Black and white chenille strands, woven with an over hand weave
Hackle: Grizzly

Outlaw

Tied by: Bryan Toothaker, Waterford, ME
Hook: Nymph, #6, weighted
Thread: Black 6/0
Tail: Red bucktail hair
Body: Sage green Estaz
Wing: Olive-brown marabou feather fibers
Belly: Black marabou feather fibers
Hackle: Purple

Perch Metamerpus

Tied by: Nadear Youssef, Pullman, WA
Hook: Mustad 796665 keel hook, #2
Thread: Olive 3/0
Tail: Olive marabou, green Krystal Flash strands
Body: White, orange, and yellow bucktail hairs, butt ends covered with pearl Polar Lite Dubbing
Topping: Green Krystal Flash strands, peacock herl strands, and olive wool
Throat: Red calf tail hair
Sides: Olive hen feathers, lower sections cut as shown
Cheeks: Olive hen feathers
Eyes: Orange/black prismatic

Pierre's Mouse

Tied by: Pierre Benoist, Hackettstown, NJ
Hook: Mustad 94845, #18
Thread: Gray 8/0
Tail: Light dun feather fibers
Rib: Gray thread
Body: Olive, brown, and gray dubbing, mixed

Purple Lemire

Tied by: Don Joslyn, Eagle Point, OR
Hook: Alec Jackson 2051, #3, weighted
Thread: Black 3/0
Tail: Pearl Krystal Flash strands
Body Hackles: Yellow and turquoise marabou
Body: Chartreuse yarn
Wing: Purple marabou feather fibers
Head: Purple chenille

Rabid Skunk

Tied by: J. Mullin, Casper, WY
Hook: Mustad 9672, #6, weighted
Thread: Black 6/0
Tail: Black and white yarn fibers, mixed
Shellback: White chenille, 2 strands
Body: Black chenille
Head: Black metal cone

Redneck

Tied by: Doug Fullerton, Menominee, MI
Hook: Mustad 9672, #4, weighted
Thread: Red 6/0
Tail: Gray peacock marabou feather fibers
Body: Peacock herl
Collar: 12 black ostrich herl strands
Neck: Red floss
Head: Gold bead

RP's Bass Worm

Tied by: Roy Powell, Danville, CA
Hook: TMC 8089, #4-#6, weighted, 20lb. mono weed guard
Thread: Fire orange UNI-Thread 8/0
Tail: Fire orange marabou feather fibers, 2 hot orange saddle feathers, 2 orange grizzly feathers, 4 strands of copper Flashabou
Body: Yellow marabou feather, twisted and wrapped
Wing: Fire orange marabou feather fibers, Aztec style

Sheldon's Hellgrammite

Tied by: Sheldon Fedder II, Millville, PA
Hook: Mustad 9575, #6, weighted
Thread: Black 6/0
Tails: Black goose biots
Gills: Black goose biots, trimmed
Body: Equal parts of black Angora goat and black Hare-Tron dubbing, mixed
Rib: Black Swannundaze
Legs: Black Hare's Ear dubbing brush strands, bent to shape
Wing Case: Black Swiss straw
Antennae: Black goose biots
Comments: A small mouth bass fly, to be used in the riffles and rocky areas of streams.

Silver Side

Tied by: Bob Sloan, Taunton, MA
Hook: Mustad 34066, #4
Thread: Black, white
Tail: Tag ends from body material
Body: Pearl Flex Cord, top colored with black marker
Wing: Pearl Flashabou, 4 strands on each side
Throat: Red Krystal Hair fibers
Eyes: Red/black 3D plastic eyes, coated with epoxy

Silverside Minnow

Tied by: Jack Pangburn, Westbury, NY
Hook: Streamer
Thread: Black
Rib: Silver oval tinsel
Body: Silver tinsel
Wing: White calf tail hair, gray squirrel tail hair
Throat: Red feather fibers

Sims' Fighting Craw

Tied by: A. Ray Sims, Dallas, TX
Hook: Mustad 34011, 1/0, 20lb. mono weed guard, lead barbell eyes painted black
Thread: Brown 6/0
Pinchers: Olive and orange rabbit strips, glued together, trimmed to shape
Antenna: Black Krystal Flash strands
Body: Olive, tan, and orange wool, stacked, trimmed to shape
Legs: Green pumpkin Sili Legs
Tail: Tan wool, coated with Silicon glue
Eyes: Orange/black plastic

Sims' Salamander

Tied by: A. Ray Sims, Dallas, TX
Hook: Bass 1/0
Thread: Black 6/0, 20lb. hard mono weed guard
Tail: Black rabbit strip, with short purple rabbit strip glued to end
Body: Black wool, stacked, trimmed to shape
Legs: Black round rubber strands, knotted
Eyes: Yellow/black painted lead barbell

Sluggo Fly

Tied by: A. Ray Sims, Dallas, TX
Hook: Mustad 80300 BR, #1/0, weighted
Thread: White
Body: Pearl Extaz
Wing: White Streamer Hair, pearl Flashabou strands, gray Streamer Hair, pearl Krystal Flash strands, black Streamer Hair
Head: Gray wool over white wool, stacked, trimmed to shape
Eyes: Plastic

Sparkle Leech

Tied by: M. Giavedoni, Maple, ONT
Hook: Streamer, #8
Thread: Black 6/0
Tail: Gold Krystal Flash strands, black rabbit strip
Body: Black rabbit strip, wrapped
Head: Black metal cone

Squirm

Tied by: Ted Cabali, River Ridge, LA
Hook: TMC 8089, #10, mono weed guard
Thread: Black 3/0
Tail: Chartreuse grizzly Sili Legs furled, attached to hook with a loop of 20lb. mono
Collar: Chartreuse grizzly Sili Legs, tied in 3 separate bunches along hook shank
Body: Black Krystal Chenille, wrapped between legs
Eyes: Yellow/black painted lead barbell eyes

Steve's Cone Craw

Tied by: Steven Wascher, Greenhurst, NY
Hook: Dai-Riki 930, #2, hook point-up
Thread: Black Dynacord
Underbody: 3 strips of .015 lead, affixed to the top of the hook shank to act as a keel
Feelers: Root beer Living Rubber, 2 strands
Pinchers: 2 brown grizzly feathers
Body: Orange UNI-Stretch Floss
Collar: Deer hair, spun, trimmed to shape
Head: Gold cone head

Streaker Sculpin

Tied by: Mark Hoeser, Stockton, CA
Hook: Mustad 79580, #1, weighted
Thread: GSP brown
Rib: Gold braid tinsel
Body: Fiery orange SLF dubbing
Wing: Peacock sword feathers, peacock Angel Hair
Fins: Ring-neck pheasant feathers, dyed green
Gills: Fiery orange SLF dubbing
Collar/Head: Red, green, orange and blue dyed deer hair, stacked, trimmed to shape
Eyes: Yellow/black solid plastic, 7 1/2mm

Trick or Treat

Tied by: Jerry Jeffery, Long Beach, CA
Hook: Streamer, #4-#8
Thread: Orange
Tail: Black rabbit strip
Body: Orange deer hair, spun, trimmed to shape
Comments: Fish fly with sinking line.

Weedless Streamer

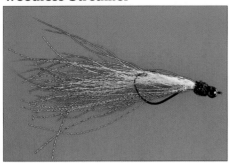

Tied by: Wade Malwitz, Portland, OR
Hook: Mustad 37187, #10, bent to shape
Thread: Black 6/0
Wing: Orange and white bucktail hairs, pearl Krystal Flash strands
Body: Peacock herl
Head: Black brass bead

Woven Ebony & Ivory

Tied by: Boyd Elder, Spiro, OK
Hook: Mustad 3366, #1
Thread: Black 6/0
Tail: Grizzly marabou feather fibers, silver Krystal Flash strands, and white Sili Legs
Body: Black and white chenille strands, woven with an over hand weave
Eyes: Red/black painted lead barbell

Woven Rabbit

Tied by: Boyd Elder, Spiro, OK
Hook: Mustad 3366, #2/0
Thread: Black 6/0
Tail: Grizzly marabou feather fibers, silver Krystal Flash strands, and white Sili Legs
Body: Black and white chenille strands, woven with an over hand weave
Wing: Black rabbit strip, Zonker style
Eyes: Red/black painted lead barbell

Woven Rabbit Crawdad

Tied by: Boyd Elder, Spiro, OK
Hook: #4, weighted
Thread: Black
Tail: Rust marabou feather fibers, rust rubber leg strands, root beer Krystal Flash strands
Body: Brown and rust chenille strands, woven with an over hand weave
Wing: Rust rabbit strip, Zonker style
Eyes: Red/black painted lead barbell

Bluegill Surface Patterns

Albino Panfish Beetle

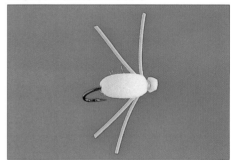

Tied by: Rich Bogardus, Schenectady, NY
Hook: Mustad 94840, #10
Thread: White
Underbody: Pearl Lit Brite
Shellback: White closed-cell foam, cut to shape
Legs: White round rubber strands

Bumble Bee

Tied by: Jack Pangburn, Westbury, NY
Hook: Mustad 9671, #8-#10
Thread: Black 8/0
Tail: Grizzly feathers, splayed
Hackle: Grizzly
Body: Yellow/black foam popper
Legs: Black Krystal Flash strands
Eyes: Yellow/black stick-on

Crane Fly

Tied by: Jack Pangburn, Westbury, NY
Hook: TMC 200R, #8
Thread: Tan 8/0
Abdomen: Brown foam strip
Thorax: Tan dubbing
Legs: Black plastic brush fibers, bent to shape
Wings: Rust Swiss straw, cut to shape
Hackle: Brown

Eyed Bug

Tied by: Nadear Youssef, Pullman, WA
Hook: Daiichi 1130, #14
Thread: Red 3/0
Tail: Black deer hair, tips from body
Body: Black deer hair, bullet style
Eye: Small doll eye, glued to bottom of body

Fire Tiger Panfish Pill

Tied by: Jeff Lingerfelter, Browns Valley, CA
Hook: TMC 100, #12
Thread: Fluorescent fire orange 8/0
Body: Yellow and orange 2mm Fly Foam, laminated, cut to shape and sanded, marked with black waterproof felt-tipped pen
Legs: Small black round rubber strands
Hackle: Green grizzly
Post: Yellow 2mm foam
Comments: Cut a slit in the foam body after forming. Use CA glue to attach body to thread wrapped hook shank.

Hare & Peacock Falcon

Tied by: Jack Pangburn, Westbury, NY
Hook: 3906B, #6-#18, weight optional
Thread: Black
Tail: Brown feather fibers
Rib: Gold oval tinsel
Body: Peacock Prism Flash dubbing, picked out
Wing: Brown rabbit fur, or color of choice

Jack's Beetle

Tied by: Jack Pangburn, Westbury, NY
Hook: Mustad 94840, #8-#16
Thread: Black
Shellback: Iridescent Flashback
Underbody/Legs: Bronze peacock Prism Flash dubbing, picked out
Body: Black closed-cell foam

Jack's Black Ant

Tied by: Jack Pangburn, Westbury, NY
Hook: Mustad 94840, #10-#16
Thread: Black
Body: Black foam, cut to shape
Legs: Black Krystal Flash strands

John's Foam Cricket

Tied by: John Ridderbos, Kalamazoo, MT
Hook: TMC 5212, #12
Thread: Brown 6/0
Tail: Root beer Krystal Flash strands
Body: Arizona dark peacock dubbing
Wing: Tan 2mm craft foam cut to shape, topped with deer hair and root beer Krystal Flash strands
Legs: Tan round rubber, rear legs knotted
Head: Tan 2mm craft foam, cut to shape, folded

Jolly Rancher

Tied by: Stephen Lopatic, Harrisburg, PA
Hook: Mustad 9672, #14
Thread: Purple 6/0
Tail: Purple poly yarn, furled
Abdomen: Purple poly yarn
Post: Purple poly yarn
Thorax: Red dubbing
Hackle: Black

Lady Bug

Tied by: Jack Pangburn, Westbury, NY
Hook: TMC 246Z, #14-#16
Thread: Black 8/0
Shellback: Orange foam, cut to shape, black painted dots
Body: Black thread
Hackle: Dun

Little Bluegill Bugger

Tied by: Ralph D'Errico, Jr., Tucson, AZ
Hook: TMC 5210, #12
Thread: Green 6/0
Tail: 2 brown feathers inside 2 olive feathers, splayed
Hackle: Ginger
Body: Olive and white deer hair, spun, trimmed flat on bottom, top and sides tapered
Eyes: Black plastic

Orange Bluegill Bug

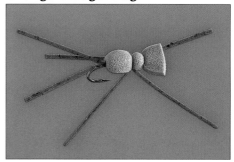

Tied by: Steve Potter, Tracy, CA
Hook: Mustad 9672, #10-#12
Thread: Orange 6/0
Tail: Orange Sili Legs
Body: Orange foam, cut to shape
Legs: Orange Sili Legs

Panfish Wasp

Tied by: Chris Helm, Toledo, OH
Hook: Daiichi 1190, #10
Thread: Black 6/0
Underbody: Olive-brown dubbing
Overbody: 2mm black foam strip, cut to shape
Wing: Yellow elk hair
Legs: Yellow round rubber strands
Head: 2mm yellow foam strip, cut to shape, folded

Para-What

Tied by: Robert Schreiner, Southampton, PA
Hook: TMC 947BL, #10
Thread: Black 8/0
Tail: Red marabou feather fibers
Abdomen: Black Thin Skin strip, wrapped
Post/Wing: Black Antron yarn
Thorax: Black dubbing
Hackle: Black
Legs: Black round rubber strands

Pond Bug

Tied by: Ed Kraft, Lancaster, PA
Hook: Mustad 998480, #8-#10
Thread: Tan 6/0
Tail: Deer hair
Shellback/Head: Deer hair
Body: Orange dubbing
Wings: Deer hair

Predator

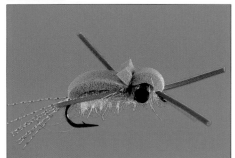

Tied by: Chris Helm, Toledo, OH
Hook: Dry fly hook, 2X long, #8-#10
Thread: Chartreuse 6/0
Tail: Lime Krystal Flash strands
Shellback: 2mm green foam strip
Body: SLF insect green dubbing
Eyes: Black plastic barbell
Head: Tag end from shellback folded back
Legs: Orange round rubber strands

Sheldon's Spider

Tied by: Sheldon Fedder II, Millville, PA
Hook: Mustad 94840, #14
Thread: Yellow 6/0
Body: Yellow foam, cut to shape
Legs: Black rubber strands

The Skipper

Tied by: Don Brown, Riga, MI
Hook: Mustad 94840, #10-#12
Thread: White 10/0
Tails: White Microfibetts
Abdomen: Red Antron dubbing
Wing Case: Mottled Fly Film strip
Thorax/Legs: Deer hair, spun, trimmed to shape
Wings: Mottled Fly Film, cut to shape with wing cutter

Walt's Bug

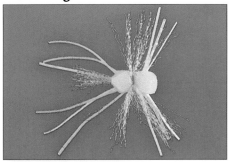

Tied by: Walt Alexander, Gridley, CA
Hook: Mustad 9671, #10
Thread: Fluorescent Chartreuse 6/0
Tail: Fluorescent chartreuse Krystal Flash strands
Legs: Yellow and white round rubber strands
Body: Yellow foam, cut to shape
Wings: Fluorescent chartreuse Krystal Flash strands

White Miller Wulff

Tied by: Jack Pangburn, Westbury, NY
Hook: Mustad 94840, #10-#16
Thread: Tobacco
Tail: Light deer hair
Body: Cream dubbing
Wings: Clear Antron yarn, divided
Hackle: Ginger

Bluegill Sinking Patterns

Bluegill Buster

Tied by: Ron Beasley, St. Louis, MO
Hook: Mustad 9671, #12-#14, weighted
Thread: Black 6/0
Tail: Tag end of body material
Rib: Silver oval tinsel
Shellback: Pearl Mylar tinsel
Body: Fluorescent orange chenille, or color of choice
Hackle: Mottled brown hen

Caught in the Middle

Tied by: Boyd Elder, Spiro, OK
Hook: Mustad 9672, #8, weighted
Thread: Black
Tail: Black squirrel tail hair
Body: Black, white, and black chenille
Hackle: Black

Ebony & Ivory Spider

Tied by: Boyd Elder, Spiro, OK
Hook: Mustad 9672, #10, weighted
Thread: Black 6/0
Tail: Black marabou feather fibers
Body: Black, white, and black chenille
Legs: White round rubber strands

Eyed Oreo Spider

Tied by: Boyd Elder, Spiro, OK
Hook: Mustad 3906B, #6-#8, weighted
Thread: Black
Tail: Black marabou feather fibers
Body: White and black chenille
Legs: White round rubber strands
Eyes: Silver bead chain

Faux Cherry

Tied by: Doug Fullerton, Menominee, MI
Hook: Mustad 94840, #10
Thread: Red 6/0
Body: Fluorescent red Antron dubbing
Wings: Silver Krystal Flash, 6 strands per side
Comments: Fish fly with a sinking line.

Flash Back Baby

Tied by: M. Giavedoni, Maple, ONT
Hook: Mustad 9672, #10-#14, weighted
Thread: Olive 8/0
Tail: Olive Z-lon fibers
Rib: Copper wire
Shellback/Wing Case: Silver tinsel
Body: Olive dubbing, thorax fibers picked out

Furry Foam Dragon

Tied by: Curtis Kauer, Salina, KS
Hook: TMC 2457, #8
Thread: Black Monocord
Underbody: Peacock Antron dubbing
Body: 2 strips of olive Furry Foam glued together, cut to shape, darkened with brown waterproof marker
Legs: Brown hen feather
Eyes: Black bead chain

Garden Hackle

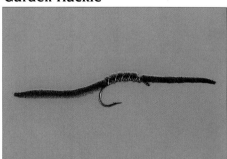

Tied by: Jack Pangburn, Westbury, NY
Hook: TMC 2487, #10
Thread/Rib: Fine copper
Underbody: Fine copper wire
Rib: Fine copper wire
Body: Rust/red Vernille, ends melted

Get-N-Jiggy

Tied by: Body Elder, Spiro, OK
Hook: 1/64 jig hook
Thread: Black
Tail: Black marabou feather fibers
Body: Black, white, and black chenille

Meal Worm

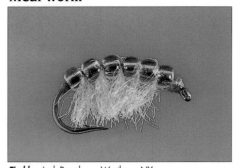

Tied by: Jack Pangburn, Westbury, NY
Hook: TMC 2487, #10
Thread: Rust 6/0
Body: Amber beads
Legs: Gold Prism Flash dubbing, pulled down, trimmed to shape

Nothing but Attitude

Tied by: Body Elder, Spiro, OK
Hook: Mustad 3665A, #8, weighted
Thread: Black 6/0
Tail: Black squirrel tail hair
Body: Black, white, and black chenille
Wing: Black squirrel tail hair

Panfish Caddis Nymph

Tied by: Chris Helm, Toledo, OH
Hook: Scud, #10, weighted
Thread: Black 8/0
Tail: Orange Anton yarn fibers
Body: Insect green Nymph Skin
Legs: Orange round rubber strands
Head: Peacock Antron dubbing

Sure Thing

Tied by: Boyd Elder, Spiro, OK
Hook: Mustad 9672, #8, weighted
Thread: Black
Tail: Black marabou feather fibers
Body: Black and white chenille
Hackle: Black

CHAPTER 12

Atlantic Salmon, Steelhead, and Sea Trout Patterns

Atlantic Salmon

Atherton Squirrel Tail

Tied by: Jack Pangburn, Westbury, NY
Hook: Partridge salmon
Thread: Black
Tag: Silver tinsel
Tail: Red brown feather fibers
Rib: Wide flat silver tinsel, overlaid with narrow embossed silver tinsel
Body: Black wool yarn
Throat: Red brown feather fibers
Wing: Fox squirrel tail hair

Black Eyed Orange Bomber

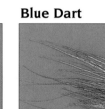

Tied by: Jack Pangburn, Westbury, NY
Hook: Partridge salmon or Mustad 80500BL
Thread: Orange 6/0
Tail: Orange calf body hair
Body: Orange deer hair, spun, trimmed to shape
Wing: White calf tail hair
Eyes: Black plastic barbell

Black Squirrel

Tied by: Gordon Mackenzie, Syderstone, England
Hook: Salmon
Thread: Black
Rib: Oval Silver tinsel
Body: Silver tinsel rear 2/3, black dubbing front 1/3
Body Hackle: Black squirrel tail hair, spun in dubbing loop, wrapped over front 1/3 of body
Wing: Dark blue gray squirrel tail hair, black squirrel tail hair
Hackle: Gray squirrel tail hair, spun in dubbing loop

Blue Dart

Tied by: Carl Ritter , Sedona, AZ
Hook: TMC 200R, #8
Thread: Black 8/0
Tag: Silver tinsel
Rib: Red floss
Body: Blue Body Braid
Wing: Blue bucktail hair, polar bear hair
Hackle: Pink

Blue Hobo

Tied by: David McCants, Pleasant Hill, CA
Hook: TMC 7999, #4
Thread: Black 6/0
Tag: Fine silver tinsel, red silk floss
Tail: Red golden pheasant crest fibers
Butt: Black ostrich herl
Rib: Gold oval tinsel
Body: Silver doctor blue silk floss
Throat: Guinea fowl feather
Wing: Jungle cock saddle feather
Cheeks: King fisher feathers (legal—purchased through Spirit River)
Topping: Red golden pheasant crest fibers

Comet

Tied by: Jack Pangburn, Westbury, NY
Hook: Partridge salmon
Thread: Orange 6/0
Tag: Fine oval gold tinsel
Tail: Gold Krystal Flash strands, orange bucktail hair
Rear Body: Orange chenille
Mid-skirt: Golden pheasant tippet fibers
Front Body: Red chenille, ribbed with round gold cord
Hackle: Long soft barbed brown feather or brown spey or schlappen feather

Dee Modern Highlander

Tied by: David Burns, McCall, ID
Hook: Partridge HE2, #3/0
Thread: Black
Tag: Gold oval tinsel, yellow silk
Tail: Golden pheasant crest, tippet fibers, barred wood duck feather fibers
Butt: Black ostrich herl
Rear Body: Buttercup silk, ribbed with silver tinsel, veiled above and below with bright yellow CDC feather fibers
Front Body: Black ostrich herl, green seal substitute dubbing, ribbed with silver tinsel and gold oval tinsel
Hackles: Green marabou, yellow mallard flank feather
Wing: Natural, yellow, orange, and green mottled turkey tail feather sections, married
Sides: Jungle cock eye feathers, drooping
Cheeks: Indian crow substitute, drooping
Topping: Golden pheasant crest fibers, drooping

Gordon

Tied by: Ron Hicks, Twin Falls, ID
Hook: Salmon
Thread: Black
Tag: Silver oval tinsel, yellow silk
Tail: Golden pheasant crest fibers
Butt: Black ostrich herl
Ribs: Sliver oval tinsel, silver flat tinsel
Body: Yellow silk, claret silk
Body Hackle: Claret
Throat: Blue feather
Wings: Golden pheasant tippet feather, peacock herl strands, feather sections from bustard, blue and green swan, married, golden pheasant crest fibers
Cheeks: Jungle cock eye feathers

Green Highlander

Tied by: Henry Hoffman, Warrenton, OR
Hook: Alec Jackson, #4
Thread: Yellow and black 14/0
Tag: Yellow floss
Tail: Golden pheasant crest fibers, barred wood duck feather fibers
Butt: Black ostrich herl
Rib: Silver oval tinsel
Body: Rear 1/3 yellow floss, front 2/3 green rooster soft hackle, tied in tip first, wrapped, the chickabou fibers at the base of the feather make the last 2 turns
Throat: Yellow chickabou feather fibers
Wing: Golden pheasant tippet fibers, green bucktail hair, gray squirrel tail hair
Cheeks: Jungle cock eye feathers

Inconnue

Tied by: Jack Pangburn, Westbury, NW
Hook: Salmon
Thread: Black 6/0
Tip: Gold tinsel
Tag: Golden yellow floss
Rib: Gold braid or tinsel
Body: Green chenille
Wing: White Antron yarn, Gold Angel Hair fibers, chartreuse bucktail hair
Throat: Bright blue yak hair
Topping: Golden pheasant crest fibers

Jak's Yak Bak (yellow)

Tied by: Jack Pangburn, Westbury, NY
Hook: Mustad 34007, #2/0
Thread: Chartreuse 6/0
Tail: Tan bucktail hair, root beer Krystal Flash strands
Shellback/Lip: Yellow foam
Body: Tan or natural rabbit fur strip, wrapped up hook shank

Kyle's Royal Bugger

Tied by: Kyle Hicks, Berwick, NS
Hook: Salmon hook, #12
Thread: White 8/0
Tag: Gold oval tinsel
Tail: Orange feather fibers, silver Krystal Flash strands, golden pheasant crest fibers
Butt: Fluorescent orange floss, golden pheasant crest fibers
Body Hackle: Orange saddle
Body: Deer hair, spun, trimmed to shape, red floss, deer hair, spun, trimmed to shape

Lady "D"

Tied by: Robert Schreiner, Jr., Southampton, PA
Hook: Partridge 01, #8
Thread: Black
Tail: Lady Amherst pheasant tippet fibers
Butts: Peacock herl
Rib: Fine oval gold tinsel
Body: Copper tinsel
Throat: Lady Amherst pheasant tippet fibers
Wing: Green, white, green, white, green, and black strips from goose shoulder feathers, married
Eyes: Jungle cock eye feathers

Lavender Princess

Tied by: David McCants, Pleasant Hill, CA
Hook: Daiichi Alex Jackson Spey Hook, #3
Thread: Black 6/0 UNI
Tag: Embossed silver tinsel (medium)
Tail: Golden pheasant crest fibers with red tips
Butt: Yellow ostrich herl
Rear Body: Red floss, ribbed with gold tinsel
Butt: Yellow ostrich herl
Front Body: Claret Angora goat dubbing, ribbed with silver oval tinsel
Body Hackle: Lavender guinea fowl feather, tied in at second turn of tinsel rib
Throat: Pintail flank feather (1 turn)
Wing: Lavender guinea fowl feathers (from front edge of shoulder), golden pheasant crest fibers with red tips
Cheeks: Conure breast feather fibers (molted gift from Siskiou Aviary—Kate's great!)

Mac's Purple Practitioner

Tied by: Gordon Mackenzie, Syderstone, England
Hook: Salmon
Thread: Black
Tag: Silver oval tinsel
Tail: Purple gray squirrel tail hair, spun in dubbing loop and wrapped
Eyes: Black burnt mono strands, extended
Rear Body: Pearl Mylar rope
Rear Wing: Purple gray squirrel hair
Middle Hackle: Purple gray squirrel tail hair, spun in dubbing loop and wrapped
Front Body: Purple dubbing, ribbed with silver oval tinsel
Wing: Purple gray squirrel tail hair
Hackle: Purple gray squirrel tail hair, spun in dubbing loop

Married-Wing Spirit

Tied by: Gordon Olson, Three Hills, AB
Hook: Alec Jackson Spey, #3
Thread: Black
Tag: Fine oval silver tinsel, light yellow silk
Tail: Golden pheasant crest fibers, blue macaw feather sections
Butt: Black ostrich herl
Rib: Fine silver wire
Body: Green silk, green hackle, pink silk, pink hackle, and purple silk
Throat: 2 peacock neck feathers
Wing: 2 yellow feathers, married feather sections from blue macaw, Lady Amherst pheasant, peacock, turkey, teal, yellow and green goose shoulder feathers, topped with golden pheasant crest fibers
Cheeks: Jungle cock eye feathers

Midnight Muddler

Tied by: Mark Hoeser, Stockton, CA
Hook: Daiichi 2271, #1
Thread: Black
Tail: Curassow feather section
Body: Medium copper braid
Wing: Golden badger rooster neck feathers, 2 pair
Shoulders: Golden pheasant tippet feathers
Collar: Natural coastal deer hair
Head: Black deer hair, spun, trimmed to shape
Eyes: White solid plastic, 4 1/2mm

Orange & Black Rainlander

Tied by: Henry Hoffman, Warrenton, OR
Hook: Partridge 01, #4
Thread: Black 8/0
Tag: Flat gold tinsel
Tail: Orange grizzly feather tips
Butt: Flame floss
Rib: Flat gold tinsel
Body: Black chickabou feather, tied on at tip and wrapped
Body Hackle: Orange soft hackle, the soft hackle tip section of a rooster breast feather removed and the remaining fluffy part is wound on
Horns: Narrow orange grizzly saddle feathers
Hackle: Black rooster soft breast or flank feather

Pete's Reel Bomber

Tied by: Pete Toscani, Bristol, CT
Hook: Mustad 34007, #1/0
Thread: Chartreuse 3/0
Tail: White calf body hair
Body Hackle: Brown saddle
Body: Chartreuse deer hair, spun, trimmed to shape
Wing: White calf body hair

Powell's Atlantic Salmon

Tied by: Roy Powell, Danville, CA
Hook: TMC 7989, #4
Thread: Black
Tip: Silver tinsel
Tag: Silver tinsel, over-wrapped with red small Vinyl rib
Rib: Silver oval tinsel
Body: Black UNI-Floss
Body Hackle: Red saddle
Throat: Black saddle hackle
Wing: Red saddle feathers, 2 or 4
Cheeks: Black hen cape feathers
Eyes: Jungle cock eye feathers

Red-Black Bullet

Tied by: John Moneyhun, Rapid City, SD
Hook: TMC 7989, #4-#8
Thread: Black 6/0
Butt: Peacock herl
Body: Olive damsel body material
Wing: White Z-lon fibers, teal flank feather
Head: Red and black fibers from marabou feathers, bullet style

Roger's Fancy

Tied by: Dorothy Shorter, Williams Lake, BC
Hook: Mustad 9672, #10
Thread: Black 6/0
Tag: Silver oval tinsel
Tip: Green floss
Tail: Peacock sword feather fibers
Rib: Silver tinsel
Body: Green dubbing
Collar: Chartreuse deer hair
Wing: Fox hair

Royal Rat

Tied by: Floyd Franke, Roscoe, NY
Hook: Partridge CS10, or Mustad 80525bl, #8-#4
Thread: Red 6/0
Tag: Gold oval tinsel
Tail: Peacock sword feather fibers
Rib: Gold oval tinsel
Body: Red floss, peacock herl
Body/Veil: Red floss strand
Wing: Gray fox hair
Cheeks: Jungle cock eye feathers
Hackle: Grizzly hen saddle

Seahawk

Tied by: Ronn Lucas, Sr., Milwaukie, OR
Thread: Black
Tag: Fine silver tinsel, yellow floss
Tail: Golden pheasant crest and red tippet fibers
Butt: Black ostrich herl
Body: Orange floss, ribbed with fine silver oval tinsel, veiled with black Impeyan feathers, black ostrich herl, maroon floss ribbed with medium oval silver tinsel
Hackle: Blue eared pheasant (from second rib in front part of body), 3 turns at head
Wing: Blue fronted Amazon feathers
Sides: Jungle cock eye feathers
Topping: Golden pheasant crest fibers
Horns: Red macaw feather fibers

Silent Killer

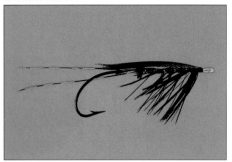

Tied by: Ronn Lucas, Sr., Milwaukie, OR
Thread: Black
Tag: Small silver oval tinsel and yellow floss
Tails: Golden pheasant tail feather fibers, set low
Butt: Black ostrich herl
Body: Maroon floss
Rib: Medium oval silver tinsel
Hackle: Black or dark brown schlappen feather with a fast taper, starting at the second rib and 3 turns at head
Wing: Bronze mallard feather sections, spey style

SLH (Santa's Little Helper)

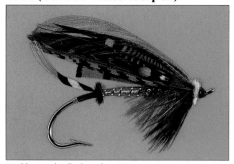

Tied by: Neal Selbicky, Talent, OR
Hook: Salmon fly hook
Thread: Black
Tag: Silver tinsel, red floss
Tail: Golden pheasant crest fibers, wood duck flank feather sections
Butt: Black ostrich herl
Ribs: Rear—fine silver tinsel, front—medium silver tinsel, fine gold oval tinsel
Body: Rear half—orange floss, front half—peacock herl
Hackle: Stiff orange hackle over peacock herl
Throat: Red guinea fowl feather
Wing: Golden pheasant tippet section, married strips of Amhurst pheasant tail, yellow, red, and green swan shoulder, dark turkey tail, light turkey tail, and golden pheasant tail feathers, married strips from barred wood duck and teal feathers, sided as a wing veiling, topped with bronze mallard strips and a golden pheasant crest fiber
Sides: Jungle cock eye feathers
Cheeks: Light green parrot feathers
Horns: Red macaw tail feather fibers
Head: White ostrich herl, red thread

Solduc

Tied by: Gordon Mackenzie, Syderstone, England
Hook: Salmon
Thread: Black
Tag: Silver oval tinsel
Feelers: Pearl Krystal Flash, 4 strands
Tail: Yellow and orange gray squirrel tail hairs, spun in dubbing loop and wrapped
Eyes: Black mono strands, extended
Rear Body: Orange dubbing, ribbed with gold oval tinsel
Rear Wing: Orange squirrel tail hair
Middle Hackle: Yellow squirrel tail hair, spun in dubbing loop and wrapped
Front Body: Orange dubbing, ribbed with gold oval tinsel
Front Wing: Orange gray squirrel
Collar: Deer hair, spun, trimmed to shape
Head: Red deer hair, spun, trimmed to shape, lip coated with Dave Flexament

Wiley

Tied by: Don Joslyn, Eagle Point, OR
Hook: Daiichi 2055, #1.5
Thread: Black 3/0 UNI
Tag: Blue silk, orange silk
Body: Orange Scintilla Caliente Dubbing
Wing: Coyote tail hair
Head: Black Scintilla Caliente Dubbing

Winter Rat

Tied by: Ken Sykes, Englewood, CO
Hook: Daiichi 2161, #2
Thread: Purple
Tag: Small oval silver tinsel
Body: Rear 2/3—purple Ice Yarn
Veil: Purple SLF Hank fibers
Body: Front 1/3—silver tinsel chenille
Wing: Gray fox tail hair
Hackle: Purple grizzly

Steelhead

Avenger

Tied by: Eric Reiter, Transfer, PA
Hook: Partridge Salmon, #2-#8
Thread: Red 14/0
Tip: Silver oval tinsel
Tag: Yellow floss
Butt: Yellow ostrich herl
Rib: Large oval silver tinsel
Body: Sunset orange floss
Thorax: Burnt orange Angora goat dubbing
Hackle: Yellow and orange feathers, wrapped together

BC Prawn

Tied by: Wade Malwitz, Portland, OR
Hook: Mustad 36890, #1-#6, weighted
Thread: Red
Tail: Orange and white bucktail hairs, orange Krystal Flash strands, 2 moose hairs
Rib: Silver oval tinsel
Eyes: Gold bead chain
Shellback: Black Krystal Flash strands, topped with thin strip of plastic
Body: Fire orange chenille
Legs: White saddle hackle, top fibers trimmed

Black Magic

Tied by: Neal Selbicky, Talent, OR
Hook: Steelhead
Thread: Black
Tag: Silver Mylar tinsel
Tail: Golden pheasant crest fibers
Body: Black wool
Throat: Dark dun feather fibers
Wing: Black bear hair, golden pheasant crest fibers

Blue Voodoo

Tied by: Don Joslyn, Eagle Point, OR
Hook: Daiichi 2055, #3
Thread: Black 3/0 UNI
Tail: Pearl Krystal Flash strands
Body: Purple Pseudo Seal dubbing, black Krystal Dubbing
Wing: Blue guinea feather fibers
Head: Black Krystal Dubbing

Christmas Tree Spey

Tied by: Ron Hicks, Twin Falls, ID
Hook: Alec Jackson, #11/2
Thread: Black
Tag: Gold oval tinsel, emerald green floss
Tail: Red golden pheasant crest fibers
Butt: Peacock herl
Rear Body: Red floss ribbed with gold oval tinsel, veiled above and below with golden pheasant crest fibers
Front Body: Peacock herl, red and black seal fur, ribbed with gold oval tinsel, 5 turns of heron substitute
Throat: Guinea
Wing: Red goose shoulder feather sections

Classic Steelheader

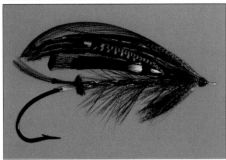

Tied by: David Burns, McCall, ID
Hook: Partridge HE2, #3/0
Thread: Black
Tag: Silver tinsel with lacquered fluorescent yellow floss over front 4/5
Tail: Golden pheasant hot pink crest fibers, veiled with fluorescent orange tippet fibers
Butt: Purple ostrich herl
Ribs: Silver tinsel and gold twist
Body: Rear-1/5 hot orange silk floss, front-4/5 purple silk floss
Body Hackle: Purple over the purple silk floss
Throat: American widgeon
Wing: Golden pheasant hot pink tippet fibers, natural, hot orange, and purple sections from mottled turkey tail feathers, veiled with teal and barred wood duck feather sections, covered with bronze mallard feather sections, topped with hot pink golden pheasant crest
Sides: Jungle cock eye feathers
Horns: Red feather fibers
Head: Translucent orange lacquer

C.J. Special Spade

Tied by: Gordon Olson, Three Hills, AB
Hook: Alec Jackson Spey, #3
Thread: Red
Tail: Golden pheasant crest fibers
Rib: Gold oval tinsel
Body: Rear—red floss, front—golden pheasant crest fibers, 10 peacock herl strands, and a grizzly hackle twisted with gold wire and wrapped
Hackle: Red and purple feathers
Cheeks: Jungle cock eye feathers
Topping: Golden pheasant crest fibers

Dream Sicle

Tied by: John Cunningham, Wenatchee, WA
Hook: Alec Jackson Gold
Thread: Fluorescent pink
Body: Orange and pink marabou feathers, wrapped
Wing: Orange Flashabou
Hackle: Blue soft hackle strands
Head: Hot Pink cone

Jackson's Egg

Tied by: J.M. Jackson, Salt Springs Island, BC
Hook: Steelhead hook, weighted
Thread: Black
Body: Hot pink Crystal Chenille, coated with epoxy
Wing: White marabou feather fibers

Kinky Pinky

Tied by: Ed Kraft, Lancaster, PA
Hook: TMC 7999, #1/0, hook point-up
Thread: Mono
Eyes: Medium nickel barbell, ends colored with red permanent marker
Tail: White Kinky Fiber
Body: Butt ends from tail material
Wing: Purple and pink Krystal Flash strands, pink Kinky Fiber
Head: Pink thread

Low Water CDC Spey B&P

Tied by: Don Joslyn, Eagle Point, OR
Hook: Daiichi 2059, #1.5
Thread: Black 3/0 UNI
Rib: Gold holographic tinsel
Body: Pink, chartreuse silk floss, black CDC dubbing
Hackle: Pink spey hackle, wrapped though rear half of black CDC dubbing
Wing: Polar bear hair

Low Water Stone

Tied by: Don Joslyn, Eagle Point, OR
Hook: Daiichi 2055, #3
Thread: Orange 3/0 UNI
Tails: Black biots
Tag: Orange thread
Butt: Brown hackle
Rib: Gold tinsel
Body: Orange thread, tangerine Scintilla Caliente Dubbing
Wing: Moose hair
Eyes: Jungle cock eye feathers, optional

Masked Black Spey

Tied by: Don Joslyn, Eagle Point, OR
Hook: Daiichi 2051, #1.5
Thread: Black 3/0 UNI
Tail: Red marabou feather fibers, short
Rib: Gold oval tinsel
Body: Orange silk floss, shrimp Scintilla Caliente Dubbing
Hackle: Black spey, through body dubbing
Head: Black ostrich herl
Mask: Jungle cock eye feathers

Midnight Rider

Tied by: Don Joslyn, Eagle Point, OR
Hook: Daiichi 2055, #5
Thread: Black 3/0 UNI
Tail: Black feather fibers
Rib: Gold oval tinsel
Body: Midnight Fire New Age Chenille
Wing: Pearl Krystal Flash strands
Hackle: Black

Monoe

Tied by: Eric Reiter, Transfer, PA
Hook: Partridge salmon, #2-#8
Thread: Black 8/0
Tip: Silver oval tinsel
Tag: Yellow floss
Tail: Lady Amherst pheasant crest fibers, golden pheasant crest fibers
Body: Black floss
Rib: Silver oval tinsel
Wing: White, blue and green bucktail hair
Throat: Guinea fowl feather fibers

Muggsie

Tied by: Don Joslyn, Eagle Point, OR
Hook: Dai Riki 270, #4, weight optional
Thread: Orange, 3/0 UNI
Body: Brown hackle, black hackle, brown hackle, and black hackle
Head: Black ostrich herl
Comments: Skates well with floatant, swims well wet, fishes well on the rocks when lead wire is added and is very easy to tie.

Mystifly

Tied by: Don Joslyn, Eagle Point, OR
Hook: Daiichi 2055, #1.5
Thread: Black 3/0 UNI
Tail: Pink hen feather fibers
Butt: Black ostrich herl
Rib: Gold tinsel, counterwrapped
Body: Pink yarn, twisted, black ostrich herl
Hackle: Pink hen saddle
Head: Black ostrich herl

Nasty Nymph

Tied by: Phillip Morphew, Rohnert Park, CA
Hook: Mustad 3906, #10, weighted
Thread: Red 6/0
Rib: Red thread, pulled up both sides of body
Body: Bright green yarn
Hackle: Ginger, trimmed

Orange Blossom

Tied by: Jack Pangburn, Westbury, NY
Hook: Partridge salmon
Thread: Orange 6/0
Tag: Yellow floss
Underbody: Dental floss, forming a smooth base
Rib: Gold tinsel
Body: Orange floss
Thorax: Yellow Seal-Ex dubbing
Hackle: Yellow and red spey or schlappen feathers

Orange Blossom Special

Tied by: Jerry Jeffery, Long Beach, CA
Hook: Mustad 94831, #6
Thread: Orange
Tail: Orange bucktail hair
Body: Orange and black chenille
Collar: Orange bucktail hair

Party Gal

Tied by: Sharie Sinclaire, Bowen Island, BC
Hook: Mustad 9672, #4
Thread: Orange 6/0
Feelers: Pearl Krystal Flash strands, orange feather fibers
Eyes: Black glass beads, with mono core
Shellback: Orange flex plastic, cut to shape
Rib: Orange thread
Body: Orange chenille
Body Hackle: Orange, front fibers trimmed short

Pete's Reel Steel Bugger

Tied by: Pete Toscani, Bristol, CT
Hook: Mustad 34007, #1/0, hook point-up
Thread: Orange 3/0
Tail: Purple marabou feather fibers, purple and pearl Krystal Flash strands
Rib: Pearl Estaz
Body: Orange thread
Throat/Wing: Orange marabou feather fibers
Eyes: Eyed metal barbell

Pheasant's Pleasure

Tied by: Ryan Sims, Salem, OR
Hook: Daiichi 2051, #1/0-#10
Thread: Black 12/0
Rib: Medium oval silver tinsel
Body: Large gold Mylar tinsel
Wing: Peacock sword feather fibers
Hackle: 2 pheasant rump feathers
Cheeks: Jungle cock eye feathers

Powell's Steelhead

Tied by: Roy Powell, Danville, CA
Hook: TMC 7989, #4
Thread: Black
Tip: Silver tinsel
Tag: Silver tinsel, overwrapped with small red Vinyl rib
Body: Black seal imitation or black Angora dubbing
Wing: Black marabou feather fibers, topped with 2 or 4 red saddle feathers
Hackle: Black and red saddle feathers

Poxy-back Rubber Legs

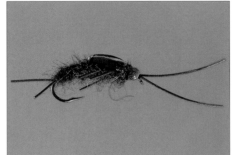

Tied by: Michael Taylor, Etna, CA
Hook: Mustad 9672, #4, shank bent down at 3/4 point
Thread: Black
Tails: Black round rubber strands
Body: Kaufmann's Black Stone dubbing
Wing Case: Black Swiss straw, topped with 3 strands of pearl Flashabou, coated with epoxy
Legs/Antennae: Black round rubber strands
Head: Hot orange metal bead

Prom Night

Tied by: Carl Ritter, Sedona, AZ
Hook: Mustad 3906B, #8
Thread: Black 8/0
Tag: Silver tinsel
Body: Red floss, peacock herl
Wing: Golden pheasant crest and tippet fibers, topped with blue-green goose secondary feather sections
Cheeks: Guinea fowl tertiary feathers
Hackle: Pink

Purple Steeler

Tied by: Sharie Sinclaire, Bowen Island, BC
Hook: #4, turned up eye
Thread: Red 6/0
Tail: Red Krystal Flash strands, purple thin tinsel, purple eared pheasant feather fibers
Tag: Silver tinsel
Rib: Silver tinsel
Body: Purple yarn
Wings: Purple mallard flank feathers
Hackles: Purple mallard flank feathers

Raider

Tied by: David McCants, Pleasant Hill, CA
Hook: TMC 7998, #4
Thread: Black 6/0
Tail: Golden pheasant crest
Rib: Medium gold oval tinsel
Body: Medium silver tinsel
Throat: Black hackle, fibers pulled down
Wing: Gray fox guard hairs, from center back of hide

Red Abbey

Tied by: Jon Hunter, Northfield, MN
Hook: TMC 7999, #4-#10
Thread: Red 6/0
Tag: Silver oval tinsel
Tail: Red feather fibers
Rib: Silver tinsel
Body: Red floss
Throat: Brown feather fibers
Wing: Red squirrel tail hair

Red Abbey

Tied by: Adam Rice, Mackenzie, BC
Hook: Mustad 39890, #4-#10
Thread: Black 6/0
Tag: Silver tinsel
Tail: Red bucktail hair
Rib: Silver tinsel, counterwrapped
Body: Red floss
Wing: Gray squirrel tail hair
Hackle: Light brown

Red Head

Tied by: Sharie Sinclaire, Bowen Island, BC
Hook: #4 1X short
Thread: Black 6/0
Rib: Halogen silver tinsel
Body: Red floss, peacock herl, red leech yarn
Wing: Red calf tail hair, pearl Krystal Flash strands, silver halogen tinsel strands
Throat: Red calf tail hair
Head: Peacock Ice Chenille

Red Shrimp

Tied by: Gordon Mackenzie, Syderstone, England
Hook: Salmon
Thread: Black
Tag: Silver oval tinsel
Tail: Orange squirrel tail hair, spun in dubbing loop and wrapped
Rear Body: Red dubbing, ribbed with silver oval tinsel
Middle Hackle: Short red and white tipped gray squirrel hairs, spun in dubbing loop and wrapped
Front Body: Black dubbing, ribbed with silver oval tinsel
Front Hackle: Red gray squirrel tail hair, spun in dubbing loop and wrapped
Wing: Black tipped gray fox guard hairs

Reel Screamer

Tied by: Dorothy Shorter, Williams Lake, BC
Hook: Mustad 9672, #6
Thread: Black 6/0
Tail: Golden pheasant tippet fibers
Body: Silver tinsel
Wing: Badger feathers, teal feather fibers, 4 peacock herl strands, yellow feathers
Throat: Badger feather fibers
Eyes: Blue feather tips

Reneg-egg Black

Tied by: Don Joslyn, Eagle Point, OR
Hook: Dai Riki 135, #6
Thread: Black 3/0 UNI
Eyes: Gold metal barbell
Body: Orange Scintilla Caliente Dubbing
Hackles: Black

Royal Bitch

Tied by: Don Joslyn, Eagle Point, OR
Hook: Dai Riki 270, #6
Thread: Black 3/0 UNI
Tail: Moose hair
Butt: Peacock herl
Body: Red floss, black CDC dubbing
Wing: Black biots
Head: Gold bead

Samish Shrimp

Tied by: Ken Sykes, Englewood, CO
Hook: Eagle Claw L144, #2-#6
Thread: Black
Tail: Black feather fibers
Rear Body: Fluorescent yellow Danville Depth Ray Nylon Wool
Antenna: Pearl Krystal Flash, 4 strands
Front Body: 3 sections of black saddle hackle and chartreuse Sparkle Chenille
Eyes: Yellow/black metal barbell

Skykomish Sunset

Tied by: Don Joslyn, Eagle Point
Hook: Daiichi 2055, #4
Thread: Orange 3/0 UNI
Tail: Deer hair
Body: Orange rabbit dubbing
Hackle: Yellow long fiber and orange short fiber marabou feathers
Wing: Polar bear hair

Soft Hackle Paint Brush

Tied by: Henry Hoffman, Warrenton, OR
Hook: L1925, #4, from Hareline Dubbing, Inc.
Thread: Flame 6/0
Body: Gold Body Braid
Body Hackle: Orange rooster breast feather
Hackle: Blue rooster breast feather

Steelhead Royal

Tied by: Mark Hoeser, Stockton, CA
Hook: Partridge CS10/1, #3/0
Thread: Black
Tag: Gold tinsel
Tail: Lady Amherst red crest fibers
Rib: Gold oval tinsel
Body: Red floss—rear 2/3, peacock herl—front 1/3
Wing: White rooster neck feathers, 2 pair
Cheeks: Golden pheasant tippet feathers
Throat: Golden pheasant rump and shelduck feathers

Steelhead Skater

Tied by: Jeff Lingenfelter, Browns Valley, CA
Hook: TMC 7989, #8
Thread: Fire orange 8/0
Tail: Fox squirrel tail hair
Rib: Copper wire
Shellback: Orange elk hair
Body: Burnt orange Antron dubbing
Body Hackle: Brown saddle
Wings: Orange elk hair, divided
Legs: Medium brown rubber strands
Hackle: Brown grizzly

Tandem Steelhead Soft-Hackle

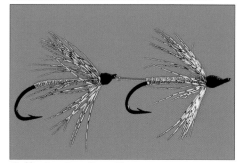

Tied by: Steve Potter, Tracy, CA
Hooks: Steelhead, #8, tied tandem with 25lb. mono
Thread: Black 8/0
Rib: Fine gold wire
Body: Persil's Gossamer yellow tying silk
Thorax: Natural Hare's Ear dubbing
Hackle: Gray partridge

Ultra Violet

Tied by: Don Joslyn, Eagle Point, OR
Hook: Daiichi 2055, #3
Thread: Translucent mono
Butt: Ultra violet & ruby Scintilla Caliente Dubbing
Body: Bare hook followed by speckled shrimp Scintilla Caliente Dubbing
Wing: Rainbow Krystal Flash strands
Hackle: Guinea
Head: Speckled shrimp Scintilla Caliente Dubbing

Wakey Wakey

Tied by: Gord Eby, Fort St. John, BC
Hook: 3X long
Thread: Black
Tag: Gold oval tinsel
Tail: Golden pheasant tippet fibers
Rib: Gold oval tinsel
Body: Purple Ultra Chenille
Wing: Black deer hair
Head: Black deer hair, spun, trimmed to shape, orange foam, trimmed to shape

White Caddis

Tied by: John Moneyhun, Rapid City, SD
Hook: TMC 7989, #4-#8
Thread: White 6/0
Body Hackle: Brown
Body: Brown dubbing
Wing: Bucktail hair, 2 pheasant saddle feathers, tied tent style, white deer hair
Head: White deer hair, spun, trimmed to shape

Wood Duck Shrimp

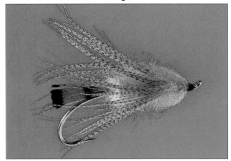

Tied by: Don Joslyn, Eagle Point, OR
Hook: Daiichi 2055, #3
Thread: Orange 3/0 UNI
Tail: Golden pheasant tippet fibers
Body: Speckled shrimp Scintilla Caliente Dubbing
Wing: Lemon wood duck feather fibers
Head: Speckled shrimp Scintilla Caliente Dubbing

Zorro

Tied by: Don Joslyn, Eagle Point, OR
Hook: Daiichi 2051, #5, weight optional
Thread: Black 3/0 UNI
Tag: Gold oval tinsel
Tail: Black hackle fibers
Rib: Gold oval tinsel
Body: Black ostrich herl
Wing: Peacock Krystal Flash strands
Hackle: Black

Sea Trout

Aderdeen Sharpe

Tied by: Jack Pangburn, Westbury, NY
Hook: Mustad 97580 or 80500BL, #6
Thread: Black 6/0
Tail: Golden pheasant crest fibers
Underbody: Dental floss for a smooth base
Rib: 2 strands of gold oval tinsel, wrap x-style
Body: Flat gold tinsel
Wing: Barred peacock secondary wing feather sections, or mottled turkey wing feather sections
Throat: Tan marabou feather fibers, burnt orange feather fibers

Braufort Badger

Tied by: Tim Moore, Winston Salem, NC
Hook: Eagle Claw, #6, 2X long, weight optional
Thread: Brown
Tail: White marabou feather fibers, peacock sword feather fibers
Rib: Silver tinsel
Body: Red chenille, tanned deer skin strip wrapped
Collar: Badger hair
Head: Brown paint
Eyes: White/black paint

Carron

Tied by: Gordon Olson, Three Hills, AB
Hook: Alec Jackson Spey, #3
Thread: Black
Ribs: Fine oval silver tinsel, holographic silver tinsel
Body Hackle: Black heron substitute
Body: Red-orange silk
Throat: Teal feather fibers
Wing: Bronze mallard feather sections

Chelsea

Tied by: David McCants, Pleasant Hill, CA
Hook: TMC 7999, #8
Thread: Black 6/0
Tag: Silver oval tinsel
Tail: Pintail flank feather fibers
Butt: Salmon ostrich herl
Rib: Silver oval tinsel
Body: Peacock herl, 5 strands
Wing: Barred wood duck flank feather sections
Hackle: Caret feather 1/2 size of silver doctor blue feather

Chri's Pink Passion Shrimp

Tied by: Chris French, East Brunswick, NJ
Hook: Mustad S2, #4
Thread: Pink 8/0
Tail: White SLF Hank fibers, pink bucktail hair, pink Krystal Flash strands
Caprice: Smoke Scud Back, cut to shape
Body: Pink Estaz

Jungle Spruce

Tied by: Floyd Franke, Roscoe, NY
Hook: Daiichi 2059, #5-#7
Thread: Black 8/0
Tail: Peacock sword feather fibers
Body: Fluorescent red wool, peacock herl
Wings: Jungle cock body feathers, tied to flare out
Hackle: Jungle cock body feather

Matuka Spruce

Tied by: Henry Hoffman, Warrenton, OR
Hook: Mustad 36890, #4-#8
Thread: Black 6/0
Rib: Fine oval gold tinsel
Body: Red floss, peacock herl
Wing: 4 well marked badger hackles, Matuka style
Hackle: Badger

Scarlet Mackerel

Tied by: Bradee Beard, Rapid City, SD
Hook: Mustad 90240, #8-#12
Thread: Olive 6/0
Tail: Golden pheasant tippet fibers
Rib: Medium gold wire
Body Hackle: Scarlet hen saddle
Body: Red Flexi Floss
Wing: Bronze mallard feather fibers

Sheepshead Minnow

Tied by: Jack Pangburn, Westburn, NY
Hook: Mustad 79580, #4, weight optional
Thread: Tan 6/0
Tail: Brown marabou feather fibers
Rib: Oval silver tinsel
Body: Brown Antron or Seal-Ex dubbing
Wing/Back: Natural rabbit strip
Eyes: Prismatic Mylar with black pupils
Hackle: Ring-necked pheasant rump feather

Powell's Sea Trout

Tied by: Roy Powell, Danville, CA
Hook: Gaelic Supreme Rangeley Streamer Hook, #1-6X long
Thread: Black
Tag: Silver tinsel
Butt: White ostrich herl
Rib: Silver tinsel
Body: Black UNI-Floss
Belly: Peacock herl, white bucktail hair
Wing: White bucktail hair, peacock herl strands, 2 black and 4 red saddle feathers
Throat: Red marabou feather fibers, on top and bottom
Shoulders: Silver pheasant breast feathers
Eyes: Jungle cock eye feathers

Smart Casual

Tied by: Carl Ritter, Sedona, AZ
Hook: TMC 200R, #8
Thread: Black 8/0
Tag: Red tinsel
Tail: Golden pheasant crest fibers
Body: Silver tinsel
Wing: Fox squirrel tail hair, golden pheasant crest fibers, mixed
Cheeks: Blue and brown feather tips
Throat: Orange feather fibers
Eyes: Prismatic eyes

Wrymouth-Cusk

Tied by: Jack Pangburn, Westbury, NY
Hooks: Standard shank #2 O'Shaughnessy hooks tied in tandem using stainless steel twisted wire or heavy mono
Thread: Black 6/0
Bodies: Wrap each hook shank with silver tinsel
Front Hook Belly: White yarn or Fish Hair fibers
Front Hook Wing: 2 black and 2 green feathers

All Black

Tied by: Vincent Paul Staley, Fredericksburg, VA
Hook: Mustad 34007, 1/0, hook point-up
Thread: Mono
Tail: Black bucktail hair, silver Krystal Flash strands
Body: Mono
Wing: Black bucktail hair, black Krystal Flash strands
Eyes: Spirit River Big Eyes, aluminum or brass, silver eyes epoxied in the sockets, attached to head using Gloop plumber's glue
Comments: One of my favorite nighttime striped bass patterns for fishing deeper currents.

Articulated Mantis Shrimp

Tied by: Earl Stanek, Cotter, AR
Head
Hook: Aberdeen light wire, ring eye, point of hook is removed after the head is cured
Thread: Color to match the natural
Feelers: Black moose mane, 4 to 6 strands
Claws: 2 Cree hen neck feathers, tinted with permanent color marker
Mouth: Red Antron yarn
Eyes: Craft flower stamen, painted with black epoxy paint
Legs: Spanflex strips, x wrapped on top of hook
Body: 30 minute epoxy, 3M Scotchlite S22 Glass Bubbles, a small amount of fabric paint mixed to match gold or green fly, I use the bottoms of beer or pop cans for mixing containers, cured on a rotary drying wheel
Hinge: Soft thin craft wire
Tail
Hook: Mustad 34007, #6, tied inverted, open the gap for better hooking
Weight: 3M Scotch Brand #422 Lead Foil Tape, cut tape to a trapezoid shape with width equal to the hook shank, tape wrapped around the hook shank
Carapace: Colored Swiss straw to match the natural, inverted
Body: Gold 2 strand acrylic yarn, green for dark fly
Rib: Gold oval tinsel
Comments: This fly has caught double digit Bones at North Riding Point, Bahamas. I use the golden colored fly for light sand flats and the green colored fly on dark turtle grass flats.

Big Eye Deceiver

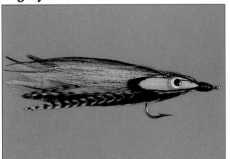

Tied by: Mal Mowbray, Waveland, MS
Hook: Mustad 34007, #1/0-#4
Thread: Black 3/0
Tail: 2 Chartreuse, 4 olive and 4 plane grizzly saddle feathers, white and chartreuse bucktail hairs, 3 to 5 peacock herl strands
Cheeks: Silver American hen feathers (Whiting), coated with Hard-as-Nails nail polish
Eyes: Yellow/black acrylic latex paint

Black and Green

Tied by: Ed Kraft, Lancaster, PA
Hook: Mustad 47011, #1/0
Thread: Black 3/0
Tail: 4 black saddle feathers per side, splayed, topped with peacock Krystal Flash strands
Body: 2 green grizzly saddle feathers, 1 chartreuse grizzly saddle feather, wrapped to mid point of hook shank
Head: Black thread with peacock Krystal Flash band in middle, coated with head cement or epoxy

Black Bird

Tied by: Henry Hoffman, Warrenton, OR
Hook: Mustad 3407, #2/0-#3/0
Thread: White 3/0
Tail: Black chickabou plumes, with 2 black grizzly saddle
feather on each side, splayed
Body: Pearl ribbon floss
Eyes: Steel or aluminum Real Eyes, from Spirit River,
optional

Chartreuse Shrimp

Tied by: Ben J Wilson, Graham, NC
Hook: Carbelo, #4, 2X, hook point-up
Thread: Nylon .004
Antennae: Chartreuse squirrel tail hair, green Krystal Flash strands
Walking Legs: Chartreuse rabbit fur
Eyes: Lead barbell, painted black
Rib: Copper wire
Swimming Legs: Grizzly hackle, top fibers trimmed
Shellback: Silver braid
Body: Peacock Crystal Chenille
Wing: Fluorescent chartreuse FisHair fibers, green Krystal
Flash strands

Crystal Shrimp

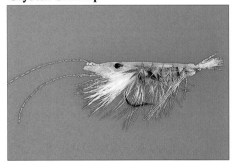

Tied by: Tim O'Sullivan, Fergus, ON
Hook: Mustad 34007, 1/0
Thread: Danville fine mono
Body: Peal Lite Brite
Shellback: Plastic Straw, cut to shape, coated with epoxy
Antennae: Pearl Krystal Flash stands
Eyes: Melted mono, ends dipped in black head cement
Rib: Fine copper wire
Legs: Grizzly hackle, top fibers trimmed
Front Feeler: White marabou feather fibers

Black Night

Tied by: Vincent Paul Staley, Fredericksburg, VA
Hook: Mustad 34007, 1/0
Thread: Mono
Tail: Black arctic fox tail hair, silver Krystal Flash strands
Body: Black crosscut rabbit strip, wrapped
Head: Brass bead
Comments: One of my favorite nighttime striped bass flies,
used in lighter currents or at flood tide.

Cocodrie Clouser

Tied by: Mal Mowbray, Waveland, MS
Hook: Mustad 34007, #2/0, bent to shape, hook point-up
Thread: Chartreuse 6/0 waxed nylon
Eyes: Umpqua Pearl eye
Wing: White bucktail hair, pearl Krystal Flash strands,
chartreuse bucktail hair, gold Krystal Flash strands, topped
with 6 peacock herl strands
Weed guard: .014 No. 3 leader wire, turned end down
Comments: This fly is a variation of the Clouser Deep Minnow
and the Flash Clouser. It was extremely effective for redfish in
the Cocodrie, Louisiana area, hence the name. The primary
variation is the bendback style of the hook and the wire weed
guard, both of which are a necessity to avoid the pitfalls of
marsh grass and oyster beds in the area. The end of the weed
guard should be rounded to slip through the marsh grass.

Doc's Salt Water Crustacean-Tan

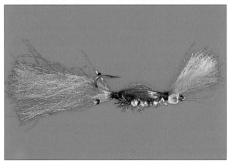

Tied by: W. Weiner, Penacock, NH
Hook: Mustad 34011, #2, barb removed with Dremel
sanding disk
Thread: Tan Kevlar
Body: Root beer Extaz Grande, 6 3mm pearl beads
Wing/Shellback: Tan yak tail hair
Eyes: Small black glass beads on 30lb. mono
Head: Ex-large pearl bead

Chartreuse Minnow

Tied by: Neville Downs, Lethbridge, AB
Hook: Mustad 34011, sized to natural
Thread: White
Tail: White bucktail bucktail hair
Body: White bucktail hair, butt ends from tail, coated with
sparkle fingernail polish
Wing: Chartreuse Krystal Flash strands, chartreuse bucktail hair
Head: White thread
Eyes: Spirit River Eyes, head and eyes coated with clear
fingernail polish

Copper Charlie

Tied by: Henry Hoffman, Warrenton, OR
Hook: Daiichi X452, #4
Thread: Tan 3/0 to tie in eyes, 8/0 for rest of fly
Body: Metallic copper ribbon floss
Wing: Barred tan chickabou feather fibers
Eyes: Gold Spirit River real eyes

Doc's Shrimp

Tied by: Bill Reddoch, Germantown, TN
Hook: Mustad 3007, #2-#10
Thread: White Monocord
Rib: Gold wire
Underbody: Lead wire, 0.10 diameter
Body: Pearl Cactus chenille
Legs: Saddle hackle, brown or color of choice, palmered, top
fibers trimmed
Shellback: Polar Hair, covered in epoxy
Throat: Pearl Comes Alive fibers, rainbow Flashabou strands
Eyes: 80lb. mono, with black glass beads, coated with epoxy
Comments: This fly can be tied in a variety of color and sizes
to match fishing conditions. The epoxy coating on the shell-
back gives the fly the natural translucence of a shrimp, which
serve as a staple in the diets of spotted sea trout and redfish.
The fly can be fished with short strips at any water depth.

Dubbing Brush Shrimp

Tied by: Floyd Franke, Roscoe, NY
Hook: F222 Jardines, #4
Thread: Mono
Mouth Parts: Pheasant tail feather fibers
Antennae: Long pheasant tail feather fibers, short grizzly feather fibers
Body: Natural Squirrel Plus Dubbing Brush
Legs: Grizzly hackle, top fibers trimmed
Shellback: Magic Shrimp Foil #11, cut to shape
Rib: Mono thread
Tail: Dubbing brush, bent to shape, coated with epoxy

Emerald Eel

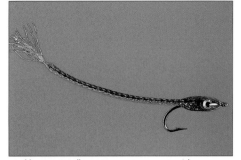

Tied by: Tim O'Sullivan, Fergus, Ontario, Canada
Hook: Mustad 34007, #1/0
Thread: Danville fine mono
Body: Wapsi 1/8-inch pearl/olive Flex Cord, heavy black mono put through Flex Cord and tied to hook shank
Tail: Butt ends from body material, tied off
Head: Olive Diamond Braid Flex Cord pull over, coated with epoxy
Gills: Red waterproof marker
Eyes: 3D stick-on, epoxied over

Epoxy Back Shrimp

Tied by: A. W. Longacre, Juneau, AK
Hook: Mustad 34011, #2
Thread: Brown 6/0
Tail: Pearl Flashabou strands, looped
Shellback: Butt ends from tail material, front strands trimmed to taper
Rib: Silver wire
Body: Tan Antron dubbing, picked out
Feelers: Orange/brown bucktail hair
Eyes: Mono eyes
Antennae: Red, pink, and rainbow Krystal Flash, 1 strand of each per side
Comments: Coat shellback and tail with epoxy.

Finny Minny

Tied by: Robert Schreiner, Southampton, PA
Hook: Mustad 34011, #1
Thread: White
Inner Body: White poly yarn, light olive sparkle flash, red yarn
Outer Body: Corsair
Top Fin: White poly yarn from inner core, colored with waterproof marker

Gartside Sparrow

Tied by: Floyd Franke, Roscoe, NY
Hook: F222 Jardine, #4
Thread: Tan 6/0
Tail: Tan grizzly marabou feather fibers
Body: Natural Squirrel Plus Dubbing Brush
Hackle: Ring-necked pheasant rump feather
Eyes: Silver bead chain
Head: Ring-necked pheasant aftershaft feather

Gulf Coast Speck Spoon

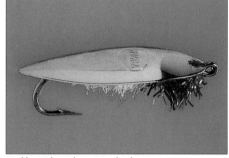

Tied by: Mal Mowbray, Waveland, MS
Hook: Mustad 34011, #1/0
Thread: Match head color
Body: White Cactus or Ice Chenille or any other color
Head: Red Cactus or Ice Chenille or any other color
Shellback: No. 4 willow leaf blade.
Comments: With a Dremel tool cut open the hole at the front of the blade. Lay a line of Super Glue down the center of the concave side of the blade. Position the eye of the hook just forward of the very end of the blade so your leader will not be cut. Hold with pressure as glue bonds the fly to the blade. Add a few drops of 5-minute epoxy at the bend and eye. Lay the fly upside down and let the epoxy dry.

Half & Half Mino

Tied by: Ed Kraft, Lancaster, PA
Hook: Mustad 34011, #1/0, hook point-up
Thread: White 3/0
Eyes: Large nickel, tied 1/4 of hook shank back from hook eye, painted in black pupil
Tail: 3 white and 1 grizzly saddle feather per side, splayed
Low Wing: White deer bucktail hair
Upper Wing: Mixed blue Krystal Flash, blue Ice Angel Hair and purple Flashabou strands, topped with white deer bucktail hair

Harley's Schooling Minnows

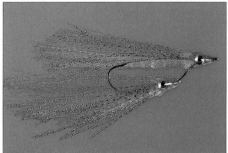

Tied by: Tim O'Sullivan, Fergus, Ontario, Canada
Hook: Mustad saltwater keel hook, #4, hook point-up
Thread: Danville fine mono
Bodies: White Super Hair fibers, silver Krystal Flash strands, topped with blue Krystal Flash strands
Eyes: 3D
Head: Epoxy
Comments: This pattern works well for striped bass, blue fish, snook or red fish. Originally Bob Popovic's Surf Candy.

Holographic Bonefish Fly

Tied by: Giuseppe Nova, Bollate, Italy
Hook: Mustad 34007, #6-#8
Thread: White
Underbody: Holographic plastic, cut to shape
Eyes: Small lead shot, CA glue into position
Body: 5 minute epoxy mixed with a very small drop of yellow Deka varnish
Wing: White calf tail hair, 2 ginger or grizzly feathers, pearl Krystal Flash strands
Hackle: Ginger

Lefty's Deceiver—Blue/Grizzly

Tied by: Chris Helm, Toledo, OH
Hook: Partridge CS 52 (Sea Prince Saltwater) #2/0-#1
Thread: White Gudebrod, size G
Tail: White bucktail hair (small bunch to reduce tail fouling on hook bend), 3 saddle feathers staggered light blue, dark blue and grizzly per side
Body: Blue Gudebrod H.T. Braid
Wing: Sides, light blue bucktail hair; top, dark blue and gray bucktail hairs, topped with blue Flashabou strands
Head: Dark blue Denecchi iridescent thread
Eyes: Stick-on red eyes, coated with thick Soft Body

Marabou Shrimp

Tied by: Rod Powell, Gypsum, CO
Hook: #6 salt water
Thread: Pink 3/0
Body: Pink Cactus Chenille
Underwing: Pearl and pink Krystal Flash strands
Wing: Pink and white marabou feather fibers, with 1 grizzly feather on each side
Eye: Gold-plated barbell

Morrison's Darodo Melt

Tied by: Greg Morrison, Brick, NJ
Hook: Mustad 34011, #1/0
Thread: Clear mono
Tail: White Polybear fibers, rainbow and pearl Sparkle Flash strands, pearl Angle Hair fibers, white and pink marabou feather fibers, 4 pink and 3 white saddle feathers per side
Body: Pearl Mylar tubing, pulled, glitter over epoxy
Eyes: Plastic white/black

Morrison's Manasquan Bunker

Tied by: Greg Morrison, Brick, NJ
Hook: Mustad 34007, #1/0-#4/0
Thread: Clear mono
Body: White bucktail hair, 2 white and 2 blue grizzly saddle feathers per side
Back/Belly: White, blue, and purple bucktail hairs, pearl Angel Hair fibers, rainbow and blue Sparkle Flash strands, topped with purple fox tail hair
Gills: Red fox tail
Eyes: Plastic yellow/black
Head: Glitter over epoxy

Morrison's Marabou Sandeel

Tied by: Greg Morrison, Brick, NJ
Hook: Mustad 34007, #1/0
Thread: Clear mono
Body: White bucktail hair, 2 white over 2 olive saddle feathers per side, pearl and olive Sparkle Flash strands, topped with white marabou feather fibers, with olive marabou feather fibers on bottom
Eyes: Yellow/black 3/16 or 7/32 metal dumbbell
Head: Glitter over epoxy

Narrow River Floating Silver Side

Tied by: Wesley Wyatt, Chepachet, RI
Hook: Mustad 34007 or 3407, #1/0-#2/0
Thread: White 3/0 Monocord
Tail: 5 to 6 strands of Strike King white rubber skirt material
Body: Medium 1/2-inch silver pearl Orvis E-Z Braid, 2 1/2-inches long, over a 2-inch piece of Rainy's 1/2-inch float foam
Wing: White bucktail hair, 1 plum of silver gray marabou, 1 plum of olive green marabou
Throat: Blood red chenille
Head: 1-inch piece of large 3/8 silver pearl Orvis E-Z Braid, over Rainy's float foam cut to shape
Eyes: Self-adhesive stick on, #6
Comments: I use this striped bass fly in the Rhode Island area. Everything about this top water fly is exciting, the way it moves on the top with a short jerk on the retrieve, and the way bass take it.

Pearl Shrimp

Tied by: Nader Youssef, Pullman, WA
Hook: Salt water 2/0, hook point-up
Thread: Mono
Antennae: 2 stripped grizzly feather stems
Eyes: Silver barbell
Underbody: Plastic worm rattle
Body: White chenille
Legs: Emu feather, top fibers trimmed
Rib: Pink or green thread
Tail: White marabou feather fibers

Permit Crab Fly

Tied by: A. W. Longacre, Juneau, AK
Hook: Mustad SS, 2/0, or sized to crab, bottom view
Thread: Brown 6/0
Tail: Pearl Flashabou strands, tan grizzly feathers 3 per side, splayed
Body: Gray Antron yarn, or colors to match the natural
Weight: Lead dumbbell, sized to crab
Legs: Black live rubber, 4 strands, epoxied body to stiffen

Pete's Reel Crab

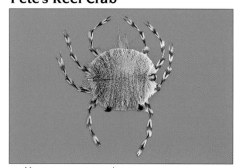

Tied by: Pete Toscani, Bristol, CT
Hook: Orvis 9034-00, #1, hook point-up
Thread: Gray Dynacord
Body: Natural deer body hair, trimmed to shape
Legs: Grizzly feathers, bent, trimmed to shape
Whiskers: Green marabou feather fibers
Eyes: Medium amber glass
Weight: Metal washer, epoxied to bottom of body, coated with brown nail polish

Pete's Reel Shrimp

Tied by: Pete Toscani, Bristol, CT
Hook: Mustad 34011, #2/0, bent to shape
Thread: White Danville flat wax nylon
Feelers: Pearl Flashabou strands, white Crazy Hair fibers, chartreuse Krystal Flash strands
Claws: 2 grizzly feathers, cut to shape
Eyes: Glass beads, epoxied on wire bent to shape
Body: Pearl Crystal Chenille, topped with pink Krystal Flash strands
Legs: Grizzly hackle, trimmed to shape
Antennae: Pink Krystal Flash, butt end from body material
Tail: Pink Krystal Flash, ends from body material, white Crazy Hair fibers
Shellback: Corsair 1/2-inch, cut out bottom, epoxied over body

Pete's Reel Squid

Tied by: Pete Toscani, Bristol, CT
Hook: Mustad 34011, #2/0
Thread: White flat wax nylon
Tail: White Crazy Hair fibers, 2 white feathers per side, splayed, pearl Krystal Flash stands, white marabou feather fibers
Inside Body: Pearl braid, wrapped, topped with pink Krystal Flash strands
Outside Body: Pearl E-Z Body 1/2-inch, coated with epoxy
Eye: Chartreuse/black stick-on, coated with epoxy

Pink Epoxy Shrimp

Tied by: Giuseppe Nova, Bollate, Italy
Hook: Mustad 34007, #4-#8
Thread: Pink
Eyes: Silver bead chain
Antennae: White calf hair, pink Krystal Flash strands
Body: Orange V-Rib
Shellback: Pink Krystal Flash strands, shellback and body coated with epoxy
Tail: Pink Krystal Flash butt ends from shellback material

Powell's Tarpon Fly

Tied by: Rod Powell, Gypsum, CO
Hook: #3/0 salt water
Thread: Olive 3/0
Tail: White bucktail hair, white and olive grizzly saddle feathers on each side
Body: Braided silver tinsel
Wing: White and green bucktail, pearl Krystal Flash strands
Throat: Red Krystal Flash strand
Eyes: Stick-on eyes, covered with Softex

Rainbow Squid

Tied by: Andy Haun, Cedar Rapids, IA
Hook: Eagle Claw L141, #2, hook point-up
Thread: Red 6/0
Eyes: White/black dumbbell
Tail: Peacock sword feather fibers, rainbow Flashabou strands, yellow bucktail hair, red bucktail hair
Body: Glittering Crystal 3D paint

Raver's Fly

Tied by: Chris Raver, Oarngevale, CA
Hook: Mustad 37187, #2-#1/0
Thread: Black nylon 6/0
Wing: Red, over orange, over blue, over chartreuse bucktail hairs, topped with 2 strands of silver tinsel and 8 strands of gold Krystal Flash
Sides: 2 grizzly saddle feathers, splayed
Eyes: Lead barbell, painted red
Head: Epoxy with blue and green glitter

Ray's Rattling Baitfish

Tied by: A. Ray Sims, Dallas, TX
Hook: TMC 8089 NP, #2-6
Thread: White Mono Cord 3/0
Tail: White marabou feathers, topped with gray marabou feather, inserted through Mylar tube, with glass worm rattle inside
Body: White Polar Aire (from Sprit River), brushed and cut to shape, marked with black marker
Cheeks: Grizzly feathers
Eyes: 3-D, epoxied on head
Comments: This shad pattern has caught largemouth and small-mouth bass, snapper, ladyfish, jacks, speckled trout, redfish and snook. It is a killer. The fly sinks slowly and actually suspends between strips, with the tail quivering. At times snook prefer a chartreuse body, while reds and speck often prefer a pink body.

Red Eye Silver Belly

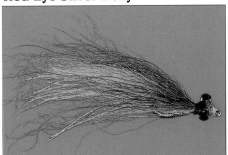

Tied by: Ben J Wilson, Graham, NC
Hook: Mustad 3407, #4, hook point-up
Thread: Nylon .004
Eyes: Lead barbell, with red eyes
Body: Silver Mylar tubing, over lead wire underbody
Gills: Red acrylic yarn
Wing: Chartreuse bucktail hair, chartreuse Flashabou strands, topped with brown bucktail hair

R.H.S. Shrimp

Tied by: Robert Schreiner, Southampton, PA
Hook: Mustad 34011, #4
Thread: White
Mouth: Pearl Krystal Flash strands, white poly yarn fibers
Antennae: Stripped pink feather stems
Eyes: Red mono
Shellback: Gray Flexibody, cut to shape
Body: White poly yarn, picked out, topped with pearl Krystal Flash strands

Rich's Buck-N-Bunny

Tied by: Richard Ross, Villanova, PA
Hook: Stainless steel ring eye, #2/0
Thread: White, black or green 3/0
Tail: Chartreuse rabbit strip, extended 1 1/4 times the length
    of hook shank, 6 strands of gold Krystal Flash
Body: Olive bunny strip, wrapped
Wings: Chartreuse buck tail hair
Comments: This fly was created for inshore striped bass fishing. The combination of bucktail and rabbit strips gives the fly a fantastic amount of movement in the surf. Fished with a slow retrieve it is as deadly as it is easy to tie. I tie this pattern in a variety of colors to suit local conditions and baitfish.

Riley's Shad

Tied by: Jim Riley, Grass Valley, CA
Hook: Streamer hook, #6-#8
Thread: Tan
Tag: Any colorful chenille
Body Float: White closed-cell foam, colored with red water
    proof marker
Body: White Antron yarn, or color to match the natural,
    brushed out, with 1 mallard flank feather on each side,
    topped by 2 strands of pearl Krystal Flash
Gills: Red micro chenille, 2 strands
Eyes: Stick-on, head coated with Loon's hard head cement,
    eyes applied to wet cement
Comments: In the Sacramento River Delta the striped bass feed around weed beds. This fly was designed to be fished near the bottom, floating just above the weeds. Use split shot 8 to 18 inches from the fly to get it down.

Sea Bee

Tied by: Ed Kraft, Lancaster, PA
Hook: Mustad 34011, #1/0
Thread: Yellow 3/0
Tail: 3 yellow and 1 short grizzly saddle feathers per side,
    topped with gold and pearl Flashabou stands, and gold
    Krystal Flash strands
Body: Yellow, black, yellow, black, and yellow hackles,
    equally space

Sill-Link

Tied by: Rick Murphy, Manitou Springs, CO
Hook: Mustad 3400, #2-#8
Thread: Tan 6/0
Eyes: Medium silver bead chain
Tail: Orange Krystal Flash strands, tan Neer Hair fibers,
    flanked by grizzly feathers
Body: Tan Ultra Chenille, with a few wraps of grizzly hackle
Legs: Brown with orange flakes Sili Legs

Silver Minnow

Tied by: Neville Downs, Lethbridge, AB
Hook: Mustad 3407, sized to natural
Thread: Mono
Tail: White bucktail hair
Body: Pearl Mylar tubing
Eyes: Spirit River Eyes, eyes and head coated with Loon Knot Glue
Comments: In April 1999 at the Air New Zealand Invitational Saltfly Tournament, this fly worked after Clousers, the #1 fly, stopped producing.

Simran

Tied by: Christopher Helm, Toledo, OH
Hook: Partridge CS 52 (Sea Prince Saltwater), #2-#6
Thread: Tan Gudebrod 6/0
Tail: Tan Fly Fur, gold Tiewell Flash strands
Hook Bend: Gold Tiewell Flash stands, wrapped
Eyes: Nickel barbell eyes or I-Balz (size to fit sink rate)
Shellback: Medium pearl Mylar tubing
Body: Flesh color rabbit fur, spun with dubbing loop and
    wrapped

Soft Shelled Crab

Tied by: Henry Hoffman, Warrenton, OR
Hook: 81 B, 3X long, #2-#4, Heters tinned jig hook, made
    in England
Thread: Tan Monocord
Weight: 2 strands of .025 lead wire twisted together to
    make a lead rope, lashed to topside of hook, this will
    cause the hook point to ride up
Claws: Bleached grizzly rooster flank feather tips, coated
    with Flexament, cut to shape
Body: Alternating bands of brown and tan chickabou
    feathers, wrapped and trimmed to shape
Eyes: Artificial flower stamens, from craft store

Sparkle Deceiver

Tied by: Tim O'Sullivan, Fergus, Ontario, Canada
Hook: Mustad 34007, #1/0
Thread: Danville fine mono
Body: 3D holographic tinsel, wrapped
Underwing: Polar bear hair
Wing: Polar bear hair, pearl tinsel strands, Sea Foam Fish
    Hair fibers, pearl Krystal Flash strands
Head: Mono, with red thread band, coated with epoxy
Eyes: 3D, coated with epoxy

Speckle Candy

Tied by: Mal Mowbray, Waveland, MS
Hook: Mustad 34011, #1/0
Thread: Match color of fly 6/0
Eyes: Plastic or lead, optional
Body: White Cactus or Ice Chenille
Head: Red Cactus or Ice Chenille
Tail/Rib: Red and gold Krystal Flash strands
Comments: Tie in the Krystal Flash behind the hook eye after finishing the body and head. Retie the thread at the bend of the hook. Equally divide strands and pull them rearward along each side of the body and secure them at the tie off position. Cut tail to length.

CHAPTER 13: INSHORE FLIES • 191

Speckle Clicker

Tied by: Mal Mowbray, Waveland, MS
Hook: Mustad 34011, #1
Thread: Black 3/0
Tail: Grizzly marabou feather fibers
Body Hackle: Grizzly
Body: 2 strands of white and 1 of black chenille, both colors tied in, the black wrapped forward and tied off, the white chenille pulled forward on each side and tied off
Head: 2 Cones, the rear head Super Glued to front of the body, so the front cone is free to slide on the hook shank

Super Shrimp

Tied by: Troy Kelly, Puyallup, WA
Hook: Gamakatsu T10-6H, #4, weight optional
Thread: Pink
Abdomen: White yarn
Thorax: White chenille
Shellback: Pink Krystal Flash strands
Legs: Pink Krystal Flash strands
Eyes: Black plastic bead chain
Feelers: Pink Krystal Flash strands

Tan Zebra Shrimp

Tied by: Henry Hoffman, Warrenton, OR
Hook: Mustad 3407, #2
Thread: Tan 6/0
Body Extension: 1 inch of brown lacquered hairpin
Claws: Barred brown/tan schlappen feather tips
Eyes: Artificial flower stamens, from craft store
Body: Tan chenille
Shellback: Barred brown/tan rooster flank feather, pre-coated with Dave's Flexament
Hackle: Barred brown/tan schlappen
Rib: Mono
Tail: Barred brown/tan rooster flank feather tips

Tarpon Treasure

Tied by: Mark Hoeser, Stockton, CA
Hook: Gamakatsu (Trey Combs), 4/0
Thread: Yellow Gudebrod 6/0
Tail: Lady Amherst pheasant tail feathers, rainbow Krystal Flash strands, and Mearns quail feathers
Collar: Silver fox body fur
Hackle: Blue peacock breast feathers
Head: Fluorescent yellow UNI-Nylon Stretch Thread, coated with Loon Hard Head fly finish
Eyes: 3-D molded prism, silver, 2.5 mm

Wide Body Whistler

Tied by: Bernard Byng, Tracy, Ca
Hook: TMC 8089 NP, #6
Thread: Black
Tail: 2 hen grizzly feathers
Body: 2 hen grizzly feathers, palmered
Cheeks: Any spotted feather
Eyes: Gold chain
Head: Red chenille

Woolly Tarpon

Tied by: Floyd Franke, Roscoe, NY
Hook: Mustad 3407, #2/0
Thread: Red 3/0
Tail: White wool fleece fibers, with red wool fleece fibers on each side
Hackle: Grizzly
Head: Tying thread

Yellow Griz

Tied by: Ed Kraft, Lancaster, PA
Hook: Mustad 34007, 2/0
Thread: Yellow 3/0
Tail: 3 yellow saddle hackles, 1 grizzly saddle hackle per side
Underbody: Chartreuse Sparkle Flash, wrapped to within 1 eye length from the eye
Collar: Chartreuse arctic fox tail hair, extending past hook bend, topped with chartreuse Sparkle Flash strands
Hackle: 2 yellow saddle feathers
Head: Fluorescent red thread

FLY INDEX

TIER INDEX

More Excellent Pattern and Tying Books

FEDERATION OF FLY FISHERS FLY PATTERN ENCYCLOPEDIA
Over 1600 of the Best Fly Patterns
Edited by Al & Gretchen Beatty

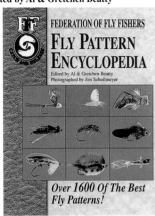

Simply stated, this book is a Federation of Fly Fishers' conclave taken to the next level, a level that allows the reader to enjoy the learning and sharing in the comfort of their own home. The flies, ideas, and techniques shared herein are from the "best of the best" demonstration fly tiers North America has to offer. The tiers are the famous as well as the unknown with one simple characteristic in common; they freely share their knowledge. Many of the unpublished patterns in this book contain materials, tips, tricks, or gems of information never before seen.

As you leaf through these pages, you will get from them just what you would if you spent time in the fly tying area at any FFF function. At such a show, if you dedicate time to observing the individual tiers, you can learn the information, tips, or tricks they are demonstrating. All of this knowledge can be found in *Federation of Fly Fishers Fly Pattern Encyclopedia* so get comfortable and get ready to improve upon your fly tying technique with the help of some of North America's best fly tiers. Full color, 8 1/2 x 11 inches, 232 pages.

SB: $39.95   **ISBN: 1-57188-208-1**

MAYFLIES: TOP TO BOTTOM
Shane Stalcup

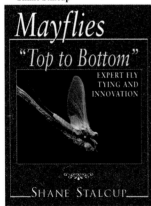

Shane Stalcup approaches fly-tying with the heart and mind of both a scientist and an artist. His realistic approach to imitating the mayfly is very popular and effective across the West, and can be applied to waters across North America. Mayflies are the most important insects to trout fishermen, and in this book, Shane shares his secrets for tying effective, lifelike mayfly imitations that will bring fly-anglers more trout. Many tying techniques and materials are discussed, *Mayflies: Top to Bottom* is useful to beginner and expert tiers alike. 8 1/2 x 11 inches, 157 pages.

SB: $29.95   **ISBN: 1-57188-242-1**
Spiral HB: $39.95   **Spiral HB: 1-57188-243-X**

SPEY FLIES & DEE FLIES: THEIR HISTORY & CONSTRUCTION
John Shewey

The Spey and Aberdeenshire Dee are among the world's great salmon rivers, their storied pools and sea-bright salmon have inspired generations of anglers. Few can fish these rivers, but we all can learn the tying and fishing techniques that made them so famous. Going straight to the source, John found much of the information in this book from the writings of the originators of the Spey and Dee flies. These salmon and steelhead flies are elegant and artfully tied—and they continue to catch fish across the globe. Beautiful photographs enhance this book destined to become a classic. 8 1/2 x 11 inches, 160 pages.

SB: $29.95   **ISBN: 1-57188-232-4**
Spiral HB: $45.00   **ISBN: 1-57188-233-2**

DRY-FLY PATTERNS FOR THE NEW MILLENNIUM
Edited & Photographed by Poul Jorgensen

Everyone has a story about his or her favorite dry flies. The Catskill Fly-Fishing Museum created Flies of the Year 2000, a very successful exhibit featuring flies from contributors around the world. First in a series, *Dry-Fly Patterns for the New Millennium* features the dry flies contributed from all over the United States. Over 360 flies are shared, along with their recipe and tying or fishing notes, creating the largest compilation of dry flies to date. The variety in these flies is amazing. Fly-fishers and fly-tiers will enjoy this book for years to come. 8 1/2 x 11, 87 pages.

SB: $19.95   **ISBN: 1-57188-244-8**
HB: $29.95   **ISBN: 1-57188-245-6**

FLIES: THE BEST ONE THOUSAND
Randle Scott Stetzer

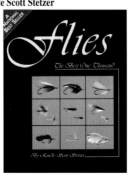

Incredibly beautiful all-color pattern and dressing guide of best flies for trout, salmon, steelhead, bass, and saltwater species. Most shown actual size or larger. Marvel at the tiers and photographer's art as you use it over and over researching flies to tie or when preparing for a trip. Stetzer is an expert fly tier as well as guide. 8 1/2 x 11 inches, 128 pages.

SB: $24.95   **ISBN: 1-878175-20-3**

THE FLY TIER'S BENCHSIDE REFERENCE TO TECHNIQUES AND DRESSING STYLES
Ted Leeson and Jim Schollmeyer

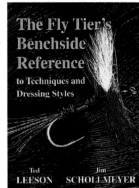

Printed in full color on top-quality paper, this book features over 3,000 color photographs and over 400,000 words describing and showing, step-by-step, hundreds of fly-tying techniques! Leeson and Schollmeyer have collaborated to produce this masterful volume which will be the standard fly-tying reference book for the entire trout-fishing world. Through enormous effort on their part they bring to all who love flies and fly fishing a wonderful compendium of fly-tying knowledge. Every fly tier should have this book in their library! All color, 8 1/2 by 11 inches, 464 pages, over 3,000 color photographs, index, hardbound with dust jacket.

HB: $100.00   **ISBN: 1-57188-126-3**
CD: $59.95 FOR PC OR MAC   **ISBN: 1-57188-259-6**

FLIES OF THE NORTHWEST
Inland Empire Fly Fishing Club

A fully revised, all-color edition of the most popular fly pattern book for the Northwest, including Western Canada, by the Inland Empire Fly Fishing Club of Spokane, Washington. The best 200 flies for trout, steelhead, and salmon. Each fly, individually photographed by Jim Schollmeyer, includes dressing, originator, and how to fish and tie it. Color paintings throughout. Full-color, 6 by 9 inches, 136 pages.
SPIRAL SB: $24.95   **ISBN: 1-57188-065-8**

MODERN ATLANTIC SALMON FLIES
Paul Marriner

Features 300 individual, detailed, color photographs of the most popular and productive modern Atlantic salmon fly patterns, wets, drys, etc. Included are complete tying recipes for each fly and a history of its origin and fishing technique use. 8 1/2 x 11 inches, 127 pages, all-color.

SB: $34.95   **ISBN: 1-57188-152-2**
SPIRAL HB: $44.95   **ISBN: 1-57188-153-0**
NUMBERED LIMITED EDITION SPIRAL HB: $75.00

Ask for these books at your local bookstore fly/tackle shop or call toll-free to order:
1-800-541-9498 (8-5 p.s.t.) • www.amatobooks.com
Frank Amato Publications, Inc. • P.O. Box 82112 • Portland, Oregon 97282

0076